Academic Disc

APPLIED LINGUISTICS AND LANGUAGE STUDY

GENERAL EDITOR

CHRISTOPHER N. CANDLIN

Chair Professor of Applied Linguistics
Department of English
Centre for English Language Education &
Communication Research
City University of Hong Kong, Hong Kong

For a complete list of books in this series see pages v–vi

Academic Discourse

Edited by John Flowerdew

Longman

An imprint of **Pearson Education**

Harlow, England · London · New York · Reading, Massachusetts · San Francisco
Toronto · Don Mills, Ontario · Sydney · Tokyo · Singapore · Hong Kong · Seoul
Taipei · Cape Town · Madrid · Mexico City · Amsterdam · Munich · Paris · Milan

Pearson Education Limited

Head Office:
Edinburgh Gate
Harlow CM20 2JE
Tel: +44 (0)1279 623623
Fax: +44 (0)1279 431059

London Office:
128 Long Acre
London WC2E 9AN
Tel: +44 (0)20 7447 2000
Fax: +44 (0)20 7240 5771
Website: www.pearsoneduc.com

First published in Great Britain in 2002

© Pearson Education Limited 2002

ISBN 0 582 41887 9

British Library Cataloguing in Publication Data
A CIP catalogue record for this book can be obtained from the British Library

Library of Congress Cataloging in Publication Data
A CIP catalog record for this book can be obtained from the Library of Congress

Transferred to digital print on demand, 2006

Typeset in 10/12pt Baskerville by Graphicraft Limited, Hong Kong
Produced by Pearson Education Asia Pte Ltd
Printed and bound by CPI Antony Rowe, Eastbourne

The Publishers' policy is to use paper manufactured from sustainable forests.

APPLIED LINGUISTICS AND LANGUAGE STUDY

GENERAL EDITOR

CHRISTOPHER N. CANDLIN

Chair Professor of Applied Linguistics
Department of English
Centre for English Language Education &
Communication Research
City University of Hong Kong, Hong Kong

Error Analysis:
Perspective on Second Language
Acquisition
JACK C RICHARDS (ED.)

Contrastive Analysis
CARL JAMES

Language and Communication
JACK C RICHARDS *and*
RICHARD W SCHMIDT (EDS)

Reading in a Foreign Language
J CHARLES ALDERSON *and*
A H URQUHART (EDS)

An Introduction to Discourse Analysis
Second Edition
MALCOLM COULTHARD

Bilingualism in Education:
Aspects of Theory, Research and Practice
JIM CUMMINS *and* MERRILL SWAIN

Second Language Grammar:
Learning and Teaching
WILLIAM E RUTHERFORD

Vocabulary and Language Teaching
RONALD CARTER *and*
MICHAEL McCARTHY

The Classroom and the
Language Learner:
Ethnography and Second-Language
Classroom Research
LEO VAN LIER

Listening in Language Learning
MICHAEL ROST

An Introduction to Second Language
Acquisition Research
DIANE LARSEN-FREEMAN
and MICHAEL H LONG

Process and Experience in the
Language Classroom
MICHAEL LEGUTKE *and*
HOWARD THOMAS

Translation and Translating:
Theory and Practice
ROGER T BELL

Language Awareness in the Classroom
CARL JAMES *and* PETER GARRETT (EDS)

Rediscovering Interlanguage
LARRY SELINKER

Language and Discrimination:
A Study of Communication in
Multi-ethnic Workplaces
CELIA ROBERTS, EVELYN DAVIES *and*
TOM JUPP

Analysing Genre:
Language Use in Professional Settings
VIJAY K BHATIA

Language as Discourse:
Perspective for Language Teaching
MICHAEL McCARTHY *and*
RONALD CARTER

Second Language Learning:
Theoretical Foundations
MICHAEL SHARWOOD SMITH

Interaction in the Language
Curriculum:
Awareness, Autonomy and Authenticity
LEO VAN LIER

Contents

PART III: Contrastive Rhetoric   165

hedpujo + modau ✓

PART IV: Ethnographic/Naturalistic Approaches   233

List of contributors

Desmond Allison,	National University of Singapore
Joyce Bell,	Curtin University of Technology, Australia
Vijay Bhatia,	City University of Hong Kong
David Bunton,	University of Hong Kong
Sally Burgess,	La Laguna University, Canary Islands, Spain
John Flowerdew,	City University of Hong Kong
Lynne Flowerdew,	Hong Kong University of Science and Technology
Ken Hyland,	City University of Hong Kong
Jane Jackson,	Chinese University of Hong Kong
Nazareth Amselom Kifle,	University of Ethiopia
Alison Love,	University of Zimbabwe
Tony McEnery,	University of Lancaster
Shirley Ostler,	Bowling Green State University, Ohio
Betty Samraj,	San Diego State University
John Swales,	University of Michigan
Chris Tribble,	University of London
Wu Siew Mei,	National University of Singapore
Tatyana Yakhontova,	State University of L'viv, Ukraine

Acknowledgements

We are grateful to the following for permission to reproduce copyright material:

Table 3.1 and Figure 11.1 after *Genre Analysis: English in Academic and Research Settings* published and reprinted by permission of Cambridge University Press (Swales, J.M. 1990). Figure 5.1 is reprinted from Thurstun, J. and Candlin, C. (1998) 'Concordancing and the teaching of the vocabulary of academic English' in *English for Specific Purposes*, volume 17(3) pp. 267–280, with permission of Elsevier Science. Figure 5.2 reprinted with the permission of Cambridge University Press.

Extracts from *Sociology* (Giddens, A. 1993) in Chapter 4 are reproduced by permission of Polity Press.

While every effort has been made to trace the owners of copyright material, in a few cases this has proved impossible and we take this opportunity to offer our apologies to any copyright holders whose rights we have unwittingly infringed.

Introduction: Approaches to the Analysis of Academic Discourse in English

John Flowerdew

The purpose of this volume is to demonstrate, through a collection of specially commissioned articles, the scope, theoretical approaches, and pedagogical concerns of the field of discourse analysis in academic contexts in English.

The study of academic discourse in English has throughout its short history been closely tied in with developments in the preparation of non-native speakers (NNSs) for study in English, English for Academic Purposes (EAP). English is now well established as the world language of research and publication (e.g. Graddol, 1997) and more and more universities and institutes of learning are using English as the language of instruction. EAP is thus a truly international phenomenon, linked in with the overall trend towards the globalisation of information exchange, communication, and education.

With this great expansion in the international use of English, there has been a parallel growth in the preparation of NNSs for study in English. This has taken place, and is continuing, in four main areas. First, in English-speaking countries such as the United States, Great Britain, Canada, and Australia, where students from overseas come to study. Second, in post-colonial territories such as South Africa, Zimbabwe, Malawi, Hong Kong, and Singapore, where the use of English, whether or not it remains a national language, has been retained in academic contexts. Third, in the countries of the former Soviet bloc, which are seeking to distance themselves from the use of Russian and, through English, connect with the wider international academic community. Fourth, and perhaps most surprisingly, in other countries where English has no official status, such as China, Japan, Western Europe, and Latin America.

In parallel to the development of EAP programmes over the last four decades or so, a considerable amount of scholarly activity has been conducted and reported in academic journals and books concerning the description of academic discourse in English. The rationale of this work is that linguistic/discoursal descriptions of the target academic genres can provide insights and frameworks for EAP pedagogy.

The earliest work in academic discourse analysis was conducted in the 1960s and focused on-the quantitative study of the formal feature of broad language varieties, or registers (e.g. Barber, 1962; Halliday, McIntosh, and Strevens, 1964). Since then, work in academic discourse analysis has steadily become 'narrower and deeper' (Swales, 1990: 3) – narrower in the sense that it has focused on specific genres, and deeper in so far as it has sought to investigate communicative purposes, not just formal features. Two specific examples are significant in demonstrating this narrower and deeper work.[1] Important research was conducted at the University of Washington on a rhetorical approach to the description of scientific and technological text (see Trimble, 1985 for overview). This work was *deeper*, in so far as it sought to analyse texts according to their rhetorical purpose: defining, classifying, generalising, describing, exemplifying, comparing and contrasting, sequencing, identifying cause and effect, etc. However, it was not always *narrower*, because it sometimes combined various genres – textbooks, technical manuals, research articles, etc. – as if they were all subject to the same purposes and corresponding discursive patterning. In parallel with this scholarly work in discourse analysis, at about the same time major textbook initiatives were undertaken, based on the new insights. Thus the *Nucleus* series edited by Bates and Dudley-Evans (1976) and Allen and Widdowson's *English in Focus* series (1974), although rather different, were English for Academic Purposes initiatives with syllabuses based upon a rhetorical approach. Other EAP coursebook projects were represented by the work done in Colombia with the *Reading and Thinking in English Series* (British Council, 1980) and at the University of Malaya with the *Skills for Learning* project (University of Malaya, 1980). Munby's model of English for Specific Purposes needs analysis and syllabus design (Munby, 1978) was similarly influenced by advances made in the communicative study of academic discourse.

Significant in its both deeper *and* narrower approach in academic discourse analysis was Tarone et al.'s (1981) study, 'On the use of the passive in two astrophysics journal papers'. This work was deeper because it focused on the communicative value of a particular syntactic feature, the passive. And it was narrower because it analysed this single feature as it was contextualised within one particular genre, the research article in astrophysics.

This deeper and narrower approach reached maturity with the book-length studies of Swales (1990) and Bhatia (1993), both of which put forward models for genre analysis – Swales in the field of academic discourse and Bhatia in business, academic, and legal genres. As with earlier work in academic discourse analysis, the work in genre analysis, as conducted by Swales and Bhatia, has always been very much 'applied' in nature, with a pedagogic purpose in mind. The models of generic structure developed (which are probabilistic rather than rule governed[2]) can be used as the basis for the development of pedagogic materials (e.g. Swales and Feak, 1994).

While Swales and Bhatia focused on some of the more predictable, formulaic aspects of certain genres ('move' structure and typical patterns of linguistic realisation), more recent genre analysis (e.g. Freedman and Medway, 1994a) – the so-called New Rhetoric school – has been more contextually than linguistically grounded (Hyon, 1996). This approach has stressed the flexible and dynamic nature of generic structure potential. It has accordingly argued for a pedagogy developed along the lines of general consciousness raising rather than overt didactics. In spite of the New Rhetoric's emphasis on context, which has been most influential in North American academic writing programmes, the more linguistic orientation has remained influential in EAP in other jurisdictions.

Important work in genre has also been conducted in Australia. This work has more in common with Swales and Bhatia than the New Rhetoric, having its roots, as it does, in Hallidayan linguistics (e.g. Martin, 1985a; Richardson, 1994). However, it has been focused more on the primary and (to a lesser extent) secondary school genres rather than those of the university (Jim Martin, personal communication, October 2000), which are the focus of this collection (although see e.g. Drury, 1991; Flowerdew, 2001, in press; Jones, 1991; Jones et al., 1989; Love, this volume; Young, 1994). Nevertheless, the range of text types dealt with in this work bears striking resemblances to the earlier work of the Washington school referred to above. Derewianka (manuscript), for example, cites a very similar range of text types as those referred to above as being studied by the Washington school.

At the same time as this work in register and genre analysis, other discourse analysts have been working in rather different paradigms, but with the same end in view, the provision of discoursal description for language teaching. These researchers have been working in contrastive rhetoric, corpus linguistics, and ethnographically influenced methods.

Contrastive rhetoric is the study of the similarities and differences between two languages and how the influence of the L1 may affect the way individuals express themselves in the L2. This research paradigm goes back to Kaplan (1966) and, while the approach has been subjected to criticism (e.g. Kachru, 2000; Mohan and Lo, 1985; Scollon, 1997), it has been given added impetus by others (Clyne, 1987a; Connor, 1996; Hinds, 1987; Mauranen, 1993a; Ventola, 1992; Ventola and Mauranen, 1996). Grabe and Kaplan (1996) explain the pedagogic rationale for contrastive rhetoric as follows:

> What is clear is that there are rhetorical differences in the written discourses of various languages, and that those differences need to be brought to consciousness before a writer can begin to understand what he or she must do in order to write in a more native-like manner (or in a manner that is more acceptable to native speakers of the target language).   (p. 109)

While there are no absolute constraints on the discourse structure of any given genre, these writers argue, there are what they refer to as 'preferred expectations about the way information should be organized' (p. 109). These preferential expectations can be examined and the resulting descriptions can form the basis of pedagogic materials.

Corpus linguistics is concerned with the collection, structuring, and analysis of large amounts of discourse, usually with the assistance of computers. Computers make possible the consistent and accurate analysis of large databases. Processing includes the operations of quantifying (counting the number of given words or phrases), concordancing (producing lists of given linguistic items with sufficient context to determine syntactic, semantic, and pragmatic properties) and parsing (syntactic analysis). Seminal in this area, although not specifically focused on academic discourse, is the work of Sinclair and the Collins Cobuild project (see Sinclair, 1991) and of Biber (1988) in register analysis. Early work within the academic registers and genres is Johns (1988) and J. Flowerdew (1992, 1994a). (see L. Flowerdew (this volume), for further references.)

Ethnography, or, more broadly, naturalistically influenced approaches, is perhaps the least recognised of the research paradigms discussed here in the field of academic discourse. If Swalesian genre analysis acknowledges the importance of context – both linguistic and situational – in the interpretation of discourse, but nevertheless makes as its primary goal the analysis of the texts, spoken or written, ethnography views text as but one feature of the social situation, which includes equally the values, roles, assumptions, attitudes, and patterns of behaviour of the participants, or text producers and receivers (Flowerdew and Miller, 1996; Van Lier, 1988; Candlin and Plum, 1999). Ethnographic methodology, accordingly, emphasises direct observation, interview, and other modes of analysing the situational context, in addition to textual analysis. For this reason, the 'New Rhetoric' approach to genre is considered in this volume as being closer to ethnographically inspired approaches than to 'genre analysis', the latter term being used to refer to the approach developed in Swales (1990).[3] As Jackson (this volume) notes, 'By bringing the cultural assumptions and expectations of professors and students to light, ethnographic research can provide a basis for improving the learning situation.' Unlike applications of the other methodologies described thus far, however, results of ethnographic academic discourse analysis may be less amenable to large-scale application to pedagogic materials. Because description is based upon a local situation, the potential for generalised application may be limited. Insights derived from one site are perhaps more likely to inform an approach to teaching in similar situations than be applied directly to the development of pedagogic materials.

ORGANISATION OF THE COLLECTION

The organisational principle of the current volume is the four research paradigms discussed above: (Swalesian) genre analysis, contrastive rhetoric, corpus-based analysis, and ethnographic approaches. There are other ways of investigating academic discourse, of course. For example, the psycholinguistic processing involved in text production and reception is an important paradigm (Van Dijk and Kintsch, 1983; Olsen and Huckin, 1990; Rost, 1994; Tauroza and Allison, 1994; Flowerdew and Tauroza, 1995), as are diachronic approaches (Bazerman, 1988; Atkinson, 1992; Gunnarsson et al., 1997). Critical discourse analysis (e.g. Bourdieu et al., 1994; Pennycook, 1996; Canagarajah, 1997) is a further approach. Finally, as already mentioned, the

Hallidayan approach to genre has also been influential. The four paradigms selected are probably the most used in academic discourse analysis and have had the most direct pedagogic application at the tertiary level.

Each section of the collection begins with a state of the art review article which overviews the approach. This is followed by a series of original empirical studies illustrating the approach in action. Each of the empirical chapters refers to the motivation and implications of the work for pedagogy, although the primary focus is on the discourse analysis itself.

It must be stated that the organisation of the book into these four categories is not watertight. Indeed, one of the purposes of the volume is to bring the different approaches together, with a view to cross-fertilisation. In recognition of this overlap, a number of the chapters might equally have been placed in more than one of the sections. As L. Flowerdew notes in her overview chapter on corpus-based approaches, a recent development in that field has been the comparison of the salient features of 'expert' academic writing (based on native-speaker corpora) with perceived differences in 'learner' writing (based on non-native 'interlanguage' corpora). This represents a coming together of corpus-based approaches and contrastive rhetoric. In recognition of this, one of the empirical chapters of the present volume (McEnery and Kifle), which embodies this contrastive corpus-based methodology, is included in the section on contrastive rhetoric rather than corpus linguistics, although it could equally well have qualified for the latter. As another example of the overlapping of approaches, two other chapters in the contrastive rhetoric section both focus on specific genres – conference abstracts (Yakhontova) and research article introductions (Burgess). Because the analysis presented in these contributions is from a contrastive perspective, however, they have been assigned to the section on contrastive rhetoric rather than that of genre analysis. As a final example of overlap, we might cite the chapter by Allison and Wu, which uses interviews and questionnaires as its primary research methodology, and is thus included in the section devoted to ethnographically inspired approaches. However, Allison and Wu also use as part of their methodology a keyword search, which is a technique derived from corpus linguistics.

In addition to cross-fertilisation of methods, another goal of this collection is to widen the range of genres which have to date been the greatest focus of attention. Because of its status as the pre-eminent academic genre – in terms of its role as a vehicle for the generation of knowledge, on the one hand, and because of its gatekeeping function, as an indicator of academic achievement and professional success, on the other – the research article (RA) has commanded the greatest amount of attention among academic discourse analysts, the work of Swales (1990) being seminal. While the reasons for the great amount of attention given to the RA are valid, it seems that many of the other academic genres also have claims for our attention. The lecture, as a genre, while still pre-eminent in undergraduate education, in spite of my earlier collection (Flowerdew, 1994b) remains relatively neglected. Some work has been done on textbooks, another important undergraduate genre (e.g. Love, 1991, 1993; Hyland, 1999b), but this work is relatively sparse.

Other genres which have been investigated are office hours interactions with foreign teaching assistants (see Briggs et al., 1997 for references), conference abstracts (Berkenkotter and Huckin, 1995; Kaplan et al., 1994), editorial correspondence (Flowerdew and Dudley-Evans, 1999; Hamp-Lyons, 1988; Swales, 1996a), seminars (Furneaux et al., 1991), research grant proposals (Connor and Mauranen, 1999; Connor, forthcoming) and theses (Bunton, 1998). But the treatment of all of these genres is relatively sparse. The present volume, accordingly, while offering two chapters on the RA (Burgess, Samraj), broadens its focus to take in textbooks (Love), Ph.D. theses (Bunton), case discussion seminars (Jackson), student essays (McEnery and Kifle), conference abstracts (Yakhontova), and examination questions and assignments (Allison and Wu).

Genres, of course, do not represent the only important form of variation in academic discourse. Another important parameter is that of disciplinary variation – how the description of a given genre may vary according to the discipline it falls within (Hyland, 2000). This is a focus of the chapters by both Bhatia and Samraj (this volume).

CONTRIBUTORS TO THE VOLUME

Another feature of the collection is the attempt to represent not just 'Anglo' perspectives i.e. research conducted in English-speaking countries by native speakers of English, but also the perspectives of researchers for whom English is not their first language or who conduct their research in locations where English is used as an auxiliary language. Thus, while not wanting to put labels on individuals, a number of contributors have English as their auxiliary language (although it should be pointed out that English is probably their first language, as far as academic research is concerned). In addition, the majority of contributions have come primarily from outside the United States and the United Kingdom, which are traditionally the main centres of academic research. The collection thus has contributions from countries as diverse as Australia, Eritrea, Hong Kong, Singapore, Spain, Sri Lanka, and Ukraine. In this way, it is representative of the truly international nature of EAP and EAP-focused research.

DISCOURSE ANALYSIS AND PEDAGOGY

As already mentioned, the underlying premise of most academic discourse analysis has been that the findings will be of value to language pedagogy. The extent to which discoursal accounts may be applied directly to syllabus and materials design or may more generally serve to inform an overall approach depends upon two important factors. First, upon the degree to which the analysis focuses on linguistic realisation, on the one hand, or contextual conditions of production and reception, on the other. And second, upon the philosophy of teaching and learning which the course designer holds to. Regarding the first of these, clearly, ethnographic accounts, with their greater emphasis on the conditions of production and reception, as opposed to the detailed description of linguistic realisation, are not likely to provide material for the development of linguistic items to be incorporated into the syllabus in the same way that corpus-based or Swalesian genre descriptions are. They may, on the other hand, provide important insights into the preferred patterns of interaction of the participants, problems they may have in processing the discourse, or cultural mismatches between students and teachers, all of which can be carried over into EAP course design. Regarding the second point, while many EAP practitioners take the view that language can be taught (as opposed to acquired), others, most notably the New Rhetoricians, maintain that genre is too flexible and unstable and that it is misleading to develop expectations in the learner of direct form–function relations, however variable these might be. The debate on this issue is ongoing (Freedman and Medway, 1994a; Johns, in press).

ISSUES OF LINGUISTIC HEGEMONY AND EMPOWERMENT

While the globalisation of English brings with it obvious benefits in the form of improved international communication, including in the field of education and scholarship, it has not been without its critics (e.g. Pennycook, 1994; Phillipson, 1992). Such critics see the spread of English as culturally intrusive and hegemonic. English brings with it Western cultural values (the so-called McDonaldisation phenomenon), which represent a threat to indigenous cultures. Alongside such arguments concerning cultural imperialism, other critics, specifically in the academic domain, have seen the increasing use of English in certain genres as impoverishing indigenous languages (Mauranen, 1993b; Swales, 1997). Certain academic genres which once existed in the L1 are displaced by English. Because academics want to publish their research findings internationally – in English – there ceases to be a need for them to write in such genres in their first language. Indeed, for many scholars, their first language, as far as academic writing is concerned is, in fact, English, although their mother tongue is some other language (Connor, 1999).

In the face of such criticism, how does one justify a volume such as the present one, devoted to the study of academic discourse in English, with an emphasis on its value for pedagogic application? The justification, I think, lies in the fact that, whether one likes it or not, English as a World Language, at least in the academic field, is more or less a *fait accompli*. While it is important to make people aware of the potential for hegemony in the use of English and the issues of power and access which accompany this potential, and while it is important to encourage cultural and linguistic plurality, to deny people access to the linguistic, social, and educational capital that English represents is irresponsible. Indeed, English is – ironically – a vehicle by means of which voices arguing for linguistic diversity can be heard loudest.

In this regard, the chapter by Yakhontova (this volume) is particularly import-ant. Yakhontova argues that, while Ukrainian scholars want to make the results of their research available to the international audience, in doing so they do not want to cast off their cultural identity as Ukrainians. She suggests, there-fore, that the academic community should accept diverse ways of presenting research (in English) and not restrict writers to a Western 'Anglo' model.

OVERVIEW OF THE COLLECTION

Part I. Genre analysis

Vijay Bhatia

The overview chapter in the first part of the book, on genre analysis, by Vijay Bhatia, makes the point that genres in the academy represent an enormous range of text-types, some of which display a significant overlap, while others may have very little in common. In one sense, these genres form a colony of academic discourse, which in applied linguistic/ESP literature has often been identified as EAP discourse. The main body of Bhatia's chapter reviews the most significant work done in investigating those genres which constitute for Bhatia the common core of EAP. At the same time the chapter raises some of the main issues involved in the analysis and identification of these genres. Emphasis is placed on the complexity and dynamism in discursive practices both within and across professional and academic communities; issues of interdisciplinarity in academic programmes and the workplace; the notion of academic literacy versus multiple literacies; conflicts and contentions within genres and across disciplinary boundaries; and resulting mixed or hybrid forms in academic discourse.

In addition, the chapter discusses to what extent the work reviewed can be used as an effective argument either for or against the use of EAP as a unified concept for a number of applied linguistic purposes, especially language teaching and learning (general as well as specific) and professional and academic communication programmes. As far as this question relates to specific pedagogic application, Bhatia emphasises the need to investigate overlap and variation in particular contexts, rather than presuming either one or the other.

Betty Samraj

Betty Samraj, in her chapter, 'Disciplinary variation in abstracts: The case of wildlife behaviour and conservation in biology', begins by noting that although there has been a growing interest in writing in different disciplines in recent years, most of the studies in this area have focused on the nature of texts written in individual disciplines (e.g. Myers, 1990; Bloor and Bloor, 1993) and have not attempted comparisons of writing across disciplines. Studies that focus on writing from a single discipline, Samraj argues, cannot fully distinguish between discourse characteristics due to disciplinary norms and features intrinsic to the genre of the text. In addition, comparisons of the results of single disciplinary studies do not provide an accurate picture of disciplinary differences in writing, as these studies tend to employ different analytic frameworks and focus on different textual features.

Samraj's chapter, which reports on a study of 40 research article abstracts published in prominent journals from two related fields, Wildlife Behaviour, a sub-discipline of Ecology, and Conservation Biology, a newly emerging interdisciplinary field, thus sets out to fill this research niche. The study reveals interesting differences in the textual norms of these two fields of enquiry at both the global organisational and lexico-grammatical levels of the abstracts. The Conservation Biology abstracts appear to perform more of a persuasive function through the presence of a Background move where justification for the research reported was provided. The Wildlife Behaviour abstracts, on the other hand, seem to fulfil a more pragmatic function of conveying the newest information by giving prominence to the Results and Conclusion moves. This comparison of article abstracts from two disciplines adds to our present understanding of the influence of genre norms and disciplinary preferences on discourse structure, Samraj argues.

David Bunton

The second of the empirical studies of Part I, 'Generic moves in Ph.D. thesis Introductions', by David Bunton, moves the focus from the research article to a lesser studied, but in many ways equally important genre, the Ph.D. thesis, focusing on the *Introduction* chapter. Differentiating the focus further, Bunton is concerned with the thesis as it is written by non-native speakers of English (in this case primarily with Chinese as their L1). Bunton's goal is overtly pedagogical, concentrating on the linguistic and textual difficulties encountered by these Chinese L1 writers with the genre. The chapter builds on the work of those who have analysed the *Introductions* of shorter genres such as the research article (e.g. Swales, 1981a, 1990), and the Masters dissertation (Dudley-Evans, 1986), but argues that the Ph.D. *Introduction*, being a chapter rather than a section, and introducing a much longer text, shows qualitative as well as quantitative differences in its generic structure.

Forty-five *Introduction* chapters were analysed by Bunton, from the faculties of Science, Engineering, Arts, Education, and Social Sciences. Notable differences were found between the structure of *Introductions* from the 'science and technology' faculties (the first two) and the 'humanities and social sciences' (the last three faculties), and two different models are proposed. The three basic moves of Swales's (1990) CARS (Create a Research Space) model are retained as a framework for the model, but differences emerge in the number and nature of the steps that make up these moves.

The research student writers in the corpus were found to have problems with the structuring and sequencing of their *Introductions*, and in not being explicit enough about what they are researching and what they believe their research is contributing to the field. In particular, some thesis writers were found not to have established a niche for their research (Swales, 1990) and others, although indicating such a niche, did not show explicitly how their research occupied it.

Alison Love

In the first of the empirical chapters of this section, by Samraj, the focus was the research article, a genre normally created by professional academics. In the second, by Bunton, our attention was turned to the Ph.D. thesis, a genre which is the result of work by apprentice scholars. With the third of the empirical chapters of this section, by Alison Love, 'Introductory concepts and "cutting edge" theories: Can the genre of the textbook accommodate both?', we go further down the academic hierarchy, with a shift to the introductory undergraduate textbook.

But Love's chapter also differs from that of her predecessors in other ways. In their adoption of a quantitative approach to the analysis of moves and their linguistic realisations, the chapters by Samraj and Bunton can be seen to fit firmly within the quantitative framework for genre analysis initiated by Swales. In contrast, Love's chapter is more qualitative in nature, focusing on just one examplar of the chosen genre, the academic textbook. In addition, Love employs a Hallidayan approach to the lexico-grammatical analysis, a feature not present in the other two chapters or in Swales's original work.

Love begins by noting that the perception of the textbook as genre has frequently been influenced by Kuhn's characterisation of scientific textbooks as 'a body of knowledge backed by a consensus of practitioners' (Myers, 1992b: 5; Swales, 1995: 4). However, while students may often be only too happy to 'see textbooks as concrete embodiments of the knowledge of their disciplines' (Hyland, 1999b: 4), there is increasing evidence that some textbooks, including some scientific ones, introduce students to the complexity and tentativeness of knowledge (Hyland, 1999b; Love, 1999). This is seen as part of the preparation for the epistemological work of analysis within their disciplines. In many social sciences, in particular, students may be exposed to competing theories and alternative interpretations (Love, 1999). It appears, then, of interest to examine whether textbooks introduce new students to the 'cutting edge' of ideas in the discipline at the time that they are written, particularly if the authors are leading theorists in the field.

The focus of Love's chapter is therefore the examination of an introductory textbook in one discipline, sociology, which explicitly sets out to incorporate specific cutting-edge ideas into its introduction to the discipline. The textbook in question is by Anthony Giddens (Giddens, 1993a), a major and controversial figure in contemporary sociological theory. By means of a systemic functional analysis of both its overall structure and the realisation of this structure at the level of lexico-grammar, Love demonstrates that Giddens uses a variety of linguistic strategies to initiate students not only into the content and theory of sociology, but also into the complex processes through which sociological concepts and theories evolve and are contested.

Part II. Corpus-based studies

Lynne Flowerdew

In her overview chapter on corpus-based approaches, Lynne Flowerdew begins by pointing out that in the the 1980s and early 1990s corpus-based research tended to centre on the exploration of lexical, grammatical, or lexico-grammatical items in what were considered at the time to be large-scale generalised corpora, such as the one-million-word Brown and LOB corpora, or the 7.3-million-word Cobuild corpus. Since then, however, the field of corpus linguistics has expanded considerably, regarding both the size and types of corpora being compiled for investigation, and the very nature of these linguistic investigations. The compilation of corpora has widened in two senses – much larger-scale, mega-corpora are now in use. For example, the original Cobuild corpus has been expanded into a 300-million-word monitor corpus, named the Bank of English, and there also now exists the 100-million-word BNC, British National Corpus. The field has also widened in another sense, to include the recognition of much smaller, specialised, genre-based corpora. Many of these corpora comprise databases of written or spoken academic discourse whose findings have been used to inform pedagogy in the field of EAP. Another development in the field is the compilation of learner corpora for academic uses.

The main focus of Lynne Flowerdew's chapter is a review of the various written and spoken, expert and learner corpora compiled for descriptive or pedagogical purposes in EAP. She divides these into English for General Academic Purposes (EGAP) and English for Specific Academic Purposes (ESAP). Within the field of ESAP she surveys corpus-based work in English for Science and Technology (EST), English for Medicine, English for Business, Finance and Economics, and Contrastive Studies, an area where comparisons are made within the same genre from different academic disciplines, between different genres within the same academic discipline, or between subgenres of a particular academic discipline. The article also demonstrates that the field of corpus linguistics is now moving away from concentration solely on the lexical, grammatical, and lexico-grammatical patterning of text to a broader perspective embracing other linguistic and social science fields such as textlinguistics and ethnography. Corpus linguistics is thus informed by these other methodologies, but at the same time corpus linguistic techniques can also be used to shed light on the discourse practices in these other areas. Lynne Flowerdew concludes by expressing the hope that in the future there will be more cross-fertilisation not only between corpus linguistics and other branches of linguistics but also within the field between the descriptive research-based work and the more applied aspect so that the domain of EAP can profitably benefit from this methodology.

Ken Hyland

Working with a large corpus of 80 published research articles from eight disciplines, Ken Hyland, in his chapter, 'Activity and evaluation: Reporting practices in academic writing', is concerned to highlight the broad disciplinary differences in the use of the linguistic/semantic feature he has chosen to investigate. He argues that reporting verbs offer writers a network of what he calls 'process' and 'evaluative' options for introducing others' research. His findings show there to be broad similarity across the disciplines in the textual environments in which reporting verbs occur, with general preferences for what he refers to as 'summary' and 'non-integral structures'. There are considerable differences, however, in the frequency of occurrence of reporting verbs in general, in the individual verbs employed, and in the categories they are drawn from. Writers in the sciences and engineering generally use fewer reporting verbs and display a preference for non-evaluative 'Research Act' verbs. Articles in the humanities and social sciences, on the other hand, contain a higher proportion of both 'Discourse Act' and 'Cognition Act' verbs and a higher incidence of verbs conveying criticism of cited work.

Hyland argues that his findings contribute to our understanding of the specialised literacy skills required in academic writing and that they have value for the preparation of discipline-specific English for Academic Purposes teaching materials.

Chris Tribble

Following on from Hyland's focused empirical study, Chris Tribble's chapter, 'Corpora and corpus analysis: New windows on academic writing', is a more general argument and exemplification of how corpus-based work can be applied to help students with their academic writing. Tribble outlines ways in which corpus resources can be used to help students to develop the knowledge they need to become effective writers within specific academic domains. The chapter starts from the premise that writers need four kinds of knowledge in order to respond successfully to writing tasks: content knowledge, writing process knowledge, context knowledge, and language system knowledge, and that students can best develop language system knowledge through the analysis of texts that are similar to those they need to write. In the following discussion an analytic framework is proposed. This draws on earlier work in genre studies, but gives greater emphasis to the distinction between contextual and linguistic analysis than has been the case in other studies. This framework is applied to a short published paper, with extensive use being made of the concordancing program *WordSmith Tools* – in particular, the *Keywords* tool – during the linguistic analysis. This section concludes with the observation that a combination of public domain text resources such as the British National Corpus Sampler and the Lancaster Oslo Bergen Corpus and the right corpus tools can be used to develop exciting insights into the linguistic realisation of specific genres of written communication.

In the second part of Tribble's chapter, suggestions are made for a corpus informed approach to EAP writing instruction. Such an approach calls for the collection of texts which are either the same as those that learners need to write, in other words, an exemplar corpus, or, where this is impossible (as is often the case), the collection of an analogue corpus which contains texts that are similar to those that learners need to learn about.

John Swales

If Tribble's chapter emphasises the positive contribution that corpus-based techniques can make to EAP pedagogy, John Swales argues that, while the recent rise of specialised micro-corpora represents a valuable additional resource in our attempts to understand academic discourse, there are nevertheless several obstacles to realising this potential. These include the procedural differences between concordance searches and discourse analysis, the limitations of a lexical approach to understanding academic discourse, the fact that a corpus – at least one without elaborate pragmatic tagging – is 'intuition-blind', and the need for applied corpus work to be guided by pedagogical questions and requirements.

In the body of his chapter, Swales illustrates some of these problems (and on occasion their partial solutions) via review of a fragment from an academic writing consultancy, and reflection on some corpus-informed advanced EAP materials. It would seem at present that the availability of appropriate corpora is valuable for finding examples for EAP purposes and for testing grammatical and lexical claims about discourse, Swales argues. However, attempts to use a corpus as some kind of 'new insight generator' do not as yet, and on balance, offer a viable return on the amount of effort expended, he concludes.

Part III. Contrastive rhetoric

Shirley Ostler

Shirley Ostler begins Part III of the collection with her overview of contrastive rhetoric by pointing out that the contrastive rhetoric paradigm has expanded considerably since the 1960s, when Kaplan (1966) first addressed the issue of ESL writing at a level beyond the sentence. Initially intended to explain to ESL writing teachers in the post-secondary setting the impact of different cultural views on the composing of an essay, the paradigm has now broadened considerably, Ostler states. The areas of research have expanded to include writing preferences outside of ESL/EFL writing, research designs have been refined, and different populations of writers and types of writing are now being studied. The initial notion was generally well received by ESL/ EFL teachers, though there have been critics who claim contrastive rhetoric to be too mechanical or ethnocentric, and those who claimed the observed differences to be developmental. These issues are explained by Ostler and the contributions which such criticisms have brought to the refining and further expansion of the paradigm are noted. Ostler concludes her chapter with a call for more contrastive rhetoric research by non-native speakers of English, and on English speakers learning other languages. She also recommends continued expansion into the variations of writing in different genres, and issues such as literacy, and pedagogy, as well as more collaboration with those doing research on the teaching of reading and foreign languages other than English.

Tony McEnery and Nazareth Amselom Kifle

The first of the empirical studies in the section on contrastive rhetoric, by Tony McEnery and Nazareth Amselom Kifle, actually uses a corpus linguistic approach to investigate its contrastive research question: the differences in the use of epistemic modality by Eritrean and British students in English argumentative essays. Epistemic modalities are expressions that help writers/ speakers to convey their claims with different degrees of commitment. This is an area of particular difficulty for second-language learners (Hyland, 1996; Hyland and Milton, 1997). With specific regard to second-language writing, the authors claim that part of the difficulty arises from the fact that many syllabuses devote attention to teaching modal verbs as the main means of expressing epistemic modality, and neglect other devices (adverbs, adjectives, lexis, and nouns) frequently used with epistemic modal effect (Holmes, 1988).

Two corpora, one of about 20,000 words and the other of about 18,000 words, were used in the study. The findings revealed that the two groups of writers show notable differences in their use of epistemic qualifiers. The native British writers use more epistemic devices than the Eritreans, and frequently employ devices which convey certainty and strong assertion. The Eritreans make use of a limited selection of devices, and have a tendency to sound more tentative in their claims. The classroom materials used by the Eritrean learners are strongly implicated as the source of the difference between the two groups.

Sally Burgess

Just as McEnery's contrastive chapter could equally well have fitted into the corpus linguistics section of this collection, so too could Sally Burgess's, 'Packed houses and intimate gatherings: Audience and rhetorical structure', have fitted into the section on genre analysis. Burgess applies Swales's three-move model of the introduction to research articles to the analysis of audience constraints on the rhetorical structure of a large sample of research article introductions in the field of linguistics. However, Burgess's chapter is contrastive in nature, hence its inclusion under the heading of contrastive rhetoric. Burgess's corpus is made up of introductions to four types of article, according to language and audience: international journals of linguistics (written in English); Spanish Hispanic Studies journals (written in Spanish); Spanish English Studies journals (written in Spanish); and Spanish English

Studies journals (written in English). Contrasting these different categories, Burgess concludes that it is the audience which constrains the differences she identifies in the rhetorical structure of the introductions more than the L1 of the writer, the language of publication, or the area of specialisation.

Tatyana Yakhontova

Tatyana Yakhontova's chapter, '"Selling" or "telling"? Towards the issue of cultural variation in research genres', analyses cultural variation in the conference abstract on the basis of Ukrainian/partly Russian conference abstracts versus appropriate English texts and equivalent texts in English written by Ukrainian and Russian speakers. Yakhontova's procedure for the analysis of the texts arises primarily from the Bakhtinian vision of genre as the inseparable unity of its thematic content, compositional structure, and style. In the spirit of this framework, three generic aspects of the abstracts are analysed: (1) their cognitive/rhetorical organisation; (2) their manifestation through the formal composition (layout) of texts; (3) and the most conspicuous aspects of the language used to realise (1) and (2).

Yakhontova's findings show there to be remarkable differences in the generic features of the three types of text. For example, English writers justify a particular piece of research by indicating a gap in previous studies, question-posing or counter-claiming, whereas Slavic authors present their investigation as a significant part of the field or as a possible solution to its urgent problems. Ukrainian texts tend to avoid criticism and the use of the words of negative evaluation that, in contrast, function in the English texts. At the same time, the texts written by Ukrainians and Russians in English possess an eclectic mixture of different generic features. These 'indefinite', transitional texts are labelled 'intergenres' by Yakhontova (by analogy with the concept of interlanguage (Selinker, 1972), as a stage in second-language acquisition distinct from both native and target tongues). As complex phenomena, 'intergenres' show not only the level of the linguistic and cultural competence of their creators, but also signal the changes in the ideology and conventionalised existence of the academic community that has found itself at the interface of two social systems. Yakhontova suggests tentative explanations for the national professional, cultural, and ideological backgrounds underlying the identified differences.

Part IV. Ethnographic/naturalistic approaches

John Flowerdew

The overview chapter, by John Flowerdew, in the section on ethnographic/ naturalistic approaches is divided into three main parts. The first of these sets out some of the key issues and principles involved in such approaches. These include an emphasis on context and group culture as much as, if not more than, actual texts; the use of multiple methods; questions of validity and reliability; data analysis, the role of theory, the writing up of an ethnographic report; and application of the findings to pedagogy. The second part of the chapter discusses four studies, selected for their diversity and to show how each at the same time applies the principles set out in the first part. In the third part of the chapter there is a detailed description of a project in which the author was himself involved. Here, there is a systematic application of the principles highlighted in the first two parts of the chapter.

Desmond Allison and Wu Siew Mei

In the first of the empirical chapters in this section Desmond Allison and Wu Siew Mei describe how they became convinced that to examine the problem of students' academic writing in English language studies at their university in Singapore, the appropriate focus of enquiry was not simply to describe and evaluate tendencies in students' written texts at different stages, but to provide an account of how 'writing development' is conceptualised and promoted (or impeded) by the curriculum, both explicitly and implicitly. Accordingly, the researchers examined not just the writing tasks, but also ways in which students and teachers conceive of academic writing in contexts of curricular practice.

Their study is thus at the same time ethnographically inspired and pedagogically motivated. It is ethnographic in inspiration in that it seeks to characterise an educational culture in some depth and detail, taking account of significant texts and practices and different participant perspectives. It is pedagogically motivated in so far as it seeks to provide solutions to students' problems in academic writing.

Jane Jackson

Like Allison and Wu, in her chapter Jane Jackson is interested in finding solutions to her students' learning problems – in her case, business students who need to take part in case-based discussions. Jackson describes the purpose of her study as 'to provide an interpretative-explanatory account of the discourse and interaction that took place in English in a business case discussion at a Hong Kong university'. The account Jackson provides focuses not just on the language, but also on the attitudes of the professor and his students. 'By bringing the cultural assumptions and expectations of professors and students to light,' Jackson argues, 'ethnographic research can provide a basis for improving the learning situation.' In doing so Jackson hopes her findings will be of value not just to the participants involved, but also to others 'trying to understand professor–student behaviour in case discussions in other second- or foreign-language settings'.

Joyce Bell

In the third of the empirical chapters in the ethnographic/naturalistic approaches section, Joyce Bell, unusually for a naturalistic study, focuses on reading. The increasing number of students from cross-cultural and overseas backgrounds, speaking other languages and with different educational upbringings, is having a profound influence on the process of education in Australia, Bell argues. Reading, in particular, has been found to be one skill which presents considerable difficulty for international students, as their reading techniques are based on different cultural and intellectual traditions. Within the context of a larger study of the reading practices and traditions of postgraduate students from Thailand and India, the focus of Bell's study is a case study of one Thai member of this group.

The methodology involves what the author describes as an ethnographic approach, grounded in a theory of framing and metacognitive theory, using individual interviews and pair think-aloud protocol analysis. The case study reveals significant changes in strategy use between the first and third semesters and the student's awareness of these changes. Dissemination of this data will assist supervisors to understand the processes which many international students undergo, enabling them to design more culturally sensitive supervisory frameworks, Bell argues.

NOTES

1. See Swales (1988) for an anthology of papers with commentary summarising the early development of academic discourse analysis.

2. That is, a genre is composed of a number of typical rhetorical stages, some of which may be obligatory and some optional. In addition, the ordering of individual stages and their component parts may be fixed or variable. So a physical description would include a core stage describing the various parts of the object in question. In addition to this core stage, however, there might be description of the function of some or all of the parts. The component parts of these different stages, as well as being obligatory or optional, may occur in either a fixed or variable position. Hasan refers to this feature of genre as 'generic structure potential' (e.g. Hasan, 1985, 89).

3. It should be noted that the last chapter of Swales (1990) incorporates an ethnographic dimension, but this is not integrated with the textual analysis of genres presented in the main body. Swales's interest in integrating ethnography and textual analysis was later developed into what he calls 'textography' in his 1998 book, *Other floors, other voices: a textography of a small university building* (Swales, 1998).

Part I

GENRE ANALYSIS

Chapter 1

A Generic View of Academic Discourse

Vijay K. Bhatia

OVERVIEW

It has become almost axiomatic to regard linguistic analysis and description as a kind of prerequisite to the development and design of any language teaching and learning activity, especially in the context of English for Specific Purposes (ESP). Although the trust in the usefulness of linguistic descriptions for language teaching has not changed in the last few decades, the nature of linguistic analysis has developed considerably. Analyses of linguistic data for pedagogical applications have gone through a variety of stages in the past four decades. They started with the characterisation of statistically significant features of lexico-grammar to the study of textualisation in discourse, i.e. a characterisation of values these features of form realise in discourse. The second stage of development extended the study of textualisation to the study of macro-structures in texts, thereby bringing into focus the notion of discourse structure. The third stage of development marked a more significant shift of focus from the object of analysis itself, i.e. text, to the context in which it is constructed, used, interpreted, and perhaps exploited. It is at this stage that the focus shifted *from text* to *what makes a text possible*, from surface structure to deep structure of discourse, from discourse to genre, and finally from 'what' to 'why' in language use, and of course in language learning and language teaching. The next stage is already in place, which connects texts to social practice, shifting focus more centrally to the study of social structures, social identities and discourse systems, and things of that kind. One may notice here a subtle shift of attention from discourse to the underlying critical concerns of power and politics of language use, domination, and empowerment through linguistic and social practices via the context of communication, culture, and cognition.

Many of these developments can be characterised in terms of a quest for thicker descriptions of language use, often incorporating, and many a time going beyond, the immediate context of situation. This quest for thicker descriptions of language use has become popular as genre analysis, where an attempt is made to offer a grounded description of language use in educational, academic, or professional settings. We can also see how linguistic

21

analyses have became much more than mere descriptions, often attempting to offer explanation for a specific use of language in institutionalised social, educational, academic, and professional settings. These efforts to offer more explanatory linguistic descriptions often attempt to answer the question 'why does a particular use of language takes the shape it does?' One way of looking at these varying perceptions of language description can be the way they relate texts to contexts, as in the following diagram.

Language Description

as

Text

What features of lexico-grammar are statistically and/or functionally distinctive?
Context: narrowly configured in terms of textual links

Genre

Why do we use the language the way we do and what makes this possible?
Context: more specifically configured in terms of disciplinary cultures

Social Practice

How do we relate language to social structures, social identities,
and social practices?
Context: broadly configured in terms of socio-cultural realities

---

It is obvious from the diagram that just as a very narrowly configured context is likely to make textual description less effective for language teaching purposes, similarly a very broadly configured context in terms of socio-cultural practices may make insights less relevant to the learning and teaching of language. Ideally, one may need to position oneself somewhere in the middle, looking at the use of language as genre to achieve non-linguistic objectives, thus maintaining a balance between the study of linguistic form, on the one hand, and the study of context, in a broad sense of socio-cultural factors, to focus on why members of specific disciplinary cultures use the language the way they do and what makes this form possible. Let me give further substance to this view of language as genre by identifying and discussing some of its main concerns.

GENRE ANALYSIS

Genre Analysis is the study of situated linguistic behaviour in institutionalised academic or professional settings, whether in terms of *typification of rhetorical action*, as in Miller (1984), and Berkenkotter and Huckin (1995); *regularities of staged, goal oriented social processes,* as in Martin, Christie, and Rothery (1987) and Martin (1993); or *consistency of communicative purposes,* as in Swales (1990) and Bhatia (1993). Genre theory, in spite of these seemingly different orientations, covers a lot of common ground, some of which include the following:

1. Genres are reflections of disciplinary cultures and, in that sense, those of the realities of the world of discourse, in general.
2. Genres focus on conventionalised communicative events embedded within disciplinary or professional practices.
3. All disciplinary or professional genres have integrity of their own, which is often identified with reference to textual and discursive (text-internal) factors, or contextual and disciplinary (text-external) factors. However, it is not always fixed or static but often contested, depending upon the rhetorical context it tends to respond to.
4. Genres are recognisable communicative events, characterised by a set of communicative purpose(s) identified and mutually understood by members of the professional or academic community in which they regularly occur.
5. Genres are highly structured and conventionalised constructs, with constraints on allowable contributions in terms of the intentions one can give expression to, the shape they can take, and also in terms of the co-grammatical resources one can employ to give discoursal values to such formal features.
6. Established members of a particular professional community will have a much greater knowledge and understanding of generic practices than those who are apprentices, new members, or outsiders.
7. Although genres are viewed as conventionalised constructs, expert members of the disciplinary and professional communities are often in a position to exploit such conventions to express 'private intentions' within the structures of socially acceptable communicative norms.

As we can see, the most important feature of this view of language use is the emphasis on conventions that all the three manifestations of genre theory consider very central to any form of generic description. Genres are essentially defined in terms of the use of language in conventionalised communicative settings, which give expression to a specific set of communicative goals of specialised disciplinary and social groups, which in turn establish relatively stable structural forms and, to some extent, even constrain the use of lexico-grammatical resources. Often such constraints can also be attributed to variations in disciplinary practices.

The second important aspect of genre theory is that although genres are typically associated with recurring rhetorical contexts, and are identified on the basis of a shared set of communicative purposes with constraints on allowable contributions in the use of lexico-grammatical and discoursal forms, they are not static. As Berkenkotter and Huckin (1995) point out,

> genres are inherently dynamic rhetorical structures that can be manipulated according to conditions of use, and that genre knowledge is therefore best conceptualized as a form of situated cognition embedded in disciplinary cultures.

Emphasis on conventions and propensity for innovation – these two features of genre theory appear to be contradictory in character. One tends to view genre as a rhetorically situated, highly institutionalised textual event, having its own what I have elsewhere called *generic integrity*, (Bhatia, 1993); whereas the other assigns genre a natural propensity for innovation and change, which is often exploited by the expert members of the specialist community to create new forms in order to respond to novel rhetorical contexts or to convey 'private intentions' within the socially recognised communicative purposes. How do we resolve this contradiction?

Although genres are associated with typical socio-rhetorical situations and, in turn, shape future responses to similar situations, they have always been 'sites of contention between stability and change' (Berkenkotter and Huckin, 1995: 6). It may be that a person is required to respond to a somewhat changing socio-cognitive need, requiring him to negotiate his response in the light of recognisable or established conventions, since genres do change over time in response to changing socio-cognitive needs. Alternatively, it may be that he or she intends to communicate 'private intentions' within the rhetorical context of a 'socially recognized communicative purpose' (Bhatia, 1993).

It is often possible for some members of the professional community to manipulate institutionalised generic forms or generate new ones, which gives them 'tactical freedom' to exploit generic resources to negotiate an individual response to recurring and novel rhetorical situations. However, as Bhatia (1995) points out,

> such liberties, innovations, creativities, exploitations, whatever one may choose to call them, are invariably realized within rather than outside the generic boundaries, whichever way one may draw them, in terms of recurrence of rhetorical situations (Miller, 1984), consistency of communicative purposes (Swales, 1990, and Bhatia, 1993), existence and arrangement of obligatory structured elements (Hasan, 1985). It is never a free-for-all kind of activity. The nature of genre manipulation is invariably realized within the broad limits of specific genres and is often very subtle. A serious disregard for these generic conventions leads to opting out of the genre and is noticed by the specialist community as odd.

Another aspect of genre theory is its versatility, which can be seen operating at various levels. The versatility of genre-based linguistic description can be seen at other levels too. Using communicative purpose associated with a specific rhetorical situation as a privileged criterion, genre theory combines the advantages of a more general view of language use on the one hand, and its very specific realisation, on the other (Swales, 1990: 58; Bhatia, 1993). In this sense, genre analysis is narrow in focus and broad in vision. The concept of communicative purpose itself is a versatile one. On the one hand, it can be identified at a high level of generalisation, whereas on the other hand it can be narrowed down to a very specific level. In addition, it may either be a single communicative purpose or a more detailed set of communicative purposes. Depending upon the level of generalisation and detail at which one specifies communicative purpose(s), one may be in a position to identify the status of a particular genre and its use of generic conventions (see Bhatia, 1995, for a discussion of promotional discourse). In academic discourse also, this versatility offers a convincing explanation for the tension between genres and disciplines, to which I shall turn briefly at this stage.

Genres, as we know, cut across disciplinary boundaries, in the sense that one can notice significant overlap in the case of genres such as research article introductions (Swales, 1981a, 1990), abstracts (Bhatia, 1993), textbooks (Myers, 1992b) and a number of others across a range of disciplines. However, it is also true that these very genres, at a different level of delicacy, display subtle variations across a range of disciplines (see Biber, 1988; Fortanet et al., 1998; Hirvela, 1997; Holmes, 1997; Bhatia, 1999a; Hewings and Nickerson, 1999; Hyland, 2000, and Samraj, this volume, among others). Often these variations appear to be more significant in the way lexico-grammatical resources and rhetorical strategies are exploited to give expressions to discipline-specific concepts, knowledge and its structure, modes of conducting and reporting research, level of rhetorical intimacy, and pedagogic approaches and concerns. These two apparently contradictory concerns in disciplinary discourses have strong implications for both the theory and practice of ESP. In the area of ESP theory, they have been very much a significant part of the history of language description ever since the early days of ESP. At the level of ESP practice, this tension between disciplinary overlap and variation underpins the tension between pedagogic convenience and pedagogic effectiveness, which has been at the very heart of EAP and ESP.

ACADEMIC DISCOURSE

Historical perspective

Academic Discourse has long been viewed as a unified register in applied linguistic literature, especially in language teaching and learning, where courses for English for Academic Purposes (EAP) have become established as a standard response to fulfilling the English communication needs of tertiary-level students in the academy. One may find a wide range of EAP courses being offered to university-level undergraduate students all over the globe in second-language learning contexts. There are also a number of textbooks available in the market, some of which have been very successful commercially and been there for a long time. Some of the notable attempts in the area are Bachman (1986), Hamp-Lyons and Heasley (1987), Jordan (1990), Adamson (1993), and several more recent ones appearing every year.

However successful some of these courses might be, it is difficult to claim that they were all based on any principled investigation of whatever interpretation of the term 'academic discourse' they may have taken. To this date there has been very little research on a systematic investigation of what we mean by 'academic discourse'. In principle, the use of the term 'academic English' presupposes the existence or at least an understanding of what might be called an 'academic core' underlying most of the discourse types used in the academy; however, in practice, the existence of such an academic core is often assumed, rather than investigated and established. This kind of assumption necessarily has a number of consequences, some useful, others problematic for the teaching and learning of English, where solutions to pedagogic problems are sought even before the problems can be identified. Textbooks in language teaching, whether for EAP or ESP, are a very competitive business, where new ideas and approaches leading to innovative materials are essential for survival; however, one often gets little time to investigate, establish, or try out innovations before they are published. Many of the EAP materials, though some of them were extremely successful commercially, were put together on the basis of the long experience and perceptive insights of the authors, rather than on the basis of any research findings. Some of them have been successful commercially because of either their timely appearance or the pedagogic convenience they offered to those teachers of English who were desperately looking for quick solutions to the problems of ESP students. However, this does not ensure that all of them are pedagogically effective as well.

Although there have been a number of interesting and very successful attempts to design and implement EAP (or Study Skills in English) programmes (notably the ones coming from the University of Lancaster, University of Malaya, and Reading and Thinking Series), a number of others have often lacked a research basis for their rationale, teaching methodology, and design of teaching materials. Some of the important decisions related to EAP programme design are often based on experience rather than on any systematic research, which often discourages innovation and creativity in materials design on any principled basis. In the circumstances it is not surprising that Hamp-Lyons, in her introduction to the Special Issue of *English for Specific Purposes* (Vol. 16, Issue 1, 1997), reflects somewhat pessimistically on the state of EAP, when she asks some of the most relevant questions, such as the following.

- Why is it . . . that we seem to understand the problems facing second language users of English in reading and listening hardly any better than we did 5 or 10 years ago?
- Why haven't we learned how to teach students to deconstruct a lecture in order to reconstruct a meaning of their own?
- Why aren't the materials getting better?
- Has the development of materials teaching text structure comprehension and text 'attack' skills helped?
- Why hasn't anyone found the perfect method, the perfect materials?

These are interesting, relevant, and insightful questions, and although some of the answers are hidden behind the issues I have raised in the introductory paragraphs, the others may need to be identified and discussed in the context of recent developments in university education, to which I shall return in the next section. However, before I do so, I would like to point out that irrespective of the lack of research basis, English for Academic Purposes has survived and has always remained an important aspect of ESP. The popularity and success of such an approach is largely attributed to the pedagogic convenience that it offers to ESP practitioners. ESP by definition is narrowly conceptualised, but in practice it is often possible to broaden the angle to cover a much larger range of disciplinary requirements. Although narrowly conceived, designed, and executed ESP courses are likely to be more pedagogically effective, they are often time-consuming, expensive, and difficult to design. On the other hand, broad-angle ESP courses (of which EAP is one of the most popular and significant examples; others include English for Technical Communication) are easy to design, less time-consuming, and more cost-effective, in that they can be delivered to larger audiences. They are significantly different from their more narrowly defined counterparts, in that they tend to undermine the role of disciplinary variations and sometimes even subtle variations in skills and abilities required for specific academic tasks. Although such broad-angle EAP courses are less likely to be as effective as some of the more narrowly designed specific ESP courses, they certainly are more convenient in terms of time and effort. In the final analysis, then, the tension between ESP and EAP can be captured in terms of tensions between pedagogic effectiveness and pedagogic convenience.

Present-day perspective

In recent years, in response to a number of interesting developments, including a sudden increase in economic liberalisation in many developing and newly developed countries and a corresponding increase in the interdisciplinary and multicultural contexts of the workplace, we have noticed significant changes in the way educational programmes are designed, offered, and evaluated. Interestingly enough, it is not only the socio-political and geographical but also the disciplinary boundaries that are being renegotiated or demolished in a complex and dynamic manner. Also, there seems to be a much stronger need now than ever before for expertise in multiple specialisms and hence the need for interdisciplinary qualifications.

In response to this dynamic complexity of present-day workplace practices, a number of universities have been radically changing the nature of their academic programmes, making them increasingly interdisciplinary. One of the essential consequences of this development has been that students interacting with different disciplines need to develop communication skills that may not be an extension of general literacy to handle academic discourse, but a range of literacies to handle disciplinary variation in academic discourse. In the areas of Business and Law, for instance, students majoring in Business Studies no longer require simply an ability to handle the discourses related to their parent discipline, but also those related to other disciplines, and the same is true of law students who need to handle business discourses as part of their legal studies. Most business programmes incorporate some aspects of law and many programmes in law include some aspects of business. Increasingly we find a number of innovative joint programmes in business and law, accountancy and law, management and law, in addition to somewhat more established interdisciplinary programmes in management engineering, and socio-legal studies, professional communication, and others. There are even university departments which display this kind of interdisciplinarity, not only in their academic offerings, but also in their establishment and structure, as in Department of Law and Accountancy, Faculty of Business and Law, etc.

However, if we look at the discourses of the individual disciplines, we are less likely to find sufficient common ground to justify the merger of such disciplinary cultures. On the contrary, we are more likely to find generic and disciplinary conflicts, which, in turn, create learning problems for those second-language learners who with their rather limited competence in the language are required to cope with such intricacies of disciplinary discourses. Consequently, many of the conventional English for Business courses are becoming increasingly inadequate to meet the complexity of the communication demands inherent in the multidisciplinary nature of the academic tasks that the learners are expected to accomplish. What the learners really need is the competence to handle several types of literacy, which may not be a simple extension of previously acquired communicative competence; it may be more a matter of developing expertise in diverse and multiple literacy practices (Chiseri-Strater, 1991) within and across disciplinary boundaries. One of the main issues in the teaching and learning of ESP relevant to academic contexts, therefore, is not simply to investigate the communicative demands placed on students in the designated disciplines, but also to find out if these demands vary across disciplines. Developments such as these raise a number of important issues for the teaching and learning of broad-angle Academic English courses. In this chapter, I would like to focus on some of the following issues related to the use of academic English in EAP/ESP contexts:

- What is the nature of academic English?
- How widely or narrowly should it be viewed?
- How do we define it?
- How significant are the disciplinary differences in the discourses of the academy?
- How effective can it be in the context of a need for multiple specialisms?

I will also discuss the implications of such findings for the theory and practice of EAP, especially in the design and implementation of such programmes.

English for Academic Purposes

Like a number of other concepts of this kind, Academic English or English for Academic Purposes (EAP) is a fuzzy concept. In ESP/EAP literature, it is generally understood very broadly, covering all areas of academic concern, i.e. teaching (undergraduate- as well as postgraduate-level textbooks, lectures, tutorials, seminars, academic discussions), research (articles, conferences, academic research reports, research grant applications, etc.), examination

(examination papers and answers, project reports and theses, essays and other written work), and sometimes even academic administration (e.g. course and programme descriptions); however, in teaching and learning contexts, it is often identified somewhat narrowly depending upon the specific application for which it is used. The broader the view we take, the more dominant the role of disciplinary variation within it. The interesting thing is that although much of the research published in the area of discourse and genre analysis of academic discourse in recent years (Alderson and Urquhart, 1985; Anderson et al., 1990; Bhatia, 1998, 1999b; Braine, 1989; Candlin and Plum, 1999; Chiseri-Strater, 1991; Faigley and Hansen, 1985; Fortanet et al., 1998; Hewings and Nickerson, 1999; Read, 1990; Tedick, 1990; and more recently Hyland, 2000) has consistently demonstrated academic discourse to be varied in terms of disciplines and genres, the EAP community have consistently taken it to be a single and uniform entity, with a 'common core' across disciplines and often genres. Similarly, the concept of academic literacy has also been treated as unproblematic for a long time and it is only in the last few years that in ESP literature we have seen this being referred to in the plural as 'academic literacies' (Chiseri-Strater, 1991; Lea and Street, 1999). Hyland (2000: 147) aptly sums up the damage such an unproblematic view of discourse can do to the learning and teaching of writing in the academy:

> The fact of multiple literacies within the academy is a further burden to students, particularly if they lack the vocabulary and analytical skills to distinguish the heterogeneity of the discourses and practices typical of the different disciplinary cultures they encounter. Presenting academic skills as universal and transferable does a serious disservice to learners as it disguises variability, and misrepresents academic writing as naturalised, self-evident and non-contestable ways of participating in academic communities.

However, there seems to be a historical explanation for these developments. Although disciplinary knowledge has always played a significant and distinctive function in the identification and designing of ESP programmes, often providing necessary psychological validity to many of the early ESP courses, as discourse analysis developed from the concept of register and moved towards genre and became increasingly interdisciplinary, the role of disciplinary variation took a back seat. This was also due to the fact that most researchers felt that disciplinary knowledge contributed little more than the use of specialist lexis. Meanwhile, with the development of genre analysis as a more popular option, the focus shifted towards rhetorical analyses, which often cut across disciplines at the expense of those that highlighted disciplinary contrasts.

   More recently, with the renewed interest in the design of interdisciplinary programmes, the emphasis, once again, has shifted to the contributions that disciplinary cultures tend to make to the construction, interpretation, use, and exploitation of academic and professional discourses; however, it is important to take into account disciplinary variations in ways that complement the genre-based view of discourse, resulting in more comprehensive analytical insights. Just as the recent genre-based view of discourse offers flexibility to analyse genres, either in their pure form or in hybrid, embedded, or mixed forms, it can similarly provide insights into disciplinary variations as well. In fact, the concept is so versatile that, on the one hand, it can account for variation across genres, while on the other hand it can also account for variation across disciplines, without creating any tension between disciplines and genres. Elsewhere (Bhatia, 1999a), discussing the versatility of generic framework, I have suggested that genres are strategically placed between 'textual space', on the one hand, and 'social space' on the other, generic knowledge covering much of the socio-pragmatic or what I call the 'tactical' space. In other words, a genre-based view of discourse can satisfactorily explore the 'textual' as well as the 'social' space, within which most discourses operate, whether one is interested in disciplinary variation or generic overlaps or 'hybridity' across a range of genres. This versatility can be visually represented as in Figure 1.1.

Current research in disciplinary variation in discourse therefore makes it necessary for applied linguists, in general, and language educators, in particular, to broaden their traditional view of language use and literacy from that of a common core academic discourse to a more differentiated view

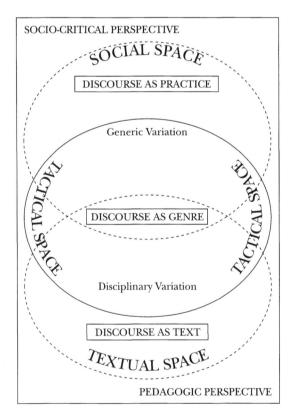

Figure 1.1 Perspectives on generic variation

based on generic as well as disciplinary models, if language education is to be pedagogically effective. As Candlin (2000) in his preface to Hyland (2000) points out, the need is to take 'a comparative view across a range of academic disciplines and across faculty boundaries so that we can . . . assess clearly how these processes of social interaction are variably realised in discipline-specific writing'. He further points out the need 'to demonstrate what is generically integral across genres, across disciplines, and what is discipline-specific', on the basis of which one may 'make broader generalisations about what is common to academic writing as an activity-type, and where genre variation and discipline-specific genre variation' becomes significant. Underlying this assertion here is the problematic concern about the assumptions in a typical traditional approach to academic discourse about the presence of a 'common core' based on generalisations across genres and disciplines without investigating the tensions within and across genres and disciplines. Let me give more substance to what I have been claiming in these sections by focusing on some of the tensions in academic discourse.

Genres and disciplines

Genres and disciplines interact in an interesting and dynamic manner, especially in academic discourses. I would like to identify some of the interesting cases, which seem to raise issues of variation in the context of the search for a common core in what is commonly understood as academic English. First, there are genres and systems of genres that are typically associated with certain disciplines. Second, we find genres that typically overlap a range of disciplines. We may also find genres within a single academic discipline displaying tensions of various kinds, as in the case of textbooks and research articles. And finally, we may consider cases where on the surface there may appear to be striking similarities in terms of textual features, but very little overlap in terms of functional domains, disciplinary uses, and pedagogic values.

Let me begin with a brief indication of typical generic systems conventionally operating within specific disciplinary boundaries, in order to see if there is any overlap across disciplines in this respect. The first thing that one can notice in this area is that there are typical sets of genres associated with each discipline and they are rather distinct in terms of their generic integrity, textual and rhetorical characteristics, functional values, and social purposes and applications, with little overlap whatsoever. These genres are typically employed in specific disciplinary cultures in the fulfilment of specific disciplinary objectives, not necessarily meant to be used in academic contexts. In some cases, these are often associated with more professional than academic contexts. The main objectives in the study of law, for instance, are to encourage legal reasoning and to pursue issues about the law through legal research. The emphasis is on deriving principles of law from the facts of life and also on applying principles to the daily affairs of the members of one's society. Strategies to promote legal reasoning are also deeply rooted in the discourses of law and have remained unchanged for a long time. Academic communication

ly depends on two of the most conventionally standardised disciplin-
ares (legislation and judgments) to construct legal knowledge, and
..... centrality is also signalled in the intertextual and interdiscursive patterning
that these mutually dependent generic constructs display in all forms of legal
discourse, including textbooks.

Business Studies, on the other hand, constitute a variety of concerns, some
of which may even have sub-disciplinary variations. Accounting, for instance,
emphasises primarily collecting, classifying, recording, analysing, and interpreting financial data, Economics emphasises devising theory, collecting and
analysing data to verify or refute theories, whereas the emphasis in marketing
is on practical applications of marketing theories. Most of these disciplines
crucially depend on business case studies and reports, letters, and memos to
construct and communicate their typical disciplinary knowledge and concerns.

In the case of Public Administration or Political Science, as Bhatia (1999a:
137) points out, conceptual identities are often viewed as being in a constant
process of change and development not because of the changing times, but
because of the changing perceptions of the people interpreting events taking
place in a particular age or place. Quite understandably therefore, the discipline heavily depends on genres such as news reports, political and policy
statements, international treaties, memoranda of understanding, etc. in order
to understand and study the changing perceptions of socio-political developments. An interesting thing about these systems of genres is that although
they are not originally written to be used in academic contexts and are not
centrally located in such contexts, they are often considered extremely important for the construction of disciplinary knowledge in the academy.

There are, however, several other factors, which make things complicated
for language educators, or, more specifically, ESP practitioners, who have a
strong interest in and commitment to interdisciplinary programmes. Let me
take up the second case now, where systems of genres are often used across
a range of disciplines. Some of the genres within the academy, such as textbooks, journal articles, projects, examination questions, essays, etc., have interesting generic overlaps across a number of academic disciplines. Although
these genres, by definition, cut across disciplinary boundaries, they do display
subtle disciplinary differences, in addition to the use of specialist lexical
realisations. Even in this narrowly identified area of academic discourse, it is
not always safe to assume overlaps. Take, for example, the genres of textbook
and research article. As instances of a broad category of academic discourse,
they do seem to display significant overlap in terms of what is popularly known
as field of discourse, especially patterns of specialist lexis and certain rhetorical
functions; however, the two genres certainly have their own 'generic integrity'
(Bhatia, 1993), which is often reflected in some of the following features.

- *Discourse content.* Textbooks incorporate established disciplinary knowledge,
  whereas research genres handle new and often contested knowledge.
- *Participant relationship.* The textbook writer is viewed as the knowledgeable
  teacher and the student as an uninitiated reader, which is a typical instance

of unequal encounter distinguished in terms of presence or lack of disciplinary expertise, whereas in research genres such a relationship is based
more on expectations of a balanced and equal participation.

- *Discourse characteristics.* Textbooks often display the use of appropriate rhetorical devices to make knowledge accessible to a range of students, which
is a function of the textbook competence of the writer, some of which
include *description, definition, classification,* etc. (Trimble, 1985; Widdowson,
1978) and *predictive structures* (Tadros, 1989); in research genres, on the
other hand, such devices are rare (Swales, 1981b, 1982).

- *Discourse strategies.* Textbooks often facilitate learning through the use of
rhetorical strategies, such as *access structures* (Waller, 1977) and *easification procedures* (Bhatia, 1983), *rhetorical questions as section headings* to lead learners
through the intricacies of discipline-based understanding, *non-linear rhetorical devices* like charts, diagrams, figures, pictures, etc. to express complex
materials (Bhatia, 1984; Trimble, 1985), *metadiscourse,* specially lexical fam-
iliarisations or word glosses (Williams, 1985) to explain difficult concepts;
however, such strategies are often dispreferred in research genres.

Similarly, it is possible to distinguish other academic genres, such as examination essays, question papers, course descriptions, and several others as independent and yet related instances of discourse within the same academic
register, but markedly distinctive in terms of their generic identities. All of
them serve quite distinctive communicative purposes and display the use
of typical rhetorical conventions and characteristics. Investigating the use of
textbook and research article genres in pedagogic practice, Myers (1992b)
quite appropriately claims that these two genres behave quite differently
when used in academic contexts. In spite of certain overlapping features,
they represent different realities in teaching and learning contexts and require
very different reading and analytical strategies on the part of learners, who
wish to come to terms with disciplinary knowledge. These genres also attract
different tasks if they have to be treated authentically in academic contexts,
even if one were to ignore subject-specific concerns.

Disciplinary cultures thus differ on several other dimensions, such as typical
patterns of membership and initiation into disciplinary cultures, knowledge
structures and norms of enquiry associated with different disciplines, in addition to expectations and standards of rhetorical intimacy and modes of expression, the specialist lexis, and typical approaches to the teaching of different
disciplines. Demarcations between broad subject areas thus not only appear
to reflect differences in the structure of knowledge systems, but also often
embody quite different assumptions about discourse and communication
(Berkenkotter and Huckin, 1995). These differences influence both the preferred modes of communication within and across different disciplines and
the rhetorical characteristics of the genres students are expected to master in
becoming competent members of a particular disciplinary culture.

So the complexities of what we commonly understand as academic discourse
show interactions between a range of factors, each influencing and creating

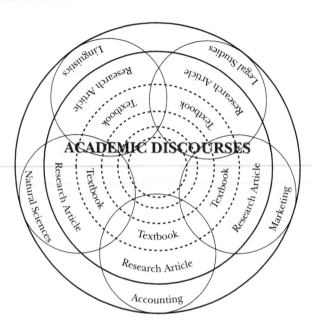

Figure 1.2 Variations in academic discourses

variation, sometimes even tension between disciplinary discourses. Some of these factors are associated with variations in disciplinary knowledge (especially the way it is structured), generic constructs (range of genres), pedagogic procedures (especially the way teaching and learning takes place in the classroom). In effect, considering the complexity and a range of variations, one may find it difficult to conceptualise academic discourse as a single entity with an identifiable common core; it may be more realistic to represent the variations quite legitimately in terms of academic discourses, in the plural rather than the singular, as in Figure 1.2.

Let me now move on to another case where a particular genre with a deceptively similar surface-level appearance across two very different disciplines behaves entirely differently in the context of the two disciplinary cultures, i.e. cases in business and law.

Cases form a significant part of the repertoire of disciplinary discourses in both business and law. These are often viewed as a record of past events, leading to the identification of problematic issues, contextualising opportunities for the discussion and illustration of important disciplinary concepts. The generic realisations also begin with a somewhat characteristic narration and description of facts, leading to the identification of problems, discussion of issues at stake, and finally to a solution or judgement based on disciplinary principles. A business case generally begins with a brief description of the company, which is seen as facing some difficulty, followed by a detailed description of facts, embedded in a situational context, eventually leading to a discussion of possible solutions, and sometimes a conclusion. A law case, on the other hand, typically begins with the identification of the case, followed by establishing of facts, and then by the arguments of the judge, which also includes deriving *ratio decidendi* and always ends with the pronouncement of the judgment. However, these surface similarities seem to be misleading, if we look at the way cases are used in the pedagogy of the two disciplines.

In business studies, cases are often originally written for business students, or sometimes for professionals for the identification and discussion of problems, invariably leading to possible solutions of identified problems, which eventually leads to more effective planning for better marketing or sales strategies or human resource management issues. In academic business contexts, cases are used for developing business skills in simulated contexts, problem identification and analysis, critical thinking and communication, understanding group dynamics, data handling and decision-making. In professional business contexts cases are used to bring an element of realism by simulating the roles of real-life executives and creating realistic business contexts for decision-making.

A law case, on the other hand, is a report of the opinion of a particular judge based on the real negotiation of justice in a court of law. Law cases are records of court proceedings to be used as precedents for future judgments. In academic contexts, cases demonstrate the nature and logic of judicial reasoning in the negotiation of justice. In law courts, cases are used to support or dispute arguments. Wisdom (1964) claims 'the process of legal argumentation in cases' is not a 'chain' of demonstrative reasoning. It is a presenting and representing of those features of the case which 'severally co-operate' in favour of the conclusion, in favour of saying what the reasoner wishes said, in favour of calling the situation by the name by which he wishes to call it. The reasons are like the legs of a chair, not the links of a chain.

Bhatia (1993: 175) points out, 'Legal cases and legislation are complementary to each other. If cases, on the one hand, attempt to interpret legal provisions in terms of the facts of the world, legislative provisions, on the other hand, are attempts to account for the unlimited facts of the world in terms of legal relations.' This can be visually represented as in Figure 1.3.

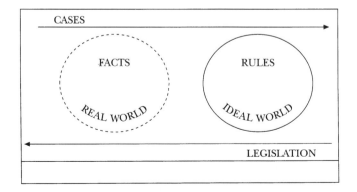

Figure 1.3   Interdiscursivity in legal genres

A related genre in law based very much on legal cases is what is popularly known as the problem-question genre, where learners are given made-up legal problems and they are expected to offer solutions to such problems using legal arguments and authorities. The expected response to such problem-questions often mirrors, though not closely, the discourse patterns they find in legal judgments. It is expected that a good response to such questions will include arguments and counter-arguments to several possible solutions, with the most favoured based on legal authorities, which may appropriately include case precedents and legislative provisions. One of the most widely read legal scholars, Glanville Williams, has the following to say to students of law:

> One of the most important of a lawyer's accomplishments is the ability to resolve facts into their legal categories. The student should therefore take pains to argue in terms of legal rules and concepts. It is a common fault . . . to give the impression that the answer is based wholly upon common sense and a few gleanings from the Sunday newspapers . . . When the problem is possibly distinguishable from the authority or authorities nearest in point, a careful analysis of possible distinction or distinctions should always be given. This is particularly important if the authority in question has been doubted by judges or criticised by legal writers. It may be that the student does not feel competent to discuss various distinctions, but even so the existence of the possible distinctions should be pointed out in the answer.   (Williams, 1982: 118, 123)

The most important aspect of this genre is thus the learner's ability to demonstrate a sound understanding of legal reasoning based on an understanding of the relevant aspects of the law in question. This is often illustrated in the discussion of a number of plausible solutions. As Harris (1997) points out, 'the law and its conceptual framework is learned through a process of matching, contrasting, classifying and distinguishing cases'; hence the importance of legal reasoning and argumentation. However, in an exercise of this kind in academic business contexts, where business students study law, it is often the case that they tend to offer a good, pragmatically convincing, but not necessarily a legal solution to the problem. This is perfectly understandable from the point of view of business concerns, and that is exactly what they are required to be doing in real business contexts, but unfortunately not in academically legal contexts. This kind of disciplinary tension is often at the heart of a successful or not-so-successful response to such a problem-question exercise. This was recently confirmed by a professor teaching law in the faculty of business in one of the universities in Hong Kong. In the course of a focused group interview in the context of an investigation into the communicative demands placed on students pursuing interdisciplinary business education in Hong Kong, she pointed out that a number of business students did not appropriately respond to such problem-questions, certainly not in the way they are expected to in legal contexts. In many cases, although the use of language is reasonably good, and sometimes the suggested solutions are acceptable, the argument, the use of relevant legal authorities, and the discussion of other possible solutions are underemphasised. The solution may be considered legitimate from the point of view of business culture from a legal viewpoint it is often less than acceptable.

To sum up, surface-level generic similarities across disciplines must be viewed with caution, when planning and designing EAP programmes. Instruction in any discipline is acculturation, which means bringing the student into the discourse community of the discipline, having specific norms, expectations, and conventions with respect to writing. Hyland (2000: 149), referring to Geertz (1983), points out that 'disciplinary communities are not simply bundles of conventions, but ways of being in the world, and this implies the use of specific ways of conceptualising problems, devising taxonomies, selecting data and processing claims through established genres. ESP has long recognised this, although it has rarely endorsed an investigative approach to communities as well as texts.'

Conclusions

I have made an attempt to highlight some of the disciplinary conflicts that may arise as a result of a tendency to introduce interdisciplinary university programmes. In the workplace context also corporations are finding it difficult to employ highly skilled individuals in narrowly defined areas of speciality. Engineers find better job prospects if they have a degree in management. Similarly, business management graduates find better opportunities if they have a degree in law as well. It is not simply a matter of economy. In the context of work, this kind of multidisciplinary expertise facilitates better understanding of issues and more effective communication prospects. In response to such demands of multidisciplinary expertise in the professions, a number of universities have started responding by introducing increasingly innovative multidisciplinary academic programmes. This has raised for the language teaching community several issues related to disciplinary and generic tensions within and across the discourses of the academy, which have often been assumed to be unproblematic. These issues have significant implications for the design and implementation of academic purpose English programmes to meet the communicative demands imposed on second-language learners in the pursuit of their academic and professional careers, some of which include:

- How do we develop sensitivity to this kind of dynamic complexity in academic and professional genres in EAP programmes, which are intended to serve not just one discipline but the demands of several disciplines at the same time?
- To what extent does the learning of various academic disciplines involve academic literacy that is uniform across a number of disciplines?
- Is it possible to assume that there is an 'academic core' underlying all academic disciplines?
- If so, to what extent does this common core provide a sufficient basis for developing a cross-disciplinary and cross-generic sensitivity in academic and professional discourse?

- If not, what is the best way to integrate the two seemingly conflicting aspects of interdisciplinary academic and professional discourse, the core and the conflict?

As learners move from one discipline to another, from primary to secondary specialisation, for example, they are faced with the problem of reconciling differences and even contradictions associated with varying disciplinary practices, including the use of genres as well as conversations with their teachers and specialist writers. In the case of the textbook genre from economics and law, for instance, one may obviously find some similarities in the two disciplines, especially in the use of rhetorical strategies to make what we understand as established disciplinary knowledge accessible to uninitiated readers. Angela Tadros (1989) rightly claims that her model of discourse prediction works for economics and law, in that in both of them one finds predictive categories like *reporting, question, advance labelling, enumeration, recapitulation,* and *hypotheticality*. However, this does not mean that there are no significant dissimilarities in other important ways, such as in the nature and development of argumentation, especially the way evidence is used to make claims, e.g. the way cases and legislation are used to make claims and to argue for them in the discourse of law; and the way numerical data are used to construct, formulate, and support argumentation in economics. Similarly the importance and function of intertextuality in the discourse of these two disciplines also vary significantly. In economics, intertextuality between textbooks and real-world numerical data is important, whereas in law, intertextual patterns between textbooks and cases and legislation are crucial to the development of argument. In law, footnotes play a significant role in the development of legal knowledge and also in the construction of legal argument, whereas in economics and, indeed, in many other disciplines, they have a peripheral role, and are fast disappearing. Moreover, the pedagogic tasks in these two disciplines are selected and performed differently (see Bhatia, 1999a, for a detailed discussion of this issue). Hyland (2000: 149) goes a step further when he points out,

> Disciplinary writing is a form of social action in which communicative purpose of the writer is a defining feature. We should . . . not view EAP teaching too narrowly to exclude the institutional and social practices in which these purposes are embedded. Instead we have to strengthen textual analysis with the insights gained from examining how writing is constructed, interpreted, and used by experienced members of the community in their everyday lives. In other words, students need to research not only the profession's principal discourses, but also the profession itself.

In most traditional EAP programmes cross-disciplinary variation is assigned a very low priority at the cost of pedagogic effectiveness. As Faigley and Hansen (1985) point out:

> If teachers of English are to offer courses that truly prepare students to write in other disciplines, they will have to explore why those disciplines study certain

subjects, why certain methods of enquiry are sanctioned, how the conventions of a discipline shape a text in that discipline, how individual writers represent themselves in the text, how a text is read and disseminated, and how one text influences subsequent texts. In short, teachers of English will have to adopt a rhetorical approach to the study of writing in the disciplines, an approach that examines the negotiation of meaning among writers, readers and subject matters.

(Faigley and Hansen, 1985: 149)

In early ESP practice, although disciplinary variation played a significant role in the identification and designing of courses for specific audiences, it was mainly used for psychological and face validity of the offerings or for lexical development. The commercial success of some of the discipline-specific ESP textbooks in the early 1970s is a good case in point. Sometimes, disciplinary variation is used to teach technical terminology, especially in LSP courses in the European context. However, cross-disciplinary variation has always been either underplayed or assumed to be least problematic. For the effective and efficient planning and designing of specialist language teaching courses in the present-day context, it is all the more necessary to take into account cross-disciplinary patterns in academic discourse, focusing on varieties of genres employed in disciplinary communication, keeping in mind the disciplinary boundaries these genres correspond to.

To conclude, I have made an attempt to outline some of the fundamental and pedagogically important disciplinary differences which may influence the teaching and learning of academic discourse within university-level academic programmes, especially those which rely heavily on interdisciplinary and multidisciplinary perceptions of knowledge. The concept of academic discourse, especially for the designing of specialist language teaching programmes, needs to be viewed in the light of the present-day trend towards the introduction of an increasing number of inter- and multidisciplinary academic programmes. Understanding and discussion of disciplinary conflicts, some of which I have alluded to here, will lead to a better and more realistic perception, understanding, construction, interpretation, and use of academic discourse. The tensions between the 'core' and the 'conflicts' that I have discussed in this chapter boil down to a tension between *pedagogic convenience* and *pedagogic effectiveness*. Although it is economical, convenient, and cost-effective in ESP course design and implementation to look for an academic core in disciplinary discourse, it could be less effective and counterproductive in a number of ways to ignore the sophistication and subtleties of variations across disciplinary boundaries. On the one hand, it is necessary to take advantage of the common ground; however, on the other hand, it is equally desirable to be aware of disciplinary distinctions. The ESP paradigm needs to develop a discourse and genre-based cross-disciplinary approach, taking into account the dynamic aspects of disciplinary boundaries, to create appropriate conditions for meeting the interdisciplinary discourse-based demands placed on apprentices in the academy.

Chapter 2

Disciplinary variation in abstracts: The case of Wildlife Behaviour and Conservation Biology

Betty Samraj

INTRODUCTION

The field of genre studies has developed in a number of different directions in the recent past (Bhatia, this volume). A number of spoken genres, such as graduate seminars (Weissberg, 1993), and lectures (Dudley-Evans, 1994b), have been studied in addition to more detailed studies of written genres, such as research articles, which have been the focus of study for a number of years. These studies on various genres, both oral and written, have informed us on the social construction of the texts, their characteristic rhetorical and lexico-grammatical features, and the ways in which they have evolved over time. Most of the studies on various genres are analyses of texts from a particular discipline. For example, Nwogu's (1990) study of research article abstracts is limited to texts from one field, medicine. Alternatively, the texts for some genre studies have come from a number of different fields in order to neutralise any disciplinary effect on genre structure (e.g. Swales, 1990).

Recent developments in genre studies have been concerned with variations within a particular genre. Genres have been shown to exhibit two types of variations. One is variation in a genre across linguistic and cultural boundaries (Melander, Swales, and Fredrickson, 1997; Ahmad, 1997) and the other is discoursal variation in a genre across disciplinary boundaries (Samraj, forthcoming). Though there have been some studies on generic variations across disciplines, most of the studies on variation have focused on cross-linguistic differences in academic discourse (see Ostler, this volume). These studies have provided evidence of the influence of cultural and linguistic factors on discourse structure. The characteristics of texts produced by non-native speakers of English and texts produced in different languages have been compared to the textual features identified in genres produced by native English speakers (e.g. Taylor and Chen, 1991; Bhatia, 1993; Jenkins and Hinds, 1987). The variations in genre structure found have been explained in terms of cultural and linguistic features. For example, the second move in research article introductions, which primarily presents the justification for the research being reported, is largely absent in introductions in linguistics research articles in Swedish (Fredrickson and Swales, 1994). The size of the discourse community and the ensuing lack or presence of competition for research space is offered as an explanation for this rhetorical variation seen across tokens of the same genre produced in two different cultural and educational communities.

The second dimension of generic variation is disciplinary proclivity of the text. A genre may not have an invariant structure within one linguistic/cultural community. Recent work on writing in the disciplines has pointed to some textual variation due to disciplinary norms (e.g. Samraj, forthcoming, on research article introductions). Disciplinary variation in text structure adds another layer of complexity to variations found in genres due to cultural and linguistic factors. Disciplinary communities within a particular cultural or linguistic community can be viewed as subcultural communities within that community with their own discursive practices.

One genre which has been the subject of studies on disciplinary variation is the research article introduction,[1] a genre which has been studied for a number of years (Swales and Najjar, 1987; Anthony, 1999). Other genres which have not been as extensively studied have also not received as much attention as far as disciplinary variation is concerned. Research article abstracts are a genre that did not receive much attention until the 1990s (Swales, 1990; Bhatia, this volume). However, since then a number of studies have analysed the schematic structure or global organisation of this genre as well as the linguistic features that characterise it. Several of these studies have focused on abstracts from a particular discipline. For example, Salager-Meyer (1992) and Nwogu (1990) have studied abstracts from medical science while Santos (1996) has studied abstracts from linguistics.

In general, though recent work on genres in the disciplines has pointed to interesting differences in textual structure of genres from different disciplines, there are few studies that are truly comparative in their focus. Some studies of writing in the disciplines merely focus on texts from one particular discipline but in this case it is not always clear whether the discourse features identified are due to generic conventions or disciplinary norms. Analysing texts from a single discipline usually does not reveal as much about disciplinary variation as does a comparison of two sets of texts belonging to the same genre but two disciplines. Such a comparison can yield information on the influence of genre norms and disciplinary preferences on discourse structure. One study of abstracts that has been both cross-disciplinary and cross-cultural in its perspective is that by Melander et al. (1997), which compared abstracts from Biology, Medicine, and Linguistics, written in English (by native speakers from the USA and non-native speakers from Sweden) and Swedish (by native speakers in Sweden). Though this study and others on disciplinary variation in research articles have given us some insight into generic variation within one cultural/linguistic community due to the influence of disciplinary values, our knowledge of the interaction of generic and disciplinary norms in text structure is still in its infancy.

In this chapter, I will discuss a study that was undertaken to further explore how the structure of research article abstracts varies across disciplines. The research article abstract is a genre that has considerable importance in academic writing and reading. Published with most research articles, abstracts are used extensively by the busy academic reader to scan the literature. As such, the analysis of abstracts has pedagogic value since it can be safely presumed that a well-written abstract, according to the norms of the discipline in question, would be more likely to attract a larger readership than otherwise. My study will build on what is already known about abstract structure but will extend our understanding with regard to disciplinary variation. As indicated above, there have been few systematic cross-disciplinary studies of generic variation. Melander et al.'s (1997) study analysed texts from widely differing fields: Biology, Medicine, and Linguistics. My cross-disciplinary study will analyse abstracts from two related fields, Conservation Biology and Wildlife Behaviour, both components of the overarching interdiscipline, environmental science. Moreöver, both disciplines in my study are biological sciences but differ considerably on the theory vs. applied dimension. Wildlife Behaviour is concerned with the life histories and behaviours of different species while Conservation Biology draws on various fields, such as resource economics and policy, ecology, and environmental ethics, in order to arrive at solutions for conservation problems. By comparing texts from disciplines that are somewhat related, this study will explore whether generic structures vary across texts which have some disciplinary affinity. The study will reveal whether texts have to belong to significantly different disciplines to show textual variation. Analysing two sets of texts from related disciplines will also indicate which aspects of the genre are most likely to vary in response to any small change in disciplinary value.

STUDIES ON ABSTRACTS

Studies on abstracts have focused on both the rhetorical moves and linguistic features found in this genre. Bhatia (1993) states that abstracts provide a summary of the research article and uses the overall organisation of the research article to arrive at the rhetorical moves found in abstracts: introduction (purpose), method, results, and conclusion. These same moves have also been used in the analysis of abstracts by other researchers such as Salager-Meyer (1990), who uses the four rhetorical moves to evaluate the quality of Medical English abstracts. In another study, also of Medical English abstracts (Salager-Meyer, 1992), she identifies the presence of other moves, such as case presentation in abstracts that accompany case reports and data synthesis in review article abstracts. Melander et al.'s (1997) study of abstracts from different disciplines and produced in different languages identifies some moves that are similar to the ones previously discussed but also notes a problem-recommendation rhetorical structure in Swedish medical abstracts. Another recent study of abstracts by Santos (1996) focuses only on linguistics abstracts and postulates five moves to account for the overall organisation. In addition to the four discussed in previous studies such as Bhatia (1993) and Salager-Meyer (1992), he also postulates a move called 'Situating the research', where writers present current knowledge in the field and can optionally delineate a problem in the research area. He maintains that this move serves the function of attracting a readership and is found in a little less than half the texts analysed in his study.

A variety of linguistic features have been the subject of previous studies on abstracts. Most common among these are tense, modality, negation, and passive voice. In addition to analysing the frequency of occurrence of different linguistic features in abstracts, at least one study has attempted to explicitly relate form to function. Salager-Meyer (1992) shows how choices in tense and modality vary across the different moves in an abstract. The modal 'should', for example, is most commonly used in recommendations that appear in the conclusions move. She also shows how tense choice is a rhetorical choice and not an obligatory constraint. Melander et al.'s (1997) study also analyses a number of linguistic features in abstracts and reveals that some features such as negation, which were claimed in earlier studies to be absent in abstracts, are indeed present in abstracts in both Swedish and English. Their study also reveals that though various sets of texts from the same discipline but in different languages may be similar as far as the frequency of linguistic features such as negatives and passives are concerned, they may still be different in terms of rhetorical structure. The results of their study underscore the need to perform both rhetorical and linguistic analyses in genre studies.

TEXT CORPUS

Twenty abstracts each from the two disciplines, Conservation Biology and Wildlife Behaviour, were analysed both for macro-organisation and a number of linguistic features. The texts were randomly selected; they were the abstracts that accompanied the first 20 research articles published in *Conservation Biology* and *Animal Behaviour* in 1995. Both journals were selected as the data source because they were deemed to be central in the respective fields by disciplinary specialists. The four moves commonly identified in earlier analyses of abstracts served as the initial framework for analysis. However, a preliminary analysis indicated that a number of the texts contained a move preceding the 'purpose' move. Therefore, Santos's (1996) 'Situating the research' move was also included in the schema. Tense choice, the use of interpersonal metadiscourse, and the presence of first-person pronouns as sentence subjects were the three linguistic features analysed in the abstracts. These linguistic features were chosen for analysis both because they have been included in previous studies of abstracts (such as Melander et al., 1997) and because they are useful in distinguishing abstracts from the two disciplines under consideration in this study.

The two sets of abstracts vary in length, with the Conservation Biology texts having an average length of 9.0 sentences and the Wildlife Behaviour abstracts being 6.8 sentences long. These differences in length can be easily explained by the word limits for abstracts set by the editorial guidelines: 300 words for Conservation Biology and 250 words for Wildlife Behaviour.

RESULTS AND DISCUSSION

Each sentence in an abstract was assigned to a move. However, in some cases a particular sentence does serve two rhetorical functions, especially when the sentence includes more than one clause. A fairly common pairing of rhetorical functions in one sentence is the purpose–method combination, such as 'Sources of sex-specific odour information were identified using a preference task in meadow voles'. In such a case, the sentence was coded for both moves. The order in which the moves appeared was also noted, though there were no significant deviations in both sets of texts from the usual linear ordering: (1) situating the research, (2) purpose, (3) methods, (4) results, and (5) conclusions.

Abstracts from the two disciplines do not appear very dissimilar in terms of the rhetorical moves that characterise them. However, though the same five moves are found in both sets of texts, there are subtle differences in the constituent parts of some moves, in the frequency with which certain moves appear, and the textual space they occupy. Table 2.1 presents the frequencies with which the five moves are found in the abstracts from the two disciplines. As shown in the table, disciplinary affiliation does not affect the frequency with which some moves appear in this genre. Results appears consistently in the abstracts and this move is obviously obligatory for this genre in these two disciplines. It is not surprising that this is the case, given that the results of a study are presumably its most important contribution to the ongoing disciplinary discourse. The statement of the goal or purpose of the paper is equally important in the Conservation Biology abstracts, but this is not the case with the Wildlife Behaviour abstracts. In the Wildlife Behaviour abstracts, results is the one move that needs to be present although there is no text in the corpus which only contains this single move.

Table 2.1   Rhetorical moves in the Wildlife Behaviour and Conservation Biology abstracts

	Wildlife Behaviour	**Conservation Biology**
Situating the research	9	18
Purpose	13	20
Methods	10	10
Results	20	20
Conclusion	16	16

The methods move is equally unimportant in the abstracts from both disciplines. This move, which discusses the methods employed in the study, is present in only 50% of the texts. This is in contrast to the linguistics abstracts studied by Santos (1996), where methods are commonly described. Editorial guidelines for the two journals differ with regard to the place of discussion of methods in the abstracts. The guidelines for *Conservation Biology* state that the 'abstract should state concisely the goals, methods, principal results, and major conclusions of the paper' (1995: 229), explicitly mentioning the place of methods in the abstract. *Animal Behaviour* omits methods in its statement of information to be included in the abstracts: 'The abstract should describe the purpose of the study, outline the major findings and state the main conclusions' (1995: iii). The low presence of methods in abstracts could perhaps be explained by editorial guidelines for the Wildlife Behaviour texts; however, the structure of the Conservation Biology abstracts indicates that macro-organisation cannot be explained solely through the explicit guidelines given to authors in journals.

The most striking disciplinary variation in this genre is the importance attributed to the situating-the-research move. Though this move is commonly found in the Conservation Biology abstracts (90% of the texts), it is found in fewer than half of the Wildlife Behaviour abstracts. Santos (1996) postulates two submoves, statement of current knowledge and statement of problem, as subcategorizations of his first move. In these two sets of texts, statement of current knowledge can either concern the real world or the research world. Before the purpose of the study is given, the authors often provide a statement regarding a certain animal behaviour, the state of affairs with a particular species, or conservation management practices, such as in the following examples:

Example 1

A variety of animals periodically shuttle between two sites, such as one containing food and another containing oxygen, water, or conditions for heat exchange. The amount of non-food resource obtained, together with its rate of use, influences travelling and foraging time. Three criteria are evaluated to examine how control of body temperature may be optimal for shuttling . . .

(WB 11: 1–3)

Example 2

A major aim of conservation today is the maintenance of biodiversity. Practically, this pursuit might involve protecting a representative sample of the current biotic diversity . . . safeguarding species with traits that may be correlated with susceptibility to extinction, or protecting those species that are currently categorized as under short-term threat of extinction. Priority areas for conservation may vary, however, depending on which of these three approaches is taken. We investigated the designation of priority areas using these different approaches for Afrotropical antelope.

(CB 20: 1–3)

In some cases, authors may provide a statement about the current state of knowledge in the field, foregrounding the epistemic construction of knowledge in a discipline, such as in example 3 below:

Example 3

The logic of demographic modeling, the apparent simplicity of its quantifiably substantiated answers, and the ready availability of software correlate with increasing use of demographic modeling as the means of applying biology to the conservation of potentially endangered populations. I investigated that use by considering a small population ... of a large, forest-dwelling mammal of the tropics, the Virunga gorilla (*Gorilla gorilla*) of Zaire, Uganda, and Rwanda.

(CB 10: 1–2)

In a number of background moves, both types of information may be provided, with a statement about animal behaviour of some kind leading to a discussion of some more theoretical issue.

An interesting difference across the two sets of texts is the element of problematisation found in this move. In most of the Wildlife Behaviour abstracts, background information on a specific animal behaviour is provided in a neutral fashion such as in example 1 above. However, in the Conservation Biology abstracts, the current state of affairs regarding a species or community is often highly problematised. Notice the numerous words with negative overtones used in the following abstract:

Example 4

Many tropical nature reserves are woefully understaffed or exist only on paper. Without effective implementation, tropical reserves cannot count on in situ enforcement and consequently are subject to a wide range of invasive threats. Weak institutional structures are aggravated by reserve designs that facilitate rather than discourage unlawful human activities. Taking into account severe financial and institutional constraints, we consider the current status of forest reserves in lowland Amazonia.   (CB 1: 1–3)

In fact, problematisations concerning either the research world or the real world of conservation are found in 12 out of the 18 abstracts containing the background move. In sharp contrast, only two of the nine instances of the background move contain any sort of problematisation in Wildlife Behaviour. Of interest as well is the fact that these two problematisations concern the research world and are in fact statements of gaps in previous research, such as is seen in the following extract:

Example 5

Although many sources of sexually specific chemical signals have been identified, few attempts have been made to identify all the sources of sex-specific information in any species or to determine whether the various cues that provide this

information have the same communicative functions. Sources of sex-specific odour information were identified using a preference task in meadow voles.

(WB 4: 1–2)

Other than for statements of gaps in previous research in two abstracts, very little attempt is made in the first move of the Wildlife Behaviour abstracts to explicitly persuade readers about the value and interest of the research being reported in the article. The Wildlife Behaviour abstracts exhibit the 'tacitness and taciturnity' that Melander et al. (1997) maintain is a characteristic of 'mature' research areas in a Kuhnian sense and which is also seen in the abstracts from medicine and biology that they studied. In contrast, a large amount of rhetorical work is performed in the Conservation Biology abstracts to enhance the importance of the research being reported. This is most commonly achieved by portraying the dire state of affairs of certain species and their habitats. Since Conservation Biology has been described as a 'crisis' discipline (Soule, 1985), that is, a discipline concerned with providing solutions to environmental crises, it is perhaps not surprising that the abstracts fulfil their persuasive function by highlighting a problem in the world. Not only do Conservation Biology abstracts provide background information relevant to the study reported before stating the goal of the study, this background information is also highly negative. The crisis nature of the situation described seems to provide a justification for the study being reported. The background information provided in the Wildlife Behaviour abstracts, on the other hand, seems to mostly situate the study being presented within the context of relevant animal behaviour and theoretical considerations.

Both sets of abstracts have a concluding move an equal number of times, as shown in Table 2.1. However, a closer analysis reveals subtle differences in this move across these two disciplines. In the Wildlife Behaviour abstracts, the conclusions are generally implications of the results reported in the study. The conclusion extends the scope of the results obtained in a particular study by relating the specific results to what is already known in the field. A couple of examples of implications in the concluding move in Wildlife Behaviour abstracts follow:

Example 6

Radiotagged non-territorial males did not preferentially intrude upon the territories of males with RO bands and the song rates, number of border disputes, mean length of border disputes, and territorial intrusion rates did not differ significantly for RO and non-RO males. **These results suggest that colour-banding willow ptarmigan with red colour bands does not have a negative or positive effect on reproductive success or survival, and thus the data do not support the coverable badge hypothesis.** (WB 6: 10–11)

Example 7

The subjects did not use the experimenter's gazing at the correct object as a cue. In contrast, they did use gazing plus pointing, and the final experiment showed that pointing was necessary and sufficient under the conditions of the study. **The ineffectiveness of the experimenter's gazing as a cue may be caused by reduced cue-response spatial contiguity, but it may also reflect a limitation of mental or visual perspective-taking in these monkeys**.   (WB 20: 3–5)

As can be seen in example 7, explanations for the results obtained may also be provided in the conclusion. The tentativeness of the claims made in the concluding move is indicated by the use of modal verbs and other hedging devices, as will be discussed later in this chapter.

Implications are also found in the concluding move of the Conservation Biology abstracts. However, in a number of these abstracts (7 out of 16), the concluding move presents recommendations for management actions. These recommendations are in fact a certain type of implication of the results. In Conservation Biology, delineating actions to be pursued is a worthwhile implication of the study. In Wildlife Behaviour, on the other hand, recommendations concerning either the real world or world of research do not appear in the conclusion. In a few Conservation Biology abstracts, a generalisation based on the results is coupled with a recommendation for future conservation action, such as in example 8, where a recommendation is followed by two implications:

Example 8

Restriction fragment length polymorphisms distinguished animals from the east and the west of Hamilton and from the north and south of Tasmania. Nucleotide sequence divergence was substantial (2.2–2.5%) between Hamilton and Tasmania. **Implications are that captive breeding and reintroduction should be designed to genetically represent the structure within Hamilton in order to minimize inbreeding and that the introduction of Tasmanian P. gunnii would not benefit the Hamilton population. It is concluded that mitochondrial DNA markers clearly can provide useful information about the history and current status of endangered marsupial populations, to the benefit of conservation management**.
                                                        (CB 8: 6–9)

Though abstracts from the two disciplines contain the same types of moves, the Wildlife Behaviour abstracts on average contain a smaller number of moves. Wildlife Behaviour abstracts contain 3.5 moves while Conservation Biology abstracts contain 4.1 moves as an average. In fact, 16 out of the 20 Conservation Biology abstracts contain at least four moves while only nine Wildlife Behaviour abstracts contain four or more moves. In addition, there are three Wildlife Behaviour abstracts that only contain two moves each. The variety of moves found in the Conservation Biology abstracts could be due to the greater length of these texts. However, it also appears to be the case that the Wildlife Behaviour abstracts contain a smaller number of moves because one move, namely, results, is often well-developed.

The textual space occupied by each move in each abstract was calculated as a percentage of the whole text in terms of number of sentences. Interestingly, the results move seemed fairly important in the Wildlife Behaviour abstracts as measured by the space devoted to it. In 15 of the Wildlife Behaviour abstracts, results occupied the most space, taking anywhere from 33% to 86% of the text. In addition, in more than half of the abstracts (12 out of 20), the results move accounted for at least 50% of the sentences in the text, such as in the abstract below, where all sentences except one report the results of the study:

Example 9

Vigilance behaviour was examined in four groups of white-faced capuchins in Santa Rosa National Park, Costa Rica. **In each group, males spent more time vigilant than females. Average time spent vigilant within each group was not significantly correlated with group size, but was negatively correlated with the number of male group members. The alpha male tended to be the most vigilant individual in each group. Males in two of the four groups were more vigilant at waterholes than in other areas; males in two of the three groups having overlapping ranges were more vigilant in areas of overlap. There was a positive correlation between absence of neighbours and level of vigilance in both sexes. Male vigilance appeared to be directed primarily towards males in other groups, rather than towards potential predators or other group members.** (WB: 1–7)

In substantial contrast, only six of the Conservation Biology abstracts have a results move that constitutes at least half the text. In general, there is a greater variety of moves in the Conservation Biology abstracts. In correspondence with this pattern, none of the moves tends to take up a substantial portion of the text. In the Wildlife Behaviour abstracts, instead of having instances of all the possible moves, there is a tendency to have a smaller number of moves.

To sum up, the analysis of the macro-organisation of abstracts from two disciplines has revealed that the discourse structure of a genre can vary across disciplines not just in the presence or absence of a particular rhetorical move or even in the frequency with which a move may appear but also in the constituent structure of a move. The situating-the-research move is clearly more important in the Conservation Biology abstracts. More rhetorical work is performed in situating the research being reported since in a large number of texts the current research is connected to a problematised real world or problematised research world. In Wildlife Behaviour, not only is this move less frequent, it also does not always create a link to a problematised research world or real world. Another key difference between the two disciplines is the constituent structure of the final move. Conservation Biology abstracts tend to conclude with recommendations, which are absent in the Wildlife Behaviour abstracts. Because of the nature of the first and last moves in the Conservation Biology abstracts, the study being presented is often found sandwiched within a Problem–Solution framework.

The two sets of abstracts were also analysed for a small number of linguistic features. The first is tense choice. In both sets of texts, the most common tense used is the past tense. Clear patterns of tense choice associated with different moves are only seen in the texts from Wildlife Behaviour. Usually the purpose, methods, and results moves are in the past tense while the background and conclusion moves are in the present tense. In fact, the transition from the results to the conclusion move is clearly revealed by the tense switch, as in example 10:

Example 10

Decreased aggression and facilitation of paternal responsiveness **occurred** most reliably after extensive exposure to pups, even if exposure had occurred more than 2 months before testing. Unlike house mice, neither copulation nor exposure to females **enhanced** male responsiveness to pups. Given that male meadow voles only **nest** with females and young during the colder parts of the breeding season, it **may be** adaptive for paternal responsiveness to be triggered by pup exposure, rather than by some aspect of earlier contact with the female.

(WB 1: 3–5)

In contrast, in the Conservation Biology abstracts there is greater variation in the tenses used in the different moves. For instance, the background move may be in the past tense. On occasion, the whole abstract may be in the present (or present perfect) tense, as in example 11:

Example 11

Recent emphasis on a holistic view of natural systems and their management **is associated** with a growing appreciation of the role of human values in these systems. In the past, resource management **has been perceived** as a dichotomy between extraction (harvest) and nonconsumptive use, but this **appears** to be an oversimplified view of natural-cultural systems. The recreational fishery of Yellowstone cutthroat trout (*Oncorhynchus clarki bouvieri*) in Yellowstone National Park **is** an example of the effects of management on a natural-cultural system. Although angler harvest **has been** drastically reduced or prohibited, the recreational value of Yellowstone cutthroat trout estimated by angling factors (such as landing rate or size) **ranks** above that of all other sport species in Yellowstone National Park. To maintain an indigenous fishery resource of this quality with hatchery propagation **is** not economically or technically feasible. Nonconsumptive uses of the Yellowstone cutthroat trout including fish-watching and intangible values, such as existence demand, **provide** additional support for protection of wild Yellowstone cutthroat trout populations. A management strategy that **reduces** resource extraction has provided a means to sustain a quality recreational fishery while enhancing values associated with the protection of natural systems.   (CB 12)

This abstract reveals that the present tense may be used even in a report of the results in Conservation Biology because the studies are not always experiments or controlled in such a manner that the results are only true for a specific occasion. In the above case, the study concerns the Yellowstone National Park and the findings of the study are a number of generalisations concerning the Park that hold true for the present time.

The abstracts were also analysed for the use of interpersonal metadiscourse. Previous research in contrastive rhetoric has focused on the use of various types of metadiscourse, which refers to language that does not add to the propositional content of a text (Mauranen, 1993a; Crismore et al., 1993). Metadiscourse has been divided into two categories, textual and interpersonal, where the former refers to language used to signal the organisation of the text and the latter to language used to signal the writers' 'attitudes toward the propositional content of the text and toward their readers' (Crismore et al., 1993: 40). Hedging, one kind of interpersonal metadiscourse, has been shown to vary across disciplines (Hyland, 1996a, 1996b, 1998) and therefore the use of interpersonal metadiscourse in the two sets of abstracts was analysed. Textual metadiscourse was not analysed because this metadiscoursal element is generally not found in short texts.

The texts were analysed for the presence of four types of interpersonal metadiscourse (following Crismore et al., 1993): hedges, certainty markers, attributors, and attitude markers. Out of these four types, hedges, where the author shows a 'lack of commitment to the truth-value of the whole proposition' (Crismore et al., 1993: 50), are most commonly found in both sets of abstracts. In addition, the Conservation Biology abstracts also contain attitude markers, which express a writer's 'attitudes toward the propositional content and/or readers rather than commitment to the truth-value' (Crismore et al., 1993: 53). These include a writer's expression of obligation regarding an action or happening, such as 'The program should be proactive rather than reactive.' It is therefore not surprising that attitude markers are found more in the Conservation Biology abstracts than the Wildlife Behaviour abstracts, given the earlier finding that recommendations are commonly found in the conclusions move in the former but not the latter. Attributors, where authorities are referred to in order to increase the persuasive force of the proposition, are not found in both sets of abstracts. This is probably due to the limits on length imposed on this genre by the conventions of the academic community and the resulting absence of reference to literature. The final type of metadiscourse, certainty markers, is hardly present in the corpus either. These markers perform a function that is the opposite of that performed by hedges. Certainty markers express the writer's commitment to the truth-value of the proposition and are expressed by phrases such as 'it is clear . . .'. There is only one instance of certainty markers in a Conservation Biology abstract. Previous research, such as that of Hyland (1996a, 1996b), has shown the prevalence of hedging in academic writing. It then would follow from this that certainty markers, which fulfil the opposite rhetorical function, should be absent in academic discourse.

In the analysis of hedges, the presence of modal verbs, reporting verbs (such as 'suggest'), and other forms of lexical items that indicate a writer's tentativeness, such as 'possible' and 'tended', were coded. Hedging is present to the same extent in the abstracts from the two disciplines. In both sets of texts, there are about 20 instances of hedges per 100 sentences. The abstracts from the two disciplines are also similar in the part that modal verbs play in hedging. In both cases, modal verbs constitute about half the hedging devices employed.

In the Wildlife Behaviour abstracts, most of the hedges (about 70%) are found in the conclusions move. It was noted earlier that this move is also characterised by the use of the present tense. By using the present tense, the claims being made are extended in scope, enabling a move beyond a particular phenomenon, an experiment, for instance. This expansion of a claim is countered by an increase in its tentativeness. As Hyland (1996a: 255) notes, hedging devices are used to 'signal a writer's anticipation of the negatability of claims'. The use of the present tense increases the negatability of a claim and the hedging device seeks to reduce this, as in example 12:

Example 12

Both males and females investigated scent from the posterolateral region of males more than those of females. **Mouth and posterolateral area may provide different information and/or have different functions compared to the sex-specific scents from urine, faeces and the anogenital area.**   (WB 4: 8–9)

Hedges are also found in the background, goal, and results moves but with very low frequencies. It can be concluded that interpersonal metadiscourse is mainly a feature of the final move in Wildlife Behaviour abstracts and that it is mostly realised in terms of hedges.

Though hedges are also the most common type of interpersonal metadiscourse found in the Conservation Biology abstracts, they are not just found in the conclusions move. Instead, though the largest portion of hedges (42%) does appear in this last move, a substantial portion also appears in the background (19%) and results (25%) moves. Hedges are present in the results move mostly because of the interpretative nature of some of the results reported in the Conservation Biology abstracts. It is not always the case that the Conservation Biology abstracts report results which are from carefully constructed experimental studies. Even when the studies lead to quantitative results, authors may provide interpretations of these numerical figures while discussing the results, such as in example 13:

Example 13

To address recent criticisms of the recovery process of the U.S. Endangered Species Act and to search for ways to improve recovery efforts, we evaluated all recovery plans approved by the U.S. Fish and Wildlife Service and the National Marine Fisheries Service as of August 1991. As expected with rare species, we found an overall lack of detailed biological information presented in recovery plans. Information on species' distributions was most common, being mentioned in 88% of the original recovery plans, while information on species' abundance, population demographics, and dynamics (in descending order) was much less available. **Biological information tended to be sparsely distributed among taxonomic groups.** We found that threatened and endangered species were at risk of extinction, yet differentiation between threatened and endangered species' status in the wild and their recovery goals was not evident.

(CB 15: 1–5)

As mentioned earlier, attitude markers are another type of interpersonal metadiscourse found in the Conservation Biology abstracts. However, it is mostly markers of obligation from this category that characterise these abstracts. The modal verbs mostly used are 'should' but there are a few instances of the stronger modal 'must', as in example 14:

Example 14

Deterministic change in habitat is a greater threat than stochastic demographic variation, and yet our ecological ignorance is such that we could not begin to model the consequences of removal of even the main food plant. We **must** add to our ability to model outcomes of demographic perturbation a far greater understanding of the processes by which the perturbations occur.

(CB 10: 6–7)

The analysis of interpersonal metadiscourse has revealed that hedging is the most important strategy used by writers in the two disciplines to express their reactions to the propositional content of the text and to characterise the type of relationship sought with the reader. However, there are some interesting differences in the metadiscoursal strategies employed. Hedging is found to a greater extent in the discussion of results in Conservation Biology than it is in Wildlife Behaviour mainly because of the interpretative nature of these results. In addition, attitude markers expressing obligation create a hortatory relationship between the writer and reader in the Conservation Biology abstracts.

The final analysis conducted on the corpus is the use of the first-person pronoun. Earlier studies of abstracts (such as Melander et al., 1997) have revealed variation in this linguistic choice across disciplines. In particular, Melander et al.'s (1997) study has revealed a dearth of first-person pronouns in biology (specifically plant pathology) abstracts. There is a remarkable difference in the use of first-person pronouns in the two sets of texts analysed here. The Wildlife Behaviour abstracts eschew the use of first-person pronouns while 15 Conservation Biology abstracts have at least one sentence subject that is a first-person pronoun.[2] In fact, first-person pronouns function as sentence subjects in 21% of the sentences in the Conservation Biology abstracts.[3] (There are also numerous instances of the possessive form of the first-person pronoun in these texts though they were not included in the coding.) Below is an example of an abstract which contains more than one first-person pronoun:

Example 15

By combining a spatially explicit, individual-based population simulation model with a geographic information system, **we** have simulated the potential effects of a U.S. Forest Service management plan on the population dynamics of Bachman's Sparrow (*Amiophilia aestivalis*) at the Savannah River Site, a U.S. Department of Energy facility in South Carolina. Although the Forest Service's management plan explicitly sets management goals for many species, most of the prescribed management strategy deals with the endangered Red-cockaded Woodpecker (*Picoides borealis*) because of legal requirements. **We** explored how a species (the sparrow) that is not the target of specific management strategies but that shares some habitat requirements would fare under the management plan. **We** found that the major components of the proposed management plan may allow the sparrow population to reach and exceed the minimum management goal set for this species, but only after a substantial initial decline in sparrow numbers and a prolonged transition period. In the model, the sparrow population dynamics were most sensitive to demographic variables such as adult and juvenile survivorship and to landscape variables such as the suitability of young clearcuts and mature pine stands. Using various assumptions about habitat suitability, **we** estimated that the 50-year probability of population extinction is at least 5% or may be much higher if juvenile survivorship is low. **We** believe, however, that modest changes in the management plan might greatly increase the sparrow population and presumably decrease the probability of extinction. **Our results** suggest that management plans focusing on one or a few endangered species may potentially threaten other species of management concern. Spatially explicit population models are a useful tool in designing modifications of management plans that can reduce the impact on nontarget species of management concern. (CB 3: 1–9)

In this abstract, the authors are the subjects of sentences reporting on the purpose, methods, results, and conclusions of the study. Hyland (1998: 181) has pointed out that the use of personal subjects in academic writing reveals 'overt acceptance of personal responsibility' for the claims being made. He argues that the use of these pronouns functions as a hedge since the claims are made to appear dependent on certain activities performed by the author(s). Interestingly, this 'personal alignment with findings, models and analyses' (1998: 182) is only found in the Conservation Biology abstracts. This difference in linguistic choice with the use of first-person pronouns results in the authors having a greater presence in the Conservation Biology texts. As a result, the claims made also appear more subjective.

CONCLUSION AND PEDAGOGICAL IMPLICATIONS

This systematic comparison of texts from the same genre but different disciplines has increased our understanding of the influence of genre and discipline on text structure. A more complex picture of discursive norms was also attained by conducting analyses of both macro-organisation and linguistic features than would have been possible with just one type of analysis.

The results of the analysis of the macro-organisation of the abstracts have revealed that the results move is the most important part of an abstract. The results have also shown that the methods move is least important to the structure of an abstract and that abstracts do not necessarily provide a simple synopsis of the research article they accompany. Another key finding is that even texts from closely related disciplines vary in their generic structure. The most important disciplinary differences are in the first and last moves. The Conservation Biology abstract provides more explicit persuasion in the situating move by problematising the real and research worlds within which the new research is situated. In Wildlife Behaviour there is less of an attempt to situate the research being presented and, if textual space is devoted to situating the research within a larger context, it is often the context of accepted knowledge of animal behaviour and previous research. It is noteworthy that it is the applied discipline which performs more justification for the research, particularly in terms of relevance to real-world conditions. In the final move again, the applied discipline makes a connection to the world of conservation by presenting management recommendations. The first and last moves result in a problem–solution framework within which the new study is placed. In contrast, there is no problem–solution framework enveloping the Wildlife Behaviour study.

The study has also shown that a genre may vary across disciplines in terms of linguistic choices, such as tense and modality. Tense choice patterns are considerably more stable in Wildlife Behaviour than in Conservation Biology, perhaps reflecting the intedisciplinary slant and emergent nature of the latter discipline. An emergent discipline may still be in the process of attaining stable discourse patterns especially at the grammatical level. The contribution of various sub-fields to this interdiscipline may also be a factor that can account for the variability seen in the texts.

The results of this study, like others on generic variation across disciplines, can be employed in EAP courses. Educators can draw on findings such as those from this study to inform their students about discursive practices in academic communities in order to facilitate their acculturation into various disciplinary communities. When teaching their students a new genre, instructors can make them aware of features that are obligatory in that genre, such as the results move in the abstract. Beyond that, students also need to be made aware of disciplinary variation in genre structure. As has been suggested earlier (Johns, 1997; Flowerdew, 1993a), students can be trained to be ethnographers of writing practices in their own disciplines. Studies on writing in the disciplines inform us of the dimensions along which a particular genre varies across disciplines. Students can be made aware of these dimensions since it will be difficult for them to discover these dimensions on their own. Students need to be made aware that some of the variation is in terms of moves that may be absent or present. However, they also need to learn that sometimes the variation could be in terms of the constituent structure of the moves, as was seen with the background and concluding moves in abstracts. This study has also shown that certain linguistic dimensions, such as tense, use of personal pronouns, and interpersonal metadiscourse, may have different values in different disciplines.

The same dimensions may not be important for disciplinary variation, for different genres and research on writing in the disciplines can inform pedagogy by uncovering the relevant dimensions for different genres. Further systematic comparisons of the same genre produced in different disciplines can increase our knowledge of generic variation across disciplinary communities. The findings from such studies together with the results from contrastive rhetoric studies can enhance our understanding of variability and stability in genre structure.

NOTES

1. Research article introductions have been referred to as a part genre (Dudley-Evans, personal communication). However, following Swales (1990), I will refer to both research article introductions and abstracts as genres.
2. There is a greater use of the first-person-plural pronoun than the singular pronoun because most of the Conservation Biology articles are co- or multi-authored.
3. Not surprisingly, there is a greater use of the passive voice in the Wildlife Behaviour abstracts: 29% of the sentences have main clause verbs that are in the passive voice in Wildlife Behaviour while only 17% of the sentences have main clause verbs in the passive voice in Conservation Biology.

Chapter 3

Generic Moves in Ph.D. thesis Introductions

David Bunton

INTRODUCTION

The Ph.D. thesis or dissertation[1] has not been researched as a text genre as much as one might expect. The Ph.D. thesis is important as the *rite of passage* to an academic career, required by universities around the world and anguished over by thousands of research postgraduate students and their supervisors/advisers.[2] The Ph.D. thesis has been the subject of many guidebooks for students, giving advice on how it should be written and the structure it should follow. Increasingly in universities today, it is the subject of workshops, or even courses, in thesis writing. But as Mauch and Birch (1993: vii) state in their guidebook, 'One of the surprising weaknesses in the thesis or dissertation process is that there is relatively little scholarly literature and a remarkably small number of empirical investigations about it.' Ventola and Mauranen (1996: vii) also note that 'innumerable guidebooks and manuals on writing up research have been published; however, very few of these are based on serious linguistic analysis of the kinds of texts that a novice academic might have to master'.

The relative lack of research into the Ph.D. thesis as a genre may have two explanations. The first is length. Swales (1990: 188) points out that the analysis of research theses and dissertations has been 'largely avoided, at least partly because of the daunting size of the typical text'. In some British and Commonwealth universities the maximum length is around 80,000 words. A 'small' sample of 13 theses at that length would surpass a million words. The second explanation may be that, generally, a person writes only one Ph.D. thesis. Having accomplished it, one does not then write a second, better Ph.D. thesis on another topic, followed by a third, gradually mastering the genre. On the contrary, one normally makes one's way in the academic community by turning to a much shorter genre, the research article (RA). And that is the genre for which much more text analysis has been done (see Swales, 1990).

This chapter reports on the genre analysis of 45 Ph.D. thesis *Introductions*. It builds on an earlier study (Bunton, 1998) that analysed the overall thesis structure of 21 Ph.D. and M.Phil. theses and their *Abstracts*, and which then focused on the *Introduction* and *Conclusion* chapters of the 13 Ph.D. theses in that sample. Insights from the analysis of those 13 *Introductions* have been used to analyse a further 32 Ph.D. *Introductions* in this study. The combined corpus of 45 *Introductions* is a representative sample from the disciplines with the highest output of Ph.D. theses at the University of Hong Kong in the mid-1990s. They come from the Science, Medical, Dental, Engineering, Architecture, Social Science, Education, and Arts Faculties and two schools/ centres not under a faculty.

Introductions are important because they play a key role in showing the relevance of the research about to be reported in the thesis to previous work in the field (Bhatia, 1993: 82). As such, they set up the reader's expectations and can make it easier to navigate the long text to follow. Yet students and supervisors have indicated that *Introductions* and *Discussions* are the most difficult sections of dissertations to write (Dudley-Evans, 1986: 134; Shaw, 1991: 205).

Genre analysis of texts can operate at many levels. For example, at a micro level, it can indicate the way certain grammatical features, like verb tense or voice, are used in different genres of writing, and in different places within the same genre (for RAs, see Oster, 1981; Heslot, 1982; Tarone, Dwyer, Gillette, and Icke, 1981 and 1998; or Malcolm, 1987). At a macro level it can analyse the overall structures of different genres (for RAs, see Hill, Soppelsa, and West, 1982; Weissberg and Buker, 1990; and Swales and Feak, 1994; and, for particular disciplines, Nwogu, 1997; and Posteguillo, 1999). This chapter looks at two related macro levels of textual genre analysis: *generic moves and steps*.

Swales (1990: 140) refers to this phenomenon as 'rhetorical movement', while Holmes (1997: 325) defines a 'move' as 'a segment of text that is shaped and constrained by a particular communicative function'. This echoes Bhatia (1993: 30), who suggests that generic or 'cognitive' structure shows the moves the writer makes in a text in order to achieve his/her communicative purpose in the genre. The communicative purpose of an RA *Introduction* is defined by Bhatia (1993: 82) as marking 'a *link* between what has gone before in the relevant field of research and the present work that is being reported', making it '*relevant* by placing it appropriately in the context of . . . previous research in a particular field of study'.

For Ph.D. theses, it is just as, if not more, important that the research it reports is shown to be relevant to the field, since one of the criteria for the award of a doctorate in many universities is that the thesis makes an original contribution to knowledge. The role of the *Introduction* in showing that relevance is therefore crucial to the thesis.

This section has considered the rationale for analysing Ph.D. *Introductions* at the macro level of generic moves. The next section reviews previous research into the generic moves and steps in RA *Introductions*. Later sections will describe the methods used to select and analyse the Ph.D. thesis *Introductions* in this corpus, present the findings, discuss the issues raised, and, finally, propose a model for Ph.D. *Introductions* that allows for disciplinary variation, together with its pedagogic implications.

PREVIOUS RESEARCH

The pioneering work in this field was Swales's (1981a: 22) analysis of 48 RA *Introductions*. These RAs came from three different areas: 16 from 'hard' sciences (physics, electronics, and chemical engineering), 16 from the biology/medical field, and 16 from the social sciences. Across these different fields, he identified four common moves with a number of possible steps within them. There is a single progression in this model from the first move to the fourth. The first move, *Establishing the field*, deals with the field in which the research topic is located and its importance. The second move is *Summarising previous research*, while the third, *Preparing for the present research*, moves on from the previous research by querying it in some way, showing an area it has not covered or indicating a way in which it could be extended. The fourth move is *Introducing the present research* by giving its purpose or outlining the work carried out.

One basic criticism of this model has been made by Crookes (1984), who found that these four moves are often not a single progression but occur in cycles, sequenced in various recursive ways, such as: 123, 23, 23, 4. Several researchers (Crookes, 1984; Hopkins, 1985; and Cooper, 1985) have also noted the absence of Moves 2 or 3 and occasionally even Move 1 in *Introductions* they examined.

After some researchers noted the difficulty of distinguishing between Moves 1 and 2, *Establishing the field* and *Summarising previous research*, Swales (1990: 141) amalgamated them in the three-move, 'Create a Research Space (CARS)' model, which is set out in Table 3.1.

Bhatia (1993: 85, 88) has argued that in avoiding one problem, Swales has 'created a more serious problem by combining the two (moves)'. He believes the literature review deserves separate status because it is a well-established

Table 3.1 'Create a Research Space (CARS)' model for research article *Introductions*

Move 1: Establishing a Territory
    Step 1: Claiming centrality, and/or
    Step 2: Making topic generalisation(s), and/or
    Step 3: Reviewing items of previous research
Move 2: Establishing a Niche
    Step 1A: Counter-claiming, or
    Step 1B: Indicating a gap, or
    Step 1C: Question-raising, or
    Step 1D: Continuing a tradition
Move 3: Occupying the Niche
    Step 1A: Outlining purposes, or
    Step 1B: Announcing present research
    Step 2: Announcing principal findings
    Step 3: Indicating RA structure

Source: Swales (1990: 141)

Table 3.2   Dissertation *Introductions*

Move 1: Introducing the field
Move 2: Introducing the general topic (within the field)
Move 3: Introducing the particular topic (within the general topic)
Move 4: Defining the scope of the particular topic by:
    (i)   introducing research parameters
    (ii) summarising previous research
Move 5: Preparing for the present research by
    (i)   indicating a gap in previous research
    (ii) indicating a possible extension of previous research
Move 6: Introducing the present research by
    (i)   stating the aim of the research, or
    (ii)   describing briefly the work carried out
    (iii) justifying the research

Source: Dudley-Evans (1986: 135)

part of research reporting and also prompts many reviewers' comments on articles submitted for publication, requiring the author to demonstrate knowledge of the relevant literature. He suggests that citations from the literature can appear in either an *Establishing the field* move or a *Summarising previous research* move, but with differing 'discoursal functions'.

None the less, the three moves of the CARS model (and their names) highlight more clearly the communicative purpose that Bhatia (1993: 82) suggests for the *Introduction*: showing the link between what has gone before and the present work. The second move creates that link between the first and third: a space or niche has to be created in the territory of established knowledge and research and it must then be occupied by the current research.

A rather different model of article *Introduction* has been proposed by Zappen (1983). It is basically a problem–solution structure in the following sequence:

Goal ∧ Current Capacity ∧ Problem ∧ Solution ∧ Criteria of Evaluation
However, this has been criticised (e.g. Swales, 1990: 138–40) on the grounds that some areas of research do not involve (or are not presented as) problem solving.

Nwogu (1997) has also produced a model for the structure and functions of medical research papers. He proposes three moves for the *Introduction*: *Presenting background information, Reviewing related research*, and *Presenting new research*. The 'niche' step is the second part of the second move: *Reference to limitations of previous research*.

The above studies have looked only at research articles. Dudley-Evans (1986: 135) analysed the *Introduction* and *Discussion* sections of a longer genre: seven Masters dissertations (M.Sc.). For the *Introductions*, he identified six moves, some with two or three possible steps within them. These are set out in Table 3.2.

The distinctive feature of this model is the initial three-move progression from field to general topic to particular topic, where Swales has only one move. Dudley-Evans (1986: 134) remarks on the lengths to which his dissertation writers go to 'place the work . . . in the context of the general literature of the field and to justify this work in terms of the previous research'. The greater number of moves may also be related to the greater length of the dissertation as a text compared with the research article. Dudley-Evans also notes that three shorter *Introductions* omitted Move 1, and that three others reversed the order of Moves 3 and 4.

Dudley-Evans's Move 5, *Preparing for the present research*, is similar to Swales's Move 2, *Establishing a niche*, in that they both create the key link between the present research and the wider field. The steps within the move are similar: both have a step in which a gap in previous research is indicated, and Dudley-Evans's *Extension of previous research* could in some circumstances be similar to Swales's *Continuing a tradition*. Swales's other categories of *Counter-claiming* and *Question-raising* add further possibilities to this key move.

It could be argued that by making it the central move of three in his CARS model, Swales is giving greater prominence to this important move, and that it loses prominence as the fifth of six moves in Dudley-Evans's model. The name for Swales's model, 'Create a Research Space', also highlights the move to establish a niche. For this reason, the CARS model has been taken as the basis for the initial analysis of moves in this study, but at the level of steps, all of those proposed in the literature, by Dudley-Evans or Swales, are considered.

It is also recognised that the chapter-length *Introductions* of Ph.D. theses in this study may reveal other, additional, steps not reported in the literature. Special attention will be paid to the way in which writers review previous research, to see whether it is a step in the move to establish territory or whether it should constitute a move in its own right – or whether it is, in the Ph.D. thesis, a separate chapter.

METHOD

As indicated at the beginning of this chapter, 45 Ph.D. thesis *Introductions* were selected. Thirteen were from students who gave consent for their Examiners' Reports to be read as part of the original study (Bunton, 1998) looking at textual and grammatical problems in theses. One of the University Senate's conditions for access to those reports was anonymity for the thesis writers. Citations from those theses, therefore, do not contain references to the subject matter of the thesis. The remaining 32 theses were selected from all departments or faculties that produce at least 3% of all Ph.D.s at the University of Hong Kong, in numbers proportional to their output. However, an upper limit of four theses was placed on the two departments with the largest output: Chemistry, and Ecology and Biodiversity. Theses in departments were selected by the order in which they appeared in the University's annual publication *Abstracts of Theses*, except where the author had not given Library users permission to photocopy and cite the thesis.

The only exception to this selection procedure was made in an attempt to have a subset of theses by research students who are not native speakers of Chinese. The reason for this is that over 80% of HKU research students are from Hong Kong or the mainland of China, so if a number of non-Chinese writers were included in the sample, it would be less likely to reflect a Hong Kong or Chinese tradition of thesis writing. Therefore wherever there was a non-Chinese author in the 1997 list of theses in the appropriate departments, that thesis was chosen. As a result, 11 of the 45 theses (about a quarter) were written by non-Chinese research students, most of them native or near-native speakers of English, from Western countries or the South Asian subcontinent. The subset of non-Chinese speakers' *Introductions* will be compared with the Chinese-speaking majority's *Introductions* in terms of the range of moves and steps they use, and their expression of research purpose.

It should be noted, however, that the danger of HKU thesis *Introductions* reflecting only a Hong Kong or Chinese tradition of thesis writing is reduced by the fact that approximately 40% of Supervisors at HKU are non-Chinese, as are 60% of the External Examiners. Furthermore, many of the Hong Kong Chinese Supervisors have done their own Ph.D.s in overseas universities. As a result there is a strong influence from the international academic community on the thesis-writing process at HKU.

The resulting corpus of 45 *Introductions* consists of 781 pages of text and about 187,000 words. These *Introductions* were analysed for moves and steps already identified in the literature (above). Where a move or step did not appear to fit with descriptions or definitions in the literature, a new category of move was proposed. As noted in the previous section, at the level of moves, the three identified in Swales's CARS model were used as a starting point for the analysis, but at the level of steps, all those identified by Dudley-Evans were considered as well as Swales's steps. After all *Introductions* had been analysed for the first time, each one was then re-analysed one or more times in the light of findings from the other *Introductions*.

Section headings within the introductory chapters were noted and compared. Since they indicate the function the writer has in mind for the section, they can give some indication of the moves or steps a section may contain.

Some analysis of later chapters was also carried out in two ways:

(i) The number of references to other authors in *all* chapters of each thesis was counted. These figures show which chapters make most reference to previous research and the literature in the field. This helped indicate whether the main review of literature is in the *Introduction* or in another chapter.

(ii) Where the *Introduction* did not contain research questions or hypotheses, later chapters were read to see if they appeared elsewhere. This helped indicate whether the main expression of research purpose was in the *Introduction* or in another chapter.

Finally, the analyses of the 45 introductory chapters were compared in order to find common features and differences.

FINDINGS

This section will now report the findings, first on length, then number of references, section headings, and finally on the moves and steps identified in the *Introductions*.

Length

Overall the 45 *Introductions* averaged 17.4 pages in length, the shortest being two pages and the longest sixty. There were considerable differences between faculties, with Medicine, Social Sciences, and Arts averaging 26 to 34 pages, while Science, Engineering, and Education averaged only 9 to 10 pages. However, there were wider differences within some faculties than others. In Medicine, the six *Introductions* were all quite long (29 to 45 pages) while in Social Sciences they ranged from 6 to 46 pages, and in Arts from 10 to 60 pages.

Number of references to the literature

One reason for some *Introductions* being longer than others is that they include the main review of the literature while others do not, leaving the *Literature Review* to another chapter. Three *Introductions* are explicitly titled or described as including a literature review. Ten other *Introductions* make more references to the literature than any other chapter in the thesis.

However, these were a minority: 32 of the *Introductions* (71%) did not have more references to the literature than any other chapter. Table 3.3 sets out the proportion of total references to the literature that appear in *Introductions*. Where this is the highest proportion, the figure is in bold. The low percentages of references in many *Introductions* indicates that reference to previous research may play a much smaller role in these *Introductions* than it does in others.

Table 3.3   References to the literature in Ph.D. *Introductions*

Faculty (School/Centre)	Proportion of references to the literature in *Introductions* **Bold** indicates more than any other chapter
Arts	**37%** 17% **46%**
Education	0% 6% 7%
Social Sciences	2% 4% 11% 21% 24% **50% 84%**
Business (School)	2%
CUPEM	8%
Architecture	13%
Engineering	0% 3% 10% 17% 19% 26% **38% 38% 58% 70%**
Science	0% 0% 0% 3% 5% 7% 8% 14% 15% 32% 38% **52%**
Dental	2%
Medicine	**26% 39%** 41% 44% **52% 56%**

CUPEM = Centre for Urban Planning & Environmental Management

It also seems to indicate that the main review of literature in most theses is not in the *Introduction*. Only in Medicine and Arts did the majority of *Introductions* make more reference to the literature than any other chapter. Ten theses have other chapters titled *Literature Review,* and eleven more theses have chapters with *Review of...,* *Theory, Approaches, Concepts,* or *Conceptual Framework* in the title, or are described as being reviews of the literature. This makes a total of 21 theses, nearly half of the 45, where chapter titles indicate that a chapter other than the *Introduction* reviews the theories, concepts, approaches, and/or literature in the field.

Section headings

Section headings are of interest because they tell us how the author sees the structure of his/her text. However, 12 of the 45 *Introductions* were not divided into sections, and so had no section headings. These tended to be the shorter *Introductions* (mostly 2 to 5 pages), but three of them were 11 to 13 pages. Most of the *Introductions* without section headings were from the Science Faculty (7), but there was one each from the Engineering, Dental, Social Sciences, and Arts Faculties and the School of Business.

In the 33 *Introductions* that used section headings, 41% of the headings were topic-specific, i.e. they related to some aspect of the research topic. The majority, however, were generic headings, i.e. they could be used in an *Introduction* on any topic, for example, *Significance of Study.* Or in other cases they were partially generic, e.g. *General Review of X Methods,* where X is a particular topic of the study. The generic or partially generic headings that occurred in more than one *Introduction* are set out in Table 3.4 with the number of occurrences in brackets. They are sequenced in the table in approximately

Table 3.4   Generic section headings in 45 Ph.D. *Introductions*

Introduction (6)
Problem (statement of) (6)
Background (3)
Overview of . . . (2)
The field (brief history of) (2)
X Approaches (5)
Y Methods/techniques (review of) (3)
Previous studies (3)
Local studies (3)

Scope of present study/investigation (6)
Aims/Objectives (8)
Research questions/issues/Hypotheses (3)
Method/Research design (4)
Definition of terms (3)
Significance of study/Contributions (5)
Organisation/structure/outline of thesis (11)

the order they appear in their *Introductions*. Those occurring five times or more are in bold type.

These generic section headings indicate two overall focuses: the first is on introducing the field, including its approaches, methods, and previous studies. It is noteworthy that three of these *Introductions* separated local studies (in this case, Hong Kong) from the wider international field as a means of moving towards the niche their study would occupy. The second overall focus is on introducing the present study. In this part of the *Introduction*, scope, aims, and objectives are all more prominent in section headings than research questions or hypotheses. Method and definitions are two aspects of the present research highlighted in these section headings but not included in the Swales or Dudley-Evans models. The heading most frequently found (although still in less than a quarter of the *Introductions*) is *Thesis structure/ organisation*, nearly always at the end of the *Introduction*.

The only section headings that in any way resembled Swales's niche move or Dudley-Evans's *Preparing for present research* move were the problem statements that often came early in the *Introduction*. This is not to say that thesis writers do not indicate niches when reviewing previous research – that will be considered in the findings of the text analysis in the next section.

Moves

Nearly all *Introductions* had sequences of text identifiable as the three moves in Swales's (1990) CARS model: *Establishing a Territory* (T), *Establishing a Niche* (N), and *Occupying the Niche* (O). The only exception was one author whose *Introduction* did not explicitly establish a niche in the previous research for his research to occupy. However, as we have seen above with the section headings, the move to establish a niche was seldom delineated by the author as a separate section – the only exceptions being six who had a section headed *Problem* or *Problem Statement*.

As with Crookes's (1984) finding, the moves were cyclical in nearly all *Introductions*. Only in three cases did the T–N–O moves follow in a single progression (one each from the Faculties of Education, Science, and Engineering). In all other cases, there were two, three, or many more cycles of moves, the highest number being 18, and the average 5.5. The lowest average number of cycles were in the Education and Science *Introductions* (2.7 and 3.6 respectively) with the number of cycles rising through Engineering, Social Sciences, and Arts to Medicine with the highest average, of 8.8 cycles.

The most frequently used cycle was not T–N–O, but T–N. This typically occurred as authors were reviewing previous research and pointing out gaps or problems or raising questions as they reviewed the literature, but did not go on to announce their own research until later. On average, there were 2.5 T–N cycles per *Introduction*, 1.4 T–N–O cycles and 0.7 T–O cycles.

Most *Introductions* (38 out of 45) began with *Establishing a Territory*. However, seven did not. Five of these began by announcing the purpose, focus, or scope of the present research (O moves) and two began with a problem statement or a claim that there had been little research in the field (N moves). In all cases, the opening O or N move was followed by a move to establish the territory (T).

An even greater majority of *Introductions* (42 of 45) ended with *Occupying the Niche*. The only exceptions were two, in Arts and Social Sciences, which ended with long moves considering the territory and reviewing its literature (a T move) and one, in Architecture, which ended with a summary restating the purpose and methods of the present research (O) and three T–N cycles summarising the state of the field.

Steps

The 45 Ph.D. thesis *Introductions* showed a much greater variety of steps than the RA and Masters dissertation *Introductions* described in Swales's (1981a, 1990) and Dudley-Evans's (1986) models.

All the 14 steps[3] identified by Swales and Dudley-Evans were found. However, 10 more steps were identified which (a) did not fit any of the descriptions in Swales's or Dudley-Evans's models; or (b) were considered distinctive enough to require a more precise category than a wider category in the earlier models, for example *Research Questions or Hypotheses* instead of the more general *Outlining purposes* step.

Table 3.5 sets out the number of *Introductions* in which each step was found,[4] and those steps found in a majority of *Introductions*, in each faculty and overall, are in bold. The newly identified steps are indicated with an asterisk. One, with a double asterisk, was found to be capable of appearing in either the first (T) move or the third (O) move.

The main differences between these thesis *Introductions* and those reported in the literature on RA or Masters dissertation *Introductions* are in the third move to introduce the present research, where ten of the 11 newly identified steps occur. It is perhaps understandable that Move 3 presents so many more aspects of the research, since the Ph.D. thesis is a much longer document and Ph.D. research extends over a considerable period of time.

Newly identified steps will be discussed in the next section, but there is one overall finding I want to consider before that. This is the comparison of the 34 *Introductions* written by Chinese-speaking research students with the 11 *Introductions* written by the subset of research students from Western countries and the South Asian subcontinent (mostly native or near-native speakers of English). When the *Introductions* of these two groups were compared, it did appear that in two faculties (Arts and Education), the non-Chinese writers used a wider range of steps, but in two other faculties (Science and Social Sciences) they used a narrower range of steps than the Chinese-speakers. Overall the non-Chinese-speaking authors used an average of 8.6 different steps in the three moves of their *Introductions*, while the Chinese-speaking majority used an average of 9.2 different steps. It cannot be said, then, that the research students from Hong Kong and the mainland of China are more limited in the range of steps they use to introduce their research when compared with the non-Chinese subset.

Table 3.5   Moves and steps found in Ph.D. thesis Introductions

Moves and steps	Faculty and no. of *Introductions* with the step							
	Arts	Edu	Soc	Engg	Sci	Med	Misc	Total
	3	3	7	10	12	6	4	45
Move 1: Establishing a Territory								
Topic generalisations/Background	3	2	6	8	10	6	3	38
Centrality/importance of topic	1	3	5	9	12	2	3	36
**Defining terms	3		2	3	1		1	10
Parameters of research			1				1	2
Reviewing previous research	3	1	7	9	9	6	4	39
Move 2: Establishing a Niche								
Gap in previous research	3	1	6	7	8	6	2	33
Question-raising	2	1	3		1	1	2	10
Counter-claiming	1			1				2
Continuing/Extending a tradition	1		3	1	1	4		10
*Problem/Need	1	2	4	9	9	3	3	31
Move 3: Occupying the Niche								
Purpose/Aims/Objectives	2	3	6	9	9	6	3	38
*Chapter structure	1		2			1	1	5
*Theoretical position		1	4				1	6
Announcing research/Work carried out	1	1	1	5	3		1	12
Parameters of research		1	1				1	3
*Research questions/Hypotheses	1	2	2			1	2	8
**Defining terms		2	1	1				4
*Method	3	3	5	6	10	3	3	33
*Materials/Subjects	2	1	3	1	2	1	1	11
Findings/Results	1	1	2	4	1		1	10
*Product/Model proposed			2	7	1			10
*Application				3				3
*Evaluation				4				4
Justification/Significance		3	6	3	5	2		19
Thesis structure	1	2	5	10	9	1	3	31

* indicates newly identified step ** indicates one which can appear in first or third moves (T or O)

Notes: Abbreviations for the faculties in Tables 3.5 and 3.6 are as follows. Edu: Education, Soc: Social Sciences, Engg: Engineering, Sci: Science, Med: Medicine, Misc: single theses from the Dental and Architecture Faculties, the Centre for Urban Planning & Environmental Management, and the School of Business.

NEWLY IDENTIFIED STEPS

There is not space in this chapter to give examples of each of the newly identified steps. I shall only illustrate the more important ones and some of those distinctive to certain disciplines.

As explained in the section on 'Method' citations from 13 of the 45 *Introductions* had to have the subject matter of the research removed in order to preserve the anonymity of the writers. This means that what is cited from those *Introductions* is the non-subject-specific language that could be used by any thesis writer – and as such it constitutes the linguistic signals of these steps and moves. The key lexical signals are in bold.

Introductions from the original corpus of 13 theses were categorised into two broad disciplinary groups, following Casanave and Hubbard (1992): the Science and Technology disciplines, designated ST, and the Humanities and Social Sciences, designated HSS. *Introductions* from the other 32 theses are designated with their year of acceptance and their HKU Library reference number, e.g. 97.W21.

First we shall look at the one step found in Move 2 to *Establish a Niche* which does not appear in Swales's or Dudley-Evans's models.

Indicating a problem or need

The move to *Establish a Niche* was realised (at least partially) in a majority of *Introductions*, across all faculties, by the indication of a *Problem* or *Need*. The only step more frequently used in this move (33, compared to 31 of the 45 *Introductions*) was *Indicating a gap in previous research*. Many *Introductions* used both.

The indication of a problem was at the centre of Zappen's (1983) model for *Introductions*, and 33 of the 45 *Introductions* in this corpus indicated a problem or need at some point of their review of previous research. Often it clearly indicated a niche which the present research then occupied. This example of a problem step is from an ST discipline:

> To extend its application to W, the X method was combined with the Y concept. This method has been successfully applied to Vs. **However**, such methods are **not generally applicable** to all Zs.   (ST.5)

This problem was immediately followed by the presentation of the present research purpose, in terms that attempt to tackle the problem of the earlier method's non-applicability to some cases. The next example is from an HSS discipline:

> So **the major problem** which emerges is how will X be interpreted and implemented in a Y environment which displays a number of features that are **in marked contrast** to Z. It is therefore important to examine how X has fared in . . .   (HSS.11)

This problem of the applicability of X to a potentially difficult environment is immediately addressed with research questions that form the basis of an examination of how X has fared in that environment. The statement of a problem has thus performed the function of indicating the niche that the present research is intended to occupy.

The indication of a need is somewhat different. This example, from a thesis in Education, follows a brief introduction to the issue of quality in education:

It **would be useful** to have a full understanding of what is required for universities to make their maximum contribution to the good of society.   (97.C)

The *Introduction* then goes on to announce the present research in narrower terms: 'This thesis has a more limited aim . . .'.

And in a thesis from the Botany Department, a brief T-move showing the centrality of the topic is followed by this statement of need:

> **In order to** obtain concentrated seed proteins, extraction procedures **are necessary** to isolate them from the rest of the seed materials.   (97.B11)

This is followed by the method and objectives of the present research.

We shall now consider steps that belong to Move 3.

Taking a theoretical position

A step found mainly in *Introductions* from the Social Sciences is *Taking a theoretical position*. This appears to be a distinctive way of moving to *Occupy the Niche*. For example, one *Introduction*, after a first sentence that indicates both the field and a general topic, continues:

> Over the decades many theories have been offered to account for the phenomenon and resolutions following from such explanations have been recommended. While it is fair to say that each of these theories has its own strengths and limitations, and we should not expect one single theory to be able to explain everything, most studies have adopted a posture that does not give sufficient status to the perspectives of . . . **The present study is located firmly within the tradition of** . . . While this tradition accepts that the various X theories have a positive contribution to our understanding of . . . this contribution is still limited in two key aspects: the importance assigned to . . . and the manner in which . . .   (HSS.9)

This appears to be a firm step, very early in the *Introduction*, to take a theoretical position that occupies the gap seen in the effectiveness of other theories. The position taken will need to be justified by the research carried out and a conclusion given later in the thesis.

Product/Model

Ten *Introductions* announced a *Product* or proposed a *Model* as a result of the research. This example of a *Model* is from Psychology:

> In an attempt to bridge these two approaches, **a** social-cognitive interactionist **model** of depression that examines the mutual influences of social and cognitive factors on depression **was proposed**.   (97.C14)

and this example of a *Product* is from Engineering:

> In chapter 2, different bit allocation algorithms for image coding will be described. In particular **a new bit allocation** based on the actual rate-distortion curves of quantizers and the Marginal Analysis Method **is developed**.   (97.F12)

Evaluation

Evaluation steps were only found in Engineering *Introductions* (4) and were always associated with a *Product* step. The *Product* step just cited in the previous section was followed by this *Evaluation*:

> This algorithm **is better than** the Wu-Gersho's algorithm in terms of speed and
> peak signal to noise ratio.   (97.F12)

Application

The three *Application* steps were all in Engineering *Introductions*. They were all associated with *Product* steps and indicated how the research product could be applied in future to a real-world use. This example is from Computer Science:

> **An application** that is able to exploit the full power of a multicomputer **is**
> **expected to be in the form of** a concurrent programme comprising a number
> of communication (sequential) processes. These processes **would be** attached
> to different processors within the multicomputer initially and at different times
> during execution, and they **would** communicate via sending and receiving of
> messages.   (97.S)

Other newly identified steps

Defining terms appeared on ten occasions in Move 1 and was concerned with the territory as a whole, but on four occasions it appeared in Move 3 and was concerned with introducing the particular research, so it is included in the model for both moves.

The step to indicate *Chapter structure* always occurred, unsurprisingly, early in the chapter. However, in four of the five instances this was not as a part of Move 1, but as part of an early move to *Occupy the Niche*.

There was a greater concentration on the *Method* of research in these *Introductions* than the Swales and Dudley-Evans models suggest. Most of the *Introductions* (33 of the 45) gave details of the methods chosen, sometimes for several pages, and in three cases devoting one or two sections to method or research design. Eleven *Introductions*, across all the faculties, indicated the *Materials* or *Subjects* of the present research; in all these cases there was also a *Method* step.

We shall now look at the most important step in Move 3, the one which announces the research purpose, however generally or specifically that is done.

RESEARCH QUESTIONS, HYPOTHESES, AND PURPOSE

Most *Introductions* (38 out of 45) have statements of *Purpose, Aims, or Objectives*. But probably the most unexpected finding is how few *Introductions* propose *Research questions* or *Hypotheses*: only 8 out of 45, and none at all in Science or Engineering.

Table 3.6 Expression of research purpose in Ph.D. theses

Expression of research purpose	Faculty and no. of theses							
	Arts	Edu	Soc	Engg	Sci	Med	Misc	Total
	3	3	7	10	12	6	4	45
General purpose	2	3	6	9	9	6	3	38
statement	67%	100%	86%	90%	75%	100%	75%	84%
Aims/Objectives	1	1	3	3	6	5	2	21
	33%	33%	43%	30%	50%	83%	50%	47%
Hypotheses/Research	1	3	7	2	2	2	3	20
questions	33%	100%	100%	20%	17%	33%	75%	44%

This raises the question of whether research questions or hypotheses occur in later chapters of the theses rather than in the *Introduction.* Later
chapters of all 45 theses were read and it was found that four more theses
had research questions in later chapters, and six more had hypotheses explicitly expressed in later chapters. There were also four theses in which a
role similar to that of hypothesis was played by arguments (Economics),
theorems (Statistics), propositions and conjectures (both Computer Science).
For example:

> **I would like to develop the argument that** A **can** serve as a bridging concept
> which mediates these two levels of analysis. On the one hand, Bs **are capable of**
> . . . On the other hand, A also draws our attention to C . . . A is also critical in that
> it **can** serve as a yardstick against which D can be evaluated. **These are large claims**
> and **I will try to substantiate them** in various parts of this thesis.   (HSS.9)

When these are taken into account, together with the research questions and
hypotheses found in *Introductions,* it still leaves us with the finding that 25 of
the 45 theses (56%) had no explicitly expressed hypotheses, research questions, or equivalents.

There are also distinct differences between disciplines in this regard: research questions and hypotheses were far more common in Social Science
and Education (each 100%) and far less frequent in Science (17%) and
Engineering (20%). Faculty figures are set out in Table 3.6.

Where they did occur, research questions and hypotheses were often clearly
enumerated, for example:

> To accomplish this purpose, this study takes a qualitative approach in examin-
> ing these phenomena. Specifically it will **address the following questions**:
> 1. What are the **changes** in A resulting from B?
> 2. What are the **impacts** upon C due to B?
> 3. What are the **possible measures** that D may take so as to strengthen E?
> 4. What are the **contributions** of F to the re-appraisal of G?   (97.X)

but in other cases they were expressed within a paragraph:

In this study the **hypotheses are that** levels of A in healthy individuals **are** genetically determined **and that** interaction with other environmental factors **might** interfere with its expression **and thus might** potentially increase the disposition of an individual to B.   (97.P)

Objectives were also enumerated on many occasions:

The **purpose** of this study is to apply the techniques of X and Y to the study of Z. The **primary objectives** of this study are:
1. To **analyse** the operation of A processes on B . . .
2. To **discern** the processes of C by analysing D . . .
3. To **reveal** the special aspects in E in the condition of F.
4. To **assess** the impact of G on H.
5. To **build up models** for I.   (97.W13)

However, the statement of research purpose is less precise in theses without research questions, hypotheses, or aims/objectives (33% of the sample), for example:

In this thesis, I **will be mainly concerned with** the X effects on the Y properties in Zs.   (97.Z11)

In the five theses (11%) that did not have any expression of research purpose, this role was played by statements of 'work carried out', to use the name Dudley-Evans (1986) gives to one of his *Introduction* steps. For example:

In this thesis, therefore, an X monitor for Y **was developed** in order to overcome all the shortcomings of the Z method . . .   (97.C112)

The prevalence of theses without hypotheses or research questions, and the presence of five theses without any statement of research purpose, suggest that this was considered acceptable at least to the supervisors and external examiners concerned. Whether this is a convention in certain fields or whether others in the same field would view this as a weakness, requires further research.

In order to see whether the absence of research questions or hypotheses could be linked to a Hong Kong/China thesis-writing culture, the subset of non-Chinese speakers was compared with the rest. In fact, a higher proportion of the Chinese-speakers used research questions or hypotheses (47%) than the non-Chinese speakers (36%). So there is no evidence in these data that this phenomenon is more typical of Chinese-speakers than of research students who come from a wider range of cultures and academic backgrounds.

A MODEL FOR PH.D. THESIS INTRODUCTIONS

In proposing a model for Ph.D. thesis *Introductions* we have to ask the question whether the model should be a purely descriptive one, or whether it should be influenced by pedagogic considerations.

If our model is to be purely descriptive, the third move should probably be called *Announcing the Present Research* rather than *Occupying the Niche*, because not all thesis writers explicitly state how their research is to occupy the niche they have indicated. All the writers in this corpus do, however, announce their own research.

It could even be argued that a purely descriptive model would not have a compulsory second move *Establishing a Niche*. The section headings used by most writers, as noted in the section on that subject, generally fall into two categories: *Establishing a Territory* and *Announcing the Present Research*. The only section headings that do establish a niche were the six *Problem Statement* sections.

However, as we have noted, the Ph.D. thesis is, by definition, written by a research student who is seeking admission to the academic community, unlike the research article which is the professional genre written by experienced practitioners as well as newcomers. The model for RAs needs to be purely descriptive, because all instances of the RA have been through the journal review process before being published. Only through descriptive text analysis can we discover what RA text structure is like. The Ph.D. thesis usually has three examiners, who may reject it or require amendments, but it is not certain that their criteria are the same as those of journal reviewers and editors. While some theses on the library shelves may have been considered excellent, others may have only been just acceptable – as a result the text analyst may not know whether the theses being analysed are good models or not. A pedagogic element to the Ph.D. thesis model may therefore be justified.

The model still needs a strongly descriptive element for two reasons: (i) there has been little research into Ph.D. text structure; and (ii) authentic Ph.D. texts may show what supervisors intuitively know about the way such research should be presented without necessarily being able to state it explicitly. But for pedagogic reasons, the model should highlight those structures that help show the contribution the Ph.D. research is making to knowledge.

When all this is taken into account, a model can be proposed that does make use of Swales's (1990) CARS three-move structure with its focus on the establishing of a niche. This link between the first and third moves is particularly important for the Ph.D. thesis as a genre, because the primary communicative purpose of the doctoral thesis is to demonstrate to its examiners that the writer/researcher has made an original contribution to knowledge in the chosen field.

Table 3.7 sets out this model for Ph.D. *Introduction*s, with newly identified steps in italics. Those steps that are characteristic of theses from certain faculties are annotated with the faculty name. This model has already been used in two ways. It has been presented at research student conferences in my own faculty, with students asking for copies to use as a guide in their own thesis writing. It has also been used in a workshop with supervisors across faculties in another university: the supervisors (mostly non-linguists) used the model to identify moves and steps in a sample *Introduction* and then discussed its applicability in their disciplines.

I believe the model is as important for supervisors as it may be for students. Supervisors will be more able than their students to see what variations

Table 3.7   Modified CARS model for Ph.D. thesis *Introductions*

Often present	Occasionally present
Move 1: Establishing a Territory	
STEPS	
1: Claiming centrality	
2: Making topic generalisations and giving background information	Research parameters
3: *Defining terms* (Eg, A, So)	
4: Reviewing previous research	
Move 2: Establishing a Niche	
STEPS	
1A: Indicating a gap in research	
1B: *Indicating a problem or need*	
1C: Question-raising (So, A)	Counter-claiming
1D: Continuing a tradition (M, So)	
Move 3: Announcing the Present Research	
(Occupying the Niche)	
STEPS	*Chapter structure*
1: Purposes, *aims, or objectives*	*Research questions/Hypotheses*
2: Work carried out (Eg, Si)	*Theoretical position* (So)
3: *Method*	*Defining terms*
4: *Materials or Subjects*	Parameters of research
5: Findings or Results	
6: *Product of research* (Eg)/*Model proposed* (So)	
7: Significance/Justification	*Application of product* (Eg)
8: Thesis structure	*Evaluation of product* (Eg)

NB The moves in this model may not occur in a single progression, but may well be cyclical. For example, the sequence of moves may be: 1–2, 1–2, 1–2–3
A=Arts, So=Social Sciences, Eg=Engineering, Si=Science, M=Medicine.
Newly identified steps are in *italics*

are conventional in their particular fields. The model can then work as a pedagogic framework around which they build the knowledge they already have, intuitively if not explicitly expressed, about the way research is presented in their disciplines.

ACKNOWLEDGEMENT

The author wishes to acknowledge the help of Christine Rwezaura in data collection and of Dr Peter Falvey in commenting on an early draft of the chapter.

NOTES

1. The terms 'thesis' and 'dissertation' are used differently in different countries and even in different universities of the same country. In most UK, Hong Kong, and

Australian universities, a 'thesis' is written for the research degrees of Ph.D. and M.Phil., while a much shorter 'dissertation' is one of the final requirements for a taught Master's degree. In many American universities the terms are reversed, with theses written at Master's level and a doctoral dissertation at Ph.D. level. This chapter uses the Hong Kong, UK, and Australian terms of a Ph.D. thesis and a taught Master's dissertation.

2. This chapter also uses the term 'supervisor' (as in many British and Commonwealth universities) for the member of staff responsible for guiding the research student through the research and thesis/dissertation writing process – for whom the term 'adviser' tends to be used in US universities.

3. Certain of their steps have been conflated. For example, Dudley-Evans's step *Indicating an extension to previous research* has been combined with Swales's step *Continuing a tradition*; and Dudley-Evans's three moves to introduce the field, general topic, and particular topic parallel Swales's two steps *Making topic generalisations* and *Claiming centrality*.

4. The *frequency* of occurrence in each *Introduction* is another matter, because most moves and many steps recurred in cycles. However, even a frequency count would not give a sense of how long or short the steps are in different *Introductions*. The single step *Reviewing previous research* sometimes continued for 10 or 20 pages.

Chapter 4

Introductory concepts and 'cutting edge' theories: Can the genre of the textbook accommodate both?

Alison Love

The genre of the introductory textbook has attracted attention from applied linguists, both because of its problematic relationship to professional academic genres (e.g. Myers, 1992b; Swales, 1995; Hyland, 1999b) and because of its centrality as a pedagogical genre (e.g. Henderson and Hewings, 1990; Love, 1991, 1993; Johns, 1997). It is generally agreed that the generic purpose of the textbook is not only to provide information, but crucially to introduce students to the epistemology of the discipline (Love, 1991; Hyland, 1999b). The perception of the textbook as genre has frequently been influenced by Kuhn's characterisation of scientific textbooks as 'a body of knowledge backed by a consensus of practitioners' (Myers, 1992b: 5; Swales, 1995: 4). Johns (1997: 46–9) provides a useful overview of some of the features which have been described, including the absence of discussion of disciplinary conflict, the 'absence of the author', and some of the grammatical structures realising this consensus.

However, while students may often be only too happy to 'see textbooks as concrete embodiments of the knowledge of their disciplines' (Hyland, 1999b: 4), there is increasing evidence that some textbooks, including some scientific ones, introduce students to the complexity and tentativeness of knowledge (Hyland, 1999b; Love, 1999), as preparation for the epistemological work of analysis within their disciplines. In many social sciences, in particular, students may be exposed to competing theories and alternative interpretations (Love, 1999). It appears, then, of interest to examine whether textbooks introduce new students to the 'cutting edge' of ideas in the discipline at the time that they are written, particularly if the authors are leading theorists in the field. This chapter will examine an example of an introductory textbook in sociology which explicitly sets out to incorporate specific 'cutting edge' ideas into its introduction to the discipline.

Many of the studies of textbooks have been concerned with the status of knowledge presented in textbooks, and so have concentrated particularly on such issues as hedges, argument, and authorial comment. However, a further – one might even say more basic – task of the textbook is to introduce students to the type of data studied in the discipline and the language used to conceptualise it. The discussion of this topic has been much more patchy. Work on economic concepts has been done by Henderson and Hewings (1990), emphasising the problems raised by the initiation into the abstract language of that discipline.

The most detailed discussion of this issue (in secondary-level textbooks) is given by Martin in 'Technicality and Abstraction' (Halliday and Martin, 1993). It has been developed in great detail by Wignell (1998), in a paper which suggests a basic difference in the creation of technical disciplinary language between sciences and social sciences. Drawing on Martin's contrast between technicality in scientific knowledge making and the abstraction of interpretation in the humanities, he argues that the social sciences first construct an abstract model of the world:

> One instance can be treated congruently, but generalisation from more than one instance often requires the intervention of abstraction. (Wignell, 1998: 313)

The social sciences then use this to construct a technical interpretation:

> social science takes as its starting point an abstract construal of experience and then reconstrues that initial abstraction technically. (Wignell, 1998: 298)

Wignell argues that the connections between the 'world' and the model are thus hidden:

> Unlike in science there appears to be little translation directly from the commonsense to the technical. Abstractions and metaphors intervene in the translation. . . . The technical framework is used as a means of interpreting the 'world' but does not seem to be derived from the 'world'. The theoretical model appears to precede its application to the 'world'. (Wignell, 1998: 323)

Wignell develops his claim through detailed linguistic analysis of both historical texts and a contemporary introductory textbook in sociology. While I shall question the generalisability of Wignell's conclusions, his model of construction of technicality in sociology is extremely useful in investigating the way in which students are introduced to disciplinary terminology.

This chapter will examine one sociology textbook, written by a leading sociological theorist, in terms of two features, its method of introducing technical sociological concepts and its approach to the status of knowledge and argument in the discipline. Both these features will be related to some of the author's theoretical positions, as they appear in his 'professional' publications. Thus the paper will attempt to examine whether a writer's 'cutting edge' ideas influence the approach to initiating novices into the discipline.

ANTHONY GIDDENS, *SOCIOLOGY* (SECOND EDITION)

Anthony Giddens is a major and controversial figure in current sociology theory. His introductory textbook to the discipline therefore provides an ideal case study for investigating whether such a theoretician attempts to introduce novice students to 'cutting edge' ideas, or presents the discipline in an uncontroversial, unproblematic manner. This book is a major under-graduate text, now used in a 'fully revised and updated' Second Edition, by, among others, our students at the University of Zimbabwe, where it is a core recommended text for the 'Introduction to Sociology' course.

Giddens is explicit about his intention to introduce new ideas into the textbook:

> After teaching at all levels of sociology for some while, I became convinced of the need to filter some of the discipline's current advances and developments into an elementary introductory text.   (Giddens, 1993a: 1)

He sets out several of his theoretical positions in the Conclusion to *New Rules of Sociological Method* (second edition) (Giddens, 1993b: 168–70). Most relev-ant to this chapter is his final point:

D1   *Sociological concepts thus obey a double hermeneutic:*

. . . (b) Sociology . . . deals with a universe which is already constituted within frames of meaning by social actors themselves, and reinterprets these within its own theoretical schemes, mediating ordinary and technical language. This double hermeneutic is of considerable complexity, since the connection is not merely a one-way one; there is a continual 'slip-page' of the concepts constructed in sociology, whereby these are ap-propriated by those whose conduct they were originally coined to analyse, and hence tend to become integral features *of* that conduct (thereby in fact potentially compromising their original usage within the technical vocabulary of social science).

This concept of the double hermeneutic, while only a part of his theories, is thus central to Giddens's position, and has attracted controversy (Giddens, 1993b: 9). Moreover, it focuses on areas which seem crucial to novices to the discipline, who need to be assisted to an understanding of the relationship between their own experience of the 'phenomena' investigated by sociology and their 'technical' description and interpretation. In particular, the ac-knowledgement by Giddens of the 'slippage' between the *language* of the two reveals a willingness to problematise this relationship, which is often pre-sented as 'given' in introductory textbooks (cf. Wignell, 1998: 323). Giddens's concept of the 'double hermeneutic' thus seems of central relevance to an investigation of the introductory textbook.

Moreover, as his introduction to the second edition of *New Rules of Socio-logical Method* makes clear, Giddens is actively engaged in theoretical contro-versy (Giddens, 1993b: 1–15). It is therefore likely that his textbook will not attempt to avoid the presentation of theoretical conflict.

In this case study I shall therefore attempt to investigate to what extent Giddens uses the introductory textbook to apprentice novice sociologists to his approach to his discipline. I shall examine the text structure of the book as a whole, and then examine sections of one chapter – that on 'Conformity and Deviance'. First I shall discuss the textual and lexico-grammatical realisation of the 'double hermeneutic', specifically in relation to the interaction between theory and experience. Secondly I shall discuss the extent to which and means by which Giddens presents theoretical controversy.

Structure of book

The overall structure of a textbook indicates its major themes, the issues it presents as most important, and the pedagogical approach of the author. In particular, the introductory chapter will offer insights into the author's approach to the student audience. The most significant difference between textbooks in the latter is likely to be that between top-down and bottom-up presentation of the discipline: does the textbook open with superordinate theoretical concepts which are then elaborated and exemplified, or does it offer descriptions which are then analysed so that the student moves inductively to the theoretical conclusions? Most textbooks are of the former type, including sociology texts, for instance that described by Wignell (1998: 316). In this basic respect, the Giddens textbook already exhibits differences. Giddens states at the outset:

> There is no abstract discussion of sociological concepts at the beginning of this book. Instead, concepts are explained when they are introduced in the relevant chapters, and I have sought throughout to illustrate ideas, concepts and theories by means of concrete examples. (Giddens, 1993a: 3)

Part I of the book, Introduction to Sociology, 'outlines the basic concerns of the subject' (Giddens, 1993a: 3). This emphasis on 'concerns' (as opposed to theories) reflects the author's desire to 'engage' the student-reader's involvement in the 'questions' of the subject, thus underlining the complexity of the 'double hermeneutic', as the reader is led through examples which contrast 'Sociology and "common sense"' (Giddens, 1993a: 12). Parts II–V cover what Giddens considers major areas of the subject. Part VI then deals with Methods and Theories in Sociology, covering first Methods of Research, followed by Development of Sociological Theory. There follows a final Part VII, which consists of Appendix and Glossaries, covering advice on library sources, as well as glossary and bibliographical information.

This organisation suggests a pedagogical approach which seeks first to engage the student in reflection on the relation of sociological enquiry to commonsense experience of the same phenomena. It then leads the student through description and analysis of the chosen areas of sociology, before providing encouragement to the student to 'become a sociologist', by adopting research methods. The history of sociological theory is delayed to the very end, suggesting that Giddens wants the student to reach their own commitment to sociological enquiry before contextualising it within theoretical schools. This is consistent with his concept of the 'double hermeneutic': if students already have knowledge of social life as participants, then a progressive engagement of them in problematisation of this knowledge and a subjecting of it to technical analysis is likely to be more effective than presenting them with a pre-given theoretical taxonomy.

Within Chapter 1, 'Introduction to Sociology', Giddens introduces several ideas in ways which are related to his approach to the discipline. Early in the chapter, he engages the student in a consideration of 'Love and marriage', pointing out the dangers of generalising from one's own historically situated experience, and comments:

> Most of us see the world in terms of familiar features of our own lives. Sociology demonstrates the need to take a much wider view of why we act as we do.
>
> (Giddens, 1993a: 9)

He elaborates on this later in the chapter:

> Sociological findings both *disturb* and *contribute to* our **commonsense beliefs** about ourselves and others.   (Giddens, 1993a: 13)

Moving beyond the students' own beliefs about social life, he paraphrases his concept of the 'double hermeneutic' thus:

> In investigating social life we deal with activities that are **meaningful** to the people who engage in them. Unlike objects in nature, humans are self-aware beings, who confer sense and purpose on what they do. We cannot even describe social life accurately unless we first of all grasp the meanings which people apply to their behaviour.   (Giddens, 1993a: 21)

Thus Giddens is at pains in his introductory chapter to sensitise students to the issues inherent in a 'double hermeneutic' approach to sociology.

Secondly, Giddens explicitly addresses the issue of the contested nature of many sociological ideas. Discussing 'objectivity' in sociology, he states:

> Objectivity in sociology is thus achieved substantially through the effects of mutual *criticism* by members of the sociological community. Many of the subjects discussed in sociology are controversial, because they directly concern disputes and struggles in society itself. But through public debate, the examination of evidence and the logical structure of argument, such issues can be fruitfully and effectively analysed (Habermas, 1979).   (Giddens, 1993a: 21)

This statement prepares students for the later chapters, in which Giddens presents differing arguments, evaluates them, and either draws conclusions or leaves the issues open. Giddens uses this introductory chapter to sensitise students to the complexity of sociology, to present it as an approach rather than a fixed body of knowledge, and to alert students to the intellectual requirements of the discipline, while linking it clearly to their own social experience. All this is in harmony with his theoretical writings.

Chapter structure

The chapter structure within the textbook also reflects Giddens's desire to engage students in problematising their existing views of social life, and hence tends to proceed from experience and example to analysis and theory.

This is in marked contrast to the comments made by Wignell on the sociology text he analyses. There

> the discourse is at its most technical and abstract at a point where it is most new
> to initiates.   (Wignell, 1998: 315)

A typical chapter in the Giddens text is Chapter 5, 'Conformity and Deviance', the earlier part of which will be discussed here.

While the chapter title is composed of technical sociological terms, the brief (untitled) chapter introduction leads the students into engagement with the social experience underlying the concepts before technical definitions are introduced. Previous examination of conformity is briefly reviewed, and then the concept of deviance is introduced as 'another side to the story':

> Not everyone conforms to social expectations all the time.
> (Giddens, 1993a: 116)

There follows a brief example from road use, followed by the introduction of (what will become) the technical term, not as an abstraction, but as a behavioural process:

> People quite often *deviate* from the rules they are expected to follow.
> (Giddens, 1993a: 116)

Thus the 'slippage' between everyday and technical terminology in sociology is clearly exemplified. After this 'engaging' introduction, sections follow which open by giving formal definitions of the sociological use of key terms *(deviance, norms, sanctions, laws, crime)*, followed by extensive exemplification and exploration of the concepts, so that students are continually shifting focus between their experience of social life and its sociological interpretation. The chapter then moves to a more theoretical approach in 'Explaining deviance'. Here a wide variety of theories are described and evaluated, leading to 'theoretical conclusions' which give a balanced but clearly positioned account of the author's views. Other aspects of deviance – punishment, mental illness – are then covered before a final speculative conclusion on 'Deviance and social order'.

This chapter structure leads the student from considering the relations between the sociological concepts and social experience to the differing attempts to explain these aspects of social behaviour. Differing theories are critiqued, some being firmly rejected, others given partial recognition and others qualified acceptance. The ways in which both 'commonsense' and sociological contestation of issues in social life is carried out are thus highlighted. Again, the chapter structure reflects the author's concerns.

Lexico-grammar and the double hermeneutic

In this section I shall discuss the relationship between Giddens's concept of the double hermeneutic and his introduction of sociological concepts as it is realised through choices in lexico-grammar. I shall look at the patterning of grammatical subjects, in terms of whether they represent real-world entities or abstractions. I shall also examine the types of verbal processes, distinguishing particularly between material and behavioural processes, which realise real-world activities, and what I shall term 'epistemic' processes, which realise mental activities within the discipline.[1]

Introducing the concepts (Giddens, 1993a: 115–19)

The first extract to be examined consists of the opening few sections, which introduce the topic and the basic concepts. This extract clearly shows how Giddens introduces students to sociological concepts and relates them to their experience of social life, through lexico-grammatical choices.

The introduction to the chapter opens with reinforcement of the concept of social order, which has already been established in an earlier chapter. This is done through a series of abstract subjects ('human social life', 'The norms we follow in our actions'), which realise concepts which occur on the border between commonsense and technical language about social experience. The pre- and post-modification of the abstract noun heads associate them here with real-world experience, and thus place them as abstractions rather than technical terms. The students' engagement is invited by the use of first-person-plural pronouns and possessives, and by the posing of hypothetical negative conditions:

> Our activities would collapse into chaos if we did not stick to rules.

The concept of deviance is introduced concretely, by examples of groups of people who may behave differently:

> Drivers sometimes disregard the rules of traffic behaviour . . .
> . . . a person may drive recklessly . . .
> People quite often *deviate* from the rules they are expected to follow.

Here the verbal processes are behavioural or material, occurring in the real world. The use of the active verb *deviate* draws attention to the social behaviour underlying the technical sociological term; the fact that it is associated with the mental process 'expect' points to the root of the technical term in societal meanings, thus emphasising the double hermeneutic. The focus then switches to the epistemic significance of such behaviour, with subjects realising epistemic activity:

> The study of deviant behaviour is one of the most fascinating tasks of sociology. It is a complex area of analysis because there are as many types of rule violation as there are social norms and values.

This is then exemplified by contrasts between nominalised material processes:

> Smoking marijuana is a deviant activity in British culture, while drinking alcohol is not. Exactly the reverse is the case in some Middle Eastern societies.

The concept of deviance is thus introduced by engaging the student in appreciation of its interest and its obviousness, once knowledge of social life is activated. The technical sociological term is introduced through interpretation of concrete experience, especially by the strategy of using the related verbal and adjectival forms, which are less 'technical' than the abstract noun, not through the process of abstraction described by Wignell (1998: 323). This can be related to Giddens's concept of the double hermeneutic, in that he leads students to draw on their social experience to recognise the sociological interest of the topic and to problematise it.

The chapter then proceeds to formal definition of the necessary terms. In the section 'What is deviance?' Giddens employs a structure of short cycles in which a technical hyper-Theme (Martin, 1992: 437) is followed by elaboration through description involving real-world grammatical subjects. While this thematisation of the technical corresponds to Wignell's findings (Wignell, 1998: 309), the elaboration provides mediation between the technical and the commonsense. The opening cycle is typical:

> (1) **Deviance** may be defined as non-conformity to a given norm, or set of norms, which are accepted by a significant number of people in a community or society. (2) No society can be divided up in a simple way between those who deviate from norms and those who conform to them. (3) Most of us on some occasions transgress generally accepted rules of behaviour. (4) Many people have at some point committed minor acts of theft, like taking something from a shop without paying for it or appropriating small items from work – such as office notepaper – and putting them to private use. (5) Large numbers of individuals have smoked marijuana . . .   (Giddens, 1993a: 116)

Here the first sentence – the hyper-Theme – has as grammatical subject 'deviance'. The fact that it is printed in bold indicates that at this point Giddens wishes the student to identify it as a technical sociological term, rather than a commonsense description of social behaviour. Thus Giddens signals a shift to the epistemic level. This is confirmed by the verbal process in the main clause, 'may be defined', which is epistemic, in the sense that it refers to a cognitive/verbal activity of the sociological community. The second sentence has a highly generalised (negative) real-world subject and an epistemic verbal process – the 'dividing up' is conceptual, not material. The third sentence invokes the readers' confirmation of the social behaviour – 'most of us' – while the verbal process is a metaphorical realisation of a material process using a fairly technical term ('transgress'). The fourth sentence has a similarly generalised subject, while the verbal process is again metaphorical, using the circumlocution 'committed small acts of theft' to redefine the examples which follow as falling under the definition of deviance. The final sentence retains the generalised subject, but here the verbal processes are material, shifting the focus to description of phenomena. Thus the cycle opens with a technical, epistemic definition, which is then elaborated by gradually 'working down' through application of the way in which the concept of deviance is operationalised until the students can appreciate fully the phenomena which fall under it.

What is most interesting here is the patterning in the verbal processes, which starts with fully 'epistemic' processes and moves through metaphorical to material ones. This can be seen as a mirror image of Giddens's strategy in the introductory section. Here, rather than enlisting the students' social experience to assist them in conceptualising the technical, he introduces the technical and then leads the students to redefine their social experience in terms of it. Thus Giddens is again concentrating on possible points of 'slippage' between the two aspects of the double hermeneutic and exploiting them to extend students' understanding.

The next section of the chapter, 'Norms and sanctions', reverses this pattern. Here Giddens again begins with the real world and 'works up' from social experience to introduce technical concepts. The following extract illustrates this:

(1) Maintaining attitudes of civil inattention towards strangers, using tact in our conversation with friends, or following the procedures establishing 'markers' between encounters – all these we usually do without even realizing that distinct rules of procedure are involved.

(2) Other types of norm we follow more in the conscious belief that the behaviour they involve is justified. (3) This is true, for instance, of the norms of traffic behaviour mentioned earlier. (4) Drivers accept that they have to observe rules like driving on the correct side of the road or stopping when the traffic light is red because if the majority of drivers did not abide by such rules most of the time, the roads would become vastly more dangerous even than they are at present.

(5) Less agreement is found about some other aspects of road behaviour – like speed limits. (6) No doubt the majority of drivers accept that speed limits of some sort are necessary to protect each other, cyclists and pedestrians. (7) But few motorists rigorously respect these limits. (8) They are likely to drive within them if they know or suspect that there is a police car nearby, but once they are confident that there are no police to be seen, many drivers will speed up to well beyond the legal maximum.

(9) This example directs our attention towards some very important aspects of conformity and deviance. (10) All social norms are accompanied by **sanctions** that promote **conformity** and protect against non-conformity. (11) A sanction is any reaction from others to the behaviour of an individual or group which has the aim of ensuring that a given norm is complied with.

Sentence (1) opens with a lengthy pre-posed theme describing examples of conventional behaviour, which is in apposition to the 'dummy' object of the empty verbal process 'do' – 'all these'; the subject, 'we', enlists agreement that these are normal practices. Sentence (2) follows the same pattern, establishing a contrast between what 'we do' 'without even realizing' and actions taken 'in the conscious belief' that the norms 'are justified'. Here the minor processes and grammatical metaphor are significant: they involve mental processes which realise social perceptions of the meaningfulness of social behaviour – the social experience element of the double hermeneutic. Sentence (3) relates these general claims to the specific example of driving behaviour, with Sentence (4) realising this connection specifically: the grammatical subject is 'real' and the verbal process is one of mental attitude, 'Drivers accept'. The next paragraph opens, in Sentence (5), with a metaphorical realisation of a contrast in mental attitude, 'Less agreement is found . . .'. The use of the abstraction and the passive verb suggest a more epistemic perspective: here the author is standing back from the social behaviour and classifying it. The following sentences elaborate this position through description. Sentences (6) and (7) have people as subjects ('the majority of drivers', 'few motorists') with verbs of mental attitude – 'accept', 'respect'. Sentences (8) and (9) then realise the material results of the mental attitudes: 'They are likely to drive . . .', 'many drivers will speed up'. However, these actions are related to specific conditions – the *perceived* presence or absence of police. The next paragraph marks the shift to epistemic. Sentence (10) labels the previous description by the epistemic term 'example' and employs grammatical metaphor ('directs our attention') to shift to the epistemic plane. In Sentence (11) the technical concepts (in bold) of 'sanctions' and 'conformity' are introduced to explain the previously described behaviour. The remainder of the section elaborates and classifies these technical terms, illustrating them with specific examples.

Again in this section Giddens exploits the 'slippage' between the two elements of the double hermeneutic to lead into understanding of the technicality. In this case the verbal processes of mental attitude emphasise the role of social perception in social behaviour, and ease the introduction of the technical concepts of sanctions and conformity. Thus, despite occasional similarities to the sociology text analysed by Wignell, Giddens's text uses resources of lexico-grammar to bridge the gap between the real world and the technical, by emphasising the role of social perception. The patterning of grammatical subjects and verbal processes in these sections of the text realises Giddens's intention to engage students with their own perceptions of social experience and use these to draw them on to technical sociological analysis of social behaviour.

Debate in Sociology (Giddens, 1993a: 122–25)

Having introduced students to the phenomena of conformity and deviance, Giddens then introduces theories which explain them. Giddens maintains, as mentioned above, that objectivity in sociology is achieved through disciplinary debate. In this section of the chapter I shall examine Giddens's endeavours to introduce students to the ways in which this debate is carried out.

In the section 'Explaining deviance', he introduces and critiques a variety of theories. The brief opening paragraph clearly signals the shift from presentation of phenomena to epistemological activity, realised in both the grammatical subjects and the verbal processes:

> (1) The nature and content of deviant behaviour vary widely both from the past to the present and from one society to another. (2) This is something we must seek to explain. (3) In the following sections, we shall discuss some of the leading theories of deviance, giving particular attention to theories of crime. (4) None of the theories provides a comprehensive explanation of crime as a whole, let alone deviance. (5) But they overlap in some ways, and can be combined together in others, to provide a reasonable understanding of major aspects of deviant behaviour.　　　　　　　　　　　　　　　　(Giddens, 1993a: 122)

Students are led from focusing on 'the nature and content of behaviour' to be involved as active participants in a world where epistemological entities are the major focus.

The sections which follow present a variety of theories, arranged in an order which allows Giddens to lead students gradually to appreciate the position he holds. While acknowledging the partial plausibility of all the theories he presents, he subjects each to evaluation. He begins with non-sociological perspectives on crime and deviance. The first such section, 'The argument from biology', is given an essentially negative evaluation. Giddens employs a number of evaluative strategies. Much of the research is presented in the past tense, indicating that it is no longer considered as part of the body of accepted knowledge. Reporting verbs emphasise Giddens's negative evaluation: 'claimed' is the commonest reporting verb, signifying disagreement (Hunston, 1993), while such expressions as 'trying to demonstrate', 'have tried to link', suggest inappropriately biased research. Each claim is countered with an adversative move, and concessions to possible plausibility are heavily modalised, for example:

> Subsequent studies carried out by other researchers claimed rather similar findings . . . However, while views of this sort still have their advocates, such research has been widely criticized. Even if there were an overall relationship between bodily type and delinquency, this would show nothing about the influence of heredity.
> (Giddens, 1993a: 123)

The concluding remarks are firmly negative:

> Yet there is no decisive evidence that any traits of personality are inherited in this way, and even if they were, their connection to criminality would at most be only a distant one.
> (Giddens, 1993a: 123)

The negative evaluation concentrates on the absence of appropriate evidence, thus emphasising the inappropriate methodology of biological research in the area of deviance.

The next section, 'The psychological view', receives similarly negative evaluation. Giddens considers that psychological accounts of criminality are no better than partial:

> psychological theories of crime can at best only explain aspects of crime. While a small minority of criminals may have personality characteristics distinct from the remainder of the population, it is highly unlikely that the majority do so. There are many different types of crime, and it is implausible to suppose that those who commit them share some specific psychological characteristics.
> (Giddens, 1993a: 124)

Giddens concedes the remote possibility of the claim being possible, but provides negative evaluation of probability, a key criterion of status (Hunston, 1993: 61), through such lexis as 'highly unlikely', 'implausible'. This evaluation concentrates on plausibility of explanation. Thus students are introduced not only to specific theories, but to criteria according to which to evaluate them.

Giddens then moves to 'Sociological theories', and the evaluation becomes strongly positive:

> A satisfactory account of the nature of crime must be sociological, for what crime is depends on the social institutions of a society. One of the most important aspects of sociological thinking about crime is an emphasis on the interconnections between crime and deviance in different social contexts.
>
> (Giddens, 1993a: 125)

The adjective 'satisfactory', which implies a wide range of positive criteria, is joined with the strong modal 'must' to produce an unusually strong assertion. Giddens believes that students of sociology must appreciate the centrality of the discipline in this area. He goes on to introduce a number of sociological explanations of crime: *differential association, anomie, delinquent subcultures*. Each of these is presented without integral evaluation, employing neutral reporting expressions, such as 'according to Sutherland', 'Merton identifies', 'They argued that'. The evaluation of these theories appears in a separate short section, where the basic ideas are given positive evaluation:

> The studies of Cloward and Ohlin and of Cohen, rightly emphasize connections between conformity and deviance.   (Giddens, 1993a: 127)

A balanced approach to their explanations is produced by partial criticisms: 'We should be cautious about . . .' and 'However, it would also be wrong . . .'. Students are thus urged to view all theories critically.

The next section, 'Labelling theory', is the longest in this sequence. It introduces the theory with immediate positive evaluation:

> One of the most important approaches to the understanding of crime has come to be called **labelling theory** . . .   (Giddens, 1993a: 128)

Importance/significance is one of the key evaluative categories listed by Lemke (1998: 37) and also falls under Hunston's macro-classification of Value in evaluation in scientific writing (Hunston, 1993: 63). In interpersonal terms it is a crucial evaluation in a textbook, as it gives a clear signal to students that this is a theory to which the author recommends they pay particular attention. Giddens then gives a very detailed account of the theory, in which the voice of the theorists and that of the author are difficult to distinguish: reporting verbs are soon abandoned. This is followed by discussion of why the theory is seen as so important:

> (1) Labelling theory is important because it begins from the assumption that no act is intrinsically criminal. (2) Definitions of criminality are established by the powerful, through the formulation of laws and their interpretation by police, courts and correctional institutions.

It is interesting to note that the positive features of labelling theory include the emphasis on the social meaningfulness attached to actions by portions of society, as realised in 'are established', 'formulation', 'interpretation'. Then follows an account of criticisms of the theory:

(3) Critics of labelling theory have sometimes argued that there are in fact a number of acts consistently prohibited across all, or virtually all, cultures, such as murder, rape and robbery. (4) This view is surely incorrect: even within our own culture, killing is not always regarded as murder.   (Giddens, 1993a: 129)

The criticisms are given serious consideration: 'argue' is a reporting verb which acknowledges the plausibility of the reported proposition. However, the proposition is firmly rejected as 'incorrect', with the addition of the evidential 'surely' to engage the readers in the reasonableness of the evaluation. Thus students are invited to join the discussion of this 'important' theory. Giddens then introduces his own criticisms of labelling theory, involving the readers:

We can more convincingly criticize labelling theory on three main grounds.

He proceeds to identify problems with the theory, but expresses them in less negative terms than in the evaluation of previous theories. He modalises his criticism so that it is less absolute:

the processes that *lead* to acts defined as deviant tend to get lost . . .

He expresses his criticism as a question:

Delinquent behaviour does tend to increase following conviction, but is this the result of the labelling itself?

Here the emphatic 'does' acknowledges the validity of the claim, while the question form is both a more polite way of challenging the interpretation than overt criticism and an invitation to students to participate in the debate. Finally he suggests a dimension missing from the theory:

Third, we have to investigate the overall development of modern systems of law, judiciary and police if we are to understand how and why different labels come to be applied.

The section ends with Giddens drawing attention to research which precisely fills this gap. Thus a favoured theory is not spared criticism: students are shown how to evaluate useful theories so as to improve them.

There then follows a further theory, 'Rational choice and "situational" interpretations of crime'. This is presented without evaluation, which is delayed until the final section, 'Theoretical conclusions'. Here the main points of the previous sections are recapitulated, with the acknowledgement that:

Each of the theoretical standpoints we have looked at has a contribution to make to understanding either some aspects or some types of crime.

However, the summaries of the applicability of biological and psychological approaches are modalised – they 'may identify personality characteristics . . .' – and the point is countered: 'on the other hand . . .'. Several positive evaluations are made of the sociological perspectives:

First, these theories correctly emphasize the continuities between criminal and 'respectable' behaviour . . . Second, all agree that there is a strong *contextual* element in the occurrence of criminal activities.

Finally, Giddens takes up a position which gives modalised support to the last two theories he presented:

> In spite of its deficiencies, labelling theory is perhaps the most widely useful approach to understanding aspects of crime and deviant behaviour. When integrated with a historical perspective, labelling theory sensitizes us . . . Situational interpretations of crime can be quite easily connected to the labelling approach . . .

Throughout this section, Giddens leads students to subject the various theories presented to scrutiny in terms of their 'methods of observation and argument'. He shows how to evaluate evidence and its interpretation, how to identify the overemphases or gaps in otherwise good theories. Thus he involves students in the process of achieving objectivity 'through the effects of mutual *criticism* by members of the sociological community' (Giddens, 1993a: 21). He does not attempt to disguise his strongly held views, but he attempts to ensure that students have followed his – sociological – process of reaching them.

Overview of analysis

In this, inevitably partial, examination of Giddens's textbook, I have attempted to show how the features of text structure and lexico-grammar contribute to Giddens's efforts to introduce students not only to the fundamentals of the discipline of sociology, but also to his particular theoretical position within it. His approach in this textbook reflects several of his positions, particularly the implications for beginning sociologists of the concept of the 'double hermeneutic', as well as his belief in the negotiated nature of objectivity in sociology. In his introduction of sociological concepts, Giddens constantly shifts between students' own social experience and the technical sociological description and explanation of that experience in a way which reflects the concept of the double hermeneutic. In his treatment of theoretical issues, Giddens initiates students into the disciplinary debate by presenting theories in the historical contexts in which they emerged, critiquing them in terms of their evidence and argument, extracting the useful elements from them, and engaging students in the argumentative process by which he has reached his own position. Thus Giddens attempts to initiate students not only into the content and theory of sociology, but into the complex processes through which sociological concepts and theories evolve.

Swales has suggested (1995: 15) that textbooks

> potentially create a unique kind of synergy which links theory to practice, past and present research to the future, task to text, and local initiative to the wider development of the field.

I would suggest that the Giddens textbook provides an example of this synergy at work in sociology, although some mediation by tutors may be needed to realise its full potential. I shall discuss such mediation in the final section.

Pedagogical implications

Genre analysis of students' textbooks can provide EAP tutors with resources to perform their complex role of mediation in their students' engagement with the discourse of their subjects. This can involve both support for full comprehension of the text and also more critical approaches to it. Johns (1997: 49) suggests useful activities which involve students in examination of their textbooks which include both 'pragmatic' and 'critical' tasks (Pennycook, 1994; Allison, 1996).

On the one hand, an understanding of the ways in which a textbook introduces students to the technical language and argumentation of a discipline will enable tutors to support students in their understanding of these features. In the case of this text, students may be asked to list the terms which emerge as technical in the treatment of the topic of deviance and then collect the examples Giddens uses – both before and after introduction of the technical term – to illustrate its meaning in the context of social experience. They can then be asked to attempt a fresh definition of the term which arises from their understanding of the examples. In this way they will engage with the author's concept of the double hermeneutic. From a more critical stance, they may be asked to discuss whether they agree with Giddens's interpretation of these examples. Particularly if they come from a different cultural context from the primary audience of the textbook,[2] they may then go on to provide their own examples from their own societal experience, and discuss whether these can be explained and classified in the same way as those of Giddens. Such activities give students the opportunity both to deepen comprehension and to critique the text.

Students can also be asked to list the theories introduced by Giddens and comment on his position in relation to each and his reasons for this. They can then discuss the validity of the author's evaluation of the arguments, examining whether they follow his logic and whether they agree with it.

Finally, since 'cutting edge' textbooks are likely to be at least partially controversial, students should be asked to compare the textbook with any others available to them, identifying differences of organisation and language as well as theoretical position. It may then be possible, particularly with the participation of a sociology informant, to assist them in seeing the connection between these differences and Giddens's theoretical positions.

Theorists who write introductory textbooks from 'cutting edge' positions are likely to want students not only to adopt their views, but engage with the processes of reaching them – to participate in their methodology and argumentation. This appears to be the case in the Giddens text. The mere 'setting' of a textbook may not lead students to such engagement, as they may treat the text as just another source of disciplinary authority. Analysis of the interaction between the author's theoretical position and their approach to disciplinary initiation can allow the EAP tutor to stimulate students to examine the text more interactively and to place it in relation to other introductions to the discipline.

NOTES

1. Thus I shall not distinguish between 'congruent' realisation and 'grammatical metaphor', in Halliday's terms (Halliday, 1994), but concentrate on the 'real-world' versus 'modelling' locus of the process.
2. For obvious commercial reasons, most textbooks are written for a primary audience in the North, and students in South countries need to recontextualise examples.

Part II

CORPUS-BASED STUDIES

Chapter 5

<hr>

Corpus-Based Analyses in EAP

Lynne Flowerdew

INTRODUCTION

In the 1980s and early 1990s corpus-based research centred on the exploration of lexical, grammatical, or lexico-grammatical items in what were considered at the time to be large-scale generalised corpora, such as the one-million-word Brown and LOB corpora (see Meijs, 1988; Kennedy, 1991) or the 7.3-million-word Cobuild corpus (see Renouf and Sinclair, 1991; Sinclair, 1987, 1991), whose exploitation has resulted in a myriad of pedagogic materials for English for General Purposes, such as dictionaries, grammars, and course-books. Corpora have also long played a role in other aspects of language studies such as historical linguistics, dialectology, and variation studies (cf. McEnery and Wilson, 1996, ch. 4, for an overview of other uses of corpora). More recently, the use of corpora has also been proposed for the raising of grammar awareness in teacher education programmes (Hunston, 1995) and taught as an academic subject as part of a degree programme (Hatzidaki, 1996; Renouf, 1997). Another area which is receiving increasing attention is the use of multi-lingual parallel corpora for translation purposes (King, 1997; Barlow, 1996). Thus, since the early 1990s this burgeoning field has had an impact on other areas in linguistics and language studies and has also expanded considerably regarding the size and types of corpora being compiled and the uses to which these corpora are put. Recent conferences such as the TALC'98, Teaching and Language Corpora Conference (http://users.ox.ac.uk/~talc98), TALC2000 (http://www-gewi.kfunigraz.ac.at/talc2000), PALC'97, Practical Applications in Language Corpora, PALC'99, the two North American symposia on corpora in linguistics and language teaching (http://www.lsa.umich. edu/eli/micase/symposium.html), the first taking place in 1999 and the second in 2000, bear witness to the growing interest in the application of corpus linguistics to language teaching. The edited conference proceedings for TALC'98 are reported in Burnard and McEnery (2000), PALC'97 in Lewandowska-Tomaszczyk and Melia (1997), PALC'99 in Lewandowska-Tomaszczyk and Melia (2000), and the First North American Symposium on Linguistics and Language Teaching in Simpson and Swales (in press). A discussion list on corpus linguistics and language teaching has also recently been created (for details see http://www.ruf.rice.edu/~barlow/cllt.html), which is yet another sign of the increasingly important role that corpus linguistics is now playing in language pedagogy.

During the last few years, the compilation of corpora has widened in two senses – much larger-scale, mega-corpora are now in existence (see Kennedy, 1998 for details of such corpora). For example, the original Cobuild corpus has been expanded into a 300-million-word monitor corpus, named the Bank of English. New text is continually being added to the database, which has been used to inform an updated series of dictionaries and grammars. There also now exists the 100-million-word British National Corpus, BNC, (Aston and Burnard 1998). In another sense, though, the field has widened to include the recognition of much smaller, specialised genre-based corpora, which was initiated by Biber (1988). Many of these corpora comprise databases of mostly written, but occasionally spoken, academic discourse whose findings have been used to inform pedagogy in the field of EAP (see J. Flowerdew, 1996: 101 for a list of small-scale corpora for EAP/ESP applications). As Aston (1997) points out, such corpora are usually in the 20,000–200,000-word range and are more specialised than the larger ones in terms of topic and/or genre. Many of these EAP corpora have been compiled for very specific research or pedagogical purposes either on an individual (e.g. Johns's Plant Biology Corpus, 1988) or institutional basis (e.g. the Wellington Corpus, Kennedy, 1995), rather than nationally or internationally.

Another interesting development in the field is the building of inter-language corpora of academic discourse (Greenbaum, 1992; Granger, 1993, 1998a; Milton, 1998, 1999). Both the International Corpus of Learner English, ICLE (Granger, 1998a), and the Hong Kong University of Science and Technology (HKUST) Learner Corpus (Milton, 1998, 1999) consist of the argumentative writing of undergraduate, non-native speakers of English. Whereas the exploration of the expert or native-speaker EAP corpora has mostly been carried out on untagged text using published concordancing software such as *MicroConcord* (Scott and Johns, 1993) or *WordSmith Tools* (Scott, 1996), both ICLE (Dagneaux et al., 1998; Meunier, 1998) and the HKUST Learner Corpus (Milton and Chowdhury, 1994) have been tagged with an error tagset devised by the compilers to aid linguistic investigation of learner errors.

A striking feature of these EAP corpora is that the majority consist of written rather than spoken academic discourse. It would seem, therefore, that corpus compilations of academic discourse are still perpetuating the severe imbalance between spoken and written data characteristic of most larger-scale corpora, such as the BNC of which only 10% is from spoken sources, a point noted by Leech (1997).

Not only does the spoken component of general large-scale corpora tend to be smaller in relation to the written component, but within the spoken component usually only a small percentage comprises speech of an academic nature, such as lectures. Although large-scale spoken corpora exist such as the London–Lund Corpus of spoken English (Svartvik, 1990), the Corpus of

Spoken American English (Chafe et al., 1991), and the Lancaster/IBM Spoken English Corpus (Knowles et al., 1996), again, academic lectures feature as one genre among a wide variety of other genres covering dialogue and monologue, and spontaneous and planned speech. The Cambridge and Nottingham Corpus of Discourse in English, CANCODE (McCarthy, 1998), which currently comprises 5 million words of English, features naturally occurring spoken interaction in a variety of largely non-formal settings; however, it does also include a pedagogical EAP context of informal tutorial conversations. It is therefore evident that although a variety of spoken corpora exist, spoken corpora specifically relating to EAP do not figure very prominently as a subsection of these.

The following review will survey the various (mainly) written and spoken, expert and non-native speaker, or learner, corpora which have been compiled for descriptive or pedagogical purposes in EAP. Under the umbrella of EAP, I distinguish between corpus-based studies for English for General Academic Purposes (EGAP) and those relating to English for Specific Academic Purposes (ESAP), an important classification noted by Dudley-Evans and St John (1998). Within the field of ESAP, I will survey both descriptive and more applied corpus work in English for Science and Technology (EST), English for Medicine, English for Business, Finance, and Economics, and various types of contrastive studies. Where discussed by the compilers/researchers, I will also briefly outline their rationale for choice of texts and the software tools and methods for extracting data for analysis, as these are important considerations in corpus-based research and its applications.

ENGLISH FOR GENERAL ACADEMIC PURPOSES

The majority of the corpus work in this area centres on the exploration of learner corpora. In order to disambiguate which grammatical structures or lexis are underused by students in academic writing, findings from a learner, or non-native speaker (NNS), corpus are either usually compared with a parallel corpus of native-speaker (NS) writing, or sometimes with a larger reference corpus of expert writing. Some early work in this field was conducted by Tribble (1990, 1991) on the use of 'speech' verbs, e.g. *say*, in a 54,861-word Student corpus mostly taken from English language examination scripts extracted from the Longman Corpus of Learners' English. Later research in the area of student, or learner, corpora has been carried out on much larger corpora which have been tagged syntactically to aid analyses – the ICLE and HKUST Learner Corpus being prime examples of this category.

For example, Granger and Rayson (1998) compared word frequency profiles from the International Corpus of Learner English (ICLE), a non-native-speaker corpus of *c.*280,000 words of argumentative essay writing by advanced French-speaking learners of English, with a control corpus of similar writing by British and American university students taken from the Louvain Corpus of Native English Essays (LOCNESS). They examined significant patterns of over- and underuse of various word categories (articles, determiners, pronouns, prepositions, adverbs, adjectives, nouns, and verbs) in the learner corpus, noting a very significant overuse of the first and second personal pronouns, but an underuse of prepositions, a category often associated with nominalisations in informative, academic writing. They thus conclude that their learner data displayed many of the stylistic features of spoken English, and practically none of the features typical of academic writing. Granger has also used the ICLE and LOCNESS corpora to compare connector usage (Granger and Tyson, 1996), collocation of amplifiers and formulaic sentence builders, e.g. *it is said/thought that . . .* (Granger, 1998b).

Similarly, Milton (1998) has compared a 500,000-word interlanguage corpus (a subsection of the HKUST Learner Corpus) consisting of Hong Kong 'Use of English' examination scripts with scripts receiving the highest grades transcribed from the Cambridge Examinations Syndicate 'General Studies' Examination held in the UK. He examined four-word strings underused and overused by Hong Kong students, concluding that there is a strong correlation between the idiomatic expressions overused by Hong Kong students, such as *All in all, In a nutshell,* and the classified lists of expressions distributed by Hong Kong tutorial schools, where high school students register to cram vocabulary and model answers before public examinations. Also examining learner language from a collocational perspective, Howarth (1998) has analysed the extent to which NNS deviate from NS phraseological norms which he established on the basis of collocational patterning in the social sciences text in the LOB Corpus and a collection of other university texts. Howarth found that the majority of learner errors were concentrated in the area of grammatical modification, e.g. *respond students' need, or lexical substitution, e.g. *do attempts.

Several studies have examined the issue of 'directness' in students' academic writing. Hyland and Milton (1997b) investigated the expressions of doubt and certainty in NS and NNS high school students' argumentative academic writing, using the same corpora described in Milton (1998). Their findings reveal that Hong Kong students do not moderate their claims sufficiently as their writing displays firmer assertions, a more authoritative tone, and stronger commitments to statements when compared with NS writing. Similar infelicities have also been uncovered in advanced German learners' use of adjective intensification by Lorenz (1998) who, again, explored two NS and two NNS corpora, of around 100,000 words each, containing argumentative essays. See also McEnery and Kifle, this volume, for the presentation of arguments by Eritrean students.

L. Flowerdew (2000), while not using a NS corpus, relied on contextual factors to determine whether various hedging devices were used appropriately in a 200,000-word corpus of 90 analytical reports written by Hong Kong learners of English. She found that in many cases students presented explanations for their data and drew conclusions as a certainty rather than based on plausible reasoning, resulting in writing which was too direct. In these recommendation-based reports one very common expression for making a recommendation was *Therefore we highly (strongly) recommend that* . . . However, this phrase was socioculturally inappropriate for the context as the undergraduate students were writing these reports to a superior in which case a more mitigating expression would be in order. As in the case of this example and many others, it would be difficult to tell from an examination of the corpus text alone if the pragmatic force of an expression was appropriate or not without having knowledge of the wider context and reader/writer relationship. For this reason, hands-on concordancing exercises may not be appropriate in certain teaching situations where interpretation of the discourse relies on contextual factors which are not immediately recoverable from the corpus itself (see L. Flowerdew, in press 2001). This instance thus indicates that one cannot always trust the text alone and for certain pragmatic aspects of text it is necessary to adopt a more ethnographic approach to the data analysis (see Part IV, 'Ethnographic/Naturalistic Approaches').

A more textlinguistic approach to corpus analysis has been taken by Green et al. (2000) who examined the effects on coherence of marked themes in a subsection (600,000 words) of undergraduate writing from the HKUST Learner Corpus. The researchers tagged two topic-fronting devices (*For* and *Concerning*) and three logical connectors (*Besides, Furthermore,* and *Moreover*) in both the interlanguage corpus and three subsections of native-speaker corpora of comparable size: expository writing from the LOB and BROWN corpora and the Cambridge Syndicate Examination (CSE) corpus. Their comparison of the items in the interlanguage and native-speaker corpora reveal that the Chinese students have a greater tendency than native speakers to place these connectors in theme position. However, when fronted as marked themes, signalling new information rather than the usual given or known information in theme position, these items were found to have a negative effect on both local and global coherence. De Beaugrande (1996: 525) touches on this aspect of thematic structure when he remarks that 'We could use the corpus to explore which types of words or collocations tend to be used for beginning or ending a sentence'.

In the studies cited above, the overuse, underuse, and misuse of lexical or grammatical items is established on the basis of a comparison of a learner corpus with a corpus of native-speaker writing or, in the case of inappropriate use, with reference to the socio-cultural context. Another way in which to determine whether certain words are being underused or overused in a learner corpus is by using the *KeyWords* tool in the *WordSmith* program (Scott, 1996). This tool can compute words of unusually high frequency in a small corpus through comparison with a larger reference corpus (in fact, this tool is also very useful for specification of genres, see Scott, 1997, 2000). Granger and Tribble (1998) compared the ICLE corpus of 280,000 words with a larger reference corpus, in this case the Core BNC of *c.*1,000,000 words, discovering that learners were too reliant on superordinate adjectives such as *important* in their academic writing.

Most of the work on learner corpora cited above focuses on descriptions of language use whereas Milton has also exploited his empirical data for pedagogic applications. For example, Milton (1998) reports on a tutorial CALL program which includes an error recognition (i.e. proofreading and editing) exercise intended to sensitise learners to the most common or serious errors exposed by the corpus analysis, accompanied by a hypertext online grammar designed to give context-sensitive feedback based on these errors. To compensate for underuse of expressions revealed by his corpus analysis Milton (1999) has also devised a wordlist-driven concordancing program (*WordPilot*) made interactively available to learners from their word processor, which calls up databases of expressions which learners are either not aware of, or avoid. This wordlist feature is also accompanied by information on the frequency and context of the expressions in various text types to enable learners to judge whether it would be appropriate to import into their own piece of academic writing. Another application of learner corpora in pedagogy is reported in Seidlhofer (2000) who describes a course in which participants act not only as analysts but also as participants in the discourse process as they 'do' corpus linguistics via their own texts and own questions.

Other applied linguists and practitioners have concentrated on the area of academic vocabulary (see Coxhead, 2000 for a description of a corpus-based academic wordlist). Pedagogic applications of academic vocabulary in EGAP corpora are reported in Pickard (1994) and Thurstun and Candlin (1998a, 1998b) whose corpus-based materials are modelled on the practical hands-on or concordance-based exercise templates described in Johns (1988, 1991, 1994) and Tribble and Jones (1990). For example, Pickard (1994) exploited five self-compiled academic corpora of *c*.50,000 words each covering a range of subject disciplines to help students with the key vocabulary (e.g. reporting verbs) of academic writing. Thurstun and Candlin (1998a, 1998b) show how *MicroConcord* has been used with the *MicroConcord Corpus of Academic Texts* (Scott and Johns, 1993) to familiarise students with the lexico-grammatical patterning of key semi-technical words related to various functions of academic writing, such as stating the topic of your writing, referring to the research literature, reporting the research of others, etc. For example, in a suite of concordance-based exercises, students are first asked to look at concordances to examine the meanings of key terms and then to familiarise themselves with the patterning as they complete a task such as the one shown in Figure 5.1. See Swales, this volume, for further suggestions of corpus-informed advanced EAP materials.

The field of EGAP is thus well represented by language descriptions derived from comparisons of NS and NNS corpora. However, with the exception of Milton's (1998, 1999) work, the findings of learner corpora are not often applied to pedagogy. Neither do the use of learner corpora feature so prominently in the ESAP field, as will be evident from the following section.

UNIT 5A
LOOK

Study these concordances, *underlining* the central group of words which can stand alone, as has been done in the first example. Then answer the questions below. You may like to look at question 1 before you start. (Don't worry that these are cut-off sentences – just familiarize yourself with the key words).

GROUP 1

- seen at puberty. *The isolation and chemical identification of several sex hormones* in the late 192 akhtin's method lies not simply in the formal identification of a genre or a subgenre or a chronotop established only after much controversy. Its identification was an early success of X-ray crystallo
- the production of muscle-specific proteins. Identification of the new muscle proteins was made pos.loration of their difficulties had led to the identification of two additional problems: <list><ite

GROUP 2

ure of construction as a whole; *the facts are identified by the principles that result.* In erapy, and that such attitudes can usually be identified by carefully analysing the patient's attemp occurrence of a linguistic form which can be identified as Arabic. Christianity has a similar cohes existence. <p> Another of many criteria to be identified could be the subsequent or continuing costs 2 BC), who rejected the idea that time can be identified with any form of motion or change. For, he 1 Greek literature, can nevertheless still be identified as a distinctive and possibly definitive ge operties. <p> Many more carcinogens have been identified since then. Some are mainly of laboratory I runs of mutual recrimination. <p> So, we have identified two characteristics of winning strategies: ver the last three hundred years or so. It is identified by a series of political causes espoused by orerunners of Islam. A later Muslim tradition identified the Rock as the point from which Muhammed a ed by Levene's tetra-structure. The sugar was identified as either ribose or deoxyribose: for a time random). Forty years later these factors were identified as bits of chromosome, and a century later er supply 20 years or so before bacteria were identified as causing the disease. Lime juice was reco Up to five stages in the life cycle could be identified, each of which might respond to a different r estimated eight hundred buildings have been identified. Her techniques and their results were by n

GROUP 3

ey do not rejoin. *If we knew enough and could identify all the individual animals alive,* say, one hu st, policies must be changed. <p> We can only identify the proper criteria correctly if we accept th the therapist's role is to help the partners identify the problems that they face as a couple and t ood is out of bounds in politics. It tries to identify the reasons which lead people to embrace this hough less widely research. Here I want to identify one feature of that relationship which seems r separate effects. Research was essential to identify the ill-effects attributable to each substanction relative to hat tradition. They hope to identify a coherent body of ideas which places them so ndon School of Hygiene, where he continued to identify the chemical constituents of fungi and discov

---

FAMILIARIZE

1) Which of the following statements do you think are true? Tick your answer in the box.

TO IDENTIFY involves naming	true ❏	false ❏
TO IDENTIFY involves describing	true ❏	false ❏
TO IDENTIFY involves imagining	true ❏	false ❏
TO IDENTIFY involves deciding what something is	true ❏	false ❏
TO IDENTIFY involves recognizing	true ❏	false ❏
TO IDENTIFY involves criticizing	true ❏	false ❏

Figure 5.1 Functional concordance-based exercise
Source: Thurstun and Candlin (1998a)

ENGLISH FOR SPECIFIC ACADEMIC PURPOSES

English for Science and Technology (EST)

The majority of the corpus work in the domain of ESAP focuses on descriptions of quantitative data of the specialised lexis of various science and engineering disciplines. One of the first specialised EST corpora to be compiled was the one-million-word Jiaotong Daxue English for Science and Technology (JDEST) Corpus, which consists of extracts from undergraduate-level textbooks from ten different subject areas in the fields of Science and Technology (Yang, 1986). In addition to identifying technical vocabulary, Yang has also identified two other categories, classifying those words which have a high distribution across fields but a lower frequency as 'sub-technical'. A high proportion of these words, e.g. *problem, result, feature, factor,* which serve as anaphoric or cataphoric signalling devices, resemble Winter's (1977) vocabulary 3 items, a category of nouns with a text-organising function. Those words which have a high distribution across fields but also a frequency peak in one field, as in the case of *work,* with a technical sense in mechanical engineering, Yang views as overlapping between technical and sub-technical vocabulary. Another early EST corpus is the Guangzhou Petroleum English Corpus (GPEC), which consists of 700 texts about 500–600 words long drawn randomly from Petroleum English writings (Zhu, 1989). Zhu compared the 50 most frequent word types in GPEC with the same word types in three other corpora, namely JDEST, Lancaster-Oslo-Bergen (LOB) and BROWN, noting that 35 of the 50 words rank among the top 50 in all of the four corpora. He remarks that what is interesting about these words is that the majority are function words 'which seem to be the mainstay of writing of all fields' (p. 31), although he also notes that some words such as *oil, gas, water, pressure* are unique to the GPEC. Another study which has examined the use of sub-technical/technical vocabulary is that conducted by J. Flowerdew (1993b). In a 104,4833-word corpus of biology reading texts and lectures for undergraduate students, Flowerdew's analysis revealed the high frequency of occurrence of these dual function items; in the top twenty most frequently occurring words, the majority are sub-technical with a specific technical meaning in biology, e.g. *wall, energy, structure, concentration, body.* See also James et al. (1997) for a lexical analysis of biochemistry, biology, and chemistry undergraduate textbooks.

In addition to identifying common content (technical and sub-technical vocabulary) and function words in EST corpora, researchers have also paid attention to the lexical and grammatical patterning of text. Lexical patterning is also the focus of Yang's (1986) research on the JDEST Corpus in which multi-word terms such as *static electric field* were identified on the basis of their stable collocational behaviour. J. Flowerdew's (1993b) work on biology texts has thrown up some interesting findings concerning grammatical patternings. The data revealed that spatial prepositions do not mostly occur as adjuncts, as they are commonly taught in textbooks, but are more often used to introduce post-modifying phrases (reduced relative clauses) as in the example *the membranes around the sap vacuole*, a syntactic construction which receives little attention in pedagogic grammars (Biber et al., 1994). Nominalisations and complex nominals, another category of grammatical patternings prevalent in academic scientific text (Halliday, 1988), have been singled out for comment in the HKUST Computer Science Corpus, a one-million-word corpus of undergraduate textbooks. James et al. (1994) note that over 97% of the 307 occurrences of *interrupt(s)* in the Computer Science Corpus are functionally nominal or adjectival, citing the following sentence (p. 45) with a particularly complex grammatical patterning as posing difficulty in interpretation for students:

> Selectively disabling interrupts on one or more levels is called interrupt masking.

The above analyses, for the main part, concentrate on individual lexical items and the lexical or grammatical patterning of text. I will now briefly consider several other studies which attempt to examine corpus-based findings from a more discoursal perspective.

King (1989), developing Yang's (1986) work on sub-technical vocabulary outlined above, compares the use of discourse-organising nouns such as *consideration, factor*, etc. in the final drafts of student projects in the fields of civil and production engineering with those found in a 114,000-word corpus of scientific and technical papers (Johns, 1994 also draws attention to the importance of such nouns in academic writing). Likewise, Wu (1992) has adopted a more discoursal approach to corpus analysis. Drawing on a corpus of engineering texts, she shows how the item *consider* can be used as a discourse signal; either to set up a particular discourse framework for the following proposition through a lexical phrase such as *Let us consider...*, or to signal the writer's evaluation of a following statement through a phrase such as *It is very important to consider... Consider* can also be used as a rhetorical organiser, fulfilling a predictive function as in the following example: *When a pavement is being examined, engineers have to consider two important questions...* Another small-scale research project which attempts to categorise items according to their rhetorical function has been conducted by L. Flowerdew (1998a) who compares the use of cause–effect markers in the Greenpeace report on Global Warming, a 40,000-word sub-corpus from the *MicroConcord Corpus of Academic Texts* (Scott and Johns, 1993), with their use in a similar corpus of student writing on the topic of pollution. She classified these causative markers according to the semantic relations of reason–result, means–result, and grounds–conclusion (Hoey, 1986). One interesting finding to surface was that in the academic corpus the prepositions *with, through, from*, and *for* were frequently used in combination with nominalisations to signal the reason–result relation between clauses, but rarely used for this function in the student corpus, a failing which is also prevalent in EAP textbooks. Pedagogic applications for this analysis using hands-on concordancing techniques are reported in L. Flowerdew (1998b). Epistemic modality at a discourse level has been investigated in science texts by Butler (1990) who explored the distribution of different modal types in relation to the macro-structure of certain text types (articles and textbooks) and subject matter (physics and biology).

In all the above-mentioned studies the analyses are primarily text-based, relying on the reader's interpretative strategies. A more ethnographic perspective to corpus analysis has been taken by Hyland (1998, 2000) who like Butler (1990) has examined the use of epistemic modal verbs used for hedging in a corpus of 80 research articles in cell and molecular biology. However, Hyland situates his research within the wider social and professional contexts in which scientists work and which motivate the use of hedging. Furthermore, in an innovative departure from the usual method of corpus analysis, Hyland reports on how he involved in the analysis four native-speaker biologists, who were all experienced researchers and writers in the field, by asking them to speak aloud their reactions to underlined features in the text and also by having them participate in small focus groups for discussion (see Part IV of this volume).

Whilst the above researchers acknowledge the usefulness of their corpus-based findings for pedagogy, these tend to remain at the level of language description and have not as yet been applied in any major way to EST materials. However, EST corpora have been exploited pedagogically on a small scale, most notably by Johns, a pioneer in this field. In Johns (1988) ideas are given for hands-on concordancing exercises using the wildcard symbol '*' meaning 'any number of characters' to extract salient vocabulary from a 100,000-word Plant Biology Corpus, and Johns (1991) reports on a set of exercises from concordanced output using a 760,000-word *New Scientist* Corpus in response to students' requests on how *should* is used. Similar examples of concordance-derived exercises designed to enhance student competence in the semantic and syntactic elements of the language of Biology undergraduate textbooks are outlined in Stevens (1991a). Practitioners are also taking advantage of the wealth of material available on the World Wide Web to construct corpus-derived materials. For example, see Foucou and Kübler (2000) for an account of teaching technical English to computer science students using documents extracted and filtered from various sources on the Internet.

It can be seen from the above overview that a considerable amount of work, both descriptive and more applied, has been undertaken in several different subject areas within EST, although the bulk of this analysis has been carried out on expert rather than learner corpora. However, as the following sections will demonstrate, much less analysis has been undertaken in other ESAP fields.

English for Medicine

Although a significant amount of research has been undertaken on the written discourse of medical English, not much work of a corpus-based nature exists in this field. Moreover, most of the corpus work on medical English reported in the literature relies on investigation of medical research articles – although see Vihla (1998) for an account of a medical corpus, *Medicor*, which comprises both professional texts such as textbook samples and research articles, and popular texts from newspapers and magazines. What is interesting about the four studies outlined below is that they attempt to investigate various lexical and grammatical features with respect to the different subsections of research articles, rather than as isolated items in word-frequency lists.

Biber and Finegan (1994) investigated the linguistic characteristics of the Introduction, Methods, Results, Discussion (I–M–R–D) sections in 20 medical research articles taken from the most recent period represented in the ARCHER corpus (A Representative Corpus of Historical English Registers). Their analysis reveals that there exist systematic linguistic differences associated with the purpose-related variation of subsections within experimental research articles. For example, the Methods sections were found to use more past than present tense verbs, reflecting the focus on reporting of past-time events and procedures. In contrast, present tense verbs were found to occur most frequently in the Discussion sections, reflecting an emphasis on the present implications of the findings.

Jabbour (1997) has conducted a similar type of research looking at shifts in tense in medical research articles, which were chosen on account of their high rank on the subject categories of the SCI (Science Citation Index). Her rationale for this method of choosing articles is that the greater the number of times an article has been cited, the more impact it has in the field and consequently, it can be seen as more representative of the journals in the field. Jabbour's findings on the use of tenses are similar to those of Biber and Finegan (1994), except that she also discusses these from the perspective of a text averral or a text attribution, a type of discourse framework that organises interaction in research articles (cf. Sinclair, 1985). For example, she notes that Discussion sections, where writers are making claims, arguing for these claims, and putting forward counter-arguments against previous research claims, are relevant to the present. Typical averrals would thus consist of verbal groups such as *would suggest* and *is not clear.*

Gledhill (1995, 1996, 2000) has also considered lexical and grammatical items from a more functional perspective, akin to the 'move structures' associated with genre analysis. Whereas Jabbour (1997) chose her medical texts on the basis of their high ranking in the SCI index, Gledhill, in order to achieve a balanced and representative corpus, asked the researchers from his survey to submit their own articles and also to recommend journals and specific papers which they considered relevant to the field. This is an important departure from the usual method of selecting text for corpus analysis as it adopts a more ethnographic approach to data collection as those specialist informants of the discourse community who shape and create the texts under investigation are consulted (see Part IV of this volume).

Gledhill (1995: 11) posits the notion of phraseology 'a system of preferred expressions differentiated by the rhetorical aims of a discourse community'. To illustrate, Gledhill (1996) examines the different phraseological behaviour of the grammatical item *in* in the titles, abstracts, results, and discussion sections of a 500,000-word corpus of 150 cancer research articles. He found that the collocational patterning associated with *in* varied in usage depending on each section. For instance, in the Results sections *in* was the most salient grammatical item in this section and was used in three different types of phrase. The most frequent expression indicated positive results involving a higher score or increased amount in terms of measurement (*increase in, higher concentrations in*), which contrasted with its use in abstracts, where *in* was seen to introduce expressions of data movement one way or the other (*decrease in, reduction in, difference in*). The second phraseology resembled its essentially spatial meaning, indicating where a specific biochemical process was found/observed in the bodies of patients or subjects (*concentration/s in human tissues, mutations in lung tumours*). The third type of phraseology functioned as a cross-reference to another section of the article (*as seen/shown in*). The prototypical phraseology of Introductions in these cancer research articles are reported in Gledhill (2000). In a similar vein, Marco (2000) has also analysed the collocational frameworks favoured by the genre of medical research papers. The frameworks *the ... of, a ... of,* and *be ... to* were found to enclose restricted sets of lexical items whose selection was conditioned by the linguistic conventions of the genre. Gledhill's and Marco's research thus indicates a departure from the analysis of single grammatical, lexical, or textual features to a more genre-sensitive approach to the analysis of linguistic and rhetorical patterning of text, but unfortunately such corpus-based findings have not as yet been applied to this field of ESAP. One pedagogical application, however, is reported in Gavioli (forthcoming), who, based on her findings of noun collocations in a 30,000-word corpus of medical research papers about hepatitis, proposes concordance-based exercises to sensitise students to the different noun collocations with *liver* and *hepatic*.

English for Business, Finance, and Economics

Most of the research in this area has focused on various types of specialised lexis. Probably the first ESAP corpus to be compiled in this domain was a small Economics textbook corpus of 20,749 words for language teaching purposes (Mparutsa et al., 1991). A much bigger corpus was compiled a few years later by James and Purchase (1996) who give a word-frequency list of a one-million-word textbook corpus, which comprises 501 sample extracts from 167 textbooks prescribed in 1994–95 for students taking courses in Business Studies, Business and Management, and Economics, as main or subsidiary subjects at first-year level in Hong Kong.

Other researchers have investigated collocational patterning in subsections of large-scale business corpora. For example, Kennedy (1995, 1998), makes use of the Economics text of about 320,000 words from the one-million-word Wellington Corpus of Written New Zealand English to explore the most frequent collocates which occur before or after common content words such as the item *increase*. Noor (1998), meanwhile, uses the commerce and finance domain of the BNC to examine the variability or fixedness of word combinations associated with common nouns. Working from a different perspective, Charteris-Black (2000) compares metaphorically motivated lexis taken from a corpus of *The Economist* magazine from 1995 to 1997 with the same words in the general magazine section of the Bank of English in order to compare their relative frequency in the two corpora. He remarks that in the economics texts animate metaphors are used to describe the economy (e.g. *growth*) and economic organisations, e.g. *parent company*, whereas inanimate metaphors are used to describe market movements, e.g. *rebounds*. To date, however, very little of these analyses has been exploited for pedagogic applications and the findings remain at the level of implications for pedagogy.

CONTRASTIVE STUDIES IN ENGLISH FOR SPECIFIC ACADEMIC PURPOSES

Several different types of contrastive studies have been undertaken in recent years. The most well-known work in this field is by Biber (1988), who proposed a multidimensional model of variation to identify quantitatively the co-occurrence of linguistic patterns by a statistical factor analysis. These dimensions are interpreted in terms of the situational and cognitive functions most widely shared by the co-occurring linguistic features and in terms of the relations among registers along each dimension. This sophisticated model can illustrate differences in register between different types of texts along various dimensions such as involved vs. informational text. For example, Biber et al. (1998) use the model to show differences between ecology and history research articles along the dimensions of narrative vs. non-narrative and impersonal vs. non-impersonal. Biber et al. report that the dimension scores for narrative vs. non-narrative features reveal that the history texts are more narrative in focus than the ecology texts as they contain a higher frequency of the linguistic features associated with narrative concerns such as past-tense verbs, third-person pronouns, public verbs, etc. (see Figure 5.2).

Biber's multidimensional analysis has also been used by Conrad (1996) to investigate variation across different types of text, namely textbooks and research articles from the field of ecology. However, see Lee (1999) for a critique of the validity, stability, and meaningfulness of Biber's results using this model.

In contrast to Conrad's research which focuses on the differences between different types of genres within the same academic discipline, other researchers have examined differences in the same genre across different disciplines, using other investigative procedures. For example, Thompson (2000) examines the use of citations in a corpus of 20 Ph.D. theses written by native speakers from different disciplines within the Faculty of Agriculture at the University of Reading. The Reading Academic Text (RAT) Corpus was tagged using a system which differentiates between integral citations (those citations appearing within the sentence) and non-integral citations (citations which are separated from the sentence by brackets and which play no explicit role in the sentence). Thompson found a comparatively low use of citations in the final chapter of the Ph.D. theses on Agricultural Economics, but

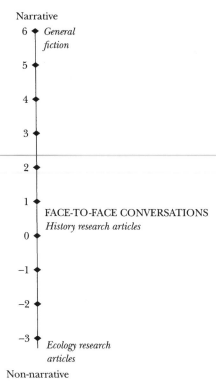

Figure 5.2 Mean scores of ecology and history research articles on Dimension 2, 'Narrative versus non-narrative concerns'
Source: Biber et al. (1998)

a significantly higher proportion of integral citations in the concluding chapters of the Agricultural Botany theses. See Chapter 4 in this volume for a genre-based account of Ph.D. theses.

Another corpus project, the Tampere Corpus of English for Specific Purposes (TESP), which is at the early stages of compilation and reported on in Norri and Kytö (1996), aims to investigate different genres both within the same discipline and across different disciplines. The purpose of this study is to investigate linguistic variation in scientific text across ten different subject fields and four levels of technicality related to the target audience and purpose for reading: (1) texts written by experts for other experts in the field (i.e. journals); (2) textbooks for university students; (3) popular scientific magazines written by experts in the field, for a wider range of readers, many of whom may not necessarily be familiar with the field; (4) magazine articles written by professional journalists on scientific topics of current interest. Preliminary research has been carried out on the pronouns *it* and *they* in a referential function in a pilot corpus consisting of 20 medical and 20 biological texts totalling 120,000 words, with the four levels of technicality each represented by five texts. The findings reveal that the use of the pronoun *they* increases notably from level 1 to level 4 technicality in both subject fields.

Norri and Kytö surmise that these linguistic forms are probably avoided because of the need for precision in level 1 technicality where words and phrases are repeated rather than replaced by referential elements which might give rise to ambiguity.

Two other corpus analyses of a contrastive nature which attempt to relate collocational patternings and grammatical structures to either the ecolect of a particular discourse community or to the wider concerns relating to society are those by Williams (1998), and Stubbs (1996) respectively. Williams (1998), using Mutual Information statistics, shows how lexical choice goes beyond individual words to prototypical lexical phrases that represent three different subgenres ('sublanguage' in his terms) in the field of Plant Biology.

Stubbs (1996) analyses two school textbooks of 80,000 and 30,000 words related to the study of the environment and compares particular grammatical features in these, namely ergative and transitive verbs, with a corpus of written English of one million words. He discusses how the different means of encoding causativity, i.e. whether the process is represented as being caused from without, or from within, as self-caused, can represent the different ideological stances of the two books. He provides examples to show that in some cases, e.g. *Young people moved away*, the agent is given, whereas in other cases, e.g. *Many jobs were lost*, the event is portrayed as natural, i.e. as self-caused as there is no explicit mention of the people involved. However, see Widdowson (2000a), who takes Stubbs to task for attaching ideological significance to a text on the basis of a particular grammatical feature, as he argues that ideological significance may well be conveyed by other features such as lexis, tense, and aspect, which were not considered in the analysis.

The contrastive studies outlined above all provide very different means, either through the application of a multidimensional factor analysis, a discourse-based tagging system, or Mutual Information statistics, for delineating variation either within the same genre from different academic disciplines, within different genres from the same academic discipline, or within subgenres of a particular academic field. It is interesting to note, however, that the research on corpus-based contrastive studies has not as yet made significant impact on pedagogy.

FUTURE DIRECTIONS

Based on the above survey of corpus-based investigations of different kinds of EAP texts representing different academic disciplines, some suggestions are made for ways in which this field could expand in the future regarding the types of corpora compiled and the approaches adopted for investigation and application.

Corpora for other languages

The focus of the above survey has been on native-speaker or non-native-speaker academic corpora of English, because this is where most of the work has been concentrated to date. However, it should not be forgotten that corpus-based research has also been carried out on other languages and that this area will no doubt assume more prominence in the future. For example, Inkster (1997) describes the building of LANFRANC, a collection of French texts from various sources. Not only did undergraduate students use it for small-scale personal research as part of their degree study, but they also contributed to the corpus-building. Corpus-based student research projects for an MA module in Modern German Studies are also reported in Dodd (1997). One large corpus-building venture being undertaken at the university of Lódź is the PELCRA (Polish–English Language Corpus Research and Applications) project. The multiple aims of this project are to exploit the learner English corpus component for investigating interference errors, and to use the corpus of native Polish for both L1 and L2 language teaching and lexicography (Lewandowska-Tomaszczyk et al., 2000).

Spoken corpora

It is strikingly obvious from the above survey that there is a dearth of spoken corpora for academic purposes. Although small corpora of academic lectures are reported in King (1989) and biology lectures in J. Flowerdew (1993b), very little mention elsewhere in the literature is made of spoken academic corpora, no doubt for the reason that compiling and transcribing spoken corpora is a far more time-consuming and difficult task than it is for corpora of written academic English. However, a recent development in this area is the compilation of a 1.5-million-word corpus of spoken American academic English, called the Michigan Corpus of Academic Spoken English, MICASE (Simpson et al., 2000). The compilers point out that academic speech is not confined to lectures but also encompasses the full range of formal and less informal speech events that occur within a university setting, such as formal lectures and tutorials in addition to more informal study groups and academic service encounters. An extremely useful feature of this corpus is that it is accompanied by a comprehensive set of speech event and speaker attributes. One of the main goals of the project is to use the analyses of academic speech to authenticate, improve, and develop the English Language Institute's spoken academic material for courses. Publications reporting various analyses of this corpus are soon to appear, e.g. Mauranen's (2000) account of reflexive talk in MICASE and Swales's (in press) analysis of 'point' and 'thing' in the metatalk of American academic discourse. A second North American academic corpus with a large spoken component, the TOEFL 2000 Spoken and Written Academic Language Corpus (T2K-SWAL), is being compiled at Northern Arizona University to provide material as an empirical basis for TOEFL development. Yet another initiative under way is the compilation of a Hong Kong Corpus of Spoken English (HKCSE) which will amount to 1.5 million words of data, comprising three sub-corpora, one of which comprises academic discourse (Cheng and Warren, 2000). All of these corpora are still in various stages of construction, but the forthcoming analyses and applications of these spoken corpora are eagerly awaited to compensate for the lack of attention hitherto paid to this area. Another avenue of fruitful research for the future would be contrastive studies of academic speech and writing.

Expansion of EAP corpora

The lack of a substantial body of corpus data of spoken English has already been noted. Although this chapter has shown that the exploration for language descriptions and exploitation for pedagogical applications of various written corpora is already a well-developed field, the compilation of written EAP corpora can still be viewed as unbalanced in several aspects. It is evident that the majority of the investigations in ESP have been carried out in the field of EST. Law and Arts subjects, such as History, Philosophy, and the Social Sciences, do not seem to be well represented in the literature. One way to redress this bias towards a narrow range of disciplines would be to make more use of the academic sub-component of large-scale corpora; for example, the Bank of English has an academic sub-corpus of about 7 million words (one million of British English and six million of American English). Another avenue for exploitation is sources from the Internet (see Foucou and Kübler, 2000, for a description of a Web Assisted Language Learning Environment (WALL)). Moreover, the majority of the work on learner corpora is in the domain of general academic English so more initiatives in building specialised learner corpora, such as the Indianapolis Business Learner Corpus (Connor and Upton, 2000), would be an area which merits further development.

Ethnographic dimension

Several studies referred to in this chapter have also been shown to take a more ethnographic, rather than purely textual, approach to corpus compilation and analysis. (see Part IV of this volume). Gledhill (1996) adopts an ethnographic approach to the choice of texts for inclusion in his corpus by consulting specialist informants on the texts which are most representative of the field in order to achieve a balanced corpus. Both Hyland (1998, 2000) and L. Flowerdew (2000) advocate a knowledge of the discourse community in which the text was produced for interpretation of certain pragmatic aspects of the text, with Hyland also involving specialist informants in the discipline in the interpretative process. Meanwhile, Stubbs (1996) shows how corpus-based analyses can reveal cultural patterns or ideological stances of writers. The ethnographic dimension therefore has both an outward and inward focus: texts can reveal ethnographic subtleties, or they are analysed in light of ethnographic considerations.

The above observations indicate that corpus-based studies cannot solely rely on the text, but must have recourse to other dimensions in which language is produced. Indeed, Barlow (1998) argues that whether corpus linguistics can assume a central position in linguistic analysis in the next decade or so is dependent on whether its practitioners can conceive of corpora being related to other sub-disciplines in the humanities and social sciences.

Textlinguistic approaches

In a recent paper (L. Flowerdew, 1998c) I argue that a decade ago corpus-based descriptions tended to concentrate on lexico-grammatical patterning of propositional content at the level of the sentence, whereas recently there has been more emphasis on analysing corpora from a more textlinguistic level whether it be genre, discourse, or systemic-functional in orientation. The studies by Gledhill (1996, 2000), Biber et al. (1998), and Conrad (1996) are genre-based, albeit from different perspectives. Tribble (2000) uses two different, yet complementary corpus tools, for establishing genre: Biber's framework is used for identifying linguistic specifications of a particular genre, whereas *WordSmith Tools* identifies genre through the unusually high frequency of keywords in a text compared to their relative frequency in a reference corpus. See also Tribble, this volume, for an approach to writing instruction which involves combining genre concepts with corpus analysis. However, as Swales, this volume, notes, the application of corpus linguistic techniques to genre analysis is somewhat problematic because of the procedural differences between the bottom-up concordance and keyword searches and the more top-down process of genre analysis which starts with the macrostructure of the text. Inserting discourse-type tags identifying the 'move structures' would be an answer, but this is only suited to texts which have a fairly formulaic rhetorical structure, such as the tagging of moves in the job application letters of the Indianapolis Business Learner Corpus (Connor and Upton 2000). It would not be a viable option for use with texts comprising mixed genres or exhibiting a wide range of move structures or embedding of move structures.

One area of systemic-functional linguistics which has received attention in EAP corpus studies is the interpersonal level, which is concerned with the writer's attitude to the message. Those studies on learner corpora described in Hyland and Milton (1997a), Lorenz (1998), L. Flowerdew (2000), and on professional science corpora (Hyland, 1998, 2000) focus on this level. However, other areas in systemics have received less attention; more explorations at the textual level or of thematic structure, such as the study conducted by Green et al. (2000), would therefore be most useful in advancing the field and taking up a question posed by Hoey (1997), 'Is the word associated with (any position in any) textual organisation?'

Pedagogic applications

Several pedagogical aspects merit attention for future development. First, although it has been noted in the previous section that some recent work in corpus linguistics draws on various textlinguistic approaches for its analysis, this work remains at the level of language description with only some brief suggestions for pedagogic applications. The same point can also be made, in general, for the transfer of EAP corpus-based findings to materials. Although such findings have been exploited on a small scale to inform materials design in specific localised contexts (e.g. Kettemann, 1997; Curado and Berzosa, 2000), it is surprising that more EAP textbooks, such as Thurstun and Candlin's *Exploring Academic English*, which derives its pedagogical content from concordances of professional academic English, have not been published.

Although there are many advocates of corpus-based pedagogy, whether in the form of hands-on concordancing activities or concordance-derived exercises, its value has been questioned by others. Widdowson (2000b) calls for a critical appraisal of corpus-based pedagogy, and other researchers (David Lee, personal communication) have expressed concern about the lack of empirical studies on using corpora in language teaching which can scientifically test the effects of using corpus methodology on students' results. There is one experimental study reported in Stevens (1991b) and another in Cobb (1997) which demonstrates that students generally performed better on concordance-based vocabulary exercises than gap-filling ones, but, sadly, such studies are few and far between. It is therefore hoped that in future more research using control groups such as in Stevens's study will be conducted to provide empirical data, rather than anecdotal accounts, to support the use of corpora in language teaching.

Another extremely important aspect concerning the transfer of corpus data to pedagogy lies in the fact that concordance data portrays 'the decontextualization of individual instances from their original communicative setting' (Aston, 1995: 260). Because the corpus is divorced from the context of situation in which it was created, Widdowson (1998: 712) argues that it can only be viewed as the textual product of a discourse as 'It cannot tell about the discourse processes whereby pragmatic meaning is appropriately achieved.'

This has important implications for pedagogical applications. For example, the two corpora of spoken academic English described previously (MICASE and HKCSE) are taken from two very different cultural settings with different discourse and social practices. In order for such language, the language for participating in tutorials, for example, to be exploited pedagogically in another academic setting, Widdowson (1998) argues that teachers have to 'authenticate' the language as discourse in their own terms and relate it to their own familiar cultural contexts and concerns.

> language teachers should indeed be concerned with pragmatic meaning, but this can only be achieved if they localise the language, create contextual conditions that make the language a reality for particular communities of learners so that they can authenticate it . . . (Widdowson, 1998: 715)

While this viewpoint is valid to some extent, it can be argued that with a comprehensive set of contextual and participant features assigned to each speech event, as in the case of MICASE, this will enable the teacher or student to judge whether a certain spoken utterance or phrase is appropriate for use in their own localised context. Another issue that has been raised by

McCarthy (2000) concerns the quality of the speech event itself. McCarthy points out that while there exists a canon of what is considered as 'good', well-formed writing (presumably, because it has been published and undergone a review process) such norms do not as yet exist for spoken corpora. This then begs the question of who, the corpus compiler or the analyst, is to judge whether an academic speech event, such as a tutorial or service encounter, is deemed successful or not. Such issues as these therefore need to be considered in the application of spoken corpora to pedagogy.

CONCLUSION

Corpus linguistics is now regarded as a branch of linguistics in its own right, much like sociolinguistics and psycholinguistics. However, as this survey of corpus-based analyses in EAP has attempted to show, this field is now moving away from concentration on the lexical, grammatical, and lexico-grammatical patterning of text to a broader perspective which now embraces other linguistic and social science fields such as textlinguistics and ethnography, respectively. Corpus linguistics is thus informed by these other methodologies, which are represented in the following sections of this book. However, at the same time, corpus linguistic techniques could also be used to shed light on the discourse patterns and practices in these other areas. It is hoped that in the future there will be more cross-fertilisation not only between corpus linguistics and other branches of linguistics but also within the field between the descriptive research-based work and the more applied aspect so that the domain of EAP can profitably benefit from this methodology, for which more empirical studies could also be conducted to support its efficacy in language teaching.

Chapter 6

Activity and Evaluation: Reporting practices in academic writing

Ken Hyland

Reference to prior research is almost a defining feature of the academic research article. Even the most original paper integrates and represents ideas, concepts, findings, and theories from other sources and, indeed, would be unlikely to reach publication if it did not. Specifically, such reporting represents in a new situation the way language was used in a previous context, and is defined for my purposes here as the attribution of propositional content to another source. Its importance in academic discourse lies in providing an appropriate context of persuasion, demonstrating how the current work builds on and reworks past utterances to establish intertextual links to the wider discipline. Put simply, academic writing depends for its success on situating current work in a larger disciplinary narrative (Berkenkotter and Huckin, 1995; Hyland, 2000; Myers, 1990). Without such links academics could neither justify their arguments by connecting their research activities to significant work in the field, nor use this disciplinary knowledge to establish the novelty of their position (Gilbert, 1976; Berkenkotter and Huckin, 1995).

By acknowledging a debt of precedent, a writer simultaneously accomplishes a number of rhetorical objectives. Interpersonally, judicious citation enables writers to display an allegiance to a particular community or theoretical orientation (Latour, 1987). It also helps them to build a credible writer ethos using citation to construct factual reliability and show they are prepared to stand behind their words. Scollon (1994), for example, has argued that attribution 'constitutes a system for the creation of the academic self' as it presents to the reader a stance or position of responsibility. Rhetorically, citation helps to define a specific context of knowledge or problem to which the current work is a contribution. But while new work reveals its disciplinary credentials by being embedded in a community-generated literature, it must also transcend this literature to create a niche for itself. Writers have to carve out a rhetorical gap from the weight of consensual knowledge (Swales, 1990), staking a claim to innovation while taking care to avoid a hostile depiction of previous work. The ability to handle citations to rhetorically construct a community consensus, and at the same time ensure that criticism stays within accepted bounds, is a central means of projecting one's insider status.

Despite this importance, however, citation represents a feature which students, and particularly non-native English speakers, find difficult to either use effectively in their writing or understand correctly in their reading (Campbell, 1990; Matalene, 1985; Pennycook, 1996a). NNS writers of academic papers frequently overuse naïve quotation with no evaluation (Bruce, 1989), and rely on a restricted range of verbs, such as 'say', to introduce these quotes (Pickard, 1993a). This problem is often more than a deficit of vocabulary, but symptomatic of a larger issue of how to appropriately acknowledge sources in academic writing. There are considerable cultural differences in how writers from different backgrounds use prior texts in argument (e.g. Bloch and Chi, 1995), and such differences also extend to notions of authorship and text ownership (Pennycook, 1996a; Scollon, 1994). However, because reporting is such an important convention of academic writing in English, it is clearly worthwhile equipping students with the means of using it successfully. In this chapter I focus on the most salient form of attribution in academic writing, the use of reporting verbs.

REPORTING SIGNALS IN ACADEMIC DISCOURSE

The significance of citation in academic writing and the obvious difficulties it poses for learners has led to considerable interest in the ways it is signalled, often as a basis for producing teaching materials.

The literature testifies to the availability of a wide range of reporting structures in English (e.g. Thompson, 1996), although academic writing appears to rely on a subset of specialised conventions from within these, principally direct quote, paraphrase, summary, and generalisation (e.g. Dubois, 1988). One attribution feature of interest to researchers has been the distinction between integral and non-integral structures (Swales, 1990: 148), the former referring to cases where the name of the cited author occurs in the citing sentence, and the latter to where the author appears in parenthesis or is referred to by superscript numbers. The use of one form rather than the other appears to reflect a decision to give greater emphasis to either the reported author or the reported message. Research has also identified the rhetorical effects of various syntactic features, such as thematic position, tense, and voice, on the reported information (e.g. Malcolm, 1987; Oster, 1981; Shaw, 1992), and the role of reporting verbs.

The use of a reporting verb is one of the most explicit ways of attributing content to another source, and represents a significant rhetorical choice. The wide range of verbs that can be used to introduce reports allow writers to convey both the kind of activity reported and whether the claims are to be taken as accepted or not (Hunston, 1993; Tadros, 1993; Thomas and Hawes, 1994). Most obviously, verbs such as *demonstrate, prove,* and *show* reveal the writer's agreement with a prior statement, while hedges like *suggest, indicate,* and *imply* open an 'evaluative space' (Thompson and Ye, 1991: 369) in which the writer can withhold full commitment to present a contrast with a new view.

Thompson and Ye (1991) provide an interesting analysis of the relationsh., between reporting verbs and evaluation, and their categorisation emphasises the important distinction between the position of the reporting writer and the source author. However, their study was confined to the introduction sections of articles, which ignores a great deal of the reporting which occurs in humanities and social science papers, and involves a rather complex categorisation system which separates evaluation from reporting and allows considerable overlap between categories. Thomas and Hawes's (1994) alternative taxonomy offers a much clearer description of the network of options available to writers in medical articles. But while this scheme is easier to apply in identifying the functions of different verbs, it does not clearly reveal their evaluative potential nor always maintain the distinction between reporting and reported writer in identifying the source of this evaluation.

So while my study draws on these systems, it also seeks to offer a clearer description of reporting conventions in academic writing, to identify the preferences for different verbs among various disciplinary communities, and, hopefully, to reveal some of the rhetorical purposes which motivate those preferences.

CORPUS AND METHODOLOGY

The study employs both qualitative and quantitative approaches, comprising frequency counts and text analyses of a corpus of published articles. The corpus of 80 research articles consists of one paper from each of ten leading journals in eight disciplines. The disciplines were selected to represent a broad cross-section of academic practice and to allow access to expert informants. Molecular biology and magnetic physics represent the pure sciences, and mechanical engineering and electronic engineering the applied sciences. Philosophy and sociology are often categorised as either humanities or social sciences, while marketing and applied linguistics might be regarded as more applied social sciences. The journals were nominated by specialist informants as among the most important in their fields, and the articles chosen at random from current issues, selecting only those based on original data to compare papers with a similar rhetorical purpose. The scanned articles produced an electronic corpus of just over 500,000 words after excluding abstracts and text associated with tables and graphics.

To locate reporting verbs, the corpus was computer searched for canonical citational forms such as a date in brackets, a number in squared brackets, and Latin references to other citations. This search left many citations unaccounted for, however, particularly where writers renewed or extended their discussions of a previously mentioned author without the repetition of a reference. I therefore concordanced all the names in the bibliographies of these articles and third-person pronouns. A citation was recorded only where the text attributed words to a specific author, thereby eliminating general references to schools or beliefs such as 'Marxists claim . . .' or 'a constructionist model suggests . . .'.

elf-citation were also ignored (see Hyland, 2001). This yielded
es of reporting verbs, about one every 220 words of text.
eloped a way of categorising these verbs, first examining sam-
corpus using the two models discussed above, and then refin-
el through a constant comparison of devices in context. This
induce...... proach allows a theory to emerge from data and produced the
model described below. Note that in the following discussion I adopt
Thompson and Ye's useful convention of referring to the person citing as the
'writer' and the cited person as the 'author'.

A MODEL - Copy for SS

FUNCTIONS OF REPORTING VERBS

Process functions

Like Thompson and Ye (1991) and Thomas and Hawes (1994), I classified
the reporting verbs according to the type of activity they referred to. This
gives three distinguishable processes:

1. **Research (Real-World) Acts**. Verbs in this category represent experimental activities or actions carried out in the real world. They generally occur
   either in statements of findings (e.g. *observe, discover, notice, show*) or procedures (e.g. *analyse, calculate, assay, explore, plot, recover*).
2. **Cognition Acts**. These verbs are concerned with the researcher's mental
   processes (e.g. *believe, conceptualise, suspect, assume, view*).
3. **Discourse Acts**. These involve linguistic activities and focus on the verbal
   expression of cognitive or research activities (e.g. *ascribe, discuss, hypothesise, report, state*).

These categories are not watertight. *Agree*, for example, is a cognition act
which carries a strong implication of verbal expression, while *conclude* is
ambiguous between a mental and a discourse process, *analyse* may refer to
physical or intellectual activities, and *solve* perhaps involves all three processes. However, it is possible to consistently attribute a particular meaning to
all the verbs using this system and the categories do provide a comprehensive
taxonomy for distinguishing the use of reporting verbs in terms of the primary aspects of the research process.

Analysis of all reporting verbs in the corpus revealed a clear preference
for reporting information as Discourse Acts, with 57% of cases in this category. Most of the remaining instances were reported as Real-World Acts,
and only 8% as Cognition Acts. Where writers chose to represent work as
Research Acts, frequencies divided almost equally between verbs describing
the author's overall findings and those commenting on research procedures.
Table 6.1 summarises these findings.

Evaluative functions

Within the process categories writers made more delicate decisions, exploiting
the evaluative possibilities of reporting verbs to take either a supportive,

Table 6.1   Distribution of verbs in process categories

Category	Totals	Average per paper	%
Real World Acts	786	9.8	35
Findings	*437*	*5.4*	*19*
Procedures	*349*	*4.4*	*15*
Cognition Acts	193	2.4	8
Discourse Acts	1308	16.4	57
Total	2287	28.6	100

tentative, critical, or neutral stance towards the reported claims. Here I depart from earlier work by representing writers' choices as a single overarching scheme of options which includes both the original author's academic activity and the reporting writer's evaluative judgements. The scheme retains Thompson and Ye's important insight, however, that while all reporting is mediated by the reporter, writers can vary their commitment by employing verbs which imply a personal stance, such as *show, demonstrate, fail*, and *ignore*, or which attribute a position to the original author (*accuse, believe, dispute, urge*).

Each of the process categories therefore has a subset of evaluative options as set out in Figure 6.1 and elaborated below.

Within the **Findings** category of **Research Acts**, writers can acknowledge their acceptance of the authors' results or conclusions with **factive** verbs such as *demonstrate, establish, show, solve*, or *confirm*. Alternatively they can adopt a **counter-factive** stance, portraying the author's judgements as false or incorrect (*fail, misunderstand, ignore, overlook*). While these verbs might seem an effective way for writers to refute prior research and establish a niche for their own alternative position, such a direct challenge to the work of a single author was a choice rarely exercised in this corpus. Academics, it seems, prefer more subtle ways of building on earlier literature. The final option is to comment on research findings **non-factively**, with no clear attitudinal signal as to their reliability (e.g. *find, identify, observe, obtain*). These verbs accounted for the majority (55%) of references in the Research Findings category. Verbs which referred to **procedural** aspects of the author's investigation contained the greatest variety of expression in my corpus with 153 different verb forms,

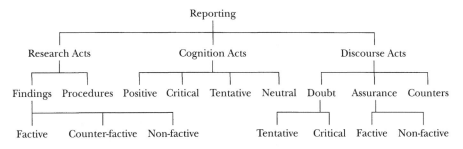

Figure 6.1   Categories of reporting verbs

36% of the total. As the following examples show, these verbs carry no evaluation in themselves but simply report research tasks neutrally:

(1) Finally, Eto et al. (1994) <u>reviewed</u> and <u>analyzed</u> the contents of
    several indicators . . .   (Mech)
    Green and Wakefield <u>compared</u> the 20 cases they found in the
    newspaper with . . .   (Soc)
    a 'layer' coupled-slot finline structure was <u>studied</u> by Mazur [7]
    and Tech et al. [8] . . .   (Phy)
    Leow (1995) <u>replicated</u> an earlier study, Leow (1993), which
    <u>investigated</u> . . .   (Ling)

Cognition Act verbs, which portray the cited work in terms of a mental process, handle evaluation rather differently. Instead of explicitly taking a personal stance on the reported information or opinion, writers here attribute a particular attitude to the cited author. There appear to be four clear options. Writers can represent the author as having a **positive** attitude to the material, accepting it as true or correct with verbs such as *agree, concur, hold, know, think,* or *understand.* Alternatively authors may be characterised as having a **tentative** view towards the reported matter (*believe, doubt, speculate, suppose, suspect*), or, more rarely, as taking a **critical** stance (e.g. *disagree, dispute, not think*). Finally, the writer can portray the author as holding a **neutral** attitude towards the proposition (*picture, conceive, anticipate, reflect*).

Writers can also employ **Discourse Act** verbs to convey an evaluation of the cited material, and here they have the option of either taking responsibility for their interpretation, conveying their uncertainty or assurance of the correctness of the claims reported, or attributing a qualification to the author. The examples below show this distinction, indicating how writers can use discourse verbs to express their own viewpoint (2) or to ascribe it to the author (3):

(2) As <u>demonstrated</u> by Baker et al. [2], the increased rate of flagellar
    RNA . . .   (Bio)
    Baddeley <u>proposes</u> a tripartite system of working memory . . .   (Ling)
    Although derived in 1965, recent work [59], <u>verified</u> that (2)
    still holds true.   (Elec)
    As Hinde (1979) <u>points out</u>, many unhappy marriages remain
    intact because of . . .   (Mkt)
    Villaruel-Ordaz, et al. (1993) <u>report</u> C. subnuda from the states
    of . . .   (Bio)

(3) Churchill <u>abandoned</u> speculative naturalism.   (Phil)
    Eckstein <u>criticizes</u> psychological reductionism, rational choice,
    and . . .   (Soc)
    Jacoby <u>accuses</u> American intellectuals of a turn to
    conservatism . . .   (Soc)
    . . . <u>dismissed</u> by some theorists as being depthless and superficial
    chatter (e.g. Baudrillard, 1988; Jameson, 1991).   (Mkt)
    Frenchio <u>urged</u> against changing . . .   (Phy)

Discourse verbs which express the writer's view directly can be separated into doubt and assurance categories. Those which express **doubt** about

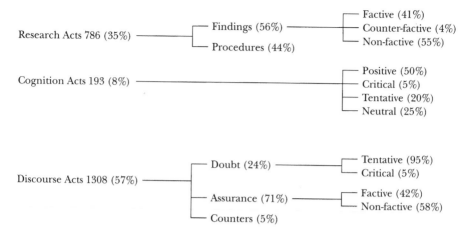

Figure 6.2   Overall distribution of reporting verbs

reported claims can be further divided into verbs which are **tentative** (e.g. *postulate, hypothesise, indicate, intimate, suggest*) and, more rarely, verbs which are directly **critical** (*evade, exaggerate, not account, not make point*). More frequent in the corpus than expressions of doubt are **assurance** verbs which introduce cited material in more positive and conclusive terms, either to neutrally inform readers of the author's position (**non-factive**) or to use that position to support the writer's own (**factive**). There is an enormous variety of verbs available for objectively passing information without interpretation, including high-frequency items such as *state, describe, discuss, report, answer, define,* and *summarise*. Alternatively, writers use assurance discourse verbs to directly bolster their own views. These signal a supportive role for the reported information in the writer's argument, often by attributing a high degree of confidence to the proposition by the original author. Examples include *argue, affirm, explain, note, point out,* and *claim*.

The final subcategory of Discourse Act verbs, **Counters**, refer to what are taken to be the cited author's own reservations or objections to the correctness of the reported message. That is, instead of taking responsibility for the evaluation as in Doubt verbs, the writer attributes these reservations to the original author. Among the examples in the corpus are *deny, critique, challenge, attack, question, warn, refute,* and *rule out*. Thompson and Ye call such attributions Author Acts (1991: 371) and writers generally drew on such author refutations either to support their own opposition to a position, or to demolish an opposing argument. The overall results are presented in Figure 6.2.

DISCIPLINARY VARIATIONS IN REPORTING PRACTICES

One issue of central concern to EAP teachers is the extent to which discourse features can be regarded as universal or as discipline-specific. Increasingly we

le 6.2   Presentation of cited work (%)

Discipline	Quote	Block Quote	Summary	Generalisation
Biology	0	0	72	38
Physics	0	0	68	32
Electronic Engineering	0	0	66	34
Mechanical Engineering	0	0	67	33
Marketing	3	2	68	27
Applied Linguistics	8	2	67	23
Sociology	8	5	69	18
Philosophy	2	1	89	8

are becoming aware of major distinctions in the ways different fields conduct their enquiries, justify their beliefs, and structure their arguments (e.g. Bartholomae, 1986; Becher, 1989; Bruffee, 1986). We are also more mindful of the ways these differences are expressed through the interactive and rhetorical features of academic writing (e.g. Bazerman, 1988; Hyland, 1998, 1999a, 2000; MacDonald, 1993). From a pedagogical point of view, then, both postgraduate students and practising academics need to be made aware of such disciplinary preferences in order to communicate with their peers using the most conventionally effective strategies. In terms of reporting structures, my analysis of this corpus suggests that while writers chose to *present* cited work in broadly similar ways, there were considerable disciplinary differences in the overall use of reporting verbs, in the frequencies of individual items, and in preferences for particular rhetorical categories.

Citing verbs do not occur in a textual vacuum. Language reports are presented in a carefully constructed reporting context which involves academic writers in conscious decisions about framing the imported material. Two central options here are how best to represent the original text and what emphasis to give to the original author. Overall, there were both broad similarities and differences in how writers in different disciplines exercised these options. Considerations of how to present a cited message mainly involve the extent to which a writer wishes to duplicate the original source material in his or her argument (Dubois, 1988; Thompson, 1996). The fundamental options are to either employ short direct quotes (of five or more words), use the original wording extensively in indented blocks, summarise from a single source, or present a generalised statement from several sources.

An analysis of half the articles in each discipline confirmed the impression that the overwhelming preference in all eight disciplines was for summary, an abbreviated statement of one work, with generalisation accounting for most of the remainder. It can be seen in Table 6.2 that direct quotation was rarely employed and did not occur in the science and engineering papers at all. In the hard sciences this may be partly related to the suppression of explicit researcher intervention, but more generally the decision of writers to express cited material in their own terms represents the most effective way of supporting their own positions. Thus while students often overuse direct

Table 6.3 Representation of author by discipline (%)

Discipline	Non-Integral	Integral
Biology	90.2	9.8
Electronic Eng.	84.3	15.7
Physics	83.1	16.9
Mechanical Eng.	71.3	28.7
Marketing	70.3	29.7
Applied Ling.	65.6	34.4
Sociology	64.6	35.4
Philosophy	35.4	64.6

Quote

quotation (Campbell, 1990: 222), expert writers tend to be sparing with it, and are only likely to employ it when they consider the author's original words to be the most persuasive means of presenting their case.

A second decision facing writers in citing material is whether to employ the reporting verb in an integral or non-integral environment (Swales, 1990). As noted earlier, integral structures (example 4 below) tend to give greater prominence to the cited author than non-integral contexts (as in example 5):

(4) . . . some can be analysed in the manner <u>suggested</u> by Lewiss . . . (Phil)
Patrick O'Niell (1990) <u>suggests</u> that the growth of black humour is a peculiarly . . . (Soc)
The study of Tadmor (1986) <u>shows</u> that fly ash and ESP ash are enriched with . . . (ME)
Barry and Diamond (1984) and Dainty (1985) <u>have argued</u> that water relation . . . (Bio)

(5) Several experiences <u>have been reported</u> in the literature on the millimeter wave interaction with snowcover [5–7] . . . (Phy)
At least one writer (Stark, 1987) <u>suggests</u> that police leniency in ghettos is largely . . . (Soc)
Reference [6] <u>shows</u> a spatial Euler-Savary analogue based on velocity and . . . (ME)
. . . recently <u>examined</u> modality differences in SLA (e.g. Kirster, 1984; Leow, 1985) . . . (Soc)

In this corpus, at least, there was again little disciplinary variation with an overwhelming preference for non-integral forms. As Table 6.3 shows, only the articles in philosophy, which typically consist of long narratives engaging the arguments of other writers, consistently included the cited author in the reporting sentence.

DISCIPLINARY PREFERENCES FOR VERB FORMS

Despite these similarities in message form and author visibility, the distribution of reporting verbs in the corpus reveals broad disciplinary differences.

pear to be community-based preferences, both for specific items
implications carried by particular semantic categories.

all the papers in my corpus included reporting verbs, they were far
evalent in the humanities and social science papers than in the hard
sciences. This in fact mirrored the more explicit role of reference to prior
research in these disciplines which occurred overall in the corpus. I have
sought to account for these broad disciplinary differences elsewhere in terms
of the distinctions between hard and soft knowledge domains (Hyland, 2000).
Briefly, I believe the higher use of citations in the soft disciplines can be
accounted for by the fact that (i) they typically have less cohesive and established frameworks of knowledge; (ii) they possess less highly formalised and
standardised codes for reporting research; (iii) they are more inclined to
explicitly recognise the role of human agency in constructing knowledge;
and (iv) they engage in more recursive patterns of investigation which involve more diverse and less predictable and abstract subjects than those
typically found in the sciences.

We can see from Table 6.4 that the density of reporting structures differed
substantially, with the average number of reporting verbs in the engineering
and science papers all below the average for the corpus as a whole. Together
there were just 619 reporting verbs in the 40 hard knowledge papers, amount-
ing to only 27% of all examples, with physics accounting for less than 3% of
the overall total. In terms of density of verbs per 1,000 words, the distribution
looks slightly more even, with both engineering disciplines similar to the
marketing figures and biology exceeding all but sociology and philosophy,
which together accounted for 44% of all the reporting verbs in the corpus.

Table 6.4 also shows the most frequent forms found in each discipline and
the proportion of total reporting verbs which these comprised. Over 400
different verbs were used to introduce citations, although the seven forms in
the totals column constituted over a quarter of all cases and nearly half the
forms in the corpus occurred only once. It appears from the figures that
writers in biology, marketing, and physics relied on a more restricted range
of items, with the most preferred five or six forms accounting for over 40%
of all cases. Clearly writers have the same potential range of items to draw on
and so this preference for a limited number suggests a higher degree of
conventionalisation in the ways that material is reported in these disciplines.

The most common verbs in the corpus were the discourse acts *suggest* (148
cases) and *argue* (103), followed by the research verbs *find* (92) and *show* (86),
and the discourse verb *describe* (86). However, there were clear differences in
the forms preferred by broad disciplinary areas. Writers in the social sciences
and humanities, for example, greatly favoured *argue* (100% of cases), *suggest*
(82%), and *study* (70%), while *report* (82%), *describe* (70%), and *show* (55%)
occurred mainly in the science/engineering articles. Of the other forms
which occurred more than 25 times in the corpus, the most marked distribu-
tional imbalances were *say* (95% in philosophy), *use* (70% electrical), *examine*
(50% physics), *report* (53% biology), *analyse* (40% sociology), and *observe* (40%
biology).

Table 6.4 Reporting verbs by discipline

Discipline	Reporting verbs		Most frequent forms	
	per paper	**per 1,000 words**	**(ranked from left)**	**%**
Philosophy	57.1	7.3	say, suggest, argue, claim, point out, hold, think	25.4
Sociology	43.6	5.3	argue, suggest, describe, note, analyse, discuss	26.8
Applied Ling.	33.4	4.8	suggest, argue, show, explain, find, point out	28.5
Marketing	32.7	3.5	suggest, argue, find, demonstrate, propose, show	40.4
Biology	26.2	4.9	describe, find, report, show, suggest, observe	55.7
Electronic Eng.	17.4	3.4	propose, use, describe, show, publish, develop	38.0
Mechanical Eng.	11.7	3.1	describe, show, report, discuss, give, develop	30.7
Physics	6.6	2.0	develop, report, study, find, expand	42.4
Totals	28.6	4.6	suggest, argue, find, show, describe, propose, report	27.3

PROCESS CATEGORIES OF REPORTING VERBS

The analysis shows a fairly clear division in the process categories which again corresponds to the traditional division between hard and soft disciplines (Table 6.5). Philosophy, sociology, marketing, and applied linguistics largely employed Discourse Act reporting verbs (averaging 61% of the total for the four disciplines), and the engineering and science papers displayed a preference for Research-type verbs (50%). Cognition verbs were infrequent in almost all disciplines and were virtually absent in the engineering and physics papers, which together contained only 11 cases, or 6% of the total.

These writers therefore clearly drew intertextual links to their disciplines in different ways, and these broadly reflected the preferred citation and argument forms of their discourse communities. The predilection for Research

Table 6.5 Distribution of verbs in process categories by discipline (%)

Process	Biology	Physics	Elec Eng	Mech Eng	Mkting	App Ling	Sociology	Phil	Totals
Total	**262**	**66**	**174**	**117**	**327**	**334**	**436**	**571**	**2287**
Research	43.1	56.0	55.2	47.0	31.2	30.5	29.1	23.5	33.5
Cognition	7.2	6.1	2.9	1.7	7.3	10.5	6.9	14.7	8.9
Discourse	49.7	37.9	41.9	51.3	61.5	59.0	64.0	61.8	57.6

verbs and corresponding deficiency of Cognition forms in the science and engineering papers, for example, together help to convey an experimental explanatory schema. This distribution contributes to an overall impression in the hard discipline papers of research activity as an inductive, impersonal, and empirically based endeavour. Here the reported facts are shown to emerge from laboratory activities rather than discursive practices, and the legitimacy of the information rests securely on the non-contingent, socially invariant standards of laboratory procedures. The following examples offer some flavour of this:

(6) Grafstrom et al. [4] have <u>studied</u> photothermal currents . . .   (Phy)
    . . . <u>using</u> special process and design [42], or by <u>adding</u> [101], or
    <u>removing</u> [83] a mask.   (Elec)
    The relevant properties from each individual tensile test have
    been reported in <u>reference</u> (11) . . .   (Mech)
    Marschner & Dell (1994) <u>estimated</u> that external hyphae of
    AM fungi can deliver up to . . .   (Bio)
    The reasons for this are <u>examined</u> in detail by Yeo et al. (1990),
    Yeo (1994), and . . .   (Bio)

The greater use of Discourse Act forms in the humanities and social sciences, on the other hand, is more appropriate in an argument schema which more readily regards explicit interpretation, speculation, and complexity as accepted aspects of knowledge. These disciplines are typically more discursive and examine relationships and features that are more subject to contextual and human irregularities than those studied in the hard sciences. Writers in the soft disciplines therefore employed arguments that made greater use of Discourse Act forms which expedited the verbal exploration of such issues, facilitating qualitative arguments which rest on finely delineated interpretations and conceptualisations, rather than systematic scrutiny and precise measurement:

(7) Lindesmith's (1965) classic work <u>indicated</u> the exclusion of
    blacks from managerial . . .   (Soc)
    Davidson <u>defends</u> this claim on the grounds that without
    creatures using sentences . . .   (Phil)
    Cass Sunstein <u>makes the case</u> that the best thing about republican
    thought is . . .   (Phil)
    Ballard and Clanchy (1991) <u>argue</u> that cultural attitudes toward
    knowledge range from . . .   (Ling)
    Over 25 years ago Hardy (1975) <u>lamented</u> that few managers
    really knew whether . . .   (Mkt)

Similarly, the fact that 85% of Cognitive verbs occurred in the humanities and social science papers admits to a greater role for personal interpretation in knowledge negotiation. In these disciplines the literature is frequently depicted in terms of the cited author's theorising and mental activities, thereby giving prominence to the role, and often the fallibility, of human agency in constructing claims. Thus, through the use of Cognition verbs, the soft domain

writers tend to represent research as proceeding from the interpretative
tions or verbal accounts of researchers, emphasising the part that rea.
and argument play in the construction of knowledge:

> (8) Chomsky <u>regards</u> scientific work as, by definition, characterized
>   by a high level of . . .   (Ling)
>   Donnelan <u>believes</u> that for most purposes we should take the
>   demonstatum to be . . .   (Phil)
>   Austin seems to <u>assume</u> that a classification of different verbs is
>   eo ipso a . . .   (Ling)
>   Jerry Fodor <u>thinks</u> that it is irredeemably disjunctive.   (Phil)
>   Julian Hochfeld <u>perceives</u> PS as the only base for a unified
>   'science of politics' . . .   (Soc)

EVALUATIVE CATEGORIES

The evaluative categories show less obvious differences, with writers in all
disciplines displaying a clear preference for neutral stances. While the selection of an appropriate reporting verb allows writers to signal their assessment
of the evidential status of information, and thus demonstrate their degree of
commitment to it, actual refutation is relatively rare. In fact, direct criticism
does not occur in my science and engineering papers at all and is mainly
confined to philosophy and sociology, where it constitutes 70% of all cases in
the corpus (46 instances):

> (9) Donnelan <u>overlooks</u> intuitions of falsity through keeping . . .   (Phil)
>   . . . and the theory of Rawls in particular, unjustifiably <u>ignore</u>
>   an unjust division of labor . . .   (Phil)
>   Lillian Faderman has also probably <u>exaggerated</u> the
>   pervasiveness of . . .   (Phil)
>   What Travers <u>fails to explain</u> is why, given these differences in
>   local context . . .   (Soc)
>   But they <u>do not explain</u> why elites no longer exhibit . . .   (Soc)

It is also worth noting that negation reporting verbs also tend to be largely
drawn from the categories of Discourse and Cognition Acts. Because these
focus on authors' interpretations or texts, rather than their research, they
are potentially a less challenging form of criticism as they avoid any direct
attack on the author's competence or reputation (cf. Thompson and Ye,
1991: 377).

Overall, however, it appears that if the writer wishes to offer a negative
assessment of another's viewpoint, this is not typically signalled by the reporting
verb. Explicit rebuttal of other researchers is a serious face-threatening act in
academic writing (Myers, 1989), and such violation of interpersonal conventions is likely to expose the writer to retaliation or the disapproval of publishing
gatekeepers (Hyland, 1998). Refutation is therefore likely to be heavily mitigated and involve considerable rhetorical work to accomplish (e.g. Pickard,
1993b). Indeed, the fact that most rebuttals in the corpus were expressed in

terms of omission, an assessment that a particular act was not performed, might itself be seen as a mitigating strategy.

Also infrequent are Counters, or cases where the writer represents the cited author as holding a tentative or negative stance to the reported information. Generally, where writers imputed positions to authors they expressed them positively or neutrally as cognition verbs. Again, the vast majority of counters occurred in the sociology and philosophy papers with almost no examples in the hard knowledge corpora:

(10) Vernon and Sewell seriously <u>question</u> the materialist premises
      of Thompson's work . . .   (Soc)
      Tilly has, in fact, <u>complained</u> that RMT 'identifies the amassing
      or spending of . . .   (Soc)
      . . . deregulation <u>has been blamed</u> for small grocery failures
      in Australia (Harty, 1994) . . .   (Mkt)
      . . . which are <u>dismissed</u> by some theorists as superficial chatter
      (e.g. Baudrillard, 1988; Jameson, 1991) . . .   (Mkt)
      . . . the idea of a characterless substructure is <u>rejected</u> by
      Aristotle in Metaphysics.   (Phil)
      . . . cited and <u>criticized</u> by Coates (1984, p. 111).   (Phil)
      . . . Donald Downs <u>decries</u> restrictions on pornography. (Phil)
      However, both Davidson and Wittgenstein explicitly <u>disown</u>
      the view . . .   (Phil)

Scientists and engineers were far more likely to report information non-factively, with 66% of all reporting verbs in these disciplines in this category. These verbs help to rhetorically represent the norms of impersonality and impartiality which are professed to characterise enquiry in the hard knowledge fields, providing an acknowledgement of prior research without appearing to corrupt it with personal judgement. This is particularly apparent where writers also chose to remove the cited author, and thus the implication of human intervention, from the reporting sentence:

(11) Ref. [9] <u>developed</u> finite formulations and corresponding code.   (Phy)
      Fig. 1 shows the CEMS spectra recorded at room temperature
      using a He/CH4 gas-flow detector <u>described</u> elsewhere [6] . . .   (Phy)
      . . . properties of a line trajectory in spatial motion are
      <u>researched</u> by Refs [21–23] . . .   (Mech)
      . . . other solutions <u>have also been published</u> [5–7]   (Elec)

Less often, these writers employed reporting verbs to signal their acceptance of prior research (22% of verbs in the hard knowledge fields). Virtually all the remaining cases were tentative Discourse Act verbs, conveying a implication of uncertainty or less than full commitment:

(12) Sacc. is <u>considered</u> a nomen confusum (Hughes, 1958) . . .   (Bio)
      These studies <u>imply</u> that microtubule penetration into . . . (Bio)
      Preliminary data (Gentzis, 1993) <u>indicate</u> U to have
      predominantly . . .   (Mech)

> Burbidge (1992) <u>suggests</u> that a manned cell should not
> contain more than . . .   (Elec)
> A theory based on the demagnetization field <u>has been suggested</u>
> by Warren et al. [13–15] . . .   (Phy)

The fact that reporting verbs were more likely to carry the writer's evaluative stance in the humanities and social science papers reflects the more disputational and discursive rhetorical style of these disciplines. Evaluation allows writers to both engage with the disciplinary literature in a continuing debate and to negotiate the value of their own contribution by opening a discursive space in that literature, building on what has gone before. This is particularly evident in the fact that writers in the soft disciplines were also more likely to evaluate cited information by adding adverbial comment to the reporting verb, often to strongly align themselves with that position:

> (13) He argues there, correctly to my mind, that . . .   (Phil)
>   Churchland correctly rejected this move . . .   (Phil)
>   Benveniste (1969: 116 and 166–168) rightly points out how the
>   act of swearing is . . .   (Ling)
>   As Dipankar Gupta correctly asserts . . .   (Soc)
>   Wilson rightly says that many important social scientific theories
>   have . . .   (Soc)

In sum, the reporting options found in this corpus appear to be more than simply the stylistic proclivities of individual writers. Instead, they can be seen as reflecting disciplinary preferences for particular forms of rhetorical expression which, in turn, instantiate the different procedures and epistemological understandings of particular fields of enquiry.

SOME CONCLUSIONS ON REPORTING AND EAP

Although reference to previous work is virtually obligatory in academic writing, I have tried to show here that the ways writers choose to present information varies according to the discourse communities they inhabit. The options offered by the network of reporting verbs are an important means by which writers are able to appropriately link their local contributions into a wider disciplinary framework and so persuade readers of their ideas. These findings, I believe, are important for novice research writers, and for those who teach them, as once again we have support for the view that students entering academic communities need to acquire and employ a discipline-specific literacy.

A growing body of research into academic discourse has demonstrated that students have specialised communicative needs which are defined by the social purposes and rhetorical practices of their specific target communities. Although initially focused on undergraduates, this research has progressively responded to the needs of more advanced groups, and the particular demands of research writing are now recognised as representing a serious challenge to both postgraduate students (Paltridge, 1997) and L2 academics seeking to publish in English (J. Flowerdew, 1999). Although reporting is often treated in EAP materials as the application of standardised conventions and advice about avoiding plagiarism (e.g. Lester, 1993), students need to know more than the necessity and mechanics of referring to an existing literature. They also have to present that literature in ways that their readers are likely to find convincing.

The selection of a particular reporting verb is a delicate choice as it is a crucial means of both situating one's work appropriately and communicating with one's peers effectively, a way of engaging with colleagues and of appealing to the epistemological and interactive understandings of one's community. Selecting a particular verb thus not only signals a reported voice, but invokes a precise context of meaning and judgement which locates the writer in a certain relationship to the reader and the reported text. This can critically influence a reader's willingness to go along with a writer and accede to her claims.

Clearly more work needs to be done. In particular, there has been no space to discuss the typical rhetorical functions of the reports in which particular categories of verb occur, and I have said nothing about the effect of negation on the use of specific verbs. Moreover, the study is restricted to research papers and does not address other academic genres that students are commonly required to read or produce, such as theses, reports, and survey papers. However, the taxonomy suggested here offers a fairly straightforward and useful way of identifying the meanings of different choices and of mapping the dimensions of difference between disciplines and genres. The need to distinguish the particular rhetorical features common to specific disciplines is a growing pedagogical imperative in university writing courses, and reporting is clearly one area where students urgently require more assistance. So, while various applications and investigations remain, this study may contribute to a fuller understanding of research reporting and to the development of materials for novice academic writers.

Chapter 7

Corpora and corpus analysis: new windows on academic writing

Christopher Tribble

INTRODUCTION

The purpose of this chapter is to outline ways in which appropriate corpus resources may help students to develop competence as writers within specific academic domains. I have discussed elsewhere (Tribble, 1997a) the sets of knowledge which writers (in general) need in order to produce appropriate and effective texts. These can be summarised as in Table 7.1.

Such a framework brings together what are commonly called *process approaches* to writing instruction (Emig, 1983; Graves, 1984; Grabe and Kaplan, 1996) and *genre approaches* (Bhatia, 1993; Cope and Kalantzis, 1993; Halliday, 1978; Johns, 1994; Martin, 1989; Swales, 1990), and provides the basis for an integrated writing instruction programme. Thus, in the case of EAP students in higher education in Britain, learners (as a result of the academic programmes they are following) will most often be the ones responsible for the content knowledge that will be realised in writing activities. Teachers, on the other hand, will have the responsibility for creating opportunities in which learners can come to a fuller understanding of (a) the processes that are necessary to the completion of a writing task, (b) the institutional and contextual

Table 7.1 What writers need to know

content knowledge	knowledge of the concepts involved in the subject area
writing process knowledge	knowledge of the most appropriate way of carrying out a specific writing task
context knowledge	knowledge of the social context in which the text will be read, and co-texts related to the writing task in hand
language system knowledge	knowledge of those aspects of the language system necessary for the completion of the task

Source: Based on Tribble, 1997a: 43

*/hich operate in the target environment and determine what
n allowable contribution, and (c) the linguistic choices which
lade in order to produce such allowable contributions.
ion then arises as to how teachers can help learners to develop
lding of the way texts work in social contexts, and how language
use and communicative purpose intersect in the genres in which they have
an interest. Language corpora may be one of the resources that teachers and
learners will want to draw on.

Although this chapter is about ways in which the computer analysis of
collections of academic texts can increase our understanding of academic
writing, I will begin my discussion by looking at a single example: a short
published paper in the Reading Academic Text Corpus (RAT).[1] (See the
Appendix for the complete text.) As the text was written by a highly regarded
scholar at the invitation of the editors of 'Plant Molecular Biology Reporter'
(published by the Plant Molecular Biology Association), we can assume that
it is felt to be 'situationally effective' (Bazerman, 1994a: 23) by members of a
particular discourse community. In other words, it is the result of what
Bazerman calls an 'expert performance' (Bazerman, 1994a: 131), and of
potential interest to apprentice writers in that field.

In the second part of the chapter, based on this example analysis, I will
make suggestions for what I will call a corpus informed approach to EAP
writing instruction. I am working this way round – from micro to macro –
because this analysis will enable me to demonstrate some of the ways in
which corpus linguistic tools and resources, combined with discourse and
genre analytic frameworks for analysis, can contribute to EAP learning and
teaching.

USING CORPORA

To date, corpus linguistics has largely been driven by the needs of lexico-
graphers, descriptive linguists, and the NLP research community (Aston, 1995;
Tribble, 1997b; L. Flowerdew, this volume). This has created an overall push
towards a 'biggest is best' view of the corpus (e.g. Sinclair, 1991), which,
while it may be valid for these communities, does not necessarily meet the
needs of teachers and learners in English for Academic Purposes programmes.
The large corpus, whether it is 'balanced' as in the case of the British
National Corpus (Burnard, 1995), or a monitor corpus as with the Bank of
English at Birmingham University (Sinclair, 1991), provides either too much
data across too large a spectrum, or too little focused data, to be directly
helpful to learners with specific learning purposes. Although they have made,
and will continue to make, an invaluable contribution to ELT lexicography
and language description, large corpora appear to have less relevance to EAP
writing instruction and other areas of ELT. It is for this reason that I suggest
that using small corpus resources *alongside* bigger corpora can be helpful in

Table 7.2 Analytic framework (Contextual)

CONTEXTUAL Analysis	
1. name	What is the name of the genre of which this text is an exemplar?
2. social context	In what social setting is this kind of text typically produced? What constraints and obligations does this setting impose on writers and readers?
3. communicative purpose	What is the communicative purpose of this text?
4. roles	What roles may be required of writers and readers in this genre?
5. cultural values	What shared cultural values may be required of writers and readers in this genre?
6. text context	What knowledge of other texts may be required of writers and readers in this genre?
7. formal text features	What shared knowledge of formal text features (conventions) is required to write effectively into this genre?
LINGUISTIC Analysis	
8. lexico-grammatical features	What lexico-grammatical features of the text are statistically prominent and stylistically salient?
9. text relations/textual patterning	Can textual patterns be identified in the text? What is the reason for such textual patterning?
10. text structure	How is the text organised as a series of units of meaning? What is the reason for this organisation?

developing an understanding of academic written discourse. Such an approach fits in with current work that focuses on the value of smaller corpora for language learning and teaching (see J. Flowerdew, 1993a; Roseberry et al. (eds.), forthcoming).

The overall analytic framework that I shall be using can be seen in a developing tradition of genre analysis (Swales, 1990; Bhatia, 1993; Johns, 1997). I have drawn on these earlier frameworks for the categories and questions I shall use in this present study, perhaps giving greater emphasis to the distinction between *contextual* and *linguistic* analysis than has been the case in other studies. The two sections of my analytic framework contain a series of headings, which can, in turn, be expressed as a question or questions. The headings and their implicit questions are given in Table 7.2, and will be used in a detailed analysis of the RAT text.

It has been my experience that such an approach provides an useful basis for contextual and linguistic awareness raising during an EAP course, and offers a coherent basis for the development of curricula for writing instruction and the evaluation of written production.

UAL ANALYSIS

Text Analysis

>wing section I shall use the questions which have been set under
Analysis to give an account of the social/cultural dimensions of the
ext.

1. Name
What is the name of
the genre of which
this text is an
exemplar?

Without privileged knowledge, naming this short text
is problematic. Six informants in Colombo, Sri Lanka
(all English-medium-educated academics) were evenly
split as to whether they would call it an *article* or
a *report*, though, in the end, most felt more comfortable with *short report*. The fact that we know it is
called a 'Commentary' helps us to situate the text as it
can now be seen as standing in an analogous relation
to similar sections in major journals such as *Nature*
which also have space for short state-of-the-art reports of
this nature. As Swales says: 'The genre names inherited
and produced by discourse communities and imported
by others constitute valuable ethnographic communication, but typically need further validation' (Swales,
1990: 58).

2. Social context
In what social setting
is this kind of text
typically produced?
What constraints and
obligations does this
setting impose on
writers and readers?

The article was written for publication in a specialist
academic journal. In writing such a short piece, the
author faces special constraints in terms of content
and extent, but also has to meet normal academic
standards of warrant and referencing.

**3. Communicative
purpose**
What is the
communicative
purpose of this text?

Given that the piece was written at the invitation of
the editors, the major explicit communicative purpose
of this text must be to share recently established
knowledge with a readership of peers. These special
conditions minimise other subordinate purposes which
may be associated with a published text – e.g. ensuring
the professional standing of the author, or (possibly)
challenging the reputation of another worker in the
same field.

4. Roles
What roles may be
required of writers
and readers in this
genre?

The readers and writers of this kind of newsletter
have largely equal status as teachers or researchers,
and the texts that are contributed to such journals are
concerned with knowledge *forming* rather than with
knowledge *transmission* (Myers, 1990, 1994). In such
journals readers expect a high level of referencing

so that claims can be seen in their research context, and claims may often be tentative and tightly restricted. However, in the present instance, claims are made forcefully and unambiguously ('No biochemist had previously proposed . . .', '. . . enabled us to break the impasse reached with the EFE . . .', 'It is now clear that EFE is . . .', '. . . plant molecular biologists need not wait . . .'). This lack of tentativeness can be accounted for by the acknowledged significance of the breakthrough being reported, and by the status that Professor John and his colleagues' team has within the discipline.

While the role relationships instantiated in this text reduce its relevance for direct *modelling* by students (J. Flowerdew, 1993a), it makes the text interesting as a focus for analysis as it permits a useful discussion of difference between the present instance and more mainstream published articles.

5. Cultural values
What shared cultural values may be required of writers and readers in this genre?

Even though the text was not subject to the full rigour of peer review prior to publication, it nevertheless displays conformity to the full panoply of Western academic tradition. The author demonstrates his awareness of the imperative obligation to avoid plagiarism and to warrant all claims by reference to empirical data or by citation.

6. Text context
What knowledge of other texts may be required of writers and readers in this genre?

Given the special nature of this particular text, the writer has more freedom of expression than he might have had if writing for another publication. Nevertheless, he demonstrates an awareness of the organisation and purpose of analogous texts in other journals (e.g. the short reports in *Nature* or *New Scientist*).

7. Formal text features
What shared knowledge of formal text features (conventions) is required to write effectively into this genre?

Apart from its use of normal paragraphing, the form of the conventional features of this text (citations, bibliography organisation, labelling or diagrams or figures) will depend on the 'house style' of the journal, and will usually be stated in explicit instructions to contributors.

XTUAL ANALYSIS: SUMMARY

rt text is a piece of written production from an established scholar in
a specialised area of scientific research. The author gives an account of
recent developments in his field to a peer readership. The specific form of
his text is informed by its interrelations with other analogous short texts in
major scientific publications. In the next part of our discussion we shall
identify the extent to which the context of production has caused the writer
to make lexico-grammatical choices which contrast with the choices that
writers in other contexts would make – that is to say, the extent to which
'social context is predictive of text'? (Halliday, 1978: 189).

LINGUISTIC ANALYSIS

In an ideal world, the writing under consideration would be Part-Of-Speech
(POS) tagged, thereby enabling a much more sophisticated analysis than is
possible with raw text. However, there is also a value in seeing how far you
can get with a bare minimum – so in this case I have worked with an ascii text
file, a PC, *WordSmith Tools v.3.00* (Scott, 1996), and *MS Word 97*. These
technical resources have been complemented by data on text differentiation
in Biber, 1988 and Tribble, 1998 and a number of reference corpora (notably the two 1,000,000-word Written and Spoken data sets which will form
the British National Corpus Sampler and a Romantic Fiction corpus derived
from the Lancaster-Oslo-Bergen (LOB) corpus of British English).

Lexico-grammatical features

What lexico-grammatical features of the text are statistically prominent and
stylistically salient?

Keywords

The first element in the analysis is to identify and investigate what Scott calls
the 'keywords' in the text (Scott, 1997). Keyword analysis is carried out by:

(a) creating a wordlist with the *WordSmith Tools* Wordlist program.
(b) creating a keyword list by referencing this wordlist against a large corpus
(in this instance a one-million-word list derived from the Written subset
of the British National Corpus Sampler). Scott (1997) outlines the statistical procedures which underlie the program. The broad gist of Scott's
explanation is that the Keywords program is able to sift out those words
which are statistically prominent in the 'target' text (either outstandingly *frequent* or outstandingly *infrequent*) when compared with the frequencies of words in the reference corpus.

Keyword analysis offers one way of coming to grips with the choices our
writer has made – in this first instance, the choices being in relation to

Table 7.3   RAT keywords

N	WORD	FREQ.
1	EFE	12
2	MEMBRANE	7
3	ENZYME	7
4	ACTIVITY	11
5	ET	7
6	ETHYLENE	4
7	AL	7
8	MOLECULAR	4
9	SOLUBLE	4
10	HYDROXYLASE	3
11	FLAVANONE	3
12	YANG	3
13	ACC	3
14	BIOLOGISTS	3
15	HOFFMAN	3
16	PLANT	4

Swales's 'content schemata'. One of the specific claims that Scott (1997) makes for the Keywords program in *WordSmith Tools* is that it gives an insight into the 'aboutness' of a text. This claim is confirmed by the results in Table 7.3 where the top ten keywords of the RAT text are listed.

The list is a clear demonstration of the way in which membership of a particular disciplinary discourse community permits and requires the use of a range of content lexis which would be unallowable in genres catering for the needs of a broader readership. The occurrence of the apparently anomalous *et* and *al* is also accounted for by this membership. Indeed, I would predict that *et al* occurs more frequently in citations in science research than it does in the humanities where collective authorship is less the norm.

Not only do keyword lists give excellent insights into the 'aboutness' of single instances of a text – they can also be used in establishing a clearer understanding of the colligational and collocational relationships which generically significant words take on in the discourse. Thus a right sorted concordance for a single noun from the keyword list (see Table 8.4) tells us that *activity* can *depend, disappear,* or can *be required, required by,* or *associated with* various phenomena. It also tells us that it can be pre-modified by single and multiple nouns (*enzyme, flavanone 3-hydoxylase, lipoxygenase*).

Such information offers significant information for learners who wish to participate in the work of this discourse community. Keywords offer a rapid way of identifying the content lexis of a text, and also provide a means of gaining insights into broader text relations and stylistic choices.

RAT 'activity'

_₎₃ the plasma membrane, and that activity depended on the maintenance
belief in everyone's mind that enzyme activity depended on membrane integri
) of the in vivo activity, and their activity disappears completely when m
because it was invariably found that activity disappears when tissue is ho
Yang and Hoffman, 1984). Some EFE activity is retained by vacuoles isol
sation of the flavanone 3-hydroxylase activity required inter alia anoxic c
en went so far as to propose that EFE activity was associated with proton t
cals which resulted from lipoxygenase activity (Yang and Hoffman, 1984). A
    itchell et al., 1988) of the in vivo activity, and their activity disappea
    t require Fe2+ and ascorbate for full activity, and it is now as amenable t

---

Frequency lists

While keyword analysis of a single instance of a genre provides an invaluable
insight into the content schemata which inform a single instance of a genre,[2]
it may offer fewer insights for other aspects of the lexico-grammar than one
can obtain from a simple frequency wordlist. In order to extend the investigation of the grammar and style of this small text sample another procedure
has been used.

(a) Create a frequency sorted wordlist for the text. Frequency sorted lists
    can be a useful starting point for text analysis (Tribble and Jones, 1997;
    Stubbs, forthcoming) as they give an immediate insight into words with
    prominent frequency.
(b) Generate left and right sorted concordances for each high frequency
    word (I have worked with the top ten in this instance). Left and right
    sorting of the contexts of the node word of a concordance is essential if
    patterning in language is to be identified (Tribble and Jones, 1997).
(c) On the basis of these lists and concordances, identify stylistically salient
    features of the text (Halliday, 1973; Leech and Short, 1981; Tribble and
    Jones, 1997; Tribble, 1998).

Initial results for the RAT text are already revealing. Although the most
frequent words in a text (prominent) are not necessarily stylistically significant (salient), they provide a good way in to a text. Given in Tables 7.5 and 7.6
are the results for the 'top ten' words in the RAT text, referenced against raw
frequency counts for the one-million-word spoken and written data sets used
in the BNC Sampler, and a 24,000-word Romantic Fiction micro-corpus
(Tribble, 1998) drawn from LOB.[3]

The first information we can get from these lists is that the text has the
high percentage of definite nouns we associate with formal written discourse.
This is evidenced by the contrasting percentages for definite article *the* for
the four text sources I have sampled. Although percentages will not give
information on statistical significance, they provide a useful rough means of
differentiating between the texts in question.

Table 7.5 RAT frequency

RAT N	Word	Freq.	%
1	THE	35	5.96
2	AND	18	3.07
3	OF	18	3.07
4	IN	13	2.21
5	A	12	2.04
6	EFE	12	2.04
7	ACTIVITY	11	1.87
8	IS	11	1.87
9	TO	11	1.87
10	THAT	10	1.70

Table 7.6 Comparators

BNC Sampler: WRITTEN				BNC Sampler: SPOKEN				LOB Romantic Fiction			
N	Word	Freq.	%	N	Word	Freq.	%	N	Word	Freq.	%
1	THE	67,075	6.21	1	THE	38,962	3.71	1	THE	1,258	4.06
2	OF	32,656	3.02	2	I	33,478	3.19	2	TO	927	2.99
3	AND	28,900	2.68	3	YOU	27,334	2.60	3	AND	805	2.60
4	TO	26,680	2.47	4	IT	26,983	2.57	4	I	656	2.12
5	A	21,958	2.03	5	AND	26,013	2.48	5	A	633	2.04
6	IN	21,184	1.96	6	S	22,236	2.12	6	HE	575	1.86
7	IS	9,954	0.92	7	THAT	22,210	2.11	7	SHE	566	1.83
8	FOR	9,590	0.89	8	TO	22,142	2.11	8	HER	559	1.80
9	THAT	8,537	0.79	9	A	20,450	1.95	9	OF	533	1.72
10	WAS	8,362	0.77	10	OF	15,916	1.52	10	WAS	530	1.71

- RAT = 5.96% of all words
- BNC Written = 6.21%
- BNC Spoken = 3.72%
- Romantic Fiction = 4.06%

This impression is confirmed when the percentage of *of* is examined. Earlier studies (Biber, 1988; Biber and Finegan, 1989; Tribble, 1998) have demonstrated that a high frequency of *of* is frequently associated with formal written English, because as the frequency of *of* increases, so does its tendency to occur in the post-modifying structures typically found in nominally dense formal written English (Halliday, 1989). This is borne out in the present case by a concordance of *of* which demonstrates that the word occurs in post-modifying structures in 12 out of 16 instances in the RAT corpus text.

UK The final step in the **biosynthesis** of the plant growth regulator, ethy embrane systems) which were capable of converting ACC to ethylene, but . E, or at least a polypeptide component of the EFE. The amino acid sequenc1 s were also started up by the **discovery** of cell-free systems (always membra clear that EFE is a member of a group of soluble oxygenases that require onsible for catalysing the **hydroxylation** of 2S-flavanones to form 2R,3R-dihy t activity depended on the **maintenance** of a membrane potential (John, 1983 . It is now clear that EFE is a **member** of a group of soluble oxygenases th et al., 1991). What then is the moral of this tale? Quite simply that pl o enzymes, which took an enzyme out of a membrane where it was not loca lia anoxic conditions, and the presence of Fe2+ and ascorbate (Britsch and on fruits there was a complete **recovery** of the au-thentic EFE activity – as of the EFE. The amino acid sequence of this polypeptide resembled that se reached with the EFE. **Stabilisation** of the flavanone 3-hydroxylase acti nce of this polypeptide resembled that of flavanone 3-hydroxylase, a solub

(d) The concordance also revealed an interesting textualisation feature (marked with **bold text** in the concordance) which we will return to in the next section – this is the preference for nominalised structures over verbal structures when describing the processes involved in experimenta-tion. Thus we find: **biosynthesis, discovery, hydroxylation, maintenance, recovery, stabilisation.** Again, this preference for nouns over verbs is typical of certain varieties of formal written English (Halliday, 1989).

Other features which arose from the raw frequency counts are consistent with the RAT text's formal written style – although the high frequency of *and* proved to be uninteresting as it is not the result of the employment of suasive rhetoric (one feature of which can be an unusually high occurrence of non-phrasal coordination[4]). Rather, it arises because of a choice about citation style (using the full form rather than *and*) and the fact we noted earlier that so many scientific papers are published under the names of more than one person. A further indication of the role of post-modifying prepositions as discriminators in written/spoken differentiation[5] comes in the data for 'in'. The percentage for *in* (2.21%) in the RAT text is comparable to the percent-age in BNC Written (1.96%) – and contrasts with the percentages for BNC Spoken (1.29%) and LOB Romantic Fiction (1.27%), where, importantly, in most cases it follows a verb (or is part of a phrasal verb) or personal pronoun rather than post-modifying a noun, as shown in Tables 7.7 and 7.8.

The final comment we will make on the raw frequency data refers mainly to the use of verbs in the passage. Items 8 (*is*), 9 (*to*), and 10 (*that*) all offer additional insights into how verbs are used in the RAT text. Item 8 (is) oc-curs 11 times and has a higher percentage occurrence than BNC Written. We could predict that this is because the RAT text has a relatively high propor-tion of passive verb phrases[6] – and we would be correct. Of the 11 instances of *is*, five are agentless passives (see Table 7.9, where they are marked **P**).

Table 7.7 RAT 'in'

ng and Hoffman, 1984). All in all, little progress was bei
), which is readily assayed in vivo by supplying tissues wi
given rise to a firm belief in everyone's mind that enzyme
, pointing the biochemists in the right direction
erting ACC to ethylene, but in these preparations ethylene
orm 2R, 3R-dihydroflavonols in the biosynthetic pathway to
progress was being made in characterising EFE. para Unt
entered the scene. In 1990 Hamilton et al. reporte
identified a gene (pTOM13) in tomato which encoded for th
ied. para The final step in the biosynthesis of the plan
me had never been studied in vitro because it was invaria
chell et al., 1988) of the in vivo activity, and their ac

Table 7.8 Romantic Fiction 'in'

urtains and let the sea breeze in before he got into bed
o leave this house . . .' I broke in on her tirade. 'That's
a minute, Mrs. Landry,' he broke in gently. 'Loss of memor
act exactly the same,' she broke in. 'Please drive back. I
m the others is that my brother's in love with Lois. He nev
lking about when tea was brought in. Diana will soon be tw

Table 7.9 RAT 'is'

991). It is now clear that EFE is a member of a group of soluble oxyg	
ant growth regulator, ethylene, is catalysed by the ethylene-forming e	**p**
activity disappears when tissue is homogenised (Yang and Hoffman, 1	**p**
pletely when membrane integrity is lost (Porter et al., 1986; Mayne and	**p**
onols and anthocyanidins. There is no obvious relationship enzymatically	
Ververidis and John, 1991). It is now clear that EFE is a member of a	
rbate for full activity, and it is now as amenable to biochemical stu	
ene-forming enzyme (EFE), which is readily assayed in vivo by supplying	**p**
ffman, 1984). Some EFE activity is retained by vacuoles isolated from le	**p**
characterising EFE. Until, that is, the molecular biologists entered the	
idis et al., 1991). What then is the moral of this tale? Quite simply	

Additionally, of the 11 instances of *to*, five are associated with verb infinitives and two with passive structures (although one is accompanied by a nonanimate agent):

biologists need not wait for their protein **to be characterised**
ethylene was shown **to be generated** by non-enzymatic reaction

That structures in the RAT text are also interesting – although again they lead us into questions of textualisation. Of the ten instances in the text, five are either introduced by a verb which comments on claims made by others:

Y *found* **that** . . .
X and Y *propose* **that** A, and **that** B . . .
X *reported* **that** . . .

or introduce a firm claim that the author is making:

It *is* clear **that** . . .

Lexico-grammatical features: conclusion

By examining a set of words that are statistically prominent in comparison with a general population of texts, along with a small number of high frequency words, it has been possible to identify the kinds of writing with which this text holds relations (formal written) and its content domain. We have also begun to see patterns in the text which contribute to the special identity of the text, and which almost certainly result from the constraints which the writer has had to respond to in order to ensure that the text is an allowable contribution to a specialist genre. The contextual analysis we have made connects with the lexico-grammatical analysis.

In the next section, we shall see to what extent other kinds of textual patterning can be identified, again using corpus linguistic tools for this purpose.

Textual patterning

Can textual patterns be identified in the text? What is the reason for such textual patterning?

We have already identified two kinds of textual patterning in the RAT text: the preference for nouns over verbs in describing processes, as was exemplified in the use of *biosynthesis, discovery, hydroxylation, maintenance, recovery,* and *stabilisation;* and the use of *that* clauses in the reporting of claims. A further example is offered here to demonstrate the potential of the kind of study we have been making in analysing a single text in relation to a large body of texts.

In this case, sentence beginnings were searched for (by looking, of course, for full-stops!). This time, however, an initial search on '*.' revealed a potentially interesting phenomenon at the *end* of sentences. Results are given in Table 7.10 which confirm this – this time based on a search for '*)'.

Out of 17 orthographic sentences in the RAT text, over 50% end with a parenthesised text citation – and another two such citations are found at coordinated clause boundaries. When compared with our reference texts, there is a striking contrast between Romantic Fiction, where (unsurprisingly) this phenomenon does not occur, and the BNC Written Sampler where it occurs 946 times (This feature is not relevant to the transcription conventions in BNC Spoken.) Space and time do not allow a detailed analysis of these results,[7] but a small sample indicates the stylistic and communicative parallels between this observed structure in the RAT text and its occurrences in the BNC.

Table 7.10   Warranting

1. a membrane potential (John, 1983). However this Mitchellia
2. activity (Yang and Hoffman, 1984). All in all, little progres
3. ogenised (Yang and Hoffman, 1984). Some EFE activity is r
4. ntegrity (Yang and Hoffman, 1984). The present author ev
5. n laboratory! (John et al., 1986). False trails were also
6. al, 1986; Mayne and Kende, 1986). para The earlier work
7. ate (Britsch and Grisebach, 1986). When these conditions
8. nzyme (Ververidis and John, 1991). It is now clear that EF
9. enzyme (Ververidis et al., 1991). para What then is the

1. f mesophyll (Guy and Kende, 1984) and by membrane vesic
2. iwifruits (Mitchell et al., 1988), but these systems ret

1. 8 or less (Mitchell et al., 1988) of the in vivo activity, a

---

Table 7.11   BNC final parenthesis

been withdrawn' (Knowles, 1978, 668). This reduction would have been
al and rural-urban (Robertson, 1961). This therefore leaves the u
compensating counter-current (Law 4). Until the recent repopulation
(what they did when they got there). Until the mid-1970s these
rising (Johansen and Fuguitt, 1984). What evidence there is from
eant (Dean **9;426;hi et al., 1984a). What was n't in doubt, th
ve method (Propst and Buyhoff, 1980). With regard to the search for
eisure time (Martin and Mason, 1976). Within this residue, which now
onsiderably (Glyn-Jones, 1979; 1982). Within the national parks'
ferent groups of housing (see fig 6). These are as follows: 1) CBD
ere noted on a rough map (see fig 3). This information was then
the pumping processes (in the dark). C is thus negative for a finit
edium) is equal to zero (modulo 2n). Each such frequency is termed

---

What we can observe here is the way in which a final parenthetic element is used to:

- warrant claims or assertions by citing a published authority;
- clarify claims or assertions by reference to a figure or other part of the text;
- clarify claims or assertions with further comment.

In each of the instances expert writers are using a convention which does not occur at all in collections of student writing such as the LOCNESS[8] collection of student essays held at the University of Louvain (Granger, 1998a), or in a collection of Polish student essays from the Polish Corpus of Learners' English (PCLE).[9] As such it constitutes an aspect of the RAT text which may be genre specific, but is more likely to be common across a broad range of texts that are used in academic discourse communities.[10] It also indicates a starting point for student research. Asking learners to look at where and how parentheses are used is an excellent way of beginning an investigation of citation practices

'n that once the parenthesised citations have been identified, it
_y to follow up how (and with which verbs, in which structures) the
. nouns which occur in such lists are used in the text.

Text structure

*How is the text organised as a series of units of meaning? What is the reason for this
organisation?*

The final area to consider is the way in which information is organised as
moves across the text. As Swales showed in the elaboration of his early CARS
model for article introductions (Swales, 1981a, 1990), identifying such moves
can be of great benefit to learners who are approaching a genre for the first
time.

Although it operates at a more abstract level than CARS, the Situation–
Problem–Response–Evaluation (SPRE) minimal discourse model proposed
in Winter, 1977 and Hoey, 1983 also offers a powerfully generative way of
viewing the relational patterns – and proves to be exceptionally apposite in
analysing the four-paragraph text in question (refer to the Appendix for the
full text). Thus the SPRE pattern maps closely on to the complete text, as is
made clear by the opening sentence of each paragraph quoted below:

- **Situation**: outlines an earlier state-of-the-art in an aspect of microbiology –
  specifically the understanding of the role of a catalyst in biosynthesis and
  the research (*The final step in the biosynthesis of the plant growth regulator,
  ethylene, is catalysed by the ethylene-forming enzyme (EFE), which is readily assayed
  in vivo by supplying tissues with its substrate, 1-aminocyclopropane-1-carboxylic
  acid (ACC), but until recently the enzyme had never been studied in vitro because it
  was invariably found that activity disappears when tissue is homogenised.*)
- **Problem**: identifies the inadequate understanding on which this view was
  based (*The earlier work had given rise to a firm belief in everyone's mind that
  enzyme activity depended on membrane integrity.*)
- **Response**: describes a revised understanding in the light of research in
  another field (*In 1990 Hamilton et al. reported that they had identified a gene
  (pTOM13) in tomato which encoded for the EFE, or at least a polypeptide component of the EFE*)
- **Evaluation**: comments on the change in understanding and its impact on
  the field (*What then is the moral of this tale? Quite simply that plant molecular
  biologists need not wait for their protein to be characterised biochemically; molecular
  biology can be a very useful prelude to the biochemistry, pointing the biochemists in
  the right direction.*)

By combining a detailed analysis of the lexico-grammar of the text with this
kind of account of the overall structure of the text, it begins to be possible to
give a very precise (and well-contextualised) linguistic specification of an
exemplar of a genre. As Stubbs says, 'the most powerful interpretation emerges
if comparisons of texts across corpora are combined with the analysis of the
organisation of individual texts' (Stubbs, 1996: 34).

RAT TEXT ANALYSIS: CONCLUSION

In the analysis so far we have seen how it is possible to use a genre analytic approach to identify the communicative context and purpose of a text, and then to develop a linguistic analysis (using corpus and discourse analysis tools) which makes it possible to identify the extent to which this context and purpose have shaped the linguistic choices the writer has made in realising the text. But how does this help us answer the questions with which this chapter started? What is the potential of a corpus approach to EAP writing instruction, and what corpus resources might be required in order to implement such an approach?

A corpus informed approach to EAP writing instruction?

In the introduction to this chapter I said that writers need four types of knowledge when producing allowable contributions to a particular genre: *content knowledge, writing process knowledge, context knowledge,* and *language system knowledge.* I hope that I have demonstrated in the sections above that genre analysis combined with corpus *tools* and corpus *resources* can make a contribution to the development of a writer's context knowledge and language system knowledge.

In the final section I would like to offer some further suggestions for developing what I shall call a corpus informed approach to EAP writing instruction.[11] I say corpus *informed* as it should by now be clear that a corpus (however well constructed) is not going to offer all the resources learners and teachers require. Content and writing process knowledge will remain areas for EAP teachers and students to address, however much contextual and linguistic investigation they might have done. What I am proposing, therefore, is the use of corpus resources in helping learners extend their understanding of written academic discourse – what Johns calls their *academic literacies* (Johns, 1997). The two areas on which I shall focus are (a) the resources which teachers might consider developing and (b) the ways in which they could use these resources to add a corpus informed dimension to their EAP programmes.

CORPUS RESOURCES FOR EAP

Exemplar and analogue corpora

We have seen that one of the main tasks that EAP learners have is finding out about the kinds of genres they want to write into. They need to understand why texts are written in particular ways and what other texts they interrelate with, and they need to be able to use the linguistic resources which are associated with these genres. I have commented elsewhere (Tribble, 1998) that in the context of writing into a new genre 'difficult' can be interpreted familiar'. Most EFL writers in British universities are competent in the ~~ties~~ required in their own academic cultures. Their problem is often ~~...~~ they do not know what the target performance looks like in English – often British academic genres are unfamiliar, and therefore difficult.[12] One reason for this is that it is often impossible (for example in the case of examination essays) to present learners with examples of the kinds of texts they are supposed to write as they are locked away in the university registry. Another reason is that the kinds of writing that undergraduates are asked to do *only* exist in educational institutions and have no clear, published analogue (Granger and Tribble, 1998; Tribble, 1997b).

One way, therefore, of developing corpus resources for EAP writing instruction is to collect texts which are the same as or, at least, analogous to the texts that your learners need to write, in other words, an *exemplar* corpus. Individual instances of such texts provide the basis for the kinds of genre analysis we have carried out here. Collections of such texts allow the learner to make generalisations about the genre which can further enhance their own written production (Bhatia, 1993). If it can be achieved, working with text collections built on production in the learners' target discourse community has many advantages, one of the greatest being that learners will be highly motivated to read the texts under consideration, and the generalisations which they are able to make on the basis of their analysis can be incorporated into their own written production. I have developed this kind of specialist corpus for project proposal writing (Tribble, 1998).

It is, however, remarkably difficult to assemble such collections, and it is often necessary to find *analogues* to the texts your learners wish to write, rather than specific exemplars (Tribble, 1997b; Johns, 1997). Tim Johns at Birmingham has taken this direction and built a corpus of *New Scientist* and science-related newspaper articles. Using this resource, he has developed a 'Virtual Data Driven Library' of activities and resources for self access use by students at Birmingham (http://sun1.bham.ac.uk./johnstf/ddl_lib.htm).

Exemplar corpora of specific genre production, and analogue corpora of close relatives of the target language production will constitute invaluable resources for language awareness raising and the investigation of grammar and lexis. Such corpora will be small and tightly focused. They will not, however, offer a basis for making generalisations about the language as a whole. Whatever the benefits of small exemplar and analogue corpora, it does not, however, mean that big corpora are bad things.

Reference corpora

Big corpora come back in to the picture when we consider the approaches to text and corpus analysis outlined in the discussion in the second part of this chapter. This approach does not depend on the compilation of a corpus of exact or analogous exemplars. Rather, it is based on the availability of a range of relevant reference corpora. The value of a reference corpus is that it permits the systematic comparison of individual instances of language use with language use in a general population of texts. This approach is inherent in much corpus linguistic work.

In developing programmes for EAP writing instruction which draw on reference corpora, teachers and learners will find themselves working with word lists and keyword lists developed by comparing examples of target language production with these large text collections. They will be identifying language use in one setting and comparing it with language use in other, clearly delineated genre contexts, and accounting for differences and similarities, and following lines of investigation similar to the one undertaken in this chapter. Working in this way, teachers will find that a combination of 'micro-corpora' of exemplar texts from their own disciplines and analogue corpora, studied in relation to large corpora such as the British National Corpus, will become increasingly important resources.[13]

CONCLUSION

In this chapter I have discussed the needs of student writers in EAP, and have attempted to outline how such students might be helped through a corpus informed approach to the analysis of written academic disource. Such an approach will draw on three kinds of corpora:

- *exemplar corpora* of texts directly related to the target writing behaviour of the learner;
- *analogue corpora* of texts which are similar to the target writing behaviour of the learner;
- *reference corpora* based on much larger text collections which will be used as a basis for the analysis of individual instances of genre production.

A corpus informed approach to writing instruction in EAP will make use of both big and small corpora, but will do so in a way which is sensitive to the needs of learners who are at different levels in their development of academic literacy. It will combine genre analysis with linguistic analysis in the early stages of EAP programmes when learners come to grips with the genres which will be important to them in their future academic careers. And it will continue to be relevant in the later stages of a programme as a means of extending the academic literacies that the learners require, and remediating problems which they discover as their confidence as writers increases.

NOTES

1. My thanks to Ron White of CALS, Reading University, for permission to use this component of RAT.
2. This is not the case if a larger sample of instances of a genre are studied. In this case, keywords can also give strong insights into the grammatical structure of a text (Tribble, 1998).

3. See Tribble, 1998 for a discussion of the potential value of these reference corpora.
4. A distinguishing feature of more suasive genres such as Project Proposals: see Tribble, 1998.
5. Biber's category 'Involved versus Informational Production' has four key components: written texts tend to have more *prepositions*, more *attributive adjectives*, a higher *type/token ratio*, and longer average *word length*.
6. Agentless passives are one of the major components of Biber's 'Abstract versus Non-abstract Information' dimension, which 'marks informational discourse that is abstract, technical and formal, versus other types of discourse' (Biber, 1988: 112–13).
7. But see Hyland (2000) for a useful discussion of citation in academic discourse.
8. My thanks to Professor Granger (granger@lige.ucl.ac.be) for permission to refer to the International Corpus of Learners' English (ICLE).
9. My thanks to Przemyslaw Kaszubski of Poznán University for permission to refer to PCLE.
10. See ch. 2 in Hyland (2000) for an extended discussion of citation in academic writing.
11. I shall assume that the reader will have access to basic technical resources – i.e. a modern PC, word-processing software (and basic skills) and a capable concordancing program. The most appropriate of these are *WordSmith Tools* (further details from Mike Scott: ms2928@liverpool.ac.uk) or *Monoconc Pro* (further details from Mike Barlow: barlow@athel.com).
12. As an extreme example, consider the 'problem' essay in legal studies.
13. It is relatively easy to use the header information to extract specific text collections from the BNC which can be saved separately from the main corpus and processed with a concordancing program.

APPENDIX 7.1: RAT CORPUS DATA (CONTACT PAUL THOMPSON [P.A.THOMPSON@READING.AC.UK] FOR FURTHER DETAILS)

How plant molecular biologists revealed a surprising relationship between two enzymes, which took an enzyme out of a membrane where it was not located, and put it into the soluble phase where it could be studied

The final step in the biosynthesis of the plant growth regulator, ethylene, is catalysed by the ethylene-forming enzyme (EFE), which is readily assayed in vivo by supplying tissues with its substrate, 1-aminocyclopropane-1-carboxylic acid (ACC), but until recently the enzyme had never been studied in vitro because it was invariably found that activity disappears when tissue is homogenised (Yang and Hoffman, 1984). Some EFE activity is retained by vacuoles isolated from leaf mesophyll (Guy and Kende, 1984) and by membrane vesicles in the juice squeezed from kiwifruits (Mitchell et al., 1988), but these systems retain only about one per cent (Porter et al., 1988) or less (Mitchell et al., 1988) of the in vivo activity, and their activity disappears completely when membrane integrity is lost (Porter et al., 1986; Mayne and Kende, 1986).

The earlier work had given rise to a firm belief in everyone's mind that enzyme activity depended on membrane integrity (Yang and Hoffman, 1984).

The present author even went so far as to propose that EFE activity was associated with proton translocation across the plasma membrane, and that activity depended on the maintenance of a membrane potential (John, 1983). However this Mitchellian EFE did not readily find experimental support, even from our own laboratory! (John et al., 1986). False trails were also started up by the discovery of cell-free systems (always membrane systems) which were capable of converting ACC to ethylene, but in these preparations ethylene was shown to be generated by non-enzymatic reactions between ACC and free-radicals which resulted from lipoxygenase activity (Yang and Hoffman, 1984). All in all, little progress was being made in characterising EFE. Until, that is, the molecular biologists entered the scene.

In 1990 Hamilton et al. reported that they had identified a gene (pTOM13) in tomato which encoded for the EFE, or at least a polypeptide component of the EFE. The amino acid sequence of this polypeptide resembled that of flavanone 3-hydroxylase, a soluble enzyme responsible for catalysing the hydroxylation of 2S-flavanones to form 2R,3R-dihydroflavonols in the biosynthetic pathway to flavonols and anthocyanidins. There is no obvious relationship enzymatically between flavanone 3-hydroxylase and the EFE. No biochemist had previously proposed an affinity between the two enzymes. Yet the structural relationship implied by the sequence homology provided the vital clue which enabled us to break the impasse reached with the EFE. Stabilisation of the flavanone 3-hydroxylase activity required inter alia anoxic conditions, and the presence of Fe2+ and ascorbate (Britsch and Grisebach, 1986). When these conditions were used to extract the EFE from melon fruits there was a complete recovery of the authentic EFE activity – as a soluble enzyme (Ververidis and John, 1991). It is now clear that EFE is a member of a group of soluble oxygenases that require Fe2+ and ascorbate for full activity, and it is now as amenable to biochemical studies as any other enzyme (Ververidis et al., 1991).

What then is the moral of this tale? Quite simply that plant molecular biologists need not wait for their protein to be characterised biochemically; molecular biology can be a very useful prelude to the biochemistry, pointing the biochemists in the right direction.

Prof. Philip John
Department of Agricultural Botany, Plant Science Laboratories, University of Reading, Reading RG6 2AS, UK

Chapter 8

Integrated and Fragmented Worlds: EAP Materials and Corpus Linguistics

John M. Swales

PRELIMINARY OBSERVATIONS

As noted by L. Flowerdew (this volume), specialised micro-corpora have been emerging in recent years as a viable pedagogical alternative to the broad-band general language corpora that dominated the field in the 1980s. These specialised corpora, especially those devoted to written texts, are interestingly varied, ranging from project proposals submitted to the European Union (Tribble, 1999) and Ph.D. theses (Thompson, 1999) to NNS undergraduate writing (L. Flowerdew, 1998a), and L. Flowerdew (this volume) provides further information on many. Indeed, some of these micro-corpora have already proved very productive in terms of findings of both potential and actual relevance for ESP, none more so than Hyland's extensive use of a corpus of 80 research articles (Hyland, 1998, 2000). Another recent contribution is Marco's (2000) investigation into certain patterns (two of which are discussed later) in a similar-sized but even more specialised corpus of medical research articles, drawn from just two leading journals, one American, the other British.

With current technology, the putting-together of such text-based corpora is technically straightforward. However, the compilation of speech micro-corpora (of around one million words or so) is an enterprise at least an order of magnitude more time-consuming, complex, and costly. Even so, two major undertakings along these lines are under way in the United States: the T2K-SWAL and MICASE corpora of academic speech, the former based at the University of Northern Arizona, and the latter at the University of Michigan; and here it is interesting to note that both of these initiatives have been primarily funded by ESL/EAP testing operations.

The proliferation of such text or transcript micro-corpora, especially if they can be accessed on the Web, as is the case with MICASE, will doubtless have a growing impact on future developments in English for Specific Purposes. Aside from issues of corpus design, and the amount and kind of syntactic and pragmatic mark-up, this relatively new corpus+concordance resource, with its puzzling and paradoxical combination of collocational power and intuitive emptiness, will probably throw the field over the next decade into some confusion, perhaps particularly with regard to English for Academic and Professional Purpose *materials*. One of the most pressing of these issues concerns how to make effective and efficient use of a specialised corpus (once it has been established) in order to gain pedagogically utilisable insight into the discourses that have been collected.

The difficulties here for the ESP practitioner have, in my view, been underestimated. For a minor example, the immediate availability of word-frequency lists (including *keywords*: Tribble, 1999) can lead to a kind of anecdotal gee-whizzery, and as a newcomer to the corporist world, I have become aware of how small gleanings about language use in a corpus can be disproportionately seductive. In the corpus of Michigan speech for instance, I have observed that the fifth and sixth most common 'lexical items' are *uh* and *um*, and that there are several hundred tokens of *I don't know* in its current 700,000 words, the former 'interesting fact' perhaps telling us something about widespread dysfluencies at my prestigious institution, and the latter one perhaps indicating unexpected levels of academic modesty and/or ignorance. At faculty meetings and the like I can find occasion to reveal these findings, often to the considerable amusement of my university colleagues, but intrinsically they are pretty meaningless, and seem most reminiscent of rather old-fashioned discussions among historical linguists and dialectologists about the minutiae of word use. Certainly, accumulations of such incidental findings provide little in the way of a *platform* from which to launch corpus-based pedagogical enterprises.

On the larger collocational front, there seems to be emerging some sense that the large volume of corpus studies published in Europe based on the major British English corpora have not always produced utilisable insights along with their incidental or quantitative findings. Obviously, there have been substantial major achievements such as the pioneering *Cobuild Dictionary* (1987) and the recent *Longman Grammar* (Biber et al., 1999). In addition, Stubbs (1996) offers convincing depictions of the negative and positive prosodies associated with certain lexical items, while Carter and McCarthy (1997) provide an excellent account of relative clauses that do not fall into the traditional grammatical categories. On the other hand, there are a good number of other studies that are less revealing, perhaps for the following reason. Although it has become increasingly recognised that it is intuition that underlies insight into and exploitation of a corpus of material, as I know to my own cost, there unfortunately seems at present to be often a huge amount of trial-and-error involved. Any such 'search' for significance involves working from small-stretch surface forms and then trying to fit these into some larger contextual frame. Alas, lack of clarity in pattern or lack of conviction in interpretation cause many initially promising lines of enquiry to be abandoned. As Kennedy observes, 'The research topics in a machine-readable corpus are potentially as various and wide-ranging as are the facts about a language and the use of that language' (1998: 274). And therein, as Shakespeare would say, lies the rub.

One compounding difficulty, at least for a person like myself, is that this procedure is precisely the reverse of the process by which I, and I suspect many others, try to understand a genre. This is typically a process which starts from macro features and only *later* tries to align these with particular linguistic realisations, and *then* looks for explanatory links between the macro and the micro. At least in terms of theory-hope, the genre analyst inhabits a more integrated discoursal world orthogonal to the enthusiastic but fragmented efforts of the corporist.

If this chapter has so far focused on problematising our deployment of the corpus-concordance resource, there is one secondary area where it has immense, if possibly short-lived, potential. Although many corporists most of the time seem to have trouble – in the present state of the art – in coming up with useful *discoveries* about the target language, they are excellently positioned to validate, modify, or reject the generalisations already made about that language in descriptive or pedagogic grammars, or in ESP teaching materials. Here is a quick illustration, which took me about an hour of work. Swales and Feak (1994) was written before we became aware of corpora, and was based on our own lengthy experiences as writing instructors. On page 19, we offer several suggestions for maintaining a formal academic writing style, such as number six: 'Place adverbs within the verb'. Our first example is as follows:

Then the solution can be discarded. →
The solution can *then* be discarded.

So, as a quick test of this dictum, I looked up *then* in the Hyland corpus and found about 500 examples *in toto*. Therein we can indeed find considerable support for mid-position use of *then*, especially with passive verbs used in exposition or procedural description; thus the generalised suggestion so far holds. However, there is a catch, and an important one. Somewhere around 130 of the occurrences of *then* (over 25%) are in the second clause following a subordinate *if* clause (plus a few others starting with *suppose* and *when*). In all these cases, except for two, *then* occurs in *initial* position in the second clause.

A quick corpus-based survey, which would have consumed a large amount of time if attempted by hand, has thus provided a useful qualification to a pedagogical generalisation. While it could justifiably be argued that I should have known about this major exception, the fact of the matter is that it never occurred to me until I switched on *WordSmith Tools* (Scott, 1996). Examples of similar validatory excursions into corpus territory can easily be multiplied, and indeed are well represented in both Stubbs (1996) and Partington (1998), but, as I intimated at the outset, it is a little unclear how long such forays will continue to prove valuable given the current pace of corpus-based descriptions, as dramatically revealed by the recent publication of the 1200-page *Longman Grammar of English Speech and Writing* (Biber et al., 1999). And, as I have also intimated, this kind of exercise, while doubtless salutary, also has a downstream and secondary quality about it.

The last of my preliminary issues is connected with the previous one and involves the more direct employment – not excluding its non-deployment – of corpus-based material in pedagogical settings. Here the concern is not so much with the advantages and disadvantages of 'data-driven learning' (Johns, 1991; Aston, 1995) *per se* as a methodological innovation, nor with deployment in class of concordance lines. On the latter, Thurstun and Candlin (1998a) provide an extremely well-balanced and interesting exploration of the opportunities and threats in doing so (see also Thurstun and Candlin, 1999). Rather, I am interested in the underlying issues of the cost-effectiveness and practicality of the EAP instructor venturing into the new virtual-corporist realm. From the discussion so far, it seems likely that in the relatively near future most published ESP pedagogical materials will need to be, at least in part, 'corpus-informed' (as in the likely revision of the mid-position adverb subsection in a second edition of Swales and Feak) if an *appropriate* corpus to be drawn upon has been selected or constructed. But that is not a small 'if'. Already there is massive confusion about one of the prime categories, 'academic prose', and about whether it should encompass textbooks (or only advanced ones?) and popularisations (or only sophisticated ones?), and this has occurred despite the efforts of Myers (1990), Swales (1995), and others to clarify the situation (see also Love, this volume). In today's unsettling and unsettled corpus linguistics context, what then are the responsibilities of ESP individual instructors *vis-à-vis* their banks of material, their classroom activities, and their individual assitance or tutorial help? In the rest of this chapter I hope to further examine a number of these issues, drawing upon my experience as a writing tutor and consultant for non-native speakers working towards doctoral degrees in a major US research university, as a classroom instructor for such students, as a materials writer, and as a person involved in a corpus project designed to capture one and a half million words of academic speech at the University of Michigan.

REFLECTIONS ON A TUTORIAL LIFE

I typically spend several hours a week in one-on-one meetings with graduate students, largely with those who are attending or have attended one or more of my writing classes. Sometimes these encounters produce moments of puzzlement or enlightenment that I can recognize as having (at least potentially) a wider role, and I dare say that my students have become accustomed to my saying things like, 'Wow, that's interesting – wait a minute while I make a note of that for future reference.' Since article usage remains a problem even for those NNS students who are extremely good writers, certainly as good and probably more published than their typical American counterparts, my antennae are particularly sensitive to such things as generic uses of articles or the occurrence or otherwise of a definite article before a noun which itself is followed by a prepositional phrase (as in 'Since *the* beginning of time'). For several years I have been offering a 'rough rule' that *the* is likely preferred before a following 'of' phrase, but likely dispreferred if the phrase is governed by another common short preposition. (The rule certainly does not work so well with a longer preposition like 'between', C. Feak, personal communication.) I happened to be working on this topic in order to add a *Language Focus* to the emerging manuscript of *English in Today's Research World* (Swales and Feak, 2000), when the 19.1 issue of *English for Specific Purposes* arrived, containing within it Marco's article on three phraseological patterns in medical research articles, two fortunately dealing with article usage in complex noun phrases. Here is part of the resulting teaching materials:

Task A
Consider the following data. What would you conclude about articles and the first noun?

1a. The increase of temperature caused the equipment to malfunction.
1b. An increase in temperature can cause equipment to malfunction.

2a. Skills in oral presentation are now expected of engineers.
2b. The communicative skills of this candidate are very impressive.

3a. Interest in this area is growing.
3b. The interest of this area lies mostly in its potential for interdisciplinary work.

4a. The contributions of this research group are substantial.
4b. Contributions to this project are truly multinational.

5a. Participants in the meeting agreed on a common goal.
5b. The members of the committee agreed on a common goal.

(When you have finished, check Note A [not given here])

Based at least on the data in Task A, we see that there is some tendency for *the* to occur before a following 'of phrase', but indefinite articles to precede noun phrases governed by other prepositions. But how quickly can you find exceptions to this probabilistic 'rule'?

Now let's look at the 'of phrase' situation in more detail, if only because it is the commonest structure. Marco's corpus of 80 medical research articles produced 9900 examples of 'the ... of ...' phrases, but only 780 examples of 'a ... of ...'. So far, so good then. It would appear 'the ... of' pattern is much more common, by a ratio of more than ten to one.

Marco provides a useful list of nouns that have an above 50% chance of occurring in the 'the ... of ...' framework – as opposed to anywhere else in the sentence! There were 12 of these in the medical corpus, the first of which is the noun *start*, which actually occurred 100% of the time in this position!

80–100%	start/basis/presence
60–79%	absence/percentage/administration/number/importance
50–59%	extent/development/effect

Overall we can see that a number of these are connected with measures (*number, percentage*), with existence (*presence, absence*) and with treatment (*start, administration, development*).

The 'a ... of ...' structure, as we have seen, is much less frequent. In Marco's medical English data, only three nouns were found a majority of the time in this context, but they are important and interesting: *a variety of/a minority of/a history of.*

Task B
Choose 'a' or 'the' for the following blanks.
1. Smokers tend to have ____ history of lung problems.
2. ____ history of the battle against smallpox is an inspiring one.
3. Side effects were noted in ____ minority of the patients.
4. Side effects were noted in ____ minority of patients who had had pre-existing conditions.
5. ____ percentage of subjects reporting stress rose sharply.
6. ____ percentage of subjects reported increased levels of stress.
7. The research group is planning ____ series of experiments to test this hypothesis.
8. After an initial setback, ____ series of experiments produced useful results.
9. ____ number of students who failed has increased over the last decade.
10. ____ number of students have failed, presumably because of poor preparation.

(See Note B for commentary on correct and less correct responses [not given here])

I would argue that there has been a useful and serendipitous conjunction of events and interests in this particular case. My painstaking and slow accumulation of individual instances of problematic and non-problematic instances of article uses and Marco's suddenly-available quantitative data in a small area of English grammar of some relevance to non-native speakers (but little discussed in pedagogical grammars) have *together* produced an adequate pair of EAP exercises. Even so, I suspect it is unlikely that many other EAP instructors will precipitously embark on devolving teaching materials from Marco's recently published research. If my own situation is typical, it would seem that ESP materials writers need to be pedagogically *primed* for uptake of this kind.

On other occasions, the tutor/instructor, whether concerned with speech or writing, needs to operate on levels that are distanced from the current capacities of concordance programs. Consider this paragraph from a draft of Chapter Four of Yao's dissertation, a humanistic architectural study of the traditional Thai house. (Yao, a pseudonym, was also an informant for Chang and Swales, 1999.) Her chapter is entitled 'Modern Bangkok: Toward Urbanization and Westernization', and what follows is the second paragraph, which in turn follows a brief historical overview paragraph on foreign influences on Thailand:

With such a long exposure to western cultures in the Thai history, one only wonders why the degree of change in the ways of life and houses in particular had been virtually unaffected, especially in comparison with the resurgence of western contacts over the last 150 years in Bangkok, the result of which is such an overturn of Bangkok's cityscape, with a by-product of the so-called identity crisis in Thai architecture. Put more specifically, what was it that ignited the outburst of western influence in the Thai dwelling architectural styles in the last one and a half century in spite of the long exposure to western lifestyles?

As it happened, our discussion was audio-recorded, and the section that dealt just with this particular paragraph ran for several minutes and involved a fair number of textual changes as I tried to get a clearer picture of what Yao was getting at in her long first sentence. Here is part of the exchange:

Y: I mean the Thai have uh have this contact, I mean is not that we have been um, kind of, secluded for a long time and then um only when we open out that uh that the western influences has affected the house style. I mean . . . why the change just happen now?

J: But you mean by 'now' you mean now or you mean in the last a hundred and fif—

Y: —in the last in the last hundred, yeah.

J: but that's quite a lot . . . that's even longer than I've been alive on the earth you know.

Y: Kind of, why in this period, um as opposed to the you know the four hundred years ago.

J: OK, well I think maybe we ought to clarify that.

And here's our clarification:

With such a long exposure to western cultures in Thai history, one can only wonder why a noticeable change in the ways of life – and in the styles of houses in particular – has only begun to take place in Bangkok over the last 150 years. As is well known, the result of this transformation has been an overturning of Bangkok's cityscape, producing in turn the so-called identity crisis in Thai architecture. The question remains, therefore, what precisely was it that ignited the upsurge of western influence in Thai dwelling architectural styles in the last one and a half centuries in spite of extensive previous exposure to western lifestyles.

The negotiation of meaning here between a young scholar attempting to communicate her specialised insights and a language facilitator seems a fair way off from any concordance enhancement, even though there was some language work to be done. Detachment from corpus-linguist input becomes even starker if we turn to the discussion regarding Yao's final paragraph in her chapter:

It is from this horizon, as different as it seems from only one and a half Centuries ago, that we look at the traditional house – *ruan thai* – and somehow find themselves yearning for it. In the journey to come, let us imbue ourselves in the experiences of four houses – Tub Kwan, Songkanong, Roy Nung Tub Nung (101/1), and Chaipranin – so as to begin to understand the essential characteristics and meanings of *ruan thai* that are perhaps absent from Bangkok houses today. Also, we will see if there is an alternative layer of meanings that might underlie and/or complement the existing historical explanations of the traditional house, and if so, what this alternative layer of meanings might be. These essentially are the questions which guide this dissertation. For now, let the journey begin.

J: I think I'm ready to leave this.

Y: I think about something to, to add. This? [pointing at paragraph]

J: yeah, this is very much your own voice. It's not what I would write <Y. Yeah. Henh!> but I think it's your, your own hermeneutic voice, so that's uh, if you want to say 'In the journey to come <[Y. starts laughing]>let us imbue ourselves in the experiences', then fine.

Y: Is it too cheesy? [still laughing] Because I know I sometimes write cheesy things.

J: Aah, I think it's, no I don't think so.

[Discussion then continues as to whether this unusual, and largely metadiscoursal, paragraph might belong better at the end of Chapter 3. It is decided that it is correctly placed here as a prelude to Yao's ethnographic and subjective responses to being *inside* the four Thai houses that are to follow.]

Even if we might, through a glass darkly, have some dim sense of what 'cheesiness' might consist of in academic writing, it is sure, in the present state of the art, that a suitable corpus and its companion concordancer are very unlikely to be able to come to our assistance in identifying potential criteria. (Partington, 1998, also notes that irony similarly escapes the concordance-user.) Certainly, I find it remarkable that even as proficient a non-native user as Yao should have introduced such an unexpected, subtle, and self-evaluative question about her writing into the discussion. Overall, in this tutorial we see in operation an engagement with text that, in terms of its historical niceties, in its problematisation of issues, and especially in its reader-on-a-journey metaphor, is far removed from any kind of computer-aided assistance.

FROM CLASS TO CORPUS AND BACK AGAIN

All foreign language instructors are from to time confronted with questions from their classes that need instant linguistic explanation and illustration. Few of us, I suspect, are honest enough to admit in public that we would like time to prepare a proper answer, and most of us do our best to respond 'on the fly', sometimes with inspired results, but more likely with limp, evasive, or even downright misleading responses. In my regular teaching of academic correspondence to doctoral students, one genre that is attended to is the request letter (now more likely transmitted in electronic form). This genre often has a pre-closing, quasi-formulaic 'I am looking forward to hearing from you in due course' or its variants. As fellow instructors will recognise, this sentence contains what most of us likely recognise as the classic lexicalisation of the *to+verb-ing* pattern, a pattern which many non-native speakers of English find counterintuitive presumably because they have been taught that verbs can be followed by either the infinitive ('She hopes to improve') or by a participle ('She hates revising'), but not, as it were, by both. In consequence, the *To+verb-ing* pattern is rarely used by non-native speakers, somewhat to their grammatical disadvantage, and hence, arguably, to some diminution of the professional impression they hope to engender in their academic correspondence.

If my own experience is typical, the NS EAP instructor also has a problem with this pattern, although of a very different kind; that is, on the spur of the moment, to come up with a sufficiently varied set of items that take this pattern, or to be able to concoct some semi-adequate response to some question like 'Fine, I now know about the "looking forward to doing something" pattern, but where else do we need to use it?' (Readers might like to pause for a moment of personal self-reflection at this point.)

In this kind of situation, having access to corpora provides an opportunity to construct adequate handouts in short order. The following extract is based on both the MICASE corpus for academic speech and the Hyland corpus for writing. I simply asked *WordSmith Tools* to search for all strings of the structure containing 'to *ing', where the asterisk is the usual 'wild card' standing for any letter or letters preceding 'ing'. Although this request produces unwanted items such as 'to sing' and 'to bring', it will also produce a useful collection of concordance lines that can then be sorted, edited, and manipulated so as to make them into a useful teaching handout. Below is what I have been able to do so far, and entirely as a result of having had access to corpora for the last year or so:

To+Verb+ing: An unusual pattern

(A) *To+Verb+ing following verbs.* Here are some of the more common ones:

> I am looking forward *to receiving* further information.
> He is committed *to teaching* all kinds of students.
> Her experience is not limited *to teaching* in the US.
> She is used *to running* complex statistical tests.
> She objected *to having* to redo the assignment.
> Certain groups are often subjected *to being* searched on entry.
> They admitted *to failing* to follow the safety procedures.

(Some others occur largely in speech, such as 'When he gets around to running the experiment, we may finally see some results', or 'All this boils down to saying that it won't work'.)

(B) *To+Verb+ing following some complex prepositions ending in 'to':*

> In addition *to working* on his dissertation, he is also teaching a class.
> Prior *to entering* the Ph.D. program, she worked in industry.
> With a view *to increasing* enrolment, the department constructed a website.

(C) *Following certain adjectives:*

> She is close *to completing* her grant proposal.
> This is crucial *to understanding* the nature of the problem.
> The Director may be open *to rescheduling* the project.
> He is resistant *to being* relocated.
> This is tantamount *to saying* that there is probably no difference.

(D) *Following certain nouns:*

> There is no alternative *to replicating* the experiment.
> She had several objections *to being* labelled a 'radical feminist'.

This is a useful guide *to constructing* similar computer programs.
His approach *to understanding* society is more psychological than sociological.
There was considerable resistance *to implementing* the curriculum reform.

Task C
Complete the following with a suitable lexical verb.

1. I am looking forward to ____ing your presentation at next month's conference.
2. The director is not accustomed to ____ing his decisions questioned.
3. The student admitted to ____ing a term-paper from the web.
4. The tax reform is being introduced with a view to ____ing benefits for the poor.
5. There can be drawbacks to ____ing on probabilistic measures.
6. She is averse to ____ing her dissertation abstract for a sixth time.

UNCONTROLLED CORPUS ENTHUSIASMS

I would like to argue that the two previous examples, while both small-scale, have been adequately motivated by pedagogic needs; certainly, they emerged out of language learner exigence rather than out of a research project *per se*, and my handouts (and the concomitant discussions) seem to have been well received by class participants. In contrast and as a final example, I now turn to a situation where the motivation for classroom materials derived, as it were, from the excitement of the linguistic chase. Discoursal research in or for EAP, and of any kind, is always prone to this kind of researcher projection, and here I need look no further for an example of 'overkill' than my over-long and unnecessarily detailed treatment of Reprint Requests in *Genre Analysis* (Swales, 1990). From a strictly pedagogical standpoint, such excursions into discoursal territories can be seen as an indulgence. However, from the position of applied discourse analysis, an argument can be made that the kinds of descriptive analyses that appear with some frequency in the pages of a journal such as *English for Specific Purposes* or *Text*, or which form the body of many ESP theses or dissertations, can be thought of (if a little idealistically) as banked intellectual resources whose pedagogical time has yet to come.

The final example begins with Biber, Conrad, and Reppen (1998), who present evidence that the frequencies of various types of English clause complementation are very different in conversation and academic prose. They observe, 'In particular, the extremely high frequency of *that*-clauses in conversation is directly linked to the frequent co-occurrence of these clauses with three matrix verbs: *think, say* and *know*. These are used to report two of the most important activities and states of humans: what they think/know and what they said!' (1998: 103). One issue that follows from this is the occurrence and distribution of so-called 'epistemic parentheticals' (Thompson and Mulac, 1991), i.e. the use of phrases such as 'he's wrong, *I think*', or 'We should move on, *I guess*'. With one splendid and highly significant exception, that of the corpus-based *Cobuild Dictionary*, these epistemic uses are little mentioned in standard reference materials, even though they are a frequent and highly significant part of ordinary and academic speech, at least as revealed by the emerging MICASE corpus.

So below I offer some current findings on epistemic parentheticals as cast in the form of draft teaching materials. My teaching notes state that these materials 'are designed to raise consciousness about the frequency, function and use of these epistemics in academic speech, and to encourage their greater employment by non-native speakers', a set of aims to which we will return.

Sample Teaching Materials

I have already mentioned the Hyland corpus of 80 research articles. In this corpus, and as you might expect, there are few examples of items such as *I think, I believe, I suppose, I guess* that are not quotations from speech. For example, the commonest verb used is *I think*, but this only occurs 50 times. Further, 46 instances have the standard 'formal' form where *I think* is followed by *that*. Here is an example:

1. But while *I think that* this does help explain why (2) is true, it does not explain why . . .

In other words, of the 50-odd examples of *I think* only four are 'parenthetical', all four of which are given in skeletal form below:

2. But it does, *I think*, justify an exploration of the possibilities for . . .
3. Yet they do not, *I think*, fully address problems of exclusion . . .
4. There are, *I think*, compelling reasons to say that . . .
5. This has implications, *I think*, for the analytic status to be accorded to . . .

As you probably know, items such as *I think* (without *that*) can move around in the sentence, especially in speech:

6a. *I think that* an MA thesis can be a good idea. (standard formal)
6b. *I think* an MA thesis can be a good idea. (standard less formal)
6c. An MA thesis, *I think*, can be a good idea. (parenthetical-medial)
6d. An MA thesis can be, *I think*, a good idea. (parenthetical-medial)
6e. An MA thesis can be a good idea, *I think*. (parenthetical-final)

If we now actually turn to the MICASE corpus of academic speech (selecting a version of the corpus of about the same size as that of Hyland's) we notice a number of differences.

Task One

Study the following table and answer the questions which follow.

1. On the basis of the data provided, how much more common is *I think* in academic speech than in academic writing? And what about its occurrence with or without *that*?
2. Look at the numbers and percentages for *I think* and *I believe*. What might you want to conclude from these? Do you have any explanations for the differences? In British English what might happen to the data for *I suppose*?
3. *Guess* is a well-established verb in English that has long had the meaning of *estimate*, as in 'he guessed that there were about 200 people present'. However, especially in spoken American English, the use of *I guess* has often

Table X. Common Epistemic Verbs with 'I' subjects in MICASE

I + VERB	TOTAL	V+ *that* (%)		V—*that* (%)	
I think	799	78	10%	721	90%
I guess	120	0	0%	120	100%
I hope	31	6	19%	25	81%
I would say	21	2	10%	19	90%
I believe	20	10	50%	10	50%
I suppose	13	3	23%	10	67%

come to function somewhat differently. For one thing, we can notice from the table that in our sample none of the occurrences of *I guess* was followed by *that*. The *Cobuild Dictionary* gives three uses for *I guess*:

    1. You say *I guess* that you suppose, think, or suspect that something is true or likely:
        'I guess I got the news a day or so late . . .'

    2. To indicate that you are reluctantly agreeing with someone:
        'Sure?' 'I guess so. Nothing else seems to make much sense.'

    3. To indicate what you are thinking, especially when you have just come to a decision:
        'I guess I must be going now'.

    4. Think of your own academic speech. Do you use *I guess* in all these three ways? Can you give examples of how you might use the phrase?

Task Two
In which of the following examples from MICASE does *guess* mean *estimate*?

1. I could make them two separate questions *I guess*.
2. So it was pretty on target *I guess*.
3. My answer *I guess* is, you know maybe 'Dangerous Minds' isn't that cheesy.
4. Fourteen out of oh *I guess* twenty-four total spoke.
5. Well *I guess* we have to, I *guess* we'll have to make it twenty minutes.

The use of *I guess* is associated with softening the speaker's utterance, often for a whole complex of reasons such as politeness, uncertainty, lack of authority, or embarrassment.

Task Three
Compare both the language and its effects on the following pairs of utterances. The second sentences are authentic data from MICASE (with some minor editing). As you do so, look for other words and phrases that combine with *I guess* to create the desired softening effect. Underline or highlight them.

1a. We need to decide who's gonna work on what we already did.
1b. Should we just sort of figure out who's gonna work on what *I guess* we kind of already did?

2a. So I concluded that language is really important for those students in terms of their affiliation with this community.

2b. So um basically what I came up with *I guess* is that language is really important to those students in terms of their affiliation with this community.

3a. I believe that women have rights to all sorts of things that they aren't
necessarily getting any recognition for . . . and so I decided to call myself a
feminist too.

3b. I believe that women have rights to all sorts of things that they aren't
necessarily getting any recognition for . . . and I thought oh *I guess* I'll call
myself a feminist too.

Task Four

In pairs rehearse the following dialogue, putting in *I guess* where you think
appropriate. Use ^ to indicate where you would add *I guess*. What other softeners
might you like to add? Would you like to change any words? Also reflect on your
tone and intonation.

T: Good to hear about that. Now we ought to have a look at your paper.
      Anything you want to say about it before we start?

S: I wrote it in a terrible hurry because I had two other papers due. I
      probably got off the point at times.

T: I have to agree with you. The end of your paper contradicts your opening
      section. I want you to rewrite your paper. This is what I want you to do.

S: I'm a slow writer. It will be hard for me to do a complete rewrite.

T: OK, I will offer a compromise.

The above has been a fairly extensive illustration of teaching materials
designed for an advanced class of largely Asian doctoral students studying in
America, and put together by an experienced materials writer with a longstanding interest in academic discourse. In addition, these closing illustrative
'corpus-informed' materials have themselves been modified as a result of two
class trials, where in each case both the perceived and expressed feelings of
the participants would seem to indicate that earlier versions of handouts lacked
direction and transparency. Indeed, the inclusion of the *Cobuild* definitions has
been a late and as-yet untested addition in an attempt to mitigate these criticisms.
Finally, this treatment of *I guess* is part of a larger set of occasional activities that
is designed to raise participants' perceptions about some of the salient differences between academic speech and writing that are emerging from the MICASE
project. But I am very unsure whether I will ever use these particular materials
again, at least not without considerable further investigation. As matters stand
at the moment, these materials have been, I believe, an educational failure. On
the one hand, I could claim that these materials are the most closely researched, from a linguistics perspective, of all the topics that I have introduced
in this chapter, and readers may concur that in some ways they are the 'most
interesting'. On the other, they are a discourse-analytic shot in the dark.
Although my aims included raising consciousness 'about the frequency, function and use of these epistemics in academic speech', in actual fact I have no
clear evidence as to how much my classes know about the functions of *I guess*.
I have absolutely no data on their own linguistic performances in this area.
And, most deleteriously, I have no real sense of how important or how relevant uses of *I guess* might be to academic and professional oral discussion.

FINAL CONSIDERATIONS

This chapter has had a somewhat personal and reflective tone to it, for which I do not think justifications are really necessary since the kinds of experiences that I have related will likely be very much part and parcel of the world of the ESP practitioner as we confront our pedagogical roles in the new century. Corpus linguistics is clearly here to stay, even though the USA has so far lagged behind some other areas such as Western Europe and Scandiniavia. Indeed, in Scandinavia, the prospects for *non-corpus* linguistics research, especially on English and by graduate students, seem to be rapidly disappearing (Christine Raisanen, personal communication), such is the momentum behind this movement. Another incipient concern is the spectre of a kind of reverse prescriptivism in which materials will be criticised *because* they do not adhere in their arrangements to corpus-derived information about frequencies of occurrence, such as those regarding English tenses. We may again need to be reminded, as we often have been in the past and again by Tribble (this volume) that high frequency does not entail high pedagogical priority.

These trends are of some concern, especially when we remember that ESP analysis and corpus work have *traditionally* started from very different points of departure, even though they share beliefs in the empirical descriptions of language and share doubts about the role of armchair reflection. As Mauranen (1997) shrewdly observes, while genre analysts have been at work in the last decade attempting to develop a richer socio-cognitive theory of non-literary genres, corpus linguistics take the concept of genre largely for granted in their attempt to cover language uses as completely as possible. Although this distance is now being reduced with the creation of the new micro-corpora, such as that of Marco discussed above, the *procedural* differences between discoursal top-down and corporist bottom-up approaches remain to be resolved. Although Partington (1998) is hopeful of a 'symbiosis' of these two approaches, the difficulties of achieving this in consistent and time-effective ways have been illustrated in the 'mixed' results presented in this chapter.

In narrowly linguistic terms, there may in fact be advantages to this working from both ends toward the middle, as I have tried to show with the illustrations of the position of *then* in research articles, or, less certainly, in the explorations of the *to+verb+ing* pattern beyond its use with a small cluster of verbs such as 'object', 'commit', or 'look forward to'. Neither of these, however, takes us far toward understanding the intersection of form and function in academic speech. For a more sociolinguistically significant corporist excursion into the MICASE data consider the recent study by Poos (1999) on the roles of *sort of/kind of* in spoken university settings. Such hedges have often been associated by scholars with various kinds of diffidence thought to more regularly accompany women's speech rather than that of men. Poos is able to show that, while such quantitative differences can indeed be attested in the MICASE data, they are in fact artefactual because of a powerful intervening variable. It turns out that there are fewer female speakers in science and engineering than in the social sciences and the humanities. In the sciences and engineering, many terms have fixed and well defined meanings (e.g. *atom* vs. *molecule*), while in the other areas, many important concepts are problematic (e.g. *class* and *culture*). It is this combination of university demographics and disciplinary variation in terminological status that actually underlies and explains the increased use of *sort of/kind of* by women in the Michigan data.

Poos' findings represent one interesting outcome of the MICASE project, as are Lindemann and Mauranen's (1999) revelation that *just* is overwhelmingly a minimising downtoner, Swales and Malcczewksi's (in press) explorations of the use of *multiple* discourse markers ('okay so now . . .'), or Ovens's (2000) study of the function of *no*+NP ('There's no point in discussing this further . . .') as a summative in academic discussion. However, these are the relatively meagre mature fruits of an investigative harvest in which the great majority of investigations have died on the vine. In more normal EAP circumstances, i.e. ones without the intellectual and material resources that the MICASE project possesses, the pickings may be even slimmer. The MICASE motto is the famous statement by Louis Pasteur made during his inaugural lecture at the University of Lille in 1954, usually translated as 'Chance favours the prepared mind'. Certainly, in the fragmented field of corpus-based observations, chance *ought* to favour the prepared mind, but, for those of us concerned with ESP materials development, that preparation would seem to require not only discoursal intuition but also what I have called 'pedagogical priming' – not to speak of Partington's symbiosis of 'top-down' and 'bottom-up' approaches. As matters stand at present, all this involves a stance that is hard to learn, and even harder to teach.

Part III

CONTRASTIVE RHETORIC

Chapter 9

Contrastive Rhetoric: An Expanding Paradigm

Shirley E. Ostler

The seminal paper on contrastive rhetoric (Kaplan, 1966) argues that cultures organise their expository prose in different patterns, and that these differences are due to the fact that rhetorical logic is shaped by the unique distribution of any given culture's religious beliefs, history, philosophy, economics, and basic value system. The initial notion of contrastive rhetoric focused on the shape of written academic discourse beyond the sentence. It was warmly received by many language teachers and the research to support it has been extensive. Although there have been various degrees of criticism (see e.g. Mohan and Lo, 1985; Scollon, 1997; Kachru, 2000), including from Kaplan himself (Kaplan, 1996), the overall research support not only has been positive, but has contributed to clarifying, refining, and expanding the notion. Contrastive rhetoric has stood the test of time. The initial paradigm Kaplan proposed, using as his basis academic discourse in post-secondary education, has been expanded until its original focus, that of ESL academic writing, has become a concept which has continued, and is expected to continue, to make important contributions to general written communication, in particular when that communication crosses cultural boundaries, including those defined by different genre.

This chapter elaborates on the expansion of the contrastive rhetoric paradigm and of new or growing aspects of this paradigm. Criticisms of contrastive rhetoric are addressed and a summary of some of the contributions contrastive rhetoric has made to cross-cultural communication in academic discourse is provided. Recommendations are made regarding further opportunities for expansion.

STRENGTHENING OF THE PARADIGM

Populations studied

Kaplan's original 1966 corpus identified three variables: the participants were university-level ESL students, thereby assuming that they were quite literate in their own languages; the corpus was academic placement essays; and the number of students participating from each specific language group was given. As the contrastive rhetoric research database has grown, it has become clear that though these are important variables, more specific variables provide better results. The paradigm has expanded so that now studies routinely include basic bio-data about the informants, the setting in which they compose, and, ideally, the purpose for which the essays used are written. The bio-data about the participants now usually include age, and general achievement levels, both scholastically and in terms of language fluency (Eason, 1995; Kamimura and Oi, 1997), whether they are graduate or undergraduate students, and their major disciplines where appropriate.

Early contrastive rhetoric studies usually ignored the distinction between graduate and undergraduate students. The accumulation of research data, however, seems to suggest a relationship between studies which reject the contrastive rhetoric notion and the mingling of graduate and undergraduate writers (e.g. Quaouicha, 1986; Xu, 1990), suggesting that these two levels of academic maturity should be kept separate. Most contrastive rhetoric data is still based on the performance of college students, but the expanding paradigm now includes occasional data from high-school students (Montãno-Harmon, 1988) and grade-school students (Jacobs, 1990; Reppen and Grabe, 1993; Mayfield, 1997), as well as an expansion into other than school-based task writing.

Research in terms of genre, mode, and type

Kaplan's first corpus was described as expository prose, exposition being one of several modes (c.f. Canavan, 1974). But in today's terminology, there is also great interest in the intended audience and purpose for which the text is being constructed. Hence the concept of genre has become important, although individual writers have different notions of what that term means. Briggs and Bauman (1992) note that generally everyone assumes they know what constitutes separate genres and what makes them distinctive. However, Swales (1990), Bhatia (1993), Mauranen (1993), and Colina (1997), for example, have divergent interpretations.

Because of the ambivalence regarding *genre* and *mode*, for the purposes of this chapter they are being used as follows: genre is the type of writing expected by a particular discipline, e.g. engineering, journalism, literature, which is further subcategorised into modes: narration, description, persuasion, etc., in other words the pragmatic intent of the discourse. An additional distinction is being made in terms of type: report, letter, editorial, professional journal article, etc. These terms are assumed to be dynamic, and both rule-governed and arbitrary. The rules are necessary to provide boundaries which differentiate them from other genres, modes, and types. They are arbitrary in that, since language changes over time and space, and is socially controlled, so it is expected that genres, modes, and types, as forms of language, will also display these characteristics. Since the form that any one of these takes is constrained by the social context in which it has been

Table 9.1   Examples of genres, modes, and types

Genre	Mode	Type
Engineering	description	report
Journalism	persuasion	letter
Literature	narrative	review
Economics	expository	journal papers

Note that within any genre several modes and types can differ. The list under each category is merely intended to be illustrative.

developed, what constitutes 'acceptable form' is dynamic and can be expected to change over time and across cultures.

In the 1960s, the concept of mode was well known, at least among English composition teachers, but genre was not discussed. In keeping with the conventions of the time, Kaplan called the original corpus expository essays. However, as our understanding of the variables entailed in written discourse has expanded, the descriptors have become more specific. Today, Kaplan's corpus would be designated as school essays (genre), placement (type), and expository (mode). This expansion, in terms of contrastive rhetoric variables, is reflected in the many genres, modes, and types now being studied.

In terms of writing for school-defined tasks, Kamimura and Oi (1997) analysed the structure their Japanese students selected to write two EFL school essays (genre), request and application (two modes) as letters (type), and Eason (1995) looked at the style expected in the school papers (genre), expository (mode), and dissertation (type) for an American university. Analysis of professional writing may seem to be out of the province of academic writing. However, the charge of most academic majors is to prepare novices to perform professional tasks. An appropriate writing style for the discipline is one of those tasks. The knowledge supplied by contrastive rhetoric can provide useful instructional materials for those preparing students to enter these fields. Such studies can be found for native speakers in Bartholomew (1993), who describes the macro-structure of professionally written engineering (genre) reports (type), assumed to be expository (mode). And St John (1987), Ward (1988), Mauranen (1993), and Burgess (this volume) write about cross-cultural scholarly papers in science, technology, and economics, respectively (genre), for non-native English-speaking professors, preparing papers (expository mode) for inclusion in English-language professional journals (type). Similar descriptions are available on the rhetorical expectations across styles of writing independent of educational settings: classified advertisements (Bruthiaux, 1993), print advertisements (Kavossi and Frank, 1990), newspaper editorials (Kenkel, 1991; Pak, 1996; Cho, 1998), news articles (Donahue, 1994), Arabic creative prose (Morcos, 1986) and business sales letters (Zhu, 1997). The scope of this survey serves to demonstrate how many more possibilities there are for further research in this area.

Non-native-speaking researchers

A welcome expansion in the number of non-native English speakers conducting contrastive rhetoric research should also be noted. Kaplan (1966) strongly encouraged such studies, recognising that only members of a particular speech community can provide native-speaker insights. Although large numbers of native English speakers continue to carry out contrastive rhetoric studies, many non-native speakers also have performed contrastive rhetoric research on their own languages rather than the other way around. Maynard (1996), Kubota (1997, 1998), Kamimura and Oi (1997) represent the native-speaker work done in Japanese; Kamel (1989) and El-Sayed (1992) in Arabic; Zhang (1990), Wong (1992), and Zhu (1997) in Chinese; Montano-Harmon (1998) in Mexican and Chicano Spanish; and Cho (1998, 1999) in Korean. We also find work on the less common languages: Ali (1987) in Bahasa Malaysia; Islam (1994) in Bengali, Fredrickson (1996) in Swedish; and Tirkkonan-Condit (1996), Mauranen (1993), and Yli-Jokipii (1996) in Finnish. These data have made valuable contributions to the expansion of contrastive rhetoric. Connor's 1996 book on contrastive rhetoric, itself written by a non-native speaker, is rich with reports of work being done in Finland and is a further contribution to the field.

Quantitative and qualitative approaches

In addition to the research aspects of contrastive rhetoric expanding in terms of types of populations, genre, mode and type, and non-native English speaker researchers, growth is noted in the type of research approach. Most contrastive rhetoric has been quantitative, with a variety of features being the focus of analysis. Kamel (1989), Lux (1991), Eason (1995), Reynolds (1996), and Clark (1997) used Hunt's (1970) t-units as one of their quantitative measures. The discourse bloc, suggested by Kaplan (1972), was used by Ostler (1987a, 1987b). Xu (1990), Dunkelbau (1990), and Clark (1997) used Richard Coe's 'discourse matrix'. Both measures are based on Christensen (1984). Some researchers, such as Kamimura and Oi (1997), count sociolexical features such as the presence of emphatic devices, and Wong (1992) searches out 'set phrases' in Chinese writing.

Some of the paradigm's expansion has been made possible through the development of modern rhetorical theory. Quaouicha (1986), Connor and Lauer (1985), and Connor (1990) used Toulmin's theory of argumentation. Wykel (1996) used Mann and Thompson's (1986) rhetorical structure theory. With the advances in electronic technology, computer-driven analyses are now possible. Reid (1988) used the Writer's Workbench and Biber developed, in the mid 1980s, a computer-driven analysis which makes it possible to describe immense amounts of data looking at the co-occurrence of specific lexical features (cf. Grabe (1984), Atkinson (1993), and Ferris (1991), among others). Corpus-based analysis is also becoming an important approach (see L. Flowerdew, this volume). Ferris (1991) is illustrative of a computer-assisted analysis. Using a computer program, Ferris explored the interrelationship between 62 separate text variables on 160 essays, a task nearly impossible to accomplish by hand. The amounts of data which can be analysed by electronic means are massive. Findings can be supported statistically and the results are easily replicable.

Important findings have come out of these new methodologies. But neither computer programs nor the traditional discourse analytical approaches can account for studies of the more individualised writing phenomena which are possible with qualitative studies. Nor can they deal with cases where the L1 texts of two or more languages differ in orthographic systems (although see L. Flowerdew, this volume, on parallel comparative corpus analysis).

After dominating contrastive rhetoric research, quantitative analysis has now given way in part to more qualitative methodologies. Included here would be native English speaker writing research such as that of Emig (1969), Perl (1979), and Heath (1983). ESL researchers, among whom are Pianko (1979), Raimes (1985), and Martin (1989), have used the protocol approach. Leibman-Klein (1992), Robinson (n.d.), and Holyoak and Piper (1997) use interviews and teaching logs to determine ESL students' attitudes regarding L1 literacy practices, and the learners' awareness of rhetorical contrasts. Soucy (1994) completed a longitudinal study entailing reflective logs and interrelated open-ended interviews. No quantitative measure can reveal the personal perceptions elicited by these types of studies. In order to amass a fuller description of the ways in which rhetorics contrast and the ways they do not, as well as to understand some of the causes of the differences, it is clear a variety of research approaches are needed.

Literacy

Within the field of ESL in general and contrastive rhetoric in particular, there has been increasing interest in how literacy practices are culturally and socially constructed. Researchers have focused on what, within a given culture or society, are considered good literacy practices, what skills constitute literacy, in what manner it is transmitted, and for what purposes it is used (Purves and Hawisher (1990), Connor (1996), Leki (1991)). This interest was foreshadowed by Kaplan (1966) when he wrote that logic is culturally defined and the writing product which reflects that cultural logic is socially constructed.

Rhetorical patterns vary across languages because of differences in the value systems of heritage cultures. Rhetoric, like other aspects of language, is socially constructed, and, as do other linguistic phenomena, changes as the society whose values it articulates changes. That cultures evolve writing styles appropriate to their own histories and the needs of their own societies has been demonstrated by Cho (1999), Fox (1994), Morcos (1986), and W. Zhu (1992). Literacy practices are embedded in the culture. Education, whose main task in the society is to perpetuate the values of that society, will reflect that particular culture's values. Some cultures do not provide overt instruction in expected composition norms, beyond basic graphemes. In that case, the students learn the expected conventions by first utilising their oral discourse patterns and then altering them as needed to meet the approval of their teachers (Holyoak and Piper, 1997). Given the pivotal role the schools play in the development of literacy, it is not surprising when Folman and Sarig (1990) conclude that, due to different instructional norms, American and Hebrew high-school students use different rhetorical patterns. Li (1992) finds that American and Chinese composition teachers differ as to what criteria constitute good writing. These differences merely reflect differences in cultural values and serve to substantiate contrastive rhetoric. The distinction between literacy practices also occurs outside academia. Fredrickson (1996) shows that in the filing of legal briefs, though the genre (legal) and the type (briefs) are the same, the pragmatic force, the mode or intention, is not. Yli-Jokipii (1996) demonstrates that business letters in Finland, England, and the United States all differ in degrees of explicitness and the use of social power.

Reading

Because their focus is fundamentally communicative, the skills of reading and writing are closely linked to social experience and conventions of text construction, in terms of both content and formal organisation (Carrell, 1984). Current models of reading hold that readers construct meaning from the text, based on their own schemata or experiences. The more closely matched the shared schemata, the more easily the reader processes the text (Leki, 1992). Clearly, not only writing but also reading is affected by the differences in discoursal patterns across languages and cultures. If ESL students are to be efficient readers, a knowledge of the formal schemata of written discourse which contrastive rhetoric can provide would facilitate achieving that efficiency. The formal schemata in written text vary from culture to culture and from genre to genre and this variation impacts upon ESL students regardless of their academic discipline.

Unfortunately, the amount of contrastive rhetoric research on reading is limited (but see Bell, this volume). Both Blyler (1991) and Pak (1996) recognise the cultural dynamics involved in cross-cultural reading. Blyler argues that American business letters must build consensus between reader and writer to be successful. Readers who come from another culture, including if that culture is another discipline, often lack the schemata to recognise the rhetorical strategies required to most effectively process text. If the schema of the writer is not that expected by the reader, communication of the intended message is impaired. Pak (1996) analyses editorials taken from major newspapers in three separate countries, substantiating the findings suggested by his data by interviewing sub-editors of each of the three papers. The distinctions he found were due, at least in part, to the socially constructed expectations of the different groups of particular readers. The editorials of a Mexico City newspaper take a different stance to serve the socially-constructed expectations of its reading public than do the editorials written in Madrid, and they both differ from those written for a New York City audience. Samoeil (1996) analyses the preferences of American student readers, in terms of the structure of narratives, with those of non-native speakers, finding that the non-native speakers preferred metadiscourse elements while American students did not.

Pedagogy

If English language learners are to function effectively in their chosen careers, their post-secondary education must prepare them to communicate in the requisite discourse patterns. Contrastive rhetoric findings about writing preferences in the several disciplines facilitate communication in English, not only for ESL/EFL students but also for those in the political and business areas.

Many strategies have been suggested about how to teach contrastive rhetoric, beginning with Kaplan's ideas in the 1966 paper where he suggests having students unscramble sentences of a paragraph (later tested by Santiago (1968)). Other ideas may be found in Grabe and Kaplan (1989), and Panetta (1997). Leibman-Klein (1992) and Robinson (n.d.), both anthropologists, have used a self-discovery approach.

Further, a careful survey of the findings in the literature will reveal some characteristic tendencies among particular groups which language teachers of writing might consider. Arabic writers tend to have long, what appear to Westerners almost unconnected, introductions (Morcos, 1986; Koch, 1983; Ostler, 1987a); Spanish and Arabic writers tend to use long, rather elaborate sentences, while Japanese writers often use much shorter ones (Ostler, 1987b). Chinese writing is frequently constructed of carefully woven sayings (Wong, 1992). But, in looking at these findings and other suggestions, it is crucial to remember that the individual student will have her/his unique ways of expression. Just as language students learn other aspects of language at their own paces, so it is the case with the differences in rhetoric. Stereotypes may be reinforced or even created if differences are overemphasised.

Some students, and not a few researchers, have been offended by the notion that one group of people organise and present their ideas differently from others. But there is also a positive side to the pedagogical aspect of contrastive rhetoric. Leki (1992) notes in her chapter on pedagogy (see also Leibman-Klein, 1992; and Robinson, n.d.) that there is an additional and quite valuable advantage to teaching L2 students about contrastive rhetoric. Once these students realise that these are fairly systematic differences, many of them feel relieved; this is a cultural difference, not a personal shortcoming.

ISSUES OF CULTURAL INTEGRITY AND GLOBAL ENGLISH

An issue of great concern for those working in World Englishes and 'critical linguistics' deals with the encroachment of the English language over the native languages of less dominant cultures. Kubota (1998) and Wong (1992) express concern about Western rhetoric imposing Western traditions on non-native speakers.

The encroachment of one style over another, whether it be languages or rhetorical styles, is a natural consequence when any two cultures, major and subculture, come into contact. For example, at the discipline level, Mauranen (1993) notes that part of socialising young scholars is to expose them to the culture of their chosen academic disciplines. The entire premise of freshman composition is to introduce the young academic into the discourse of the scholarly community (Kaplan and Ramanathan, 1996).

Some contrastive rhetoric studies have documented the effect of English discourse style on other languages. Eggington (1987) demonstrates that two types of academic discourse are prevalent among Korean scholars: those who have been trained in the United States use the conventions found in that discourse; those who have been trained in Korea use the traditional conventions. Zhu (1997) discloses that the business sales letter, as a genre and type, is just beginning to be developed in the PRC, the result of forty years when such writing was not needed. Although the study finds some indications that the traditional proscriptions are in force, there are still clear influences from the West. How far reaching these encroachments will be can be measured only with time.

In contrast, some research suggests that these encroachments are sometimes rejected. St John (1987) reports that experienced Spanish scientific writers resisted advice in revising their English writing to conform to the approved academic style. Holyoak and Piper (1997), in interviewing accomplished non-native speakers of English, learned that they considered themselves quite capable of resisting the influence of English, and 'viewed as patronizing any suggestion that they were impotent victims of a dominant culture' (p. 140). Li (1992) documents his attempt to build dialogue between American and Chinese teachers on what constitutes 'good writing'. The two groups simply value different criteria. In each of these studies, the informants remind us that, though they are influenced to some degree by the West, their personal tastes and native cultures are important to them (see also Burgess, this volume).

The acquisition of a new language or the language of a new discipline may indeed compromise the fluency of the first language. But not learning to use those new patterns of discourse also has consequences. The result of making necessary changes means passing a written exam, getting a committee to accept a dissertation, or a journal editor to accept a research article. The individual must make that decision. As Lu (1987), Shen (1989), and Fox (1994) clearly demonstrate, that decision is not an easy one, and an even more difficult one to implement.

However, following the lead of B. Kachru and World Englishes, this doesn't mean that those who hold the keys ought not to become better informed. As Wong (1992) cogently argues, these encroachments are no small matter to those who feel their cultures are under assault. She suggests that many of these issues are centred 'around perceived stereotypes, educational inequality, and power' (p. 73). In the same way that feminists, ethnic studies scholars, and critical theorists have sought to raise the consciousness of the academic community in the ways that gender and race are constructed to rationalise inequity, so those who work with cross-cultural communication 'must include a careful analysis of power relationships and constructions of difference' (p. 74).

EXPANSION OF THE PARADIGM THROUGH CRITICISM

Language and thought

No concept can remain viable for over a third century and not be criticised. In most instances, these criticisms have stimulated research, resulting in further expansion and refinement of the paradigm. The earliest criticism of contrastive rhetoric was that it was too closely allied with the Whorf-Sapir hypothesis, which argues that language and patterns of thinking are closely related. As Freed and Broadhead (1987) note, studies on how language use varies by speech communities could be dated back to the beginning of modern linguistics, from the work of historical linguistics, of dialectologists from the mid eighteenth century forwards until the more recent work of Labov and ethnologists such as Gumperz, Fishman, and Hymes. All fall under this category. The difference with Whorf is that, rather than merely observing and describing the language use of a speech community, he sought to explain why the differences occurred. Heath (1983) also asked why, but her rationale was based on socialisation rather than thought patterns, an approach which is apparently seen as less objectionable.

There is no question that Kaplan linked his notion to the Whorf-Sapir hypothesis. His 1966 paper is titled 'Cultural thought patterns in intercultural education'. By claiming that the rhetorical differences he observed in his corpus were the result of culturally coded thought patterns, he demonstrates that, like Whorf, he too was looking for a reason. This position was clearly a reflection of his times. The Whorf-Sapir hypothesis that language forms shape thought patterns was being hotly debated in the 1960s. Though a discussion of the strengths and weaknesses of the Whorf-Sapir hypothesis is beyond the scope of this chapter, its influence on early contrastive rhetoric can hardly be ignored. Today, few researchers in contrastive rhetoric refer to Whorf, unless it is to moderate this early position. However, before automatically condemning the hypothesis, the serious scholar might look at some recent work which examines Whorf-Sapir ideas in a fresh light. Lucy's (1992) book on the hypothesis provides not just a history but also a thorough examination of the concept and its implications. Kowal (1994) re-examines the hypothesis, urging the critics to reread Whorf in the context of his time, for a better understanding. Cho (1999) provides extensive details to illustrate that Confucian and Aristotelian rhetoric derive from quite different world views.

The relationship between language and conceptualisation can differ importantly from culture to culture, and from language to language. Koch's (1983) study of an interview of the Ayatollah Khomeini by a Western journalist describes a clash between the Ayatollah, who uses the rhetorical position which Koch calls absolute truth, and that of the Western journalist of providing evidence and support, so familiar to Western writers. Maynard (1996) claims that the Japanese see the world as a whole, another manifestation of Confucian influence, while a Western view of the world sees individual agents at work. Taylor and Chen (1991) and Cho (1999) demonstrate that thinking in a hierarchical fashion is very difficult for one socialised in a Confucian society.

The differences are developmental

Perhaps the best-known scholarly criticism of contrastive rhetoric is Mohan and Lo (1985). Among their objections are: (1) that developmental factors are responsible for the observed differences in international student writing; (2) that there are examples of different rhetorical patterns in Chinese, not just deductive; and (3) that the eight-legged essay given in Kaplan (1972) as evidence of the indirectness of the Chinese writing style is no longer in force. These charges are enlightening to analyse because they have had a significant effect on research designs and conclusion statements used by contrastive rhetoric researchers.

Though the development notion was eagerly accepted by some, it has been empirically refuted. Ostler (1987b), working with 160 essays written by Arabic-, Japanese-, English-, and Spanish-speaking ESL students whose English fluency level was intermediate or higher, was able to demonstrate that there were distinctions between and among all four groups at the sentential and the rhetorical levels. Reid (1988), working with 768 essays written by Arabic, Chinese, English, and Spanish speakers, came to the same conclusion. Hafernik (1990) set out specifically to test the Mohan and Lo claim by selecting for her corpus essays written by ESL basic writers whose first languages were Chinese, English, Japanese, and Norwegian. Basic writers would be those most likely to demonstrate that rhetorical differences were developmental. But her findings were remarkably similar to those of Ostler and Reid, whose data drew on more fluent ESL writers. Three researchers, working independently and using separate quantitative measures, analysing a total of six languages, constitutes a strong refutation of Mohan and Lo's developmental notion. Such a range of distinctions would not occur were the differences merely developmental.

However, further contrastive rhetoric research has shown that the level of fluency and cultural familiarity, variables not considered in earlier research designs, is important. Ferris (1991) found that, although there are significant sentential and rhetorical distinctions uniquely marking the four language groups in her study, there are also markers of fluency. More proficient writers use more cohesive devices, more referential rather than lexical cohesion, and exhibit a greater variety of syntactic and lexical choices.

Other researchers have noted that the greater familiarity with the culture, the less likely that the rhetorics will contrast. Kamimura and Oi (1997) discovered that, although there are demonstrable differences in rhetorical strategies among and between groups, fluency and cultural familiarity are important enough factors to be considered in future research designs.

In response to the contention that the eight-legged essay is no longer a valid writing pattern, Cai (1993) as cited in Connor (1996) presents a thorough description of the historical role of the eight-legged essay, asserting it is still an important pattern for Chinese writers. Regarding Mohan and Lo's insistence that the Chinese writing style is not indirect, Scollon (1994b) and Cho (1999) argue that the concept of self held by the Chinese makes it very difficult for them to be direct in their writing, or to assert their opinions, whereas the Western writer is taught to be self-reliant and individualistic. Intuitively, given these different philosophical positions of the East and West, two rhetorical stances would result. In an attempt to achieve harmony between the two positions, Wong (1992), in suggesting that there are two forms of linear writing, one direct and the other indirect, strongly reflects the need of a Chinese writer to achieve harmony.

Process vs. product

The other major criticism of contrastive rhetoric has come from the advocates of process writing. Some adherents of this approach, concerned as they are with the many factors involved as a text is developed, assume that since contrastive rhetoric focuses on the finished product, it is necessarily prescriptive and advocates a linear approach to composing a text. This contention is largely one of misunderstanding. The term 'linear' is used by Kaplan to describe how English expository prose tolerates fewer digressions from the topic than do preferred styles from some other cultures. The same term used by process researchers describes a process of writing, that of producing a text linearly, from an outline and with little genuine revision. Obviously, 'linear' has a separate meaning for each field.

Those who teach native-speaker composition and those who teach ESL writing are actually more rather than less compatible. They share many of the same objectives. They both consider the social construction of text. They both recognise that among the factors in the composing task are the topic, the audience, and the purpose. They are both interested, ultimately, in a final product, for why does one compose if it is not to produce a product? The two approaches are actually complementary: one focuses on the process of composing, the other on the shape of the finished product and the reasons it is shaped as it is.

Indeed, both groups have much to gain from cooperation. ESL instruction in writing has generally followed that of native-speaker research, so there is much familiar there. But contrastive rhetoric can also contribute to native-speaker composition theory. There is strong evidence that rhetorics contrast not only across cultures but also across disciplines (Bazerman (1988), Bartholomew (1993), Bhatia, Bunton, Hyland, Samraj, this volume). Since the task of freshman writing is to prepare novice academics for work in their major fields, and since contrastive rhetoric research also explores rhetorical differences across genres, then the ways in which the writing styles in these disciplines contrast can be informative to native-speaker writing research and pedagogy.

CONCLUSION

Expansion of the paradigm: what have we learned?

Kaplan's initial work has had far-reaching effects. Contrastive rhetoric research has clarified that rhetorical patterns are an essential component of language, just as are phonological, lexical, syntactical, and semantic phenomena. Rhetorical patterns behave in the same manner, changing over time and space, arbitrary yet rule-governed, and socially constructed and transmitted. Contrastive rhetoric research has shown that rhetorics do contrast across cultures, whether those are defined as major cultures or smaller sets of those cultures such as newspaper editorials, legal briefs, or economic reports.

Observed differences found in ESL writing across cultures are valid. Though there are some mitigating effects due to language fluency and cultural familiarity, the preferred patterns of the primary culture are demonstrably transferred into the second language. These contrasts are dynamic because they are socially coded, and change as the society which supports them changes. Individual performances may vary, though the variance is usually constrained within the conventions of the primary culture, again, whether that is defined as a major culture or a subculture. The conventions of a particular rhetorical preference have an effect on the ability to write acceptable prose in a target language and probably on the ability to read effectively and efficiently. This information is especially crucial for those entering any one of the several academic discourse communities.

Many of the differences in rhetorical conventions can be taught, though some individuals appear to have a more difficult time than others in adding new patterns, and some conventions may be more difficult to master than others. We have learned that changing from one rhetorical style to another is not a trivial task to accomplish; for some learners it may be very difficult to do emotionally as well as functionally. Though there are strong indications, from research showing transfer from other languages to English, that differences in preferred writing patterns may be the result of different thought patterns, until there is substantial research evidence of transfer from English to other languages, the question of whether different writing pattern preferences reflect differences in thought patterns cannot be answered.

IMPLICATIONS: WHERE THE PARADIGM CAN BE FURTHER EXPANDED

Research designs

Contrastive rhetoric researchers have learned that their research needs to be more carefully designed. Variables now take into account more specific populations in terms of physiological and educational maturity and gender as well as cultural familiarity, level of fluency, the type of task and its purpose from the perspective of the composer of the text. There are probably other variables about which we should be aware and include in contrastive rhetoric studies. Continuing research will most likely reveal these as it has those which have been discussed in this chapter. Types of texts are now more specifically identified. Although the types of research are expanding both horizontally across cultures and vertically across genre, modes and type, even greater growth needs to occur.

In terms of genres, modes, and type, in addition to school-generated essays, we are now seeing analyses of texts from outside academia. Expansion in these areas will provide a much better understanding of the many genres, and the patterns found in the modes and types of those genres. This expansion is vital to academia: the more we understand and implement information on how journalists, attorneys, and business executives construct prose, the better prepared will be the graduates of academic programmes to enter into these specialised fields.

In terms of research populations, that is those whose writing is being studied, we also need to expand the research into more writing from high school and junior high school, the better to inform those who teach freshman writing. We need to learn about the age when young writers are cognitively capable of both processing and creating texts from different modes in order to provide more realistic expectations for those preparing to teach in elementary and secondary school settings. We need to differentiate between integrative (i.e. immigrant) and instrumental (learning to write in English for a specific goal) ESL writers. We need to make a distinction between genuine texts, those which were composed for a purpose important to the writer, and less authentic ones, those which were composed for the needs of the researcher. This condition, almost a given for non-academic texts, is often not the case for academic corpora. Also, horizontally, more work needs to be done, or made more widely available, on the languages of Europe and the Pacific Basin countries other than China and Japan.

Research is beginning to be done vertically on various genres in the same languages. This also needs to be expanded, so that we can begin to support contrastive rhetoric through replication. Related to this is the need to use the same or similar quantitative measures. Currently, though there are many studies on some languages, especially Arabic, Spanish, and Chinese, it is almost impossible to correlate the findings of two or more studies. A promising movement is the research designs implementing both qualitative and quantitative data used by Pak (1996) and Reppen and Grabe (1993).

Crucial to the continued vitality of the contrastive rhetoric paradigm are two types of studies, research which looks at English speakers learning the rhetorical forms of other languages, and those conducted by non-native speakers of English. Contrastive rhetoric has been accused of not being sensitive to the issues of power dominance and inequality (Kachru, 1997; Kubota, 1998). For a discipline which purports to be deeply concerned about cultural equity, this is a major criticism. The contributions of non-native English speakers to contrastive rhetoric work is one way to mitigate that criticism. Another is to make comparisons between languages other than English. This has been done, at one level, in the four-way studies of Ostler (1987b) and Reid (1988), and the three-way study of Hafernik (1990); but these researchers are all native English speakers. Among valuable contributions would be research on two languages other than English and studies of three or more languages by non-native English speakers. Research conclusions should also include teaching suggestions for helping English writers write more effectively in another target language. After all, if Spanish writers have a challenge learning to write in English, it should be expected that English writers will have just as much a challenge to write effective Spanish.

If we are to understand the needs of language learners, we must know more about how literacy is delivered in those learners' home countries. Leibman-Klein (1992) introduced this idea, and Li (1992) provides some information regarding practices in Chinese schools. This research needs to be expanded. A basic set of information would include whether writing skills were taught in the home schools and what genres, types, and modes, how frequently, and what criteria were considered important. Other interesting questions would be how literacy is utilised and valued in the learner's non-school world in terms of availability and use of libraries, distribution of newspapers, etc.

Reading

The paradigm needs a greater expansion into reading. Indeed, reading research and contrastive rhetoric should be complementary disciplines. Especially important is research into how non-native speakers process texts in L2, and what strategies are most effective. By utilising basic reading theory, contrastive rhetoric research should be quite productive. Studies need to be developed to discover what impact different schemata have on reading comprehension. It may be the case that training language learners to identify particular modes and types so they can expect certain rhetorical patterns will make a substantive improvement on their processing and comprehension of second-language texts. Perhaps students who have been trained in contrastive rhetoric principles in writing classes will be able to transfer that knowledge to their reading skills. Such questions deserve to be explored.

Pedagogy

Though, as has been mentioned earlier, there are many suggestions about how to use contrastive rhetoric in the classroom, there is no study, to the knowledge of this writer, which has demonstrated the particular effectiveness of any given approach. There are a few anecdotal reports: Leki (1992) stating that knowing rhetorics differ across cultures eases student tension, and the ethnographic approaches of Leibman-Klein (1992) and Robinson (n.d.) to teach the principles of contrastive rhetoric are useful, but there is a tremendous amount of work to be done on this topic. In addition, it is appropriate to suggest that work to improve the teaching of writing to those who are cross-ing cultures needs to occur at the point when teachers are being trained. Unfortunately, many ESL teacher-training programmes focus too much on grammar, and disparage or ignore issues of text construction beyond the sentence, including contrastive rhetoric.

Native-speaker studies

Throughout this chapter references have been made to differences across genre and type as well as across cultures. Contrastive rhetoric needs to con-nect with these genres. A few scholars have been looking at the value of contrastive rhetoric to their field, especially in teaching ESL students to do technical writing. More is needed, for example with foreign language instruc-tion and translation. Contrastive rhetoric researchers also need to improve communication with those in rhetoric and composition. Second-language instruction has borrowed a significant amount of pedagogy from native-speaker writing theory, some of which has been transferred uncritically. This practice needs to be examined and specific distinctions made between native-speaker and non-native-speaker writing pedagogy. Further, contrastive rhetoric has much to offer native-speaker writing programmes, in terms of providing genre- and type-specific descriptions.

Power dominance issues

Finally, contrastive rhetoric needs to become more sensitive to the issues of power dominance. Several suggestions have been included above, the imple-mentation of which would alleviate this problem. More needs to be done. At the least, every contrastive researcher should acknowledge that rhetorics which differ do so in both directions and that cultures develop their preferred forms to serve the needs of their own social groups. As such, within the context of their own social units, they need to be accepted, respected, and perpetuated.

Chapter 10

Epistemic modality in argumentative essays of second-language writers

Tony McEnery and Nazareth Amselom Kifle

INTRODUCTION

In this chapter we will use learner corpora to examine how learners of English qualify the claims they make in argumentative essay writing. In doing so, we will be working within the tradition of contrastive rhetoric, but using the corpus methodology. Learner corpora are collections of language data gathered from non-native speakers/writers of English. Though the precise origin of the idea for the construction of learner corpora remains contentious, it is uncontroversial to say that during the 1990s an increasing number of learner corpora have been collected, such as the ICLE,[1] LLC[2] and HKUST corpora.[3]

In our examination of the argumentative writing of learners of English we will be contrasting their language use with that of native speakers of English. For almost four decades native corpora, typically of professional authors, have been used in the description of English (see Granger (1998a) and L. Flowerdew, this volume). We will not use corpora such as these in this chapter – the comparison of learner English against that of journalists, authors, and the like hardly seems relevant. Rather we will be comparing learner English against argumentative essays produced by non-professional native-speaking writers of English. However, before we begin this comparison, we would like to focus on the role of epistemic modality in the formation of argument.

EPISTEMIC MODALITY

Epistemic modality is concerned with the different levels of commitment that a writer brings to her/his writing. Coates (1983: 18) says, 'Of the many types of modality recognised by logicians, epistemic modality is the one which most clearly is relevant to normal language.' She defines epistemic modality as being concerned 'with the speaker's [writer's] assumptions or assessment of possibilities and, in most cases, it indicates confidence (or lack of confidence) in the truth of the proposition expressed'. Palmer (1986: 51) says that epistemic modality should also include evidential usage such as 'hearsay', 'report', and the evidence of the senses.

Traditionally only modal verbs were identified as having an epistemic function. However, studies of the semantic function of modality by Lyons (1977), Leech and Svartvik (1983), Quirk et al. (1985), Halliday (1994: 89) and Hoye (1997) as well as studies of modality and hedging such as that of Hyland (1994, 2000) include epistemic expressions which are not based upon modal verbs.[4] The whole picture of epistemic modality includes different parts of speech: verbs, adverbs, lexical verbs, adjectives and noun groups.[5] It is this broader view of epistemic modality which is taken in this chapter.

There are two basic degrees of confidence denoted by epistemic modality: these are *possibility* and *necessity* typically marked by *may/might* and *must* respectively. Epistemic possibility denotes the speaker's lack of confidence in the truth of a proposition and can be paraphrased with the words 'it is possible that . . .'. Epistemic necessity, as Coates (1983: 41) says, denotes 'the speaker's confidence in the truth of what he[she] is saying, based on a deduction from facts known'. Yet between these two cases lie a range of degrees of certainty/uncertainty. So it is hardly surprising to find that gradience is used by many linguists to clarify epistemic classification. Instead of discrete categories of epistemic modality these linguists prefer to talk about a 'degree of modality'. For example, Leech and Svartvik (1983: 128) say:

> Instead of thinking of truth and falsehood in black-and-white terms, we can think in terms of a scale of likelihood. The extremes of the scale are impossibility and certainty (or logical necessity); other, intermediate concepts being possibility, probability, improbability, etc.

To recap, epistemic modality is not realised by modal verbs alone and it has a central role to play in determining the degree of confidence a writer/speaker has in a proposition they are expressing. Knowledge of the types of epistemic modality and the style of their presentation is important for second-language writers. These help them to have at their disposal a repertoire of devices that allow them to make claims with the exact degree of certainty or doubt that they intend. Exposure to the full range of devices is also clearly of importance if the learners are to achieve native-like competence. But what may the effect be of learners choosing from a limited range of ways of expressing epistemic modality? Epistemic modality is of central importance to the formation of argument, as the next section will show. The ability to use epistemic modality effectively ties directly into the formation of effective – or at least native-like – argument.

RHETORIC AND EPISTEMIC MODALITY

The teaching of argumentative essay writing has a long history in academic writing courses. Learners are expected to show not only their language competence but also their rhetorical skills in writing. Toulmin et al. (1979) in their book *An Introduction to Reasoning* relate modality to the six elements which contribute to the quality of argument: claim, grounds, warrants, backing, modalities, and rebuttals. These elements are adopted by Mitchell (1996) as a comprehensive model of argument. Toulmin et al. (1979: 26), addressing qualification in argument, say,

> the degrees and kinds of strength with which warrants authorise us to argue vary greatly from one kind of case to another. Some lead to 'probable' conclusions; others establish 'presumptive' conclusions; and so on. Most practical reasoning is in fact concerned with what is 'probably,' 'presumably,' or 'possibly' the case rather than with 'certainties' alone. So we shall need to look carefully at the different kinds of qualifying phrases (modals) characteristic of different types of practical argument.

Long et al. (1995: 77) discuss this in relation to the alternative point of view, i.e. the appeal to probability and possibility which are among a range of argumentative options available to a writer in a particular rhetorical situation. The mastering of epistemic devices (referred to as EDs from here) helps writers to negotiate views and ideas and qualify claims at an appropriate level of commitment. Many studies point out that both the structuring of an argument and qualifying one's own claims by means of epistemic expressions in order to create a relationship between grounds and claims are difficult for both native and non-native writers of English. As Holmes (1988: 21) says, 'There is widespread agreement among both theoretical and applied linguists that modality is a common and very important aspect of English which is not easy for first and second language learners to acquire.' However, this is more problematic for second-language writers.

LEARNER LANGUAGE AND EPISTEMIC MODALITY

Studies of EDs expressing a writer's commitment to a claim are numerous. However, not much research has been dedicated to identifying the ways second/foreign-language learners qualify their claims as writers in their own right (Hyland and Milton, 1997b). As will be made clear in this section, Hong Kong has been an important centre for such work.

Hu, Brown, and Brown (1982) demonstrated that Chinese second-language writers seem more direct and authoritative in tone and make more use of EDs from the 'certainty' end of the epistemic continuum than native speakers (referred to as NS from here). Allison (1995) supports this finding by demonstrating that Hong Kong writers make more unjustified, strong assertions more frequently than NS writers. Hyland and Milton (1997b) compared Hong Kong learner writing with NS writing, and found that both groups use a narrow range of EDs, especially modal verbs and adverbs. However, these tendencies were more pronounced among non-native speakers (referred to as NNS from here). They concluded that the manipulation of expressions of doubt and certainty in academic writing is particularly problematic for NNS students. The picture which can be built up from the studies so far – which have largely been carried out in Hong Kong – is that learners seem prone to choosing epistemic modal expressions from the 'certainty' end of the continuum and that they have a limited repertoire of devices at their disposal for realising epistemic modality. Obviously these findings may be specific to the context – both cultural and pedagogical – within which language learning was taking place. Consequently, we decided to examine a different context – language teaching in Eritrea – to see how NS and NNS use of epistemic modality compared, in part to see how generalisable the Hong Kong results were, but also to see what explanations from the pedagogical context could be developed for any differences observed.

CORPORA AND METHODOLOGY

The corpora used in this study

We compiled two corpora for this study, both of approximately 22,000 words. Our learner corpus was compiled from 92 short argumentative compositions written by Eritrean second-year university students, who were around 20 years of age when the essays were written. The students had all taken the English Foundation Course at the University of Asmara which prepares them to pass the IELTS test (International English Testing System). The second corpus was a corpus of argumentative essays by English native speakers. These brief essays were written by British school children of around 16 years of age.

All of the essays were originally handwritten and were typed into a word processor by the authors of this chapter to make them into machine-readable texts. Spelling mistakes in the original scripts were not normalised during this process, as we intended in a later study to examine misspellings in the corpus. Not correcting the spelling was to prove a problem for our study, as will be noted later (see 'Starting the analysis').

All compositions in both corpora contain metadata about each text – the name of the institution where it was produced, the genre and topic of the text, and the name/sex/age of the informants. A basic text-encoding initiative compatible mark-up (Sperberg-McQueen and Burnard, 1994) was given to the texts to allow such metadata to be systematically encoded and retrieved. In addition, the texts were part-of-speech tagged using the CLAWS part-of-speech tagger (Garside, Leech, and Sampson, 1987).

Having described the collection and computerisation of the data, it seems useful at this point to comment on how comparable the two groups of students are. Variables, such as age, year of study, and course of study are very often different for NS and NNS groups in learner corpus-based studies. This is somewhat inescapable, as the educational environments being compared are so different that simply matching age groups and educational levels is meaningless. Such is the case here – the Eritrean school starting age is nominally 7 but in many areas schooling does not start until 11. This contrasts with the British context in which schooling begins towards the end of a child's fourth year. Eritrean students who complete secondary education go straight to university. They do not have any pre-university preparatory course. Their education is barely comparable to students in the UK of the same age. However, there are some points of comparison between the British teenage writers and the Eritrean writers in question – both NS and NNS informants are writing argumentative essays on general topics for exams. Also, the Eritrean students have just finished basic secondary schooling and the British students are just coming to the end of their basic secondary schooling. While matching populations perfectly in learner corpora studies is always problematic, we believe that the comparison undertaken here, while not perfect, is defensible.

Starting the analysis

In order to call up EDs from the NNS and NS corpora, a list of the most frequent EDs in academic writing was prepared from Holmes (1988) and Hyland and Milton (1997b). This consisted of 100 items (see Appendix 10.1).

WordSmith Tools (Scott, 1996), specifically the *concordance* feature of the program, was used to capture all of the instances from the corpora of the EDs identified in Appendix A. The concordance output was then subjected to qualitative analysis in order to isolate true EDs from other entries. For example, we found 499 modal verbs in the Eritrean students' corpus and 650 in the native-speaker corpus. However, since not all modal verbs may act epistemically in a given context, epistemic modal verbs were identified in their context and unwanted entries were deleted, resulting in an adjusted count of 231 epistemic modal verbs for the non-native speakers and 249 for the native speakers.

We also retrieved concordances of misspelled EDs common in the data, e.g. *blief, bilieve, beleive, possibily, normaly,* in order to include them in the results. It was at this point that we discovered that normalising the spellings in the corpus would have been useful.

Having identified the EDs in the corpus, we introduced a simple annotation in each corpus to mark epistemic modality. As part of our annotation of each ED in the corpus, we decided to attach a marker to indicate roughly where the word fell on the probability continuum, along the lines argued by Leech and Coates (1979), Leech and Svartvik (1983), Quirk et al. (1985), Coates (1983), and Halliday (1994). While the placement of individual examples into concrete categories remains to some degree subjective, we argue that many linguists have found an attempt to roughly divide up the continuum for purposes of research useful (see Halliday, 1994; Holmes, 1988; and Hyland and Milton, 1997b). We also used best practice in corpus annotation to achieve consistent results by applying 'case-law' decision-making criteria across the corpora (see Garside, Leech, and McEnery, 1997 for a comprehensive overview of practices in corpus annotation). Throughout, independent verification of decision making was undertaken and reference was made to arbitrating linguists where necessary.

Turning to the specifics of the annotation scheme itself, we decided that we should follow the work of Halliday (1994: 357) and Hyland and Milton

(1997b: 193) in adopting three categories of epistemic commitment. The three degrees of epistemic commitment we used placed EDs on a continuum of probability, which contained three categories: *certainty* (highest probability), *probability* (medial probability), and *possibility* (low probability).[6] Having carried out this annotation we were able to embark upon a comprehensive comparison of the use of EDs by both NS and NNS writers, which is summarised in the next section.

RESULT AND DISCUSSION

Total frequency of devices in the NNS and NS corpora

The NNS and NS show a remarkable difference in the total frequency of the EDs they employ (see Figure 10.1).

EDs in the NNS and NS corpora total 439 and 686 respectively. The NS writers use roughly half as many EDs again as the NNS writers. As Table 10.1 reveals, the native speakers use three devices per hundred words while the non-native speakers use two devices per hundred words.

Neither group uses all of the 100 EDs we examined, but the NS writers do use a wider range of EDs than the NNS writers (59 and 49 respectively). Some of these devices occur much more frequently than others, however. Table 10.2 shows that certain devices occur with very high frequency (e.g. five EDs occur with a frequency of between 50 and 100 uses in the NS corpus) while others are used infrequently (e.g. 23 devices occur only once or twice in both the NS and NNS corpora).

The top ten items account for 70% and 64% of the total frequencies of EDs in the NNS and NS data respectively (see Table 10.2). Even though the number of devices used differs, both groups show significant similarities in their use of those devices listed among the ten most frequent (see Table 10.3).

Six devices (shown in bold in Table 10.3) are common to both groups although the frequency of occurrence for each such word is noticeably different between the groups. For example, *may* is at the top of the list for the NNS writers and third for the NS writers, making up 26% and 9% of the top ten devices for NS and NNS writers respectively.

Yet in spite of superficial similarities between the uses of EDs by the NS and NNS writers, Tables 10.3 and 10.4 actually show some very real differ-

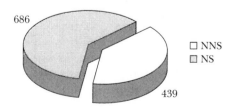

Figure 10.1   The proportion of devices in the NNS and NS corpora

le 10.1   Total number of devices per 100 words

	Corpora	Total no. of devices	Devices per 100 words
NNS	22,000	439	1.99
NN	22,000	686	3.12

Table 10.2   Variety of epistemic items in the NNS and NS data.

Frequency of occurrence of device	Number of epistemic devices in the frequency band	
	NNS	NS
100–50	2	5
49–10	7	10
9–5	10	12
4–3	7	9
2–1	23	23
Total	49	59

Table 10.3   The ten most frequent epistemic devices in the NS and NNS corpora

Rank	Non-native speakers		Native speakers	
	Device	Frequency	Device	Frequency
1	**may**	121	believe	119
2	**will**	60	**would**	107
3	**argue**	37	**may**	63
4	**would**	18	**think**	59
5	perhaps	18	**will**	51
6	might	15	view	26
7	could	15	**argue**	19
8	**always**	13	**always**	16
9	**think**	13	opinion	16
10	maybe	10	should	12
Total		320		488

ences in ED usage between the two groups. Most noticeably, *believe,* which is not among the top ten devices for the NNS, is the preferred device in the NS data. Moving on to consider words which are shared, *would,* the second device in the NS list, occurs six times more frequently than in the NNS list, a statistically significant difference. Devices of epistemic possibility such as *may, perhaps, might, could,* and *maybe* make up 56% of the ten most frequently used devices in the NNS list, while devices of epistemic possibility make up only 14% of the top ten devices in the NS data. It is little surprise that these differences are statistically significant.

Table 10.4   Tests of significance for differences in shared top ten ED devices

Word	NNS	NS	Significance test
may	121	63	8.13*
will	60	51	3.42*
argue	37	19	4.26*
would	18	107	−5.99*
always	13	16	.65
think	13	59	−3.77*

Note: Significant differences are asterisked. The significance test we carried out was a test for significant proportions, developed by Dr Damon Berridge, Applied Statistics Dept., Lancaster University. Figures in the range below −2.56 and above +2.56 are significant at the 1% level.

Table 10.5   Top ten EDs used by part-of-speech

Part-of-speech of ED	Non-native speaker	Native speaker
Modal verb	229	233
Lexical verb	50	197
Adverb	41	16
Noun	0	42
Adjective	0	0

Finally, when we consider the part-of-speech used to realise epistemic modality by the two groups, further differences become apparent (see Table 10.5). While both the NS and NNS writers most often use modal verbs to realise epistemic modality, the NS writers use a wider range of lexical verbs more frequently for this purpose. Similarly, NNS writers use a wider range of adverbs more frequently than NS writers for this purpose. Most noticeable is the use of certain nouns by NS writers, as nouns are completely absent from the NNS top ten.

These preferences, clear in the top ten, largely hold throughout the corpus, as shown in Table 10.6. NS writers employ substantially more lexical verbs and epistemic nouns than the NNS writers. Non-native writers rely

Table 10.6   Epistemic grammatical categories in non-native and native corpora

Epistemic grammatical category	NNS	NS	Significance test
Modal verbs	231	249	−4.78*
Adverbs	121	103	4.78*
Lexical verbs	87	232	−5.46*
Nouns	27	84	−3.54*
Adjectives	9	18	−0.71
Total	**439**	**686**	

Note: Significant differences are asterisked.

more on modal verbs and adverbs. Both groups of learners use relatively few epistemic adjectives, although the NS writers use slightly more adjective qualifiers than the NNS writers. Indeed, the differences in ED usage by part-of-speech are statistically sigificant across the board, with the exception of the least numerous category for both group, adjectives. This final result in itself may have been derived largely because of the few examples of either group using adjectives as EDs.

Gradience and epistemic modality in the corpora

The two groups of learners are similar in the items they use, despite many significant differences related to frequency of usage. For example, in the 'certainty category': *argue, think,* and *will;* in the 'probability category': *believe, seem,* and *would;* and in the possibility category: *may, might,* and *could.* Both the NS and NNS writers frequently employ strong forms of usuality which make up 80% and 65% of the EDs for NS and NNS writers respectively. However, beyond this similarity differences emerge.

Table 10.7 shows the result of the analysis of all the individual devices in their context in order to categorise them according to the degree of commitment they convey.

This analysis reveals that the two groups of writers differ in the degree of certainty or doubt they employ in their writing (Table 10.7). The results seem to contradict the views of many NNS writing researchers. For example, Hyland and Milton (1997b: 193) say learner writers use 'firmer assertions, more authoritative tones and stronger writer commitments when compared with native speaker discourse'. While this may be true of the Hong Kong context, it does not appear to be true of the Eritrean context.

Table 10.7 shows that the Eritrean learners use less assertive language than the native speakers and make use of a considerable number of epistemic possibility devices. The native speakers use more devices from the higher commitment band and devices of epistemic probability. In the NNS result the frequency of the epistemic possibility devices is higher than either of the other categories. There is also a tendency towards polarisation in the NNS writing, with devices drawn largely from either extreme of the certainty continuum, and medial devices being disfavoured.

Having arrived at a broad description of the differences between native and non-native speakers in the employment of EDs, we decided to check

Table 10.7 Frequency distribution of the degrees of epistemic meaning in NNS and NS

Categorical meaning	Frequency count NNS	Frequency count NS	Significance
A. Certainty	130	279	−2.16
B. Probability	92	235	−2.38*
C. Possibility	189	126	.35

Note: The remaining cases not reported here fall in the usuality continuum.

back with the pedagogical context within which English was learned by the students in order to seek explanations for the differences we could observe. We decided to examine the materials used to teach English to the students, partly because this was clearly a potentially useful source of explanation, but also because we lacked the resources to undertake a systematic study of cultural differences between the Eritrean and English students. Similarly there is no corpus of Eritrean to use as a source of evidence for interference errors. Nonetheless, as will be shown in the next section, the classroom materials the students had used in Eritrea to learn English furnished an ample explanation for most of the differences we had observed.

EXPLANATIONS

As noted, we decided to investigate what role classroom materials may have had to play in the differences we have observed. In focusing on classroom materials our task was greatly simplified by the fact that all of the students we had contact with in Eritrea had been learning English from an in-house publication of the University of Asmara, *Foundation English (Coursebook EN202)*. This textbook has no one author, and is available only within Eritrea. There was no evidence that students used other coursebooks in their own study time – or even had contact with other sources of written English. So we had both a conveniently limited study and also a context within which the influence of the coursebook could be very strong.

In this section, we want to examine a couple of differences between the NS and NNS speakers and trace those back to what we claim are the roots of that difference – *Foundation English*. We will first look at an explanation of the difference between NS and NNS speakers in terms of levels of commitment, and then move on to consider the preference for modal verbs and adverbs the NNS writers had.

The use of tentative EDs in the NNS corpus

It is no surprise that, when *Foundation English* was reviewed by us, we found that it puts emphasis on tentative and weak EM devices. It is probable that the Eritrean learners have been influenced by this to use more devices of epistemic possibility than devices of epistemic probability – in short, if the students are not sure, rather than grading their uncertainty they use EDs which express as little commitment to a proposition as possible. The model of argument which the NNS were given in *Foundation English* highlights devices such as 'perhaps' which also appear among the top devices to express epistemic possibility. The Eritrean students are told to use more tentative and uncertain language (*Foundation English*: 1):

> Hedging devices . . . protect us when we write . . . making our conclusions less certain . . . This is a characteristic of scientific writing.

Following this statement, the students are presented with examples of EDs with a marked preference for weak devices. This fact alone may account for the polarisation of EDs between strong and weak in the NNS data. This is persuasive evidence to suggest that differences between the NNS writers and NS writers are at least to some degree attributable to the texts the NNS writers learned from. Culture may or may not form a part of the explanation of the differences between NS and NNS writers. Textbooks almost certainly do. Let us look more closely now at the primacy of modal verbs and adverbs in the NNS data.

The preference for modal verbs and adverbs as EDs in the NNS corpus

There is little doubt that modal verbs as EDs receive inordinate attention in the syllabus followed by English-language learners in Eritrea, which pays scant attention to other EDs. This is no surprise – as Holmes (1988) says in her analysis of the treatment of epistemic modality in ELT textbooks, 'Many (textbooks) . . . provide an unjustifiably large amount of attention to modal verbs, neglecting alternative linguistic strategies for expressing doubt and certaintly.' The Eritrean coursebooks present the students with a limited range of options for expressing epistemic modality – *Foundation English* (p. 5) presents a list of EDs formed of modal verbs, adverbs, and quantifiers without any indication as to which of these devices are more frequently used and with no reference to other parts-of-speech which may help form epistemic modality. This fact alone may account for the startling primacy of modal verbs and adverbs over all other parts-of-speech in realising EM as shown in NNS writing in Table 10.5. This is evidence to explain the overuse of modal verbs and adverbs by the NNS as EDs.

Both of the examples covered here illuminate how crucial the role of the textbook may be in forming the language use of NNS writers. This is especially true in a context such as Eritrea, where access to resources which may balance out the views of one particular textbook (e.g. other texbooks, NS writing) is severely restricted.

PEDAGOGICAL IMPLICATIONS

Learner corpora are of paramount importance in the teaching of language. The analysis of learner language gives information on the learners' linguistic competence and areas of difficulty they experience. This information can be used to revise syllabuses and teaching materials in order to make them meet learners' needs without wasting time on those language areas which are not of immediate importance to the learners.

Second- and foreign-language syllabuses often present language content from 'expert' native speakers corpora, which in most cases have undergone various stages of editing and which do not inform us of the level of difficulty experienced by particular learners. This can now be rectified through reference to the analysis of learner corpora.

In this present study the comparison of NS and NNS corpo strates differences in the total frequencies of the devices they emplo information may help in the revision and teaching of EDs in NNS coursebo and syllabuses. As Holmes's (1988) and Hyland's (1994) evaluations of ELT textbooks have shown, most materials do not give due attention to EDs. In most cases the semantic function of EDs is disregarded and emphasis is put on the syntactic aspect of modals. Moreover, epistemic modal verbs are taught as principal types of epistemic modality and less treatment is given to adverbial, lexical, adjectival, and noun groups. Therefore, our analysis of the NNS data would help to balance the teaching of EDs.

CONCLUSION

The comparison of the NNS and NS writers reveals that the former group uses more tentative and weak devices and the latter employs stronger devices which convey a higher degree of confidence. Crucially, the NS speakers employ devices of medial certainty much more frequently than the NNS writers, who tend to use polarised EDs. The NNS learners were trained not to use strong devices and to sound more tentative in making claims. In their coursebook they were given few devices, which they then tended to overuse in their writing. However, since the choice of using one device over another depends on the learners' personal beliefs, attitude, and confidence, textbooks should not prescribe which degrees of confidence are appropriate for the learners. Learners should be given a balanced inventory of EDs to allow them to develop their own epistemic language strategies.

With this said, there are some points of caution to be sounded. First, we are dealing here with only one genre of writing. As Hyland (2000) clearly demonstrates, patterns of usage of epistemic modality may vary by discipline. One should not assume that patterns of usage revealed in argumentative essay writing will be replicated in scientific writing, for example. Secondly, we are not able to rule out cultural style as a possible explanation of the differences between NS and NNS writing we have seen. Here we return firmly to the field of contrastive rhetoric. Although the quantitative, corpus-based aspect of contrastive rhetoric is important, we feel it would be equally informative to relate such results to the context of language learning via site visits to gather learning materials from the classroom context and explorations of the culture of the NNS writers. It is such activity, we feel, which allows the corpus work to proceed from description to explanation and which would allow a fuller exploration on the possible role of culture in explaining differences in the use of epistemic modality between NS and NNS writers.

NOTES

1. International Corpus of Learner English, a project coordinated by Granger (1994, 1998a).

ers' Corpus, compiled by Longman and available for pur-
rposes from them.

ity Science and Technology corpus, organised by John Milton
KUST.

te that – as is often the case in linguistics – there is terminolo-
the definition of types of modality. For example, Quirk et al.
clough (1989: 126), and Halliday (1994: 89) all use slightly differ-
in categorising types of modality, yet all seem to arrive at roughly
iption of the phenomenon.

5. For example see Appendix 10.1.

6. Another scale along which EDs vary is the scale of *usuality*, running from strong (*always*) to weak (*sometimes*). We did not carry out an analysis of usuality in our data as the number of usuality EDs used by either group was very small – there are only 28 NNS and 46 NS examples of words drawing on the usuality scale. Consequently we have limited our analysis to the probability scale, where by far the largest number of EDs for both groups are drawn from (see Table 10.6 for details).

APPENDIX 10.1 100 ITEMS FROM THE MOST FREQUENT EPISTEMIC DEVICES IN ACADEMIC WRITING

The following list is compiled from Holmes (1988) and Hyland and Milton (1997b). It is a result from the analysis of the Brown and LOB corpus of the most frequent epistemic devices in written language. This is substantiated from the literature on modality by Coates (1983), Leech and Svartvik (1988), and Quirk et al. (1972).

Modal verbs
could
couldn't
may
might
should
shouldn't
would
wouldn't
will
won't

Adjectives
apparent
certain
a certain extent
clear
likely
obvious
evident

possible
probable
sure
unlikely

Nouns
assumption
belief
certainty
chance
claim
danger
doubt
estimate
evidence
explanation
fact
fear
hope
idea

opinion
possibility
tendency
theory
view

Lexical verbs
appear
argue
assume
believe
claim
doubt
estimate
expect
indicate
know
predict
presume
propose

seem
speculate
suggest
suppose
tend
think

Adverbs
about
actually
almost
always
(not) always
apparent
approximately
around
certainly
clearly
commonly
definitely

definitely
doubtless
essentially
evidently
frequently
generally
in fact
in general

in theory
in X's opinion
indeed
largely
likely
maybe
never
naturally

necessarily
normally
obviously
of course
often
perhaps
possibly
presumably

quite
rarely
relatively
sometimes
surely
undoubtedly
usually

Chapter 11

Packed houses and intimate gatherings: Audience and rhetorical structure

Sally Burgess

INTRODUCTION

Interest shown in academic discourse by applied linguists, sociologists of science, and teachers of languages for specific purposes has produced a substantial and diverse body of research. A particularly rich seam running though the academic discourse literature is work which can be broadly described as 'genre analytic', spanning, as it does, studies carried out by Systemic linguists in Australia and beyond, by the North American New Rhetoricians, and by those, like myself, who are primarily concerned with teaching English for academic purposes.

Work in all three 'schools' now goes back almost two decades, landmark publications being Hasan's (1985) exposition of 'generic structure potential', Miller's (1984) articulation of genre as social action, and Swales's (1981a) initial study of research article (RA) introductions in which he presented his four-move schema. While the first two publications I mention have had enormous impact well beyond the particular 'schools' to which they might be ascribed, their influence on applied linguistics research into academic discourse is arguably less immediately apparent. The work of John Swales, however, led directly to a flurry of publications in the 1980s and early 1990s in many of which the RA is the focus of attention. A number of these studies deals with the introduction section while others have been concerned to arrive at move analyses of other subgenres such as the abstract (Salager-Meyer, 1990, 1991) and the discussion section (Hopkins and Dudley-Evans, 1988). Neither has the research been restricted to the RA. An entire issue of the Brazilian journal *ESPecialist* was devoted to genre analysis in the Swales tradition and includes papers on the research interview (da Silva, 1991) and the research questionnaire (de Souza, 1991). Bhatia's (1993) volume extended the applications of a Swalesian approach to other professional discourses and has, in turn, inspired an impressive body of work. There have also been several attempts to validate Swales's (1981a) four-move model empirically, the best-known of which is Crookes (1986). Two contrastive studies which also sought to validate the first of Swales's models are Taylor and Chen (1991) and Gnutzmann and Oldenburg (1991).

While interest in genre studies remained high throughout the 1980s, the publication in 1990 of Swales's *Genre Analysis* saw even greater attention being paid to his work and a further series of publications making use of his framework of analysis. Many of these focused on research article introductions and set out to apply Swales's account of rhetorical structure to publications in specific disciplinary areas. Once again there were also those who sought to arrive at a description of the move structures of other elements of the macro-structure of the RA, a case in point being Brett's (1994) analysis of the results sections of sociology articles. Interest in the model also saw its further application in contrastive studies in which publications by speakers of languages other than English were examined (see, for example, Duszak, 1997). Some of these studies, like that of Taylor and Chen (1991), not only compare publications produced by mother-tongue English speakers with similar publications in the L1s of non-English-speaking background (hence NESB) writers but also examine these writers' publication *in English*.

Contrastive studies of L1 and L2 writing of speakers of a range of languages have a history almost twice as long as that of genre analysis (for a very complete survey of this work see Connor, 1996). The assumption has generally been that differences that emerge between the rhetorical preferences of non-English-speaking background writers and those from an English-speaking background have their origins primarily in the language culture of the writer. Increasingly, 'language culture' is understood as involving far more than the writer's L1 to encompass features of the rhetorical and cultural context. Many contrastive rhetoric studies focus on this context by direct examination of other genres such as style manuals and school writing instruction (Leki, 1991), examiners' reports (Clyne, 1987b) or try to gain information about the rhetorical context less directly through, for example, examination of students' perceptions of instructors' preferences (Degenhart and Takala, 1988).

There are also those who have undertaken contrastive genre analyses of the RA and other academic genres. The preferred approach has been either to analyse a corpus of texts in a language other than English using one or other of the Swales models or to compare the rhetorical structures of these texts with texts written by ESB scholars. More recently (see, for example, Čmejrková, 1996) researchers have used the more complete design originally applied by Taylor and Chen (1991) and have looked at NESB writers writing *in English* as well as in their L1. Although the written output of speakers of Spanish was initially a focus of a number of contrastive rhetoric studies (Connor, 1996 cites Santiago, 1970 and Santana-Seda, 1970) it has until comparatively recently received less attention from genre analysts based in Europe than have eastern and northern European languages.

In the study presented here, I examined the rhetorical preferences of Spanish English Language Studies specialists (ELSS) publishing in *both English and Spanish* and compared these preferences with those of writers in another two groups: Spanish Hispanic Studies scholars publishing exclusively in Spanish

(SpHSS) and English-speaking background scholars publishing their work in international linguistics publications (ILSS). My objective was to look closely at the role of the writer's language background in variation in rhetorical structure across the four groups. My suspicions were that other factors, namely size and nature of audience, had a bigger 'say' in what went on.

Like much other work in genre analysis, my study focused on the RA introduction. There are good reasons, I believe, for our continuing scrutiny of the research article as a whole and the introduction in particular. Publication of research articles continues to be seen as a reliable measure of a scholar's academic productivity and plays a major part in determining academic status. The introduction section is a particularly crucial subgenre in that the writing of introductions is for most, if not all of us, a major rhetorical hurdle. Novice researchers and those forced to publish in languages other than their own can find it even more daunting. The more we know about this subgenre the better able we are to make it a surmountable hurdle for all who need to make use of it.[1]

For readers too, the introduction of the RA is particularly significant. According to Swales (1990: 137) the introduction is the section that readers read first in normal circumstances, though Berkenkotter and Huckin (1995) in their study of the reading behaviours of molecular biologists found that this was not the case. Their readers read the various sections of the RA in order of their 'newsworthiness'. Be that as it may, aside from presenting newsworthy research, RA authors must establish their credibility with the discourse community they address and this they do via the introduction (Berkenkotter and Huckin, 1995: 31–2). Ordinary readers, Berkenkotter and Huckin suggest (1995: 38), rely on journal editors and peer reviewers to test this credibility through close readings of those sections of the RA with lower news value. The introduction is a case in point. Even if normal readers do not read introductions first (or perhaps ever), editors and reviewers do and the researcher must get past these gatekeepers if the knowledge claims she makes are to be certified through publication.

Myers (1992a) sees RAs as sites for the presentation of these knowledge claims to the community. Decisions about the community's views on what is research-worthy or otherwise will influence not just the 'what' of research but the 'how'. This influence is revealed in the discourse conventions writers use to present their work in such a way that they appear neither naively prolix nor arrogantly abrupt. Judgements as to what is acceptable in the stages leading up to the knowledge claim vary from one community to another and this variation, as Taylor and Chen (1991) suggest, is more likely to occur in the introduction than it is in some other sections of the RA (viz. methods and materials or results sections).

By applying Swales's (1990) CARS model (see Figure 11.1) it might be possible to see how writers' judgements vary from one rhetorical context to another. They might, for example, choose not to put their energies into creating a niche for their research – Swales's (1990) Move 2 – because they view the problem they address as entirely uncharted territory for their readers.

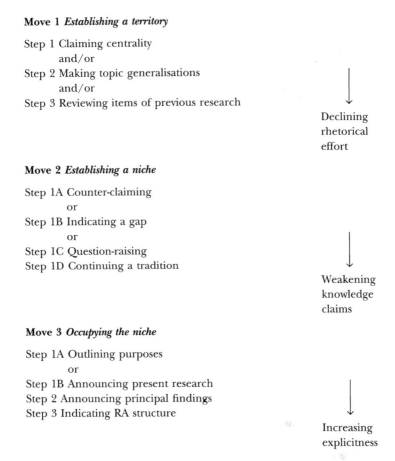

Move 1 *Establishing a territory*

Step 1 Claiming centrality
    and/or
Step 2 Making topic generalisations
    and/or
Step 3 Reviewing items of previous research

Declining
rhetorical
effort

Move 2 *Establishing a niche*

Step 1A Counter-claiming
    or
Step 1B Indicating a gap
    or
Step 1C Question-raising
Step 1D Continuing a tradition

Weakening
knowledge
claims

Move 3 *Occupying the niche*

Step 1A Outlining purposes
    or
Step 1B Announcing present research
Step 2 Announcing principal findings
Step 3 Indicating RA structure

Increasing
explicitness

Figure 11.1   Swales's (1990) CARS ('Create a Research Space') model

They may prefer in such cases to give greater weight to Move 1, step 2 ('Making topic generalisations') or to providing an extensive historical review of the literature (Move 1, step 3). Publication of a research article signals willingness on the part of the community to entertain the knowledge claim the writer makes. A writer addressing a national or local community may be able to make a higher- or lower-level knowledge claim or, borrowing Swales's ecological metaphor, to establish a much larger niche, or indeed a much smaller one, than she would if she were to address the international community, and still get her work into print. What is unsurprising in one community (and therefore unpublishable) may be newsworthy in another.

Even a cursory glance at RA introductions published in Spanish journals suggested to me that they were distinguishable from their international counterparts in terms of the kind of knowledge claim a writer could make and the way the ground is prepared for that knowledge claim. More to the point it seemed that the Spanish writers were adopting different strategies in different publication contexts, viz. Hispanic Studies journals (SpHSJs) and English

Language Studies journals (ELSJs). I wanted to look further at the nature of the groups of readers addressed by the two publication contexts and their role in shaping rhetorical structure.

DISCOURSE COMMUNITY AND AUDIENCE

I used the term 'groups of readers' deliberately in my last paragraph though I have already referred to 'discourse communities' on several occasions in citing the work of others. I would like now to turn to what for me remains a major question: What is a discourse community and what is its relationship to other similar characterisations of groups and, in particular, to audience?

In the literature one encounters a range of apparent precursors of the term 'discourse community', which shed light on how the concept evolved and on what mechanisms determine membership of such a group. Becher uses 'disciplinary culture' in an early study (1981) and 'academic tribes' in the title of a later work (1989) comparing the discourse practices of academics in a range of disciplines. Geertz (1983: 157), to whom the initial impetus for the ethnographic study of these 'academic tribes' might be attributed, uses the term 'discourse community' himself, but quotes Kuhn (1970) as using 'disciplinary matrix' and Boyle 'invisible colleges'. Fish (1989: 349) quotes Bruffee as advocating introducing students to 'knowledge communities'. Thus, we might infer that members of a discourse community share knowledge, customs, and practices but that they need not necessarily occupy some shared space in real time (hence their invisibility). By the late 1980s we find many scholars, Berkenkotter et al. (1988) and Russel (1990) among them, apparently at home with the term 'discourse community'.

Others, however, are less content. Miller (1994) prefers the term 'rhetorical community', raising concerns about examples of 'discourse communities' in the literature that might suggest they are more tangible entities than she believes they are, one such example being Swales's (1990) Hong Kong Study Circle.[2] She sees the need for a reassessment of the way 'community' has been construed in rhetoric and linguistics in terms of Harré's (1981, cited in Miller, 1994: 73) distinction between 'taxonomic' and 'relational' communities. The former exist only in the mind of the researcher, who groups individuals together because of shared characteristics. For Miller, 'speech communities' are taxonomic in that members share linguistic behaviours but do not necessarily interact with one another, nor is any interaction that takes place the focus of analysis. Relational communities, as the term suggests, are those groups whose members do, in fact, have real relationships. Miller posits a third category, 'virtual community', which she defines as 'a discursive projection, a rhetorical construct . . . the community as invoked, represented and presupposed or developed in rhetorical discourse'. It is into this third category that she places 'rhetorical community'.

Bex (1996: 64), like Miller, questions Swales's use of the Hong Kong Study Circle example, though on slightly different grounds. He argues that by choosing such a small, tight-knit group with limited social functions Swales might tempt others into regarding more loosely defined groups as falling outside the parameters of 'discourse community'. To avoid this potential distortion Bex uses Milroy's (1987) social network theory in which closeknit or 'multiplex' social networks are contrasted with looseknit or 'uniplex' networks. While members of multiplex networks are interconnected in many ways, connections among members of uniplex networks are much less dense. According to Bex we might valuably think of discourse communities as falling along a looseknit/closeknit cline. He ultimately adopts Barton's definition, which I too will quote:

> A discourse community is a group of people who have texts and practices in common, whether it is a group of academics, or the readers of teenage magazines. In fact, discourse community can refer to the people a text is aimed at; it can be the people who read a text; or it can refer to the people who participate in a set of discourse practices both by reading and writing.
>
> (Barton (1994: 57), quoted in Bex, 1996: 65)

So, for Barton and Bex the community might be a virtual or an actual group engaged in either reception or production or indeed in both.

Jolliffe and Brier (1988: 38) suggest that discourse community 'corresponds roughly' to the concept of *audience* in rhetoric, but draw some distinctions between 'knowledge of audience' and 'knowledge of discourse community', discussing the implications of these different types of knowledge for the writer. They note that in Aristotelian rhetoric, knowledge of audience involves determining who the audience is and analysing their knowledge, emotions, and beliefs so as to craft a discourse that will bring about change in what these individuals know, feel, or believe. Because, they claim, writers addressing academic discourse communities can normally rely on a readership that is essentially in a relationship of solidarity with them, adopting the classical approach to audience is unnecessary (Jolliffe and Brier, 1988: 40). Instead writers must devote their attention to displaying knowledge of a shared rhetoric by adhering to the discourse community's conventions.

Their task is complicated, however, by the fact that discourse communities are multidimensional. Jolliffe and Brier (1988), echoing Barton in Bex, see them as comprised of a series of concentric circles. The outer circle would be made up of all those who might feasibly be interested in the knowledge claim the writer is making; greater degrees of interest, and expertise, are then represented by successively smaller and smaller circles. Knowledge of 'audience as discourse community' involves understanding just how one's research can be presented to readers in each of these circles. Myers (1989: 3), while acknowledging that it is impossible to determine the true readership of a scientific article, also sees the putative audience as being divisible into at least two groups. These are: (i) a general scientific audience with general knowledge of the area concerned; and (ii) a much smaller group made up of researchers who the writer knows are dealing with the same problem or closely related problems. This smaller group is the one the writer addresses and the general audience, as Myers puts it, 'listens in'. Writers must learn to mitigate Face Threatening Acts (Brown and Levinson, 1987) perceivable as such by both these audiences. Thus, although terminology may not be glossed, citing of landmarks in the literature is done as if the readers were being told about these studies for the first time. A third writer to point up the multidimensionality of discourse community is Freedman (1994), who expresses the relationship between genre and discourse community very neatly through the metaphor of tennis. She suggests that the texts writers produce essentially 'play their partners' – the discourse communities to whom they are addressed.

> In order to do so, [the text] must represent its partner – previous, current, future, fictional or ideal. The rules of such representations are an integral part of any genre in precisely the same way as the rules of any game include the rules of interaction of partners. But texts may, and frequently do, play several games – and thus several partners – at once.   (Freedman, 1994: 48)

Many of those who write about discourse communities acknowledge that playing the genre game – just like playing any other – involves constraints not only on what writers can write or how they can write it, but on what they can know. Sullivan (1996: 224) provides an excellent review of the literature on these constraining effects but goes on to say that although the writer must demonstrate disciplinarity through exercise of the community's norms, she must also 'present some kind of news'. This janus-like task, Sullivan holds (1996: 225), produces a 'conservative yet progressive environment' in which the writer is expected to go further than her predecessors but demonstrate mastery of established practices and conventions. The process of acquiring these conventions is often painful and may on occasions, as Bizzell (1992) holds, demand the abandonment of signs of allegiance to other communities with competing discourse norms. Fully-fledged members of communities too may be discomfited when their multiple affiliations imply a conflict of interests.

Bizzell (1992: 222) argues that discourse communities parallel 'interpretative communities' in having a regulatory quality. The ability to resist or ignore the community's constraining power, she suggests, is dependent on realising that one is in fact a member in the first place (Bizzell, 1992: 226). She goes on to state that unless one remains relatively unaware of one's membership of a discourse community it is impossible to comfortably do the work that community membership implies (Bizzell, 1992: 227). Keeping the community's regulatory power over us below the level of consciousness is a mechanism that academic communities must make use of, Bizzell (1992: 229) argues. If they did not, she suggests, then the whole business of the creation of a body of canonical knowledge would be called into question, and to question knowledge making itself is hazardous for those whose livelihood depends on it.

Even where the community's paradigms are not explicitly questioned, members frequently maintain multiple affiliations. Berkenkotter et al. (1988) in their study of a postgraduate student's writing, conclude that signalling affiliation to one discourse community does not imply a rejection of the values and practices of other communities to which one might belong. Their subject, Nate, had previously taken a series of creative writing courses and despite growing mastery of the discourse conventions of the social sciences, continued to make use of his expertise in the expressive domain, something they suggest may have even facilitated his acquisition of social science norms.

Indeed, on occasions, the knowledge of alternative conventions might point up dissatisfaction with the community's modes of expression. Ivanic and Simpson (1992) chart an adult undergraduate writer's efforts to resist the tendency in academic writing to use impersonal language. This resistance grows out of dissatisfaction with perceived attempts to disguise the constructedness of academic discourse through the use of impersonal language. Ivanic and Simpson suggest that this preference for impersonal constructions, and the ideology that underpins it, can and should be contested.

This discussion of multiple membership and the degree to which discourse communites create knowledge boundaries for members has particular relevance to the issue of how far genre analysis can be applied in the classroom. I will return to this issue below.

RESEARCH QUESTIONS AND APPROACH

The research questions that motivated this study all arose from an interest in characterising the Spanish ELSS discourse community in relation to other communities of linguists publishing in Spain and internationally. A given discourse community possesses certain genres, primary among which is the RA. It is here that many of the community's discourse norms are realised because it is through the research article that members of the community present knowledge claims to their peers. As I have argued above, the introductions to research articles are a focal point for such claims. A comparative study of the introductions to RAs published in international linguistics journals (ILJ), Hispanic Studies journals (SpHSJ) and the two types of ELS publications (English and Spanish) was seen as revealing how these groups go about making knowledge claims through this genre and in what ways the strategies they adopt might be differentiated.

Comparing the groups obviously rests on the existence of a discernible repeated rhetorical pattern for each group. In the case of the ILJ texts I posited on the basis of Swales (1981a), in which the corpus included introductions drawn from linguistics journals, that the pattern would closely reflect the CARS schema, that is that introductions:

- would include all three moves;
- would include these moves in sequence;
- would not include moves not contemplated by the schema.

Assuming some consistent body of discourse norms in terms of the Swales schema was in fact discernible for the ILJ texts, I then posed the following initial research question:

(1) Do Spanish writers operate different discourse norms to their international counterparts that are discernible in the move structures of RA introductions?

If the move structure of the RA introductions drawn from the Spanish journals emerged as distinguishable from that of the ILJ introductions a further question would arise as to the origins of these differences, viz.,

(2) Is the operation of a different body of discourse conventions attributable primarily to the language background of the writer?

In order to answer this question it was initially essential to determine whether or not the three groups of Spanish writers operated a consistent preference for a particular move structure. If language background were the only factor producing differences in discourse structure, then one might expect to find that the introductions published by the three groups of Spanish writers would have many features in common including a preferred move structure, thus indicating a shared rhetoric. Those writers publishing in English would be seen as transferring the discourse norms of their own culture to their writing in English.

If, however, it turned out to be the case that no such consistent pattern emerged, then language background could not be 'the culprit'. Three possible candidates remain: area of specialisation (Hispanic versus English studies) and language of publication (Spanish or English) or the nature of the audience addressed. I, therefore, posed a further question:

(3) Are differences among the three groups of Spanish texts attributable to area of specialisation and language of publication or to differences in the nature of the audience?

If language of publication and area of specialisation were the factors exerting the most powerful influence on rhetorical structure, I anticipated that it would be possible to position the four groups of texts along a continuum (see Figure 11.2). The SpHSJ texts would be at one extreme showing the greatest degree of variation from the CARS model; the ELS texts published in Spanish (ELS1) would be next, closely corresponding to the SpHSJ texts, but with some variation as a result of their authors norming towards the conventions of the international community by virtue of their specialisation, viz. English Language Studies; at one remove on the continuum would be the ELS texts published in English (ELS 2) with some L1 interference differentiating them from the ILJ texts, which, logically, would be positioned at the other end of the cline.

If, on the other hand, differences in rhetorical structure were primarily the product of variation in the relationship between the writer and the discourse

The CARS Model————ILJ texts————ELS2 texts————ELS1 texts————SpHSJ texts

Figure 11.2   Variation from the CARS model: a posited continuum

community or audience, then one would expect a more complex pattern to emerge. For example, the texts drawn from the Hispanic Studies journals and English Studies journals might exhibit as much variation one from the other as they do from the international group.

METHOD

The corpus[3] of introductions was made up as follows:

- 27 ILJ texts;
- 29 SpHSJ texts;
- 20 ELS1 texts (those published in Spanish);
- 28 ELS2 texts (those published in English).

Each text was analysed by the writer and one independent analyst using Swales's (1990) CARS model. The following possible departures from the CARS model were posited:

(a) Deletion of one or more moves.
(b) Elaboration of move structure (through reiteration of moves).
(c) Variation in the move sequence.
(d) Addition of a move not envisaged in the Swales schema.

In addition to the move analysis a word count was done for each text and the number of references calculated. To provide a qualitative dimension the texts were analysed to the step level and compared in terms of specific realisations of those steps, with particular attention being paid to instances of Move 3.

RESULTS

None of the groups of texts exhibits a high level of consistency with the CARS model, that is to say a high proportion of texts include all three moves in sequence without recycling. However, when we come to look at the texts in terms of all the move deletion permutations to the CARS model (Table 11.1)

Table 11.1 Permutations of the CARS model

Permutation	ILJ	SPHSJ	ELS1	ELS2
Deletion of Move 1 only	–	–	–	–
Deletion of Move 2 only	3(11.1%)	4(13.8%)	8(40%)	8(28.6%)
Deletion of Move 3 only	2(7.4%)	6(20.7%)	1(5%)	4(14.3%)
Deletion of Moves 1 & 2	–	5(17.2%)	–	–
Deletion of Moves 1 & 3	–	–	–	–
Deletion of Moves 2 & 3	–	2(6.9%)	3(15%)	5(17.8%)
Total texts with deletions	5(18.5%)	17(58.6%)	12(60%)	17(60.7%)

with deletions of each move and combination of moves a pattern begins to emerge.

These data point to an affirmative answer to the first research question in that the texts drawn from the two types of Spanish publication (SpHSJs and ELSJs) show a much higher incidence of move deletion than occurs in the international linguistics journals. Furthermore, this high proportion of texts with instances of move deletion is maintained across the three Spanish groups, suggesting that these writers do indeed operate a discernibly different body of discourse conventions.

Nevertheless, it is possible to distinguish between the three groups (SpHSJ, ELS1, and ELS2) when examining the figures for deletions of specific moves. All four groups of texts show occurrences of Move 2 deletion. But while the percentages for the ILJ and SpHSJ texts are relatively low, in both groups of ELS texts Move 2 is deleted frequently: in over a quarter of the texts written in English and in almost half the ELS texts written in Spanish. For the ELS writers it is this move that is deleted more frequently than any other and this tendency sets them apart from both their Hispanic Studies counterparts and from the writers publishing in the international linguistics journals.

Turning to Move 3, once again all four groups of texts have incidences of deletion of this move, though it too acts to differentiate the four groups of texts. For the SpHSJ writers it is in fact this move that is most frequently deleted. Both the ILJ group and the ELS1 group show very low incidences of deletion of this move. While this permutation occurs more frequently in the ELS2 group, incidence is considerably lower than it is for deletion of Move 2. In the case of Move 3, then, it is the SpHSJ writers that stand apart. It should be noted also that this tendency is not reflected in the writing of their colleagues writing about English Studies in Spanish.

The importance of Move 2 in distinguishing between the three groups of Spanish texts is pointed up by the figures for deletion of both Moves 2 and 3. Here once again the writers publishing in the ELS journals delete both moves more frequently than their colleagues in Hispanic Studies. When it comes to combinations of moves the SpHSJ group of texts stands alone as the only group with incidences of deletion of Moves 1 and 2. Yet again this pattern clearly separates the SpHSJ texts from the two other groups of Spanish texts, leading us to answer the second research question in the negative, that is to say, language background would not appear to be the prime factor motivating differences in discourse structure since no shared preference emerges for the three groups of Spanish writers.

On the basis of these results the soundness of posited cline must also be questioned. Although all three types of Spanish text share a high incidence of move deletion, the percentages for deletion of Move 2 alone and for deletion of Move 2 with Move 3 (i.e. an introduction consisting solely of Move 1) along with incidences of deletion of Moves 1 and 2 (i.e. an introduction consisting solely of Move 3) lead to different conclusions about the factors motivating preferences for certain rhetorical structures. The ELS texts share a much greater tendency to delete Move 2, which distinguishes them

Table 11.2 Elaboration, sequence variation, and additional moves

Feature	ILJ	SPHSJ	ELS1	ELS2
Elaboration	23(85.2%)	15(51.7%)	8(40%)	14(50%)
Sequence variation	21(77.7%)	22(75.8%)	14(50%)	7(35%)
Additional moves	–	6(20.7%)	–	–

from the SpHSJ texts. However, this does not mean that they share more features with the ILJ texts. In fact they differ most markedly from the ILJ texts though they are clearly distinguishable from the SpHSJ texts as well. The ELS texts stand apart.

Elaboration, sequence variation, and additional moves

An elaborated structure occurs frequently throughout the corpus. Sequence variation again is a common occurrence in all four groups of texts, whereas incorporation of additional moves occurs only in the SpHSJ part of the corpus. The raw figures and percentages of each of these features are depicted in Table 11.2.

In terms of elaboration it is the ILJ group that stands as a case apart, with much higher numbers of texts showing this feature than any of the three groups of Spanish publications, where the percentages are very similar.

Sequence variation sees the four groups of texts divided roughly down the middle, with the ILJ and SpHSJ groups on this occasion sharing a relatively high incidence of the feature and the ELS groups, while still including a number of texts with sequence variation, showing a markedly lower incidence.

It is only in the SpHSJ part of the corpus that text segments outside the parameters of the Swales schema occurred.

All four groups of texts vary substantially along these dimensions from one another and, it must be emphasised, from the CARS model. Although the three groups of Spanish texts would seem not to share the marked preference of the ILJ writers for an elaborated structure, sequence variation groups the ILJ and SpHSJ texts together and distinguishes them from the ELS texts. Neither the ELS texts nor the ILJ texts share the tendency of those writing for the SpHSJs to use moves outside the parameters of the CARS model.

These results confirm the answers to the research questions reached in the preceding section. Language background does not correlate with preferences in terms of elaborated structure of variation. Similarly, the choice of English Studies as an area of specialisation and English as a language of publication does not appear to lead to a preference for the elaborated structures and sequence variation that prevail among the ILJ writers.

Predominating patterns

The predominating patterns that emerge from the analysis highlight the distinctiveness of the ILJ texts in that this is the only group in which Move 1

Table 11.3 Relative frequencies of move structures

Move structure	ILJ	SPHSJ	ELS1	ELS2	TOTAL
1	–	2(6.9%)	3(15%)	5(17.8%)	10(9.6%)
13	1(3.7%)	2(6.9%)	6(30%)	3(10.7%)	12(11.5%)
123	1(3.7%)	–	1(5%)	4(14.3%)	6(5.8%)
1213	3(11.1%)	–	1(5%)	1(3.5%)	5(4.8%)
1212[13]3	7(25.9%)	–	2(10%)	–	9(8.6%)
3	–	5(17.2%)	–	–	5(4.8%)

is never used in isolation and in which highly elaborated text structures are favoured. Likewise, the SpHSJ texts stand alone in using Move 3 in isolation, while the two groups of ELS texts share the frequent use of the 1–3 sequence.

The emergent patterns again lead us to dismiss language background as the prime factor distinguishing the preferences of these writers since the SpHSJ texts are clearly distinguishable from both groups of ELS texts. At the same time the patterns lead us to question the posited cline. The ELS texts in both languages share some features with both the ILJ and SpHSJ groups, viz. instances of elaborations of the 1–2–3 sequence and of Move 1 used in isolation respectively. They do, however, have more in common with each other than they do with either of the other two groups of texts. This finding is all the more patent when we look at the relative frequencies of predominant patterns in the four groups as depicted in Table 11.3.

The frequency with which the ELS writers use the Move 1 and Moves 1–3 patterns is much greater than it is for the ILJ texts and considerably greater than for the SpHSJ texts. Furthermore the ELS writers do not make frequent use of either of the preferred move patterns of the ILJ and SpHSJ groups.

Summary of findings

The first finding to emerge from the analysis is that writers in none of the four groups consistently realise the CARS schema, though the ILJ texts show a lower instance of move deletion and can be said to be closer to the CARS schema than the texts in the other three groups. Secondly, no consistent rhetorical preference emerges across the three groups of Spanish texts, thus suggesting that language background alone does not play a significant role in preferences for certain generic structures. Thirdly, instead of the cline that was posited for the four groups, what emerges is a situation in which the two groups of ELS texts can be characterised as sharing a tendency to delete Move 2. These texts can also be said to be comparable in that they do not show a particular preference for variation of the 1–2–3 move sequence, whereas the texts in the ILJ and SpHSJ parts of the corpus do indeed show such a preference. The move structures that predominate in the ILJ and SpHSJ parts of the corpus do not in fact predominate in the two sets of ELS texts.

Table 11.4 Mean word counts and numbers of references

	ILJ	SPHSJ	ELS1	ELS2
Mean no. words	63	512.7	351.8	567
Mean no. references	16.2	7.2	1.75	4.07

This would suggest that choice of language of publication plays no particular role and that area of specialisation does not exert the influence posited, i.e. that of causing writers to norm towards the practices of the international discourse community.

References and length

I also compared the texts in terms of number of references to previous research and length.[4] It is useful to quantify these features since they have a strong relationship to move structure: length to cyclical structures and number of references to occurrences of Move 1, step 3. Table 11.4 provides mean number of words and mean number of references for each part of the corpus.

The ELS1 texts have a much lower mean number of words and references than the other three groups. The ELS2 are closest to the ELS1 texts in terms of number of references and positioned at the mid-point between the SpHSJ and ILJ texts in terms of number of words. Both groups of ELS texts share a mean number of references that is considerably lower than the SpHSJ texts and much lower than the ILJ texts.

These findings once again confirm the conclusion that although the Spanish texts differ markedly from the ILJ texts, variation in discourse conventions is not solely the result of the language background of the writer. Nor would these results allow us to maintain the posited cline since both in terms of number of references and length the ELS2 texts (those written in English) have more in common with the SpHSJ texts than they do with the ELS1 texts.

CONCLUSIONS

In this study the language background of the writer did not play the major role in determining the rhetorical structure of the RA introduction. Spanish writers working in the field of English Language Studies can be said to differ as much from their colleagues in Hispanic Studies in terms of discourse conventions as they do from their colleagues writing for the international linguistics journals. Instead, it is suggested that the relationship between the writer and the discourse community accounts for differences that emerge in the rhetorical structures of these texts. The nature of these relationships not only helps to explain the commonalities between the two groups of ELS texts, but also the distinctive dominant rhetorical structures of the ILJ and SpHSJ texts, viz. the highly elaborated structure in the former and the use of Move 3 alone in the latter. The variation we have seen in the four groups of texts is also reflected at the step level.

For the ILJ texts we have the complex reiterative patterns such as 12(12 . . .)123 and 1213(13 . . .), initial Move 2, the use of direct questions, along with the many instances of what Swales (1990) presents as alternative steps being used in concert with one another. Linguists writing in these journals ground the knowledge claims they make in sometimes extensive reviews of the literature. Another feature these introductions share is the frequent use of Move 3, step 3, showing an awareness on the part of linguists of the role advance organisers play in easing the reading task.

In the case of the SpHSJ texts, there are introductions composed entirely of Move 3 and more elaborate introductions which open with a statement of the purpose of the study reported. On occasion these writers opt for intro-ductions in which there is no explicit statement of purpose or announcement of the research. They seldom indicate the structure of the rest of the RA in the introduction. Use of footnotes to cite previous research and the rhetor-ical purposes of citations are also features that distinguish members of this group from their ILJ colleagues. The use of footnotes perhaps facilitates the exercise of a preference these writers have for longer research histories with much earlier starting points than those in the ILJ texts. Descriptions of meth-ods and procedures were also a more frequent feature of these introductions than they were of the ILJ texts, while explicit appeals for a sympathetic reading by presenting one's research credentials or defending methodology employed were additional strategies this group had available to them.

The ELS1 writers share some features with their colleagues in Hispanic Studies, but differ from them as well. Readers are, once again, provided with extended coverage of the background to the research reported and often with indications of where this research should be situated in relation to a long research tradition. The extended referencing of the Hispanic Studies texts is, however, not prominent here. When research is announced or its purposes stated, this is done almost reluctantly, thus rendering these texts distinguishable again from those published in the Hispanic Studies journals, which frequently open with Move 3, step 1A or 1B or consist solely of this move. The ELS1 texts share with the SpHSJ texts a preference for inclusion of details of method and, because of this, often have more in common with the abstracts than they do with the introductions of the ILJ articles. Once again, like their Hispanic Studies colleagues, these writers do not see the need to indicate the structure of the rest of the RA.

The ELS2 writers share with their colleagues publishing in Spanish (ELS1) a preference for lengthy provisions of background information once again without the large number of citations in some of the SpHSJ texts. Where research niches are created it is often by quite heavily mitigated intimations of deficiencies in previous research. While these writers do introduce their research, often at the end of a sequence including realisations of Swales's (1990) Moves 1 and 2, the announcement of research or statement of purpose comes rather abruptly after the extended treatment of background information, i.e. while long text segments are devoted to Move 1, Move 3 often merits only a single sentence or clause. RA structure is indicated by the minority, but this is not generally done as explicitly as it is in the ILJ texts.

In sum, the following are the features the ELS1 and ELS2 share and which distinguish them from the other two groups:

- a tendency to delete Move 2;
- lengthy realisations of Move 1, step 2;
- a lower incidence of Move 1, step 3 in comparison to the other two groups and a tendency to cite fewer items;
- 'abrupt' onset of Move 3, step 1A/1B.

DISCUSSION

Scollon (1993) sees the apparently distinguishable discourse norms of Chinese speakers as an artefact of the relationship between writer and audience. For Scollon, the maintenance of relationships between participants is always privileged over topic introduction. Where this relationship is stable, topic can be introduced early. Where it is not, the writer must first attend to the relationship.

This view of rhetorical strategies, I believe, brings us closer to an understanding of why the four groups of writers make the choices we see exemplified in the findings. We saw that the SpHSJ writers sometimes simply announce their research without previously establishing centrality or establishing a niche. Following Scollon (1993), I would suggest that this is because Hispanic studies is a relatively small community in which there is a clearly established research agenda and in which the writer is very likely to know key members of the community well (or at least better than the ILJ writers, who must appear to be addressing a much larger notional audience). If the writer is an established member of the community she can, therefore, assume the relationship is stable and dispense with the rhetorical efforts demanded of her ILJ colleagues. In the same group of writers we also saw a strategy that involved the omission of Move 3 altogether in favour of lengthy realisations of Move 1, sometimes followed by Move 2. This I see as evidence of a sense of uneasiness on the part of some of the writers about the relationship with the discourse community: perhaps because they are relative newcomers who, therefore, feel uncertain about the level of knowledge claim the audience will countenance or perhaps because, though established, they address a topic that is not their usual domain. Both sets of circumstances may lead writers to avoid explicitly announcing their research in the introduction. The Hispanic Studies writers can thus be said to have two possible strategies available to them, depending on the degree of stability they perceive in their relationship with the community.

In contrast, the two groups of English Language specialists have little option but to attend primarily to the relationship with the reader, using

Move 1, step 2 (making topic generalisations) and on occasions devoting the whole introduction to this step. This strategy is, in my view, a response to the fact that the journals for which these people are writing are general English Studies journals with articles and a notional readership drawn from the full spectrum of interests in English Philology departments in Spain. The writers are, therefore, involved in engaging a potential audience that knows little or nothing about the issue they address. Although the community is small and individual members of the audience may be known to them, this inevitable knowledge gap creates a potentially face-threatening situation in which the writers are left with little option but to spend more time on laying a foundation for their research. Furthermore, they must lay this foundation in such a way as to downplay the reader's lack of background. Thus Move 1 is the essential move, and the preferred step, step 2. Move 2 can be dispensed with as there is little point in creating a niche when the reader does not even know the territory.[5]

The relative lack of referencing can also be explained by looking at the dilemma these writers face. It will be recalled that the ILJ and SpHSJ texts share a view of the introduction as one of several possible sites in the RA for acknowledgement of the work of others. The shared reluctance among the ELS writers, in contrast to their ILJ and SpHSJ colleagues, I would see, once again, as a response to the specific relationship that pertains between writer and discourse community. The non-expert reader will not, of course, be aware of (or even interested in) the narrative of the particular area the writer addresses and may in fact be irritated by extensive referencing of items that are completely unknown to her. A display of disciplinarity involving extensive citing of other researchers' work is potentially face-threatening to a readership without topic-specific knowledge and these writers respond to this situation by citing only widely known key figures (e.g. Halliday and Chomsky) or simply stating that the topic has a lengthy research history without referring to any of the milestones in that history.

The ELS writers are in a strange double bind: they must do disciplinarity while *appearing* to address an audience that knows little about the topic but with whom, at the same time, the writers may be personally familiar, having met them at national conferences, on thesis and tenure examination committees, and so on. It is not, of course, a real relationship between a real reader and a real writer, but the authors of these texts must demonstrate their willingness to play by the rules of the game and, even though their actual readership may be non-existent, to get past the editor of the journal and any peer reviewers they must seem to address a larger group of readers with whom they are likely to be personally familiar. Since the relationship is one of familiarity it might be said to be a stable one of peer addressing peer. However, these writers address peers who are almost inevitably non-experts and it is this, I contend, that destabilises the relationship. The writer must, therefore, set about realigning reader and writer roles, while carefully avoiding or mitigating threats to face. The safest strategy is to produce an introduction which charts the territory for the reader without pointing up her almost complete ignorance of it.

IMPLICATIONS FOR THE EAP CLASSROOM?

Trzeciak (1996: 75) questions the deficiency notion of NESB writing in the following terms:

> It is too easy to view development as leading towards an idealised norm that may itself be highly culturally determined and intolerant of deviations that challenge its canon . . .

He is, at the same time, cautious about a view of NESB text that 'uncritically' tolerates all instances of variation. Trzeciak's position is entirely coherent in the context of EAP courses taught at 'inner circle' universities. But one's attitude to the writing of a group that would perceive itself as 'expert', and that achieves considerable academic success through publishing in national and local journals, must be very different. In my case, it is not a question of exercising tolerance because it is not my province to tolerate discourse norms that are different from those that constrain me nor is it my business to criticise these norms. Hargan (1995: 231), discussing the teaching of academic writing in the Italian university system, points up the fact that much work in EAP is 'anglophone-centric'. She calls on EAP practitioners and researchers to go beyond the examination of textual patterns to look at 'the ways in which different educational cultures produce and transmit knowledge' when they are concerned with communicating that knowledge within their national or disciplinary boundaries. I would argue that an understanding of the variable relationship between writers and the discourse communities they address forms a crucial part of research into academic discourse across cultures. In situations such as Italy and Spain where English may be used as a medium of knowledge production and transmission alongside Italian or Spanish and where writers will need to make use of the genres and conventions of their own language culture as well as those of English, it would be a lopsided research agenda that privileged the norms of academic genres in English over those of local or national communities. What is required in such settings, I would argue, is an approach to academic writing research that draws on participants' attitudes to and relationships with the discourse communities they address. It is also my view that such an approach to research can be readily translated into some learning contexts.

Returning to the three 'schools' of genre analysis, we find considerable variation in terms of views held on how, or indeed if, this translation to the learning context should be achieved. The ESP genre analysts (Hyon, 1996 cites Bhatia, 1993; J. Flowerdew, 1993a; Swales, 1990) would appear to advocate a direct application of genre analyses, viz. explicit teaching of the structures arrived at. The New Rhetoric researchers argue, on the other hand, that genre knowledge is acquired through a process of socialisation into the discourse community and that pedagogical shortcuts such as providing information about text structure simply will not work. On this basis they reject the notion of genre analysis as applicable to the EAP classroom, particularly the undergraduate classroom. In the Australian context genre-based pedagogy has found followers in the secondary system, in TAFE (Technical and Further Education) and in adult migrant ESL programmes, though it has also attracted detractors many of whom fear that teaching genre means short-circuiting the acquisition of writing skills through process approaches.[6]

None of the three views of the implications and potential applications of genre analysis is in fact a response to circumstances like those of the NESB academic. There is often a sharply felt need for support in the mastery of international academic genre and register conventions by these individuals – individuals who have already achieved status and success within their own local discourse communities. But too prescriptive an approach runs the risk of patronising and antagonising people who are already experts, by suggesting that their own discourse norms are somehow unworthy. What is needed is a pedagogy that draws on these writers' genre knowledge of their own discourse communities as the basis for the acquisition of international norms. The approach I, and many other teachers (see for example Swales, 1990; Swales and Feak, 1994; J. Flowerdew, 1993a cited in Hyon, 1996), advocate is one in which course participants actually engage in genre analysis so as to arrive at a heightened awareness of rhetorical practices (be they local or international) and the social purposes those practices fulfil. Where 'instructor' and 'students' embark on this process of investigation as equal partners, such an approach has even greater potential to provide participants with the mastery of the genre conventions they require.[7]

NOTES

1. Another reason for continuing to look at this much-analysed subgenre is that conventions change over time. Since genres are 'typified responses to social contexts' (Freedman and Medway, 1994b: 10) and since these social contexts constantly change, so too do genres. As Bazerman (1988: 318) puts it, in a bid to create novel claims scientists 'use, transform and invent tools and tricks of the symbolic trade'. We need to know about how these uses, transformations, and inventions come about, become familiar, and ultimately fall into disuse.
2. A society whose members collect Hong Kong stamps.
3. In the case of the ILJ texts I chose five linguistics journals and drew the corpus from issues of these journals published from 1985 to 1991. The twenty-seven RA introductions were randomly selected from a total population of some 655 articles. This gave five articles each from the *Journal of Linguistics, Language Learning,* and the *Journal of Memory and Language* and six each from *Text* and *Diachronica.* For various reasons it was necessary to use stratified random sampling in the case of the Hispanic Studies journals. I selected twelve articles from *Español Actual,* twelve from *Lingüística Española Actual,* five from *Revista de Filología Española,* and one from the *Revista Española de Lingüística.* Both the ELS1 and ELS2 introductions were drawn from the following journals: *Anglo-American Studies, Anuari d'Anglès, Anuario de Filología, Atlantis, BELLS (Barcelona English Language and Literary Studies), Cuadernos de Investigación Filológica, ES (Revista de Filología), Miscelánea, Revista Canaria de Estudios Ingleses, Revista Alicantina de Estudios Ingleses,* and *Stylus: Cuadernos de Filología de la Universidad de Castilla y La Mancha.* Because these journals all include

articles on literary studies, cultural studies, and linguistics random sampling was not possible. I located all appropriate articles (i.e. articles on English Language Studies) and used these in the corpus.

4. Any statements about variation in length across the four groups must be seen in the light of the difficulty of determining the bounds of the introduction. In the cases of the SpHSJ and the ELS1 and 2 texts the boundaries of the introduction were not always marked by headings or numbering.

5. Ahmad (1995) arrives at a similar explanation for the omission of Move 2 in RA introductions written in Bahasa Melayu by Malaysian academics. She too sees the nature of the discourse community and more particularly the fact that it is often very small as the major factor in determining this rhetorical pattern.

6. Coe (1994), addressing the acquisition/learning issue, asks whether the process of socialisation view might not amount to little more than a restriction of access to power by those who have already achieved it through the self-same process of socialisation. He concludes by asking what role teachers might have in the transfer of genre knowledge: 'we should also remember to ask whether teachers with explicit genre knowledge might help students acquire genres, explicitly or tacitly, more successfully – just as coaches do now for all sorts of athletic skills' (Coe, 1994: 185).

7. EARLI (the European Association for Research on Learning and Instruction) launched an on-line academic writing course in September 1996 aimed at its members: academic staff from a range of disciplines in European universities seeking to publish in the EARLI journal *Learning and Instruction* or in other journals. The course, which seems to realise many of the elements in the approach I outline, was described to EARLI members in the following terms: 'As well as being a serious course, EARLI Academic Writing Online is an experiment to explore the potential of the World Wide Web (WWW) to facilitate and accelerate the teaching and learning of genre conventions through the creation of an online community of EARLI researchers' (Wegerif and Stratfold, 1996). The course coordinators planned to measure the success of the course through calculating the number of articles published.

Chapter 12

'Selling' or 'Telling'?
The issue of cultural variation
in research genres

Tatyana Yakhontova

LANGUAGES, CULTURES, AND GENRES: OVERVIEW AND
PRELIMINARIES

The close interrelationship between language and culture has already become well established, supported, in particular, by cross-cultural investigations of English research writing and the appropriate discourses in other
languages (Mauranen, 1993b; Clyne, 1991; Bloch and Chi, 1995; Vassileva,
2000; Burgess, this volume; Ostler, this volume). The rising interest in such
studies is connected with (1) the current role of English as an international
medium of transmitting world knowledge, and, consequently, with (2) the
rapid expansion of the global market for English language teaching and
learning. Due to the sociopolitical changes in the countries of the former
socialist bloc this market now has a tendency to increase significantly; as
Crystal notes, a particular growth area (for ELT business) is 'central and
eastern Europe, and the countries of the former Soviet Union, where it is
thought that nearly 10 per cent of the population – some 50 million in all –
are now learning English' (1997: 103).

Indeed, newly independent states are currently experiencing a boom in
learning English – English in general as well as different varieties of English
arising from various contexts, academic in particular; and though proficiency
in spoken and written English has not yet become a 'must' for ex-Soviet
researchers (in contrast to their Western colleagues), it is nevertheless treated
as an important and highly desirable professional accomplishment for a
scholar. Like other non-native speakers of English under similar circumstances, former Soviet researchers experience both linguistic and intercultural
problems caused by insufficient awareness of certain culture-specific features
that differ in Anglo-American and source discourses. In such a situation,
an appropriate contrastive textlinguistic research can provide important
data that may be further utilised for both theoretical linguistic and applied
(pedagogical) purposes.

In this chapter, these general insights are incorporated into a study of academic English and the discourses in Ukrainian and Russian that dominate the sphere of scholarship in Ukraine. A certain amount of comparative research on scientific writing in some Slavic languages (with a more or less deep explanation of specific cultural backgrounds) has already been conducted (Nichols, 1988; Čmejrková and Daneš, 1997; Duszak, 1997; Prozorova, 1997; Vassileva, 2000). These studies have demonstrated cultural proximity among Slavic discourses that allows us to contrast them (not necessarily separately) to pan-Western English academic written discourse. However, the above works focus mostly on the dominant discursive features and do not consider the generic organisation of the texts investigated. At the same time, genre-oriented approaches that highlight the cognitive organisation of the compared texts in connection to their most important verbal peculiarities seem to be more promising from a pedagogical perspective, due, perhaps, to the more exhaustive view they provide.

In this chapter, I will analyse cultural variation in such an academic genre as the conference abstract on the basis of Ukrainian/partly Russian versus English texts. The choice of the conference abstract as a subject of investigation has been determined by two reasons: (1) it is a widespread and important genre that plays a significant role in promoting new knowledge within scientific communities, both national and international; (2) for Ukrainian scholars nowadays it is a kind of a 'pass' to the world science market and research community that provides, if accepted, various opportunities for professional contacts and communication.

According to Swales (1996b), conference abstracts are stand-alone texts that enter a competition for the available slots on the conference programme. Comparing conference abstracts with the so-called 'homotopic' journal ones, Swales and Feak note that the former are 'much more of a "selling job"' (1994: 214). At the same time Swales states that 'the conference abstract is neither highly visible nor that easily obtainable: it is one of those "occluded" academic genres, exemplars of which rarely appear in print' (1996b: 46).

Although neglected as the objects of investigation in Soviet and post-Soviet scholarship, Ukrainian conference abstracts cannot be viewed as 'occluded'. They are usually rather lengthy (from a standard one page up to three pages) and appear in a book of abstracts separately from a conference programme; they are stored in libraries (if a conference is broad-scale enough) and are available to the reader. The practice of submitting both longer and shorter versions of abstracts is rather rare in Ukraine; some conferences establish editorial boards 'responsible' for the books of abstracts that slightly revise, if necessary, the language of the texts. At the same time, conference abstracts in Ukraine are not considered to be 'legitimate' publications, in the sense research papers or conference reports are. Despite some differences, Ukrainian abstracts undoubtedly share with their English counterparts similar communicative goals: to impress a review committee and, further, to appeal to a broader audience of professionals in the same area. However, the ways and strategies of achieving these goals, as will be shown, are subject to obvious cultural variation.

INTERCULTURAL DIFFERENCES IN THE GENRE OF THE
CONFERENCE ABSTRACT: THE DESCRIPTION OF OBSERVATIONS
AND FINDINGS

Corpus and analytical framework

The analysed corpus consists of forty-five texts, of which fifteen are written in
English by native speakers (they will be labelled henceforth as EE abstracts),
fifteen in Ukrainian (10) and Russian (5) (U/R group), and another fifteen
again in English, but this time written by Ukrainian and/or Russian speakers
(EU/R texts). Both Ukrainian and Russian (quite different lexically) share
not only some similar syntactical and stylistic features, but also (which is
more significant for this study) the common ideological and intellectual
heritage of the totalitarian period that is still traceable in the rhetoric of
their academic discourse. Despite the state policy of Ukrainisation, Russian
preserves some influence on the functioning of scholarship in eastern Ukraine,
while Ukrainian dominates academic communication in the western and
central parts of the country.

All the investigated abstracts belong to the field of applied linguistics. This
discipline has been chosen not so much (as it might be suspected) as the area
most familiar to the author, but rather as an 'Anglicised' and, to a certain
extent, one of the most dynamic fields of Ukrainian scholarship. Being more
open to influences from the West due to a higher level of English language
awareness of Ukrainian applied linguists (as compared to that of representatives of other domains), this field also bears some ideological imprints of
earlier times, and thus appears to be an interesting area for the investigation
of this much-spoken-about 'transition' period characteristic not only of current sociopolitical life in Ukraine, but of its intellectual and academic spheres
as well. Since applied language studies are a rather versatile field, the investigation has been restricted mostly (but not exclusively) to the abstracts dealing with discourse analysis, testing, and their pedagogical implications.

Within this particular area, forty-five abstracts were chosen at random. They
were submitted for individual presentation and appeared in the appropriate
sections of the books of abstracts (for the names, dates, and abbreviations of
the conferences see the Appendix). The mean length of abstracts is 300 words,
but there are also some texts that deviate from this average. The EE texts
were written for international conferences, the U/R abstracts for national
events, and the EU/R group for two rather specific types of Ukrainian
conferences. The first type are the conferences that also invite speakers from
the other former Soviet states and establish three working languages (in the
order of their priority): Ukrainian, English, and Russian. Approximately one-
tenth of the abstracts submitted to such conferences are written in English.
The second type are TESOL–Ukraine conferences that involve and address
predominantly the national audience, but with some invited US speakers and
guests (these are conducted in English and accept only the abstracts in this
language). Needless to say, being included in the conference books of

abstracts, they were all successful and, consequently, have become appropriate data for the investigation of this genre. However, it has been assumed from the very beginning of the study that the conference abstract is quite sensitive to the influence of such multiple factors as the type of a conference, the proclivities of the research area itself, the selection criteria of reviewing committees, their personal preferences, etc. The observations described in this chapter and their explanations cannot be viewed as exhaustive; rather, they will be treated only as the *prevailing tendencies of rhetorical and textlinguistic choices*.

The procedure for the analysis of the texts arises primarily from the Bakhtinian vision of genre as the inseparable unity of its thematic content, compositional structure, and style that 'are equally determined by the specific nature of the particular sphere of communication' (1986: 60). In the spirit of this framework, three generic aspects of the abstracts were analysed: (1) their cognitive organisation; (2) its manifestation through the formal composition (layout) of texts; and (3) their language, restricted, however, to the description of the most conspicuous linguistic features.

Cognitive organisation of texts

The regularities of the cognitive organisation of research texts were investigated by interpreting it as a series of consecutive moves (Swales, 1990) that reflect the conventionalised structuring of genre determined by its communicative purpose. These moves are, in fact, rather stable functional units that belong to certain genres; however, the concrete rhetorical strategies of their realisation in different texts depend, on the one hand, upon the individual preference of a writer (within the scope of possible rhetorical choices of this or that genre), and, on the other hand, upon the socio-cultural context of the genre origin and functioning.

The analysis of three groups of abstracts has allowed us to identify five basic moves of the conference abstract that are labelled in this chapter as follows:

1. Outlining the research field.
2. Justifying a particular research/study.
3. Introducing the paper to be presented at the conference.
4. Summarising the paper.
5. Highlighting its outcome/results.

In any of the three groups some texts possess all possible moves, while others lack one or even two of them, these deviations being quite natural for the texts of any genre, and therefore not significant, at least for the purposes of this study.

The distribution of each of the moves in the three groups compared is shown in Table 12.1.

As seen, the number of texts in any group that share this or that move with their counterparts in another two abstract sets is quite comparable, if not identical, with the sole exception of the 'Introducing the paper', move which is strikingly rare in the U/R group. This and the rest of the major

Table 12.1 Quantitative distribution of moves

Moves	EE	U/R	EU/R
1. Outlining the field	11	13	11
2. Justifying a research	14	13	11
3. Introducing the paper	12	6	11
4. Summarising the paper	12	15	14
5. Highlighting its outcome	11	15	8

differences become more visible when we start to consider separately *the rhetorical and textual strategies of the realisation of these moves in each group.*

The first cognitive move, 'Outlining the research field', is realised rhetorically in the EE texts by (a) the reference to established knowledge, (b) previous research, or (c) importance claim. These strategies, quite recognisable already in the first sentence, acquire the form of rather concrete statements ultimately related to the theme/subject of the paper, e.g.:

(1) The role of figurative language has been explored chiefly from the viewpoint of the research scientist and the act of discovery.   (LSP: 20)

The strategies employed by Slavic writers in both groups of abstracts also involve the reference to established knowledge and importance claim, though previous research is mentioned only in two (out of thirty) abstracts. Unlike native writers, Ukrainian and Russian authors tend to refer to familiar, shared knowledge through rather global statements of sometimes a declarative character:

(2) Teaching and testing are two inseparable aspects of the teacher's task.
                                                                   (TSLU: 53)[1]

Frequently, this reference is combined with an importance claim that presents the chosen field as a significant part of a still broader domain, e.g.:

(3) *Odnim iz vedushchikh vidov rechevoj dejatel'nosti v nejazykovom vyze javliaetsa chtenije.*   (TLSP: 121)

     One of the leading types of speech activity in a technical university is reading.[2]

In three abstracts, this option is linguistically marked (as in (3)) by the presence of the combination 'Odyn z' (Ukr.), 'odin iz' (Rus.) – 'one of' – which is quite typical of Ukrainian and Russian academic discourse.

Another strategy for realising an importance claim revealed in five non-native texts and absent in the EE abstracts consists in referring to the current sociopolitical or economic situation in the home country. This rhetorical option allows the preparation of a space for a particular research that will be further justified in the second move as an adequate and timely response to societal needs or as a possible solution to the urgent problems of the outlined field. Here is an example of both 'Outlining the research field' and 'Justifying a particular research/study' moves in a Ukrainian text:

(4) *Lingvistychni aspekty vykladannia inozemnykh mov v protsesi pidgotovki vysokokvalifikovanykh fakhivtsiv u galuzi rynkovoji economiki z kozhnym rokom nabyvajut' shche bil'shoji <u>aktyal'nosti.</u> Vazhlyvoju skladovoju uspikhu je nablyzhennia teoretychnykh doslidzhen' z tekstolingvistyki ta lingvistyki tekstu za fakhom do vyrishennia konkretnykh zavdan' uchbovogo protsesu v praktytsi fakhovo-orientovanogo vykladannia inozemnykh mov. Na ekonomichnykh fakultetakh vuziv vykladannia inozemnykh mov dotsil'no bazuvaty na vyvchenni realij economichnogo zhytia na materiali oryginal'noji fakhovoji literatury z rynkoznavstva'.*   (PTFL: 127)

> The linguistic aspects of foreign languages teaching in the process of train-ing highly qualified specialists in market economy are gaining more and more importance. The important part of the success is connected with the application of theoretical research in textlinguistics and the linguistics of professional text to solving the concrete tasks of teaching and learning process in the practice of professionally-oriented teaching of foreign lan-guages. Foreign languages teaching for the departments of Economics must be based on the studies of the realities of economic life on the basis of authentic professional texts in market economy.

It is worth noticing here that the rhetoric of two starting moves in Slavic abstracts is strikingly oriented towards emphasising the context-bound, con-tinuing character of a particular research; this strategy is universal in the U/R texts, but only partially present in the EU/R group.

At the same time, *none* of the U/R abstracts realises the second move by such popular strategies in EE texts as indicating a gap, question-raising, or counter-claiming. However, these rhetorical preferences do appear in the English abstracts produced by Ukrainian and Russian speakers. In fact, the linguistic and stylistic features of their textual realisation seem in some cases to be quite similar to those of the EE texts, as in the following excerpts that demonstrate the rhetorical strategy of counter-claiming:

EE

(5) While figurative language is an integral feature of everyday speech, we do not think of it as central to scientific explanation. In this paper, I have tried to show that it *is.*   (LSP: 20)

EU/R

(6) Most teachers believe that their main aim is to teach their students English thus taking on full responsibility for their students' progress. Such accent on teaching is the result of naive mechanistic ideas characteristic of the totalitarian school and still held dear by many teachers that all pedagogical influences are projected directly into the child. This approach does not take into account some rather obvious facts . . .   (TSLU: 12)

As we proceed deeper into the analysis, the differences between the cog-nitive structuring of the EE group on the one hand, and the U/R and EU/R texts on the other are becoming more visible. The third move – 'Introducing the paper' – marked by predominantly descriptive metadiscourse, is found in twelve EE texts but only in five of each U/R and EU/R group. These instances

that do not differ significantly from the metadiscourse of the EE abstracts
can be exemplified by the following excerpt from the EU/R group:

(7) Our research of business communication is focused on the analysis of
prototypical situations in professional partnership . . .   (TSLU: 32)

However, the fourth obligatory move, 'Summarising the paper', is realised
in strategically different ways in the EE on the one hand and the U/R and
EU/R groups on the other. In the English abstracts, it is a brief overview of
the paper (in general, or its logical parts in a consecutive order) usually
structured with the help of the appropriate text organisers (metadiscourse):

(8) The article examines dominant metaphoric themes – such as war and hunt-
ing, family – and other relationships . . . It also analyzes some of the linguistic and discourse patterns used in various figures of speech; for example,
the use of markers . . .   (LSP: 20)

These short summaries have an obvious tendency to emphasise the
author's central idea or his/her claim for the novelty or originality of the
research to be presented in a paper, e.g.:

(9) It will be argued that in designing a test the question of authenticity may
not be as important as previously considered.   (LTRC: 17)

In contrast, the Slavic abstracts in both Ukrainian/Russian and English
provide rather lengthy descriptions of the *content* of a paper (and not of its
main points or structural parts) written in a neutral, objectivised style, without any metadicourse references. These descriptions appear in the texts immediately after a 'Justifying a particular research' move and begin in a
rhetorical manner, quite typical of Soviet Ukrainian and Russian academic
discourse: either by clarifying the conceptual tools of research – its basic
notions, their definitions, and appropriate terminology – or by providing
generalised statements relevant to the theme of the paper that are gradually
'narrowed', reduced to the theme/content itself, as illustrated by the example of this move in an EU/R abstract:

(10) Situations of professional interaction are complex social events, which
involve knowledge of different aspects and levels . . . Such integrative paradigm of knowledge, which includes cognitive, linguistic phenomena, can
be fully manifested through *frame approach*, where the above mentioned
aspect of knowledge can be structured on different levels. Multifaceted
hierarchical frame helped greatly in acquisition of communicative competence, which is improved in two aspects . . .   (TSLU: 32)

From the viewpoint of the amount of rhetorical effort, the situation reverses in the last move of the abstracts. While the English texts highlight the
outcome in rather diverse and not necessarily emphatic ways (by indicating
the most important results and their possible applications and implications),
the U/R abstracts solemnly announce the significance of their findings. It is,
however, difficult to trace any explicit tendencies in this move of the EU/R
group: some texts show here the evidence of transfer of the U/R strategies

marked by a high degree of authorial commitment towards the findings, whereas the others adopt a more neutral tone of merely stating the results. At the same time, the EE texts tend to emphasise the originality of their outcome, but frequently without actually describing it in the abstract itself.

The following excerpts have been chosen to illustrate the most typical patterns (in the order of increasing rhetorical intensity) in each group:

EE

(11) Tentative explanations for the apparently unusual results are offered.

(LSP: 9)

EU/R

(12) The mentioned factors describe the complicated environment of ESL/ EFL teaching that must be reflected in the Grammatical Syllabus if it has the goal of helping the students to attain communicative competence in both speaking and writing.   (TSLU: 15)

U/R

(13) *Vvazhajemo perspektyvnym vklyuchennia do programy uchbovogo kursu na ekonomichnykh fakultetakh praktykumu z reklamy, pobudovanomu na riznykh typakh anglomovnogo RT. Tse dopomozhe posylyty fakhovi orientatsiji navchannia studentiv ta aspirantiv i spryatyme podal'shomu rozvytkovi jikh navychok volodinnya suchasnoju anglijskoju dilovoju movoju.*   (PTFL: 128)

We consider the inclusion of the specialised English course on advertising built on the different types of ad texts into the language syllabus of Economics departments to be promising. It will facilitate the professional orientation of language teaching to under- and postgraduates and promote further development of their Business English skills.

Formal layout of texts

So far, I have shown the most obvious differences in the cognitive structuring of three groups of abstracts chosen for the analysis. The picture will be, however, incomplete if we do not consider the distribution of the moves within the texts, in particular their correlation with the paragraph structuring of the abstracts, and such important textual elements as titles.

Paragraph structuring

The differences observed within the second dimension of analysis are indeed remarkable. First of all, the number of paragraphs in the texts of each group vary strikingly, as shown in Table 12.2.

Thus, the EE abstracts consist on average of three paragraphs with five as the longest variant and one as the shortest possible. Most typically, the first and the second moves are realised in the initial paragraph, while the following one introduces and summarises the paper, and the third paragraph highlights the outcome. In the texts consisting of two paragraphs the last move is

Table 12.2   Paragraphs: quantitative data

	EE	U/R	EU/R
Number of paragraphs in a text (range)	1–5	4–12	4–8
Number of paragraphs in a text (average)	3	8	5

not marked as a separate paragraph and usually follows a paper summary as a last sentence (or sentences) of the abstract. In any case, the introductory moves 'Outlining the research field' and 'Justifying a particular research' occupy no less than one-third of the text (in four-paragraph texts where they are realised through two paragraphs, their specific weight is still greater). It should also be noted that the paragraphs in the EE texts tend to be alike if not similar in their length.

At the same time, the U/R abstracts have an evident multiparagraph structure ranging from four up to twelve paragraphs with a mean number of eight. The textual distribution of moves here is, however, explicit: the first paragraph is devoted to outlining the research field and justifying a particular research, the last paragraph highlights the results, while the rest summarise, or, more exactly, tell briefly the content of the paper to be presented. As in other genres of Ukrainian and Russian academic discourse, there is no uniformity in the length of paragraphs, which can vary considerably.

Within the EU/R group, the picture is less clear. As Table 12.2 shows, the number of textual paragraphs here is less than in the abstracts in the Slavic languages, but larger than in the authentic English texts. The introductory first and second moves are realised mostly through two initial paragraphs and occupy more textual space than their U/R counterparts. However, the paragraphs that introduce and summarise the paper unmistakably reveal their 'hidden' Slavic origin: they are as variable in their length as the U/R texts. Thus, on the scale between the clearly structured, quite 'abstract-like' EE texts and the U/R group, the EU/R conference abstracts are somewhat in an intermediate position – perhaps slightly shifted towards the texts in the Slavic languages with their elaborated formal layout that makes them seem more like a mini research paper than an abstract *per se.*

Titles

And now a few observations on another important component of content and formal structure of conference abstracts – their titles.

The brief analysis of the structures of the titles investigated in this chapter has again shown that, similar to other genre-relevant features, they are subject to a certain variation that seems to be related to the type of group they belong to. The most homogeneous set of titles is that of the U/R texts with twelve abstracts headed by the titles in the traditional nominal form (a noun/ nominalised verb phrase in the nominative case):

(14) *Lingvo-dydaktychni etapy audytornoji roboty z fakhovym tekstom.*   (TLSP: 218)

Linguo-didactic stages of a classroom work with a professional text.

Within the EE group, the structure of titles seems to be more diverse. Seven of them follow the nominal pattern described above, while another seven have a more complicated structure consisting of two parts separated by a colon. Of these seven, two titles have an 'eye-catching' structure of a nominal phrase + a question separated by a colon:

(15) Youser-friendly (*sic*) metalanguage: what effect does it have on learners of
       English?   (LSP: 9)

The stylistic expressiveness of this title is intensified by a coined attribute 'youser-friendly', the meaning of which is clarified in the body of the text.

And, finally, one title follows a quite different, but not less impressive pattern of a heading-question (in fact, it even consists of two questions):

(16) Authentic for whom? Does text authenticity really matter?   (LTRC: 17)

As for the EU/R group, it reveals (as might now be expected) a rather eclectic variety of the titles that follow both Slavic and English models (but with some tendency towards the use of colon-structures observed in 40% of abstracts), e.g.:

(17) Using The History of the English Language Course as a Means of Under-
       standing the Social Identity of English Speaking People.   (TSLU: 18)

(18) Ukrainian Double-talk Still Alive: Translating Government Documents into
       English.   (TSLU: 9)

Example (17) obviously signals the transfer of source languages stereotypes, while the one following it is quite English-like. Overall, the titles written in the English language (both by native and non-native speakers) are rather diverse and tend to employ more impressive, appealing constructions than those produced in the two Slavic languages.

Some insights into the language of abstracts

The consideration of the third generic aspect of the conference abstracts – their language – will be restricted in this chapter to the description of two features that seem to be important for the genre: the functioning of pronouns 'I'/'we' and that of evaluative words.

Pronouns 'I'/'we'

Table 12.3 shows the quantitative data illustrating the number, occurrences, and distribution of two personal pronouns in the texts investigated. As seen from the table, Ukrainian and Russian abstracts of both groups definitely outweigh their English 'genre-mates' in the number of the texts that employ 'we' as well as in the number of occurrences of the pronoun in a text. The functions of 'we' in the Slavic abstracts are more diverse, the common one

Table 12.3 Distribution and occurrence of 'I', 'we' pronouns

Pronouns	EE	U/R	EU/R
I+we (for more than one co-author)			
1. Number of texts (out of 15)	4	4	4
2. Average number of occurrences in a text	1.8	1.8	2.5
We (single author)			
1. Number of texts (out of 15)	3	7	6
2. Average number of occurrences in a text	1.8	2.4	2.4

with the English texts being that of the reference to shared knowledge or experience (this is the only role of 'we' in the EE group), e.g.:

EE

(19) We can make the greatest contribution in our education/training programs . . . by infusing the content with the skills necessary to operate successfully within a variety of intercultural communication environments . . .

(LSP: 108)

EU/R

(20) Theoretically speaking, we know very much about ESP . . .   (TSLU: 31)

This 'we' is considered to be inclusive as it involves addressees in the range of referents of the pronoun (Vassileva, 2000).

The dominating 'we' in the Slavic texts, however, is the exclusive authorial 'we', widely used in the expressions of personal views as well as in the moves 'Introducing the paper' and 'Summarising the paper', where it, in fact, compensates for the absence of textual organisers (metadiscourse), e.g.:

(21) One of our tasks was to pinpoint these viruses in order to prescribe treatment. We analysed the reproductions of GD made by both native and non-native English speakers . . .   (TSLU: 9)

This explanation also seems to account for the higher occurrence of both 'I' (and 'we' referring to co-authors) in the EU/R group. It is difficult, however, to trace any regularities in their use, in so far as the pronouns appear here in various contextual situations in each of the three sets of abstracts. In general, their function here is rather traditional – to individualise discourse and emphasise the responsibility of the authors for their writing, e.g.:

EE

(22) My earlier work on 'imitation' is also not so appropriate to this investigation . . .   (DAC: 16)

U/R

(23) *U mene bula mozhlyvist' provesty aprobatsiju danogo vydu roboty v grupi studentiv ekonomichnogo fakul' tetu . . .*   (PTFL: 105)

I had an opportunity to test this kind of work in the group of students of the Economics Department . . .

EU/R

(24) I will concentrate mainly on the problem of the discourse analysis in fiction.   (TLSU: 65)

In brief, the main differences observed here are as follows: the Slavic writers tend to use a depersonalising exclusive 'we' that is entirely absent from the EE group; English authors use inclusive 'we' only; personal pronouns and those possessive pronouns semantically related to them compensate for the lack of textual organisers in the abstracts written by Ukrainian and Russian writers.

Evaluative words

Another important linguistic feature of the abstracts – evaluative language – seems to be more prominent in the U/R and EU/R groups than in the English texts. The words of positive evaluation dominate the lexical composition of the abstracts written in the Ukrainian and Russian languages. They occur in the beginning of the texts as part of the verbal realisation of importance claim, e.g.:

(25) *V galuzi metodyki vykladannia inozemnykh mov odnym iz providnykh napryamkiv stalo navchannia stylistychno dyferentsijnogo usnogo movlennia . . .*
                                                                            (TLSP: 218)

Teaching stylistically different oral speech . . . has become one of the leading trends of the methodology of teaching foreign languages.

or, still more typically, in the concluding parts of the abstracts emphasising the significance of the findings or observations:

(26) *Takym chynom, electronni teksty ye ne tilky dzherelom aktyalnoji informatsiji, ale j tsinnym materialom dlia udoskonalennia znan' z inozemnoji movy.*   (TLSP: 64)

Thus, electronic texts are not only a source of important information, but also a valuable material for the improvement of foreign languages knowledge.

The EE texts tend to be more reserved and to avoid direct positive evaluations either in the beginning of the texts or when highlighting the outcome. At the same time, these abstracts contain words with negative lexical meanings or connotations that occur in the second move of their cognitive structure:

(27) Unfortunately, it is rare for theorists to make clear what the practical implications of their theories are . . .   (LTRC: 8)

The Ukrainian and Russian abstracts do not show any verbal traces of criticism, which is quite natural for texts without a rhetorical sub-move of indicating a gap in research.

However, the EU/R abstracts are replete with both positive and negative language; they have obviously 'inherited' the Slavic patterns of evaluating the field of research and its outcome, as well as adopted to a certain extent the verbal style of criticising previous investigations. Here are two examples of the beginning and ending paragraphs of the EU/R abstracts that contain a variety of evaluative words:

> (28) Still, stylistic 'viruses' prevail in non-native speakers' translation. There could be only one reason for this – inadequate knowledge of English
> (TSLU: 9)

> (29) One of the greatest benefits of this technique is that it doesn't allow the students and the teacher to focus on teacher/pupils' behavior in class, ... but provides an excellent opportunity for practicing the target language at the same time.   (TSLU: 103)

Thus, evaluative language is a salient feature of the Slavic version of the genre, while it is less noticeable in the texture of the English abstracts.

Summary of the observations and findings

In brief, the major observations of this study are as follows.

The English native texts and Ukrainian/Russian abstracts differ significantly, if they do not oppose each other in all the features considered. On the other hand, the features within each of the two groups are consistent, that is they work together for the creation of a certain 'integral' image of a text. Thus, the EE abstracts produce the impression of clearly cut and quite 'abstract-like' texts that emphasise the originality of a particular piece of research and try to impress or even intrigue the reader. Ukrainian and Russian abstracts in these languages look like short research papers, tend to be rather global in describing their research, and are in general more impersonal than their English counterparts, emphasising not so much the novelty of the investigation, but rather its continuing and non-conflicting character. However, the EU/R group possesses such an eclectic mixture of different features (perhaps, with a slight domination of the Slavic ones) that it is difficult to outline briefly the general character of these texts; they will be considered in more detail in the section on 'Intergenres' below.

DISCUSSION AND TENTATIVE EXPLANATIONS OF THE
OBSERVATIONS AND FINDINGS

National professional, ideological, or cultural proclivities?

The variation in the genre of the conference abstract in English and Ukrainian/ Russian is probably due to a number of factors that seem to overlap and complement the influence of each other. First, some features of the texts may be determined to a certain extent by the specific conditions of the organisation of a conference. In Western countries there is a tendency to plan large-scale national and international events in advance, and prospective presenters, therefore, usually have to submit their abstracts almost a year before the beginning of a conference. Under such circumstances, the research presented in an abstract is frequently incomplete and naturally resembles a general outline with such features as a short 'Summarising the paper' move that gives the brief overview of a presentation or partially highlighted outcome in the form of some preliminary suggestions. In Ukraine the period of time between the first call for papers and the deadline for abstracts is usually about six months or even less. Under these different time requirements, Ukrainian academics prefer to write and talk about already achieved results. The evidence of this completeness of research can be seen in such features of the U/R and EU/R texts as a long and detailed description of the paper or a rather confident presentation of the outcome. These are, however, only partial explanations. Another more important group of factors seems to stem from different social and ideological contexts, in particular, from the market orientation and competitiveness of Western society and the rather collaborative, communal character (at least up till recent times) of Ukrainian life and scholarship.

Western scholars are known to experience ever-increasing demands in promoting their research during the process of struggling for publishing opportunities, academic positions, or additional funding. This reality of market society – the necessity to win the attention and recognition of target addressees, to 'sell' a research product – inevitably influences academic discourse, making it persuasive and self-promotional. Such features can be traced on the different levels of the EE texts: in particular, they include the rhetorical strategies of indicating a gap, question-posing, and counter-claiming that facilitate the presentation of research as novel; strong claims for originality; clearly cut, reader-friendly structuring of texts that promotes better and quicker perception of their main points; and, simultaneously, 'eye-catching' titles, promising hints in the end of abstracts that might impress or intrigue a reviewing committee or potential audience.

In contrast, Ukrainian society has only recently started to gain market experience that affects its academic spheres, mostly in an indirect way.

As predominantly homogeneous, collaborative (at least within a limited number of research groups), and non-conflicting, Ukrainian scholarship was formed during the Soviet era, when the Communist ideology was considered to be the only methodological foundation of research and, therefore, any explicit deviation from it was simply impossible. Thus, all research was presented as fitting this broad ideological context (though in many cases it was merely a ritual convention of Soviet academic writing). The 'imprints' of such rhetoric are traceable in the beginning of the U/R abstracts where the field of investigation and a particular research area are presented as parts of still wider and significant domains. Also, frequent reference in the Slavic texts to a current sociopolitical or economic situation is undoubtedly a 'remnant' of the Communist discourse with its constant emphasis on the superiority of societal (communal) values over individual ones. This ideological (and ethical) factor may also account for a less personal and rather formal general tone of the Slavic abstracts as compared to that of the EE texts.

On the other hand, some of these (as well as other features) seem to be shaped by certain cultural and intellectual traditions. In particular, Galtung (1985) notices that Russia and Eastern Europe experienced the impact of the so-called Teutonic (German) intellectual style due to certain historical circumstances. The features of this style (described also by Clyne, 1994; Čmejrková and Daneš, 1997; Duszak, 1997) include special emphasis on theoretical issues, the relatively greater significance of the content of writing than its form, and weak interactive properties of written texts that require from the reader certain intellectual efforts to be properly understood. Within this tradition, knowledge is transmitted to the reader in such a way as to provide the stimulus for thought or even intellectual pleasure.

In contrast, Anglo-Saxon texts are writer-responsible, that is, they are arranged in such a way as to ensure their most adequate perception and unambiguous understanding by the reader; the English writers also favour a straightforward, rather independent style for the expression of their thoughts and ideas that may be attributed to the traditional domination of individualism and appropriate ethical values of Western society.

The influence of these different cultural contexts can be noticed in the overall generic features of the investigated abstracts. While the EE texts are reader-oriented, use helpful (for the addressees) metadiscourse and have a distinct cognitive and formal structure, the Slavic abstracts seem to be preoccupied with the content, avoid textual organisers and any formal structuration, and reveal an inclination towards theorising and generalisations (through global statements at the beginning of the texts). These cultural backgrounds also determine the specific features of 'interestingness' that vary so strikingly in the two 'opposite', EE and U/R groups.

What is 'interesting' for different academic cultures?

Berkenkotter and Huckin (1995) investigated a large number of abstracts submitted to a particular conference (a composition convention) and came to the conclusion that a dominant rhetorical feature of conference abstracts is 'interestingness' created by the appropriate selection of a topic, convincing problem definition, and novelty. One of its features (though not necessarily outweighing others) is 'the way the authors define the issues and develop them' (1995: 111). This particular framing of the discourse 'in an interesting and interestingly problematic way' (Swales, 1996b: 47) is obvious in the EE texts with their preliminary scene-settings that show the importance and novelty of the research, intriguing concluding parts, 'eye-catching' titles, and appealing language. At the same time, the formal and 'serious' Ukrainian and Russian abstracts look rather 'uninteresting' – however, only for an outsider. Those familiar with Slavic academic culture and intellectual style will identify their specific 'interestingness' created not by the specific framing of the presentation, but through a deep professional contextualisation of the research, its incorporating an appropriate theoretical background, and a detailed description of the paper and its findings that establish or emphasise the scholarly credibility of the author as a worthy member of his/her research communities. Thus, the Slavic abstracts appeal to their addressees by 'telling', while the promotional English texts do their 'selling job' (Swales and Feak, 1994: 214); so far, both groups appear to be different, if not opposing each other, in the ways they realise the main goals of the genre.

'Intergenres'

And now a final insight into the EU/R group – the abstracts with an eclectic and even eccentric blend of different features coexisting in one text. The majority of them seem to be closer to their Slavic 'genre-mates' although some abstracts successfully follow the Anglo-Saxon standards; certain abstracts show the evidence of the over-application of target generic features (like the one that justifies the research by posing eleven (!) questions), that is, however, typical for texts that emerge partly as imitations. On the other hand, the steady occurrence of these features testifies that at least some of them have already been adopted, under the appropriate influences from the West and in conformity with current changes in the intellectual life of Ukraine. In fact, these 'indefinite', transitional texts are different from the other two groups and might be therefore called 'intergenres', on the analogy with the well-known concept of interlanguage (as a stage in second-language acquisition) distinct from both native and target tongues (Selinker, 1972). As complex phenomena, EU/R 'intergenres' not only show the level of the linguistic and cultural competence of their creators, but also signal the changes in the ideology and conventionalised existence of the academic community that has found itself at the interface of two social systems. The role of the English language as a 'catalyst' for 'verbalising' these new realities is, however, a decisive factor: as has been shown, the abstracts in the Ukrainian and Russian languages are resistant towards any 'marketisation' of their discourse or generic features.

PEDAGOGICAL CONSIDERATIONS AND MORE

As any kind of applied contrastive research, this study also has certain pedagogical implications. In particular, it may raise a broader issue of the degree to which the conventions of the genre have to be accepted.

It is well known that the process of learning and acquisition of genres in foreign languages inevitably includes some psychological problems. Not surprisingly, scholars writing in a non-native language may even intuitively seek a certain 'rhetorical compromise' and choose 'softened', less frustrating strategies. In fact, the 'intergenres' – the EU/R texts – reveal the signs of this almost unavoidable negotiation of cultural values that makes the process of genre construction and writing less painful. On the other hand, the toleration of such 'intergenres' by the Western Anglophone audience could also ease the way of the representatives of other cultures into international scholarship.

This final consideration that might be treated as a contradictory issue lies, however, outside the scope of this chapter. Summing up, I can conclude that the conference abstract is a genre sensitive to cultural influences, able to react to their changes rhetorically, and, furthermore, even to exist in a rather indefinite state of intercultural transition and flux.

ACKNOWLEDGEMENTS

This work was supported by the Research Support Scheme of the Open Society Institute/Higher Education Support Programme, grant no. 285/97, and through a National Academy of Education/Spencer Postdoctoral Fellowship.

NOTES

1. All examples from the English texts written by Ukrainian and Russian speakers are given without any correction to their language or style.
2. Here and henceforth, the translation of the Ukrainian and Russian examples (undertaken by the author of the paper) is close to word-by-word in order to retain the rhetorical flavour of the original.

APPENDIX 12.1 LIST OF CONFERENCES

DAC   Developing Discourse Awareness in Cross-Cultural Contexts. International Conference. Radziejowice, 9–11 May 1996.

LSP   The 11th European Symposium on Language for Special Purposes. Copenhagen, 18–22 August 1997.

LTRC   Eighteenth Annual Language Testing and Research Colloquium. Tampere, 31 July–3 August 1996.

PTFL   *Lingvo-dydaktychni problemy vykladannia inozemnykh mov na ekonomichnykh fakultetakh* (Linguo-didactic Problems of Teaching Foreign Languages at Economics Departments). West Regional Conference of Teachers of Foreign Languages. Ternopil, 13–14 May 1997.

TLSP   *Strategiji ta metodyki navchannia movam dlia spetsialnykh tsilej* (Strategies and Methodologies of Teaching Languages for Special Purposes). Third International Conference. Kyiv, 24–25 April 1997.

TSLU   2nd National TESOL–Ukraine Conference, 'The Art and Science of TESOL'. Vinnytsia, 20–22 January 1997.

Part IV

ETHNOGRAPHIC/ NATURALISTIC APPROACHES

Chapter 13

Ethnographically inspired approaches to the study of academic discourse

John Flowerdew

INTRODUCTION

Ethnography can be defined briefly as the study of a social group or individual or individuals representative of that group, based on direct recording of the behaviour and voices of the participants by the researcher over a period. An important dimension of any ethnographic study is the part played by language, but language is considered within the context of its production and reception, rather than in isolation, simply as text. Ethnographic and naturalistic approaches to academic discourse therefore take a broader, more contextual view of discourse than do the other approaches represented in this collection.

There are many ways of approaching an overview article. Possible ways of organising this chapter on ethnographic and naturalistic approaches to researching academic discourse might be according to any of the following:

- the language macro skill(s) focused upon (writing, reading, listening, speaking);
- the size of group studied (case study, multiple case study, whole group);
- the dimensions of the study (cross-sectional, longitudinal);
- the disciplines studied (sciences, arts, social sciences, etc.);
- the academic level of the participants in the study (secondary, tertiary undergraduate, postgraduate);
- the location of the study (L1 contexts, ESL contexts, EFL contexts).

This list is only partial and there are no doubt many other ways in which this chapter could be organised.

When one begins to compile a list of the work which has been done, however, one finds that none of these systems of organisation is really appropriate, because there is not enough material available to sustain whole sections on each of these categories. The first of those systems listed – language macro-skills – might be the most feasible. However, if one attempts this, one soon realises that there is a disproportionate amount of work which has been done on academic writing (e.g. Belcher, 1994; Candlin and Plum, 1998; Casanave, 1995; J. Flowerdew, 2000; Herrington, 1985, 1988; Lea and

Street, 1999; Leki and Carson, 1997; McCarthy, 1987; Prior, 1998; Ramanathan and Atkinson, 1999; Spack, 1997; Walvoord and McCarthy, 1990). There are a few studies on listening (e.g. Benson, 1988, 1994; Flowerdew and Miller, 1992, 1995, 1996; Mason, 1994). I know of only one study on speaking (Furneaux et al., 1991). As for reading, I am not familiar with any ethnographic approaches to this skill in academic contexts (although see Bell, this volume). Another drawback of approaching this chapter according to macro-skills would be to distort one of the main findings of ethnographic work into academic discourse, namely its interdiscursive nature, how any one discourse activity is situated within the context of many others, so that writing, for instance, emanates from a complex interaction of listening, speaking, and reading, prior to and during the production of the actual text (Candlin and Hyland, 1999).

I have therefore decided to select a small number of studies for review which I find particularly interesting for various reasons and – because the purpose of this article is primarily to demonstrate the potential of an ethnographic approach – I will then devote considerable space to an analysis of some of my own research (with my colleague Lindsay Miller), highlighting what I consider to be the ethnographic dimensions of this work. Before these two review sections, however, I will set out some of the basic principles of ethnography and naturalistic research as they apply to the study of academic discourse.

Using this system of organisation, I hope to be able to provide the reader with some idea of the potential of ethnographic methods in studying academic discourse, with an indication of some of the work that has been done; and some of the important principles involved.

WHAT ARE ETHNOGRAPHY AND NATURALISTIC METHODS?

For some researchers, ethnography is synonymous with other forms of naturalistic research and methods. For example, Miles and Huberman (1994: 1) state that 'the terms *ethnography, field methods, qualitative inquiry, participant observation, case study, naturalistic methods,* and *responsive evaluation* have become practically synonymous' (see also e.g. Hammersley and Atkinson, 1983: 1). For others, ethnography has very specific procedures and criteria. Johnson (1992: 134)), for example, states:

> although other approaches to research may involve similar field techniques, many visits or long stays at the research site, and good descriptive accounts, they are not ethnographies unless they involve holistic study of cultural phenomena and cultural interpretation of behavior. Interestingly, many respected ethnographers are very cautious and selective about applying the terms 'ethnographic' and 'ethnography' to their studies.

In the field of TESOL and ethnography often-cited references are an article by Watson-Gegeo (1988) which responds to the questions 'What is ethnography? And what can it do for us in ESL?' and Heath's earlier, nearly a decade-long model study, 'Ways with words' (1983).

For the purposes of this chapter, it might be useful to distinguish ethnographic or qualitative/naturalistic *methods* from *ethnography* proper.

Ethnographic methods

Ethnographic methods are based on watching and asking. A variety of methods can be used in this process:

* participant and non-participant observation;
* reflective/in-depth interview;
* questionnaire survey;
* focus group discussion;
* biographical history;
* diaries.

Notice how these methods focus upon the context of production and reception of texts, not just upon the texts themselves.

Validity and reliability

To ensure reliability and validity of findings ethnographers rely on *triangulation, prolonged engagement,* and, to a lesser extent, *participant verification.*
　Patton (1987) distinguishes four types of triangulation:

* Data sources – conclusions are developed from more than one set of data, e.g. interview transcripts and participant observation field notes;
* Investigator – more than one investigator is involved in the study;
* Theory – the same data is analysed using different theories;
* Methods – more than one data collection method is used, e.g. interviews and participant observation.

　Prolonged engagement means long periods of time spent in the field until there is *saturation of data,* i.e. repeated observations and questioning reveal no new information about the categories; researchers consciously look at different individuals and groups to find differences. When researchers continually find similar instances of data and no differences they become 'empirically confident that a category is saturated' (Glaser and Strauss, 1967: 61).
　Participant verification (Ball, 1988) refers to the recycling of the results of the analysis, or the ongoing analysis, to the participants for their validation.[1] As participants in the culture being described, do they agree with, or what is their reaction to, the analysis? Participant verification has the added advantage that it can be beneficial in raising participants' awareness of their language practices, often an important goal in ethnographic/naturalistic studies itself.

Data analysis

Data analysis is *recursive,* i.e. the researcher begins by establishing a set of categories for the data collected, but then refines these categories, making more or less and organising them in different ways, in order to account for all of the data.

Analysis can be assisted by various software packages, such as the *Ethnograph*, NUDIST, ATLAS, or WINMAX. These allow the researcher to tag extracts of data – field notes, interview extracts, diary extracts, etc. – according to the categories set up. These can then be retrieved by the software. Traditionally this was and still is done by some researchers by the use of index cards or cutting and pasting with the photocopier.

Software can also assist in adding a *quantitative dimension* to qualitative research, which can provide added validity and reliability. Of course, a quantitative dimension can be introduced without the use of software. With small numbers, however, researchers should be careful about drawing strong conclusions from such statistics.

The recursive nature of the analytical method means constant return to the field either for further observation, or – more likely – to ask further questions on specific issues. Even at the stage of writing up the report it may be necessary to substantiate or extend the findings. For example, it may be useful in the report to indicate approximately what proportion of the participants held a particular opinion on a given issue. This information might be obtained by simply e-mailing each of the participants and asking them this particular question.

How many participants should be involved in an ethnographic study?

As long as the participants are representative of the group and its culture (bearing in mind that the term 'culture' can refer to a heterogeneous group), then there is no fixed criterion for the number of participants. Sometimes, a single case study will reveal a lot about the culture. Other times, several cases may be more revealing – they are likely to provide a comparative dimension. Larger numbers, on the other hand, may suggest more reliable findings for the group as a whole.

If using multiple cases, then it is appropriate to have criteria for choosing participants who represent different aspects of the culture – for example, in an ESL context, if using three participants, one might choose one high proficiency participant, one low and one average. Or one might select participants as representative of different disciplines – for example, one biologist, one chemist, and one physicist.

The role of theory

In *grounded* approaches (Glaser and Strauss, 1967), a local theory is created out of the data. The researcher starts with as few preconceptions as possible about what is likely to be found. In practice, however, there will always be some implicit theory with which the researcher is working. In other types of qualitative research, the researcher may seek to apply a specific theory. Where interpretation is involved – a necessary dimension of ethnographic research – then we can say that a local theory is created.

The ethnographic report

In spite of criteria for maintaining reliability and validity, ethnography acknowledges the subjective role of the researcher and the 'artistic' dimension of the research report (see Atkinson, 1990). The powerful ethnographic account creates a vivid image of the culture being described and interpreted. It is therefore important that an ethnographic report should describe the setting, the participants, and what they do and say effectively.

Important techniques in effective ethnographic reporting are *vignettes* (short descriptions of situations and activities) and *quotations* from participants collected either through interviews or field notes.

Application of the findings

Because they focus on one particular group or individual, ethnographers cannot make claims as to the generalisability of their findings. It is for others to decide to what extent the findings of a given ethnographic study might apply to situations with which they themselves are familiar. For example, a study of how lectures are conducted in country A may or may not apply to the way they are conducted in country B. For this reason it is very important that as much detail about the situation as possible is provided in the ethnographic account so that others have a basis for comparison with other situations. Ethnographic accounts are often very useful, however, in addressing social and educational problems in specific contexts. Ethnographic studies may therefore often conclude with specific recommendations for consciousness-raising or direct action.

Ethnography, discourse, and text

Because ethnography is concerned with social groups and how they interact, the discourse of such groups is an important feature to consider. Typically, an ethnographic approach to language research will focus more on the social context than the actual text (spoken or written). Ethnographic approaches can be distinguished from *genre analysis* in so far as although in the latter there is an ethnographic dimension, the main thrust of the analysis is on the text. In ethnography, however, there will be more focus on the social context and the text analysis will be used to support theories about the social group.

SOME SELECTED STUDIES

Academic seminars in a British university

This study (Furneaux et al., 1991) has been chosen, first, because it is a relatively early example of an ethnographic approach to academic discourse, and, second, because it focuses, on a skill – speaking – which has received little attention subsequently.[2] The researchers began with a problem encountered in staff–student interactions in a British university. Based on their own experience, anecdote, and the literature on seminar strategies in EAP courses, their awareness of this problem was reinforced by an initial video recording of a seminar which indicated to the researchers that the students were not perceiving correctly what was expected of them in this situation. Instead of responding to the questions posed by the lecturer, they took notes, while the lecturer was reduced to answering his own questions. The investigators felt that this inappropriate seminar behaviour was likely to be 'a cultural, or at least socio-pragmatic, problem as much as a linguistic one' (p. 74). This general problem was broken down into a number of research questions, which the researchers summarise as trying to find out 'whether NNS students really have a problem, and whether it is different in kind from that which faces NS students' (p. 75). The results of the study are quite complex and difficult to summarise. However, amongst the findings were that there was a considerable variation in the structure of seminars across disciplines, that there was not such a great discrepancy between staff and students' expectations of seminar participation as had been anticipated, and that NS students considered asking questions more important than NNSs did. Recommendations resulting from the study include the following:

- EAP teachers needed to find out what types of seminars their students should expect;
- EAP teachers needed to pass this information on to their students;
- Student training was needed in listening for instructions from lecturers on what to read for the next seminar; oral presentation skills; asking questions; and collaborative problem-solving skills.

Methods used in this study included pre-course questionnaires administered to both staff and students, seminar observation, and audio recording of seminars. As the researchers themselves point out (p. 83), further research would benefit if interviews were used to supplement the questionnaire data. Thus, although the study is entitled 'The ethnography of academic lectures', while the methods used are commonly used in ethnographic methodology, the study cannot be classed as a full-blown ethnography.

Language classrooms in Chinese universities

The authors of this study (Cortazzi and Jin, 1996) describe their goal as 'to understand language classrooms in China in terms of participants' own understanding of what it means to be a good teacher or a good student' (p. 169). This, they claim, 'will form an important part of the ideological model of what teachers and learners expect from each other' and that '[t]his is part of a *culture of learning* [original emphasis] which may be a determining factor on what happens in language classrooms and what is judged to be successful language learning' (p. 169). They point out that in studying classroom behaviour '[w]hat matters is not only what happens in the classroom but how participants interpret events and what they expect to happen' (p. 172). In common with many naturalistic researchers (including Furneaux et al., 1991, above), Cortazzi and Jin bring a comparative dimension to their study, in their case, between Western teachers and Chinese learners in China: 'The emphasis here is on how participants construe the meaning and purpose of classroom activity; teachers may have one view, students may have quite another' (p. 172). Because of the emphasis on the socio-cultural context on the culture of learning, Cortazzi and Jin devote sections of their article to describing the socialisation of Chinese learners in kindergarten and primary school and the socio-economic background affecting attitudes towards the teaching and learning of English among Chinese during the current period of rapid modernisation. The main focus of the article, however, is the *English Intensive Reading Course*, which is the premier language course at all stages of learning, from school to university throughout China. Cortazzi and Jin's interest is at the university level and mismatches between the perceptions of Western teachers concerning this course and those of Chinese learners.

Data collection in this study was by means of classroom observation, interview, written responses to open-ended questions, and essays written on the theme of 'Western ways of teaching and Chinese ways of learning' by Chinese university students who were being taught by Western teachers. Reporting of the results makes use of ethnographic description of typical classroom exploitation of the *English Intensive Reading Course* and extensive use of quotations from the other data.

The results emphasise how Western and Chinese views of what constitutes an appropriate culture of learning differ, how '[t]he Western and Chinese cultures of learning sometimes weave past each other without linking' (p. 190). The observation data and research literature show that, despite its name, the *English Intensive Reading Course* is not designed primarily to develop reading comprehension. Instead, it uses texts as a basis for the development of grammar and vocabulary. This method has been much criticised by Western teachers and by some Chinese teachers, but, the researchers claim, it is difficult to change the system, because 'the teaching approach has become institutionalised as part of a Chinese culture of learning' (p. 184). As the ethnographic data indicate, the method conforms with traditional Chinese approaches to teaching and learning (if one can talk in such a unitary way), even though Chinese culture and society in general are currently undergoing rapid change in many areas (p. 198).

In their article, Cortazzi and Jin are at pains to point out that '[i]n principle, there is no reason to suppose that one culture of learning is superior to another' (p. 174). They also make the important point, however, that cultures of learning may be subject to change (p. 198). Nevertheless, different cultures of learning may be more or less appropriate to the larger cultures within which they are located. Equally, 'there is no reason, in principle why different cultures of learning should be mutually exclusive. Rather, different ways might be reconciled or interwoven.' This paves the way for Cortazzi and Jin's recommendations. Because of the mismatch between Chinese and Western conceptions of teaching and learning they recommend what they call 'cultural synergy'. Western teachers, on the one hand, can move closer to the Chinese culture of learning, but do not have to abandon the strengths of their approach. Chinese learners, on the other hand, may learn from Western teaching methods used by Western or Chinese teachers, but not at the expense of abandoning their society's own culture of learning.

Critical ethnography in a South African university

In this study (Thesen, 1997), the author is interested in 'how previous experience, particularly nonschool experience, affects access to academic discourse'. The setting is the University of Cape Town in post-apartheid South Africa, where Black students have difficulty in making the transition to university study. This transition is marked by a double linguistic shift: the medium of instruction is English and the new register is formal and abstract (a register deliberately not promoted in the pre-university system for Black students under the apartheid system). In addition, the university staff have failed to adapt to the new post-apartheid realities.

The database for the study consists of initial meetings with students, followed by biographical interviews, discussion of interview extracts with participants, and discourse analysis of essays written by students involving discussion with the latter on the relationship between aspects of the essays and their biographical interviews. The author describes her methodology as 'simultaneously linguistic (a discourse analysis of an essay) and ethnographic (an attempt through the biographical interviews to reach a better understanding of who the writers are and what their linguistic choices mean)' (p. 494).

In addition to its innovative use of biographical data, the study is particularly interesting for its overt *a priori* use of theory instead of relying on theory developing out of the data. The author initially applied *critical discourse theory* (Kress, 1989; Fairclough, 1992; Canagarajah, 1993; Peirce, 1995; Pennycook, 1994; McKay and Wong, 1996), and *new literacy studies* theory (Gee, 1990), theories which see the acquisition of literacy as ideologically determined and profoundly linked to social processes.[3] The author argues that while these theories are useful in providing analytical tools for describing what she refers to as 'the complex and contradictory stances that accompany the acquisition of English in complex settings' (p. 488), they are nevertheless limited in what they offer 'to the understanding of the relationship between individuals and larger social processes in periods of rapid transition' (p. 488). This reorientation of the theory is developed by the author out of the analysis of her data. Identity, for the author, her data reveal, is dynamic. Critical discourse theory, in imposing fixed identity categories (such as race, gender, ethnicity, and language), is, in her view, deterministic and deficient because it neglects individual accounts. The biographical data thus support the author's contention that there is a 'discrepancy between the institutional categories that are used to identify and define students [e.g. *disadvantaged, underprepared, second language*] and how students describe themselves as they make sense of their transitions into the university' (p. 488). The institutional labelling, which is translated in practical terms to special paths for Black students, is, for the author, both enabling and stigmatising (p. 490). One negative consequence of this situation is that students often become alienated from the curriculum, 'tending to invest more in their social lives than in their academic identities' (p. 505).

In terms of educational policy, the author has two major recommendations. The first is increasing institutional self-awareness of how students' identities may be negatively affected by the labelling process. The second is envisaging the possibility of issues of identity being incorporated into the beginning curriculum in order to build awareness on the part of both teachers and students. Two examples are provided of how this has been applied at the university where the study was conducted.

Academic writing at an American university

As already indicated, the study of writing has received more attention on the part of ethnographers than any other academic discourse skill. It is therefore a challenge to choose one study to represent this work. Alternative candidates would have been the seminal study by Berkenkotter and Huckin (1995) or the more recent work by Swales (1998), in which he introduces the term 'textography' to describe the text-oriented ethnography that this work represents, as well as many others. Both Berkenkotter and Huckin (1995) and Swales (1999) are book-length studies. The work I have chosen (Prior, 1998) is also a book-length study, representing 'the culmination of more than a decade of observation, thinking, research, reading, discussion and writing' (p. ix). As such, it is indicative of the prolonged engagement that can go into an ethnography. Situated in the context of the author's teaching of academic reading, writing, and conversation at a US university, the starting point was the question: 'What kind of communicative competence did this multicultural, multilingual and multidisciplinary group of undergraduate and graduate students need?' (p. 9). An answer is sought by means of a series of case studies of writing in graduate seminars – referred to by the author as 'thick descriptions of the contexts and processes of graduate students' writing' (p. x).

The analysis is conducted through the application of a variety of theories of writing and disciplinarity. At the same time, a range of methodologies is brought to bear, as the author strives to develop highly complex, fine-grained analyses, which, he claims, are the only way in which to make sense of what is going on, as the participants negotiate their way into the disciplines within which they operate. Data include transcriptions of seminar discussions, students' descriptions of the writing process, professors' representations of tasks and their responses to students, and the students' texts themselves.

Through this continual interplay of method and theory, the author argues that pre-conceived theories or hypotheses are not appropriate in ethnography. One of the main outcomes of the ethnographic research is to view writing not in the traditional way, as the discrete act of a writer, but as, instead, 'the confluence of many streams of activity: reading, talking, observing, acting, making, thinking, and feeling as well as transcribing words on paper' (p. xi). This leads to the conclusion that the training of graduate students is not a simple question of the induction of individuals into a set of clearly defined disciplines, each with its own specific range of neatly configured practices, but rather a complex negotiation into an ever-changing disciplinary space within which professors and mentors are but one of many influences that continually shape and reshape that discipline.

IN-DEPTH ANALYSIS OF ONE ETHNOGRAPHIC RESEARCH PROJECT

Having reviewed four studies which highlight various aspects of ethnographic and naturalistic approaches, I will now consider one example of my own work (with my colleague Lindsay Miller) in some depth, applying the principles introduced in the first part of this chapter and which were illustrated and developed in the second part.

The project which I will describe and analyse in some detail was conducted over a period of seven years. It began with a specific research problem and a small-scale initial study. A department of English at a Hong Kong university had recently established its first degree course for ESL teachers. The staff, which consisted of a mixture of expatriates and local Hong Kong Chinese, was relatively inexperienced in university degree-level teaching and was unsure about how able students would be in handling English-medium lecture-format instruction for the first time. At the same time, the departmental management team wanted to develop a research culture among its staff and a call went out for collaborative research projects. Familiar with some of the literature on second-language listening, Lindsay Miller and I had not come across any naturalistic studies of the listening process. Most research on listening we had come across had been discourse analysis of texts which were the object of the listening process or experimental studies conducted under laboratory-type conditions. We therefore thought it would be a useful departure for listening research to conduct a naturalistic study of our students listening to lectures in English for the first time. By naturalistic study, we had in mind a research methodology which would be based on observation of the lectures and talking to the students and lecturer. As well as making a potential contribution to the literature on academic listening, such a study would serve as a useful form of ongoing needs analysis which would help us in developing and refining our programme. With my colleague, Lindsay Miller, who was to become my collaborator for the full seven years of the project, we therefore embarked upon a study along these lines.

The participants who were the focus of the research were a group of 30 first-year Hong Kong Chinese in a TESL methods course and their lecturer. The analysis focused on students' perceptions, problems, and strategies in the second-language lecture experience. The results of this project were published as Flowerdew and Miller (1992).

As a development of this initial investigation, a larger-scale project was begun, focusing on a whole group of native-speaking expatriate lecturers and their students, across a range of disciplines. In this investigation, with greater familiarity of the culture under study derived from their previous work, the researchers were able to come up with more of an interpretative dimension. A theory was developed based upon the cultural conflicts in situations in the university where Chinese students received lectures from Western lecturers. The results of this study were reported in two papers (Flowerdew and Miller, 1995, 1996). I will now consider, by means of a number of questions derived from our discussion of naturalistic approaches so far, what the particular aspects of this research were that makes it ethnographic.

1. *What was the motivation for the research? What was the research problem?*
2. *What culture, as represented by an individual or group, did the study focus on?*
3. *What was the setting and who were the participants involved in the study? How detailed or evocative was the description of these contextual elements?*
4. *What types of data were collected and how? What level of triangulation was there? Was data collection systematic? Were data collection instruments developed in situ? How prolonged was the engagement with the situation?*
5. *How was the data analysed? What categories were developed and how? To what extent were participants involved in verification of the analysis?*
6. *How salient were the actual texts in data collection and analysis?*
7. *What was the role of theory? Did it come before or after the study was begun?*
8. *How were the findings reported?*
9. *To what extent might the study be generalisable to other situations?*
10. *What are the implications for application?*

1. What was the motivation for the research? What was the research problem? As indicated above, the motivation for the first study in the research was based on an initial desire to develop a new methodology for listening research.[4] To justify this departure, the researchers contrasted their method with in vitro approaches. First they stated that:

> [T]he in vitro procedure cannot replicate an authentic lecture situation. This means that information can be obtained on only limited aspects of the lecture listening process, namely the cognitive processing of incoming linguistic data. More global information on listener behaviour in lectures, such as the way listeners relate to the lecturer, the way they relate to their peers, the way they use support materials, when and how they record information, etc. is outside the scope of this approach. (Flowerdew and Miller, 1992: 62)

Second, they argued that:

> The second limitation created by the in vitro procedure ... is that lecture listening is treated as an autonomous activity, in isolation from background reading, note-taking, use of support materials such as hand-outs, etc. If listening is not autonomous ... then there is a danger that data derived in vitro from autonomous listening tasks will not be a true reflection of the lecture listening process. (Flowerdew and Miller, 1992: 62)

In addition to the desire to develop a new research methodology, as already mentioned, again, another motivation for the research was the desire on the part of the researchers to tackle a real-world educational problem, that of beginning university students listening for the first time to lectures delivered in English. Finally, the research was viewed as a contribution to an aspect of English for Academic Purposes – lecture listening – which had been relatively neglected compared with the other macro skills of reading, writing, and speaking.

By the time of the second phase of the research, the motivation was to extend the investigation to a broader range of disciplines across the university. As this research developed, cross-cultural issues came to be identified as a particularly problematic aspect of the lecture experience. The research problem thus became one of identifying and elucidating the contrasting perceptions, problems, and strategies, of the group of expatriate lecturers, on the one hand, and the Hong Kong ethnic Chinese students, on the other. As Johnson (1992: 152) notes, such cross-cultural, comparative perspectives are a characteristic of much ethnographic research.

2. What culture, as represented by an individual or group, did the study focus on? The culture represented in the research was that of a Hong Kong university where the vast majority of undergraduate students are Cantonese/Hong Kong Chinese and a considerable percentage of the lecturers are expatriate native-English speaking. The culture under study was thus a subculture of the larger university culture, which was made up of both expatriate native-English-speaking and Chinese faculty. Problems arising with this group were therefore significant within the wider culture of the university and therefore worthy of study. In a later investigation, not reported here due to reasons of space, the attention of the researchers turned to the Cantonese-speaking lecturers (Flowerdew, Li, and Miller, 1998).

3. What was the setting and who were the participants involved in the study? How detailed or evocative was the description of these contextual elements? The setting for the research was a relatively new university in Hong Kong during a time of rapid tertiary-level expansion in education within the society as a whole. Because Hong Kong is very dependent on English for its economic wellbeing, as a centre for international trade, finance, and marketing, it was important to provide considerable contextual background for an international readership. Basic information on the essential role of English in educational and professional success in Hong Kong, which is a predominantly Cantonese-speaking society outside these domains, is essential for an understanding of the importance of English in the university context. Because the research focused on classroom behaviour, the classrooms were described in some detail. Two groups were focused on in the research: the Hong Kong ethnic Chinese students and the expatriate lecturers. In the initial study, as suggested by the title, '*Student* Perceptions, Problems and Strategies in Second Language Lecture Comprehension' (emphasis added), the main focus was the students. Thirty students were selected at random out of a class of 60. Information is provided on their L1 background (Cantonese), the (limited) role of English for these students outside their studies, their secondary education (officially English-medium, but de facto primarily Cantonese for teacher exposition and English for the written materials) and their lack of exposure to the formal monologue lecture mode in English prior to entering the university. Information was obtained for each student on their proficiency level in English, based on their scores on the Hong Kong Use of English examination. Average scores on the Hong Kong Use of English examination were correlated with TOEFL, so as to provide a point of reference for comparison with non-native-English-speaking students studying overseas. It was noted that the scores of the Hong Kong students were somewhat lower than would normally be accepted for study at a US university.

In the later studies there was more emphasis on the lecturers. Although data was collected from a variety of sources, including students, the 'main orientation' to the data in these later studies is stated as being through interviews conducted with the lecturers (Flowerdew and Miller, 1995: 352). In addition to one lecturer who was used in a pilot study, ten native-speaking lecturers (British, US, Australian, and Canadian) (and their students) participated in the research. They were selected so as to provide a cross-section of faculty in the university, in terms of discipline, rank, experience – both in general terms and with Chinese students – and size of class lectured to (each lecturer was focused upon in relation to just one of their classes). This baseline data was presented in the form of a table.

4. What types of data were collected and how? What level of triangulation was there? Was data collection systematic? Were data collection instruments developed in situ? How prolonged was the engagement with the situation? In the first study, which focused primarily on students, data was collected by means of questionnaires, diaries kept by students, classroom observation over the course of the semester, in-depth interviews, recording of the lectures, and a study of various artefacts of the lecture situation (e.g. textbooks, handouts). In the later studies a similar methodology was used as in the previous research, with the addition of focus group discussion.

Various types of triangulation occurred in the research. First, there was triangulation with the multiple sources of data and methods of collecting it. Second, there was investigator triangulation, with two researchers involved at each stage of the project. Third, triangulation was provided by having participants confirm or disconfirm interpretations put upon them (participant verification).

Data collection was systematic, in so far as observations, interviews, diary keeping, etc. were conducted on a regular basis on a sample of participants that was specified in advance.

The data collection instruments were developed *in situ*. For example, the in-depth interviews with lecturers started with a broad set of questions organised around the three domains of perceptions, problems, and strategies. As more interviews were conducted and hypotheses started to be developed, then additional questions were incorporated. To take another example, concerning the students' diaries, initially, students wrote very little; when the researchers provided a more structured framework for them, however, diary entries became much more lengthy.

Concerning the length of engagement with the situation, as both researchers were faculty members in the institution concerned, they had extensive knowledge of the institutional setting. As previously mentioned, the study was continued, in various phases, over a period of seven years. At all times, in all contacts with the participants, an attempt was made to establish trust. Data was not just collected by a single observation or interview, but through sustained engagement. Many lectures were observed, for example, and more than one in-depth interview was conducted with each of the principal participants. As hypotheses were developed the researchers continually returned to participants for further data or interpretation.

Normally, such lengthy engagement might lead to the problem of the researchers 'going native'. However, given the different ethnic, linguistic, and cultural background of the investigators in the given research setting, this potential problem was alleviated and the 'strangeness' which is so important in ethnographic research was maintained.

5. How was the data analysed? What categories were developed and how? To what extent were participants involved in verification of the analysis? Data analysis was recursive. In the earlier work, photocopying and cutting and pasting of the interview, diary, and field-note data was relied upon. Subsequently, however, NUDIST qualitative software began to be used (Qualitative Solutions and Research Pty., 1994) to store and sort the much larger amounts of data collected. In the first study, data was organised in terms of perceptions (attitude, self-rating of comprehension level, what students look for in a good lecture, etc.), problems (speed of delivery, terminology and concepts, concentration, etc.) and the strategies they used to overcome these problems (pre- and post-lecture reading, peer or lecturer help, attempts to concentrate harder, note-taking, etc.). These three major categories and their subcategories were not pre-established at the outset, but, through recursive analysis, as what seemed to the researchers to be the most meaningful way of describing the lecture experience from the perspective of the student participants. The three major categories were used initially in the later studies, but were replaced by other more meaningful ones, given the different, cross-cultural focus of these studies that developed. Information on the categories finally settled upon in these later studies is given under questions 6 and 8.

Participants were involved in verification of the analysis in a number of ways. In a first stage, as the data was being analysed and hypotheses generated, participants were returned to in order to find out to what extent they agreed with the ongoing analysis. In addition, in some cases insufficient data had been collected on a given issue and further data collection was conducted. Once an initial report had been produced this was given to participants for their comment and feedback, some of which was incorporated into later versions of the report. As a further stage in continuing analysis, a number of public presentations were given to which participants and other Hong Kong lecturers and students were invited. Further feedback on the analysis was obtained in these sessions.

6. How salient were the actual texts in data collection and analysis? In the first study, while the emphasis was the lecture context, some attention was paid to the actual language of the lectures. For example, in response to students' reported difficulties with the heavy load of new concepts and vocabulary introduced, random samples of lecture extracts were analysed to get an idea of the extent of this difficulty. In addition, certain features of the discourse structure of the lectures were identified by students as helpful: for example, the systematic presentation of main points, the use of summaries, repetition, and interaction with the class. In Flowerdew and Miller (1995), vignettes were provided of individual lectures and much of the description contained in these accounts related to the actual text (see below). In their in-depth interviews, lecturers sometimes cited specific textual features, and a text extract is cited as a particularly felicitous use of a local Hong Kong example to illustrate a point. In Flowerdew and Miller (1996) the researchers report how they confronted lecturers with transcriptions of their actual lectures and how they were surprised at the complexity of the language. In a section on the use of humour, examples are cited of jokes which misfired with the non-native audiences.

In the main, however, analysis in all of the studies focuses on aspects of the production and reception of the texts and their underlying motivations rather than the texts themselves. In a later paper (Flowerdew and Miller, 1997), on the other hand – not discussed in detail in this chapter, for reasons of space – a systematic analysis is provided of one particular lecture, demonstrating how various of its linguistic and discoursal features are at odds with what is presented in English for Academic Purposes teaching materials.

7. What was the role of theory? Did it come before or after the study was begun? In this research, theory developed out of data collection and analysis. In the first study (Flowerdew and Miller, 1992), there was just a general research goal – to describe and analyse the lecture experience, primarily from the student perspective. The data collection and analysis resulted in what might be called a theory, constructed around students' perceptions, problems, and strategies. The researchers did not use this term 'theory', but the analysis does provide a means of understanding what is going on in the lectures and to this extent can be considered a theory, albeit, as in all ethnographic research, a local one.

In Flowerdew and Miller (1995, 1996), theory was again derived from the data, but in these two papers there is a more overt focus on theory-building. The first of these two papers (Flowerdew and Miller, 1995) presents a cultural framework for the analysis of the lecture situation. The model consists of four dimensions: (1) *ethnic culture* – culturally based, social-psychological; features which affect the behaviour of lecturers and students; (2) *local culture* – the local setting with which students are familiar and which may be alien to foreign lecturers; (3) *academic culture* – features of the lecture situation which require an understanding of the particular academic values, assumptions, roles, and so on of a given society; and (4) *disciplinary culture* – the theories, concepts, norms, terms, and so on specific to a particular academic discipline. The dimensions were developed out of the data and not imposed upon them *a priori*. The authors describe their research as fitting into the context of other educational ethnography, which attempts to provide 'descriptive theories capable of accounting for the ways teachers and students interact with each other and with texts, and how learning does or does not come about'. In the second of these later papers (Flowerdew and Miller, 1996), six salient socio-cultural aspects of the lecture situation where mismatches in student and lecturer perceptions occurred were identified. The subtitle of this paper – *Notes towards a cultural grammar* – indicates the theoretical thrust of the analysis – an attempt to provide the beginnings of a set of socio-cultural rules which underpin and can be used to account for the acts of the participants involved in the study.

8. *How were the findings reported?* In all three of the papers which are reviewed here, extensive use was made of direct quotations from in-depth interviews and diaries. This is in line with the objective of ethnographic research of describing the group under study from their own perspective. Direct quotations, judiciously chosen and organised, can create a genuine insider perspective. Another advantage of direct quotation, when participants are using English as a second language, is that a feel is created for their language proficiency – usually an important factor in evaluating the study.

Quotation is particularly vivid when participants use figures of speech such as analogy, metaphor or antithesis. Juxtaposition of quotations from different participants can also be an effective way of bringing out contrasting attitudes.

Another way of creating a 'feel' for the situation is in the use of 'vignettes', or short descriptions of specific scenes. The editor of the journal which published the 1995 study initially stated that although she liked the paper, she would have appreciated a better 'feel' for what a typical lecture was like at the research site featured in the study. It was at this stage that vignettes of two lectures were included, which convinced the editor to publish the paper.

While the vignettes may seem fairly straightforward factual accounts of what occurred in example lectures, it is important to note the artifice that has gone into them and how features have been selected for inclusion in the description because of their relevance to the analysis and local theory of cross-cultural lectures which is developed later in the paper. To give some examples from one of the vignettes, the reluctance to participate and emphasis on peer help noted on the part of students relate to the *ethnic* dimension of culture; the use of local examples by the lecturer relates to *local* culture; the mention of class size, description of the style of lecturing, and reluctance to ask questions can be related to *academic* culture; while the examples of problematic vocabulary and the discourse structure of the lecture are associated with *disciplinary* culture. In the references to other artefacts of the lecture situation, also, there is selectivity. For example, course objectives, assignments, and examination questions are cited as indicative of certain aspects of the academic culture.

9. *To what extent might the study be generalisable to other situations?* As stated previously, ethnographers cannot make definitive claims about the generalisability of their findings. They can only try to ensure that they provide sufficient descriptive detail to make judgements possible on the transfer-

ability or otherwise of the described situation to the situation in which transfer is to be applied (Davis, 1992: 606). To this extent, the generalisability question regarding the research discussed here has already been answered in the responses provided to some of the questions above.

Although strong claims cannot be made, therefore, regarding the generalisability of the three studies discussed here, consideration can nevertheless be given to what McGrath and Brinberg (1983, cited in Miles and Huberman, 1994: 279) refer to as 'the boundaries of reasonable generalization'. To the extent that large numbers of second-language students are experiencing tertiary-level lectures in their second language for the first time in many countries in the world, the potential for generalisability is great. It is quite possible that many of the problems encountered by the students in the 1992 study are also encountered by students who find themselves in similar situations, both in Hong Kong and overseas. Speed of delivery, vocabulary, difficulties in concentrating, etc. are quite likely to be encountered also by students of a similar proficiency level as those described in the study. For this reason it is important that the proficiency level of the student participants is reported in the study.

Regarding the two other studies, which focus more upon cultural issues, transfer is likely to be more problematic. The socio-cultural issues analysed in these papers are more likely to apply to Asian students than to students from other ethnic backgrounds. For example, the unwillingness of students to participate, which is related by the researchers to a number of possible factors, including their Confucian background, is perhaps more likely to be specific to communities of Chinese students (although I would note in passing that in recent years the term 'Confucian' has been given a range of different interpretations). Nevertheless, the cultural framework developed – which represents the theory – it can be argued, might well be applied to other cultural groups.

10. What are the implications for application? In the first study very specific recommendations were made for application. These recommendations were made under three separate headings: recommendations for content lecturers, recommendations for ESL professionals, and recommendations for learners. The overall conclusion is that there should be greater collaboration between the content of courses and language and study skills. 'In this way', it is argued, 'students similar to those in this study would be able to cope with the academic system of education faster and better, and lecturers would benefit by examining their teaching style and integrating their content with their methodology to become more effective lecturers' (Flowerdew and Miller, 1992: 78).

In the later studies recommendations were more general. In the 1995 paper, on the basis of the cultural framework, which was the theory developed in the paper, it was recommended that the model provided a means for developing cultural synergy – an awareness of the four dimensions of the culture of cross-cultural lectures on the part of lecturers and students could lead to more effective communication in the cross-cultural lecture theatre.

The 1996 paper recommended that a greater understanding on the part of lecturers and students of each others' perceptions of the cross-cultural issues identified in the study would likely be of value in the preparation of these two groups for participation in second-language lectures.

Both of these later papers recommended that a content-based model of language teaching would be appropriate in tackling the problems outlined.

CONCLUSION

In this chapter I have reviewed the main principles of an ethnographic/naturalistic approach to the study of academic discourse, illustrated a range of situations which can be investigated by this approach through the review of four selected studies, and examined in some detail a project in which I was myself involved, highlighting what I consider to be the ethnographic dimensions of this work. The methods adopted in the different studies vary because, as Hammersley and Atkinson (1983: 28) note, a research method such as that of ethnography cannot be 'programmed'. Rather ethnographic research methodology has to be learned by doing it, and, as such, researchers must be aware that they may be doing something wrong. I have not provided a comprehensive review of ethnographic/naturalistic studies within the context of academic discourse, as such work is relatively sparse and concentrated in the field of writing. In selecting studies outside the field of writing for review, indeed, I hope to encourage further work in these other fields, which have, to date, been relatively neglected.[5]

NOTES

1. The use of specialist informants also occurs in more text-focused approaches to the analysis of academic discourse analysis (e.g. Tarone et al., 1981).
2. Although see Mason (1994), which, although ostensibly a study of academic listening, demonstrates how this skill is becoming increasingly integrated with speaking in the lecture context.
3. See also Angelil-Carter (1997) for another interesting study using a critical ethnography approach.
4. In actual fact, once the research was begun, the researchers did come across one study using naturalistic methods to investigate academic listening in their review of the literature (Benson, 1989), and so the study turned out to be a further development of this approach rather than a totally new departure. Benson's study, however, was a single case study, while our research focused on a whole group of students.
5. In line with this goal, the chapters selected for inclusion in Part IV of this collection deal with skills outside the area of writing.

Chapter 14

Investigating writing development in an academic English Language curriculum[1]

Desmond Allison and Wu Siew Mei

Our chapter reports on an ethnographically inspired and pedagogically motivated investigation into academic writing development in one curricular setting. As ethnographic approaches to discourse analysis have been introduced earlier in the previous chapter in this volume (J. Flowerdew), our opening remarks focus on the rationale of the investigative approach taken to 'writing development' in our study. After introducing the setting of the research, we present a summarised account of our investigation into writing tasks, guidelines, and feedback practices in the curriculum in question, drawing on key texts and participant reactions, and presenting some discourse data. Our closing remarks suggest implications for research and pedagogy.

INVESTIGATING WRITING DEVELOPMENT

Space constraints do not permit us to review the extensive and varied research literature on students' academic writing (see brief comments in Allison, Varghese, and Wu, 1999; relevant chapters in Belcher and Braine, 1995; Candlin and Hyland, 1999). We refer selectively to the literature as we describe aspects of our enquiry.

An immediate concern for our study was how best to conceptualise and investigate 'the development of academic writing'. One approach would be to compare written work produced by students at different stages of the undergraduate curriculum, ideally through longitudinal studies of individuals over two or three years, alternatively through cross-sectional studies comparing different year groups at one time. Parameters to examine could include lexico-grammatical range, complexity and control, generic organisation and argumentative structure. Some of our work (not reported here) did examine student performance on selected written tasks. It was quickly apparent, however, that other variables, such as the discourse demands of different tasks, make comparisons difficult to interpret. For such reasons, Rijlaarsdam, Van Den Burgh, and Couzijn (1996) offer the following observation:

> In studies of writing ability, the tradition was to consider different writing practices as repeated measures of the same construct, i.e. writing ... Nowadays, the trend theoretically is to consider different writing assignments as operationalizations of different constructs.   (Rijlaarsdam et al., 1996: xix)

Rijlaarsdam et al. conclude that the probabilities of occurrence of a cognitive activity will vary for the same individual across different assignment tasks. Linguistic realisations of task responses will vary likewise. It follows that accounts of an individual's writing development as a single cognitive construct with predictable linguistic correlates will be difficult to substantiate theoretically.

We see two implications for research. One is identified by Rijlaarsdam et al. We need to see more research that compares performance on the same writing task over time. A good example is a study by Shaw and Liu (1998) that points to some evidence of increasing response complexity on one task following writing instruction.

The other, broader implication is taken up in our investigation. For pedagogic purposes, such as syllabus design, materials development, or programme evaluation, we think it would be unwise and impractical to argue that 'writing development' was too difficult and elusive a concept to work with across a curriculum. A university English Language curriculum, in particular, may be expected actively to foster students' academic writing development, although views on this will vary. An alternative orientation is to take a discourse turn, following Gilbert and Mulkay (1984) and many applied linguists subsequently, and investigate 'writing development' not so much as a cognitive or linguistic phenomenon in individuals, but rather as a discourse construction within educational communities. This perspective lends itself well to an ethnographically derived research approach, and to an explication of practice. Noting that Lave and Wenger (1991) conceive of learning itself as 'legitimate peripheral participation in communities of practice' (p. 30; see also Candlin and Plum, 1999; J. Flowerdew, 2000), we can go on to ask how far, if at all, writing practices in academic curricula encourage students' peripheral participation in research practices of academic communities.

In curricular terms, conceptions and expectations of 'writing development' are embodied, not necessarily consistently, in changing task demands over a course of study, as well as in the expressed views (perceptions, beliefs, and values) of participants, principally learners and teachers. Our investigation seeks to characterise the development of academic writing in one curriculum, taking account of significant texts and practices (notably the setting of written tasks in examinations and assignments), and of ways in which learners and teachers construct issues in their spoken and written comments.

EDUCATIONAL AND SOCIO-CULTURAL SETTING

The academic curriculum we shall examine is the undergraduate English Language (EL) programme at the National University of Singapore (NUS). A short description is offered in this section, with just enough detail to support the rest of our account. The NUS curriculum became modular in the mid-1990s, and continues to undergo changes. A fuller characterisation of one version of the EL programme appears in Allison (1997).

The undergraduate curriculum (up to 1999/2000) comprises a general BA degree, usually completed in three years, and for some students (around 20%) a fourth-year Honours degree. The general degree EL programme includes four essential modules: two first-level modules (*Analysing English*; *Studying English in Context*), and two second-level modules (*English Sounds and Words*; *English Structure and Meaning*). There is a wider range of third-level elective modules, totalling sixteen in 1997/98, from which we draw data. Prerequisites vary, but most electives require students to have completed the first-level modules. General degree modules are classified according to levels, not years, as access and progress are flexible. Most modules involve lectures (2 hours weekly) and tutorials (1 hour weekly, groups of around 10–12 students). Honours modules are more likely to be taught in 3-hour classes combining seminar and workshop modes.

Most students follow a double subject concentration for the general degree, comprising eight modules in each main subject, plus eight other modules, over three years. Students choosing a single subject concentration take 14 of their 24 modules in one main subject. All English Language Honours students take seven advanced (fourth-level) modules, including a two-module, 12,000-word dissertation component, all in English Language.

Certain characteristics of the curriculum and setting can be singled out for our purposes. The set of essential modules in the EL degree curriculum is an attempt to provide a coherent introduction to English Language studies, ranging from grammatical, phonological, semantic, and pragmatic description to the study of social, historical, and geographical varieties of English. These modules offer considerable variation not only in content, but in types and amounts of written work, including short focused answers to analytical puzzles (typical of *Analysing English*, for example), and full academic essays and a task corresponding to a small research paper (on *Studying English in Context*).

All students take a substantial number of modules in disciplines other than English Language. Students can thus be expected to encounter a range of views and expectations concerning effective academic writing, even if messages within the EL curriculum could be assumed (as they cannot) to be thoroughly coordinated and consistent. (Lea and Street, 1999, discuss different assumptions and levels of engagement in comments and guidelines that higher-education students in the UK also encounter.)

Most students enter their degree programmes from the local school and Junior College (JC) education system. This has a strong ethos of examination-oriented work, including quite rigorous preparation at JC level for General Paper (GP) essay writing. The impact of this previous training on views about effective writing is attested, and variously evaluated, in comments by students and teachers in our study.

Examinations and continuous assessment (CA) grades retain considerable importance in the undergraduate degree, though some learners and teachers deplore this tendency. Results at all levels affect potential entry to the Honours year and to subsequent employment opportunities and entry levels, especially in some areas of government service. The importance of assessment tasks, in both examinations and assignments, for an understanding of the curricular culture is another prominent theme in our study.

Examinations, which are held towards the end of each semester, account for 80% of the first-level module grades and 60% of most other grades, in line with Faculty guidelines. Most examinations last for two hours, though first-level papers last for three hours (perhaps reflecting their high weighting), as do most Honours-level papers. Numbers of examination questions to be answered vary from two (on several electives) to as many as 15 (*English Sounds and Words*, semester 1, 1997/98). Examination and CA writing tasks on different modules range from focused short answers through explanatory paragraphs and short essays (a few hundred words) to more extended essays (up to 2,000 words), occasional longer-term papers on projects, and a 12,000-word Honours thesis. Students' writing experiences vary substantially according to the modules that they follow.

English occupies a special place in Singapore, in terms of both language policy and social reality (see e.g. Foley et al., 1998; Gupta, 1994). The EL curriculum at NUS pays considerable attention to the description and status of newer varieties of English, both formal and colloquial, and to issues of language and identity, language acquisition at home and school, language education, and multilingualism. The fact that English Language is a degree subject at university is significant, as this is not the case in many English-medium universities, whether in predominantly 'native speaker of English' or 'English as second language' contexts.

INVESTIGATING THE ENGLISH LANGUAGE CURRICULUM

The aims of our investigation are to explore notions of academic writing development, as constructed in key texts and procedures and in comments by different participants within the curriculum, and to raise pedagogic and research questions in this light. In presenting the main lines and findings of our study, we focus first on how writing is characterised in assessment tasks, and subsequently on reported views of learners and teachers.

WRITING TASKS

Although we do not wholly subscribe to Horowitz's ideas of what teaching programmes for English for academic purposes (EAP) should aim to do, part of our investigation followed Horowitz (1986a, 1986b, 1989), as well as Allison and Gupta (1997), Hamp-Lyons (1988), Lewis and Starks (1997), and Reid and Kroll (1995), in devoting attention to assignment and examination prompts. We see these prompts as significant texts, within central institutional concerns, practices, and indeed rituals, for an understanding of this academic and educational culture and its expectations of student writers.

Following a study of 284 examination prompts, representing 15 departments and 29 courses at Western Illinois University, Horowitz (1986a) proposes four broad categories of examination question, whereby students might be required to display familiarity with concepts, relations, processes, or arguments. Each category is subcategorised further (details are too elaborate to review here). Horowitz's emphasis on displaying 'familiarity' reflects his view of the examination assessment practices he found, and more generally of what teachers expect (Horowitz, 1986b). This raises questions about the educational justification of such practices and requirements and their impact on students' experiences of learning and writing. For our purposes, it is particularly interesting to consider what relationship may hold between familiarity with known arguments and capacities for argumentation in academic writing.

Horowitz (1986a) acknowledges that his four main categories might prove too general to be of maximal pedagogic benefit in studies of single academic subjects. In practice, a general category such as 'familiarity with argument' can be expected to refer to very different expectations and practices, across disciplines and within them (see also Lea and Street, 1999; Candlin and Plum, 1999). For our purposes in examining a curriculum in English language studies – already an interdisciplinary label – the four general categories in Horowitz (1986a) none the less offered a useful point of departure. In the event, they also led to findings of greater interest than a subsequent microfunctional analysis, which we shall not report.

Making reference to pre-established descriptive categories, or questions, is a controversial procedure in an ethnographically inspired exploration, as it may seem to work against a spirit of receptive enquiry. In our view, however, receptive enquiry demands a sustained willingness to question, but is otherwise compatible with specified expectations, and may even benefit from them. For this study, we found it useful to think in terms of comparability within a wider research culture. From experience, we expected the teaching culture we were investigating to concern itself with familiarity with concepts, relations, processes, and argumentation. The essential point for us was not to force these (or any) analytic categories on to the data.

We soon encountered quite revealing difficulties in classifying prompts in terms of the four categories in Horowitz (1986a), and this was not only or mainly because his typology is general. We now review this stage in our research, concentrating on puzzles and outcomes rather than comparable results. Our primary motivation for this account is that the problems we encountered throw light on the nature of the writing tasks in the English Language curriculum at NUS.

We listed a total of 81 examination prompts, including sub-questions, from Semester 1 (1997/98), for 10 formally examined English Language modules in the general degree programme. Writing requirements ranged from very short answers (mostly requiring students to apply a concept to data) to full essays. We initially retained all 81 prompts for purposes of analysis, including short-answer prompts, as it is still possible to classify all prompts in terms of the cognitive demands affecting written responses, but we were very conscious of differences in rhetorical demands. The first author attempted to categorise the prompts according to the typology in Horowitz (1986a) and identified two main problems in doing so (problems 1 and 2 below). Working with another colleague (Dr S. Varghese) who looked at a subset of 30 prompts, the first author then adapted the typology (problem 1: response), and excluded six prompts from the analysis in response to problem 2.

Both authors later applied the adapted typology to the remaining set of 75 prompts. Each of us independently noted further difficulties (problem 3 below). Our initial agreement rate was only moderate (75%). Most disagreements were attributable to problem 3, and were readily resolved in discussion (final agreement rate 97%). However, the problems we identified appeared more revealing to us than the solutions reached in discussion. We remain cautious about high agreement rates obtained (as reported for example in Lewis and Starks, 1997) when raters cross-check their analyses.

Three interesting problems that we identified are now presented and discussed.

1. The most striking feature of the analysis was the predominance of tasks that required students to apply knowledge to newly presented data. This was interesting, but it posed a problem for our analysis, in light of Horowitz's description of the subcategory of argumentation called 'critical thinking'. In that subcategory:

> writers are called upon to present and defend their own theses – ideas, judgments, hypotheses, *or analyses of previously unseen data*. In general, *the prompts require the application of learning to a new situation*.
>
> (Horowitz, 1986a: 115; our emphases)

No fewer than 58 out of 75 prompts in our data required application of learning to a new situation. Some were short-answer prompts, but others involved sustained textual analysis, and invited critical commentary. One example presented two contrasting observations made at different times by Noah Webster about the autonomy, or otherwise, of the English spoken and written in America, and asked:

> What does this contradiction tell you about how it might be useful to approach the study of the development of American English?
>
> (*Studying English in Context* examination)

Students would be expected to draw on ideas discussed during the course, but there was no single expected answer. (We rely on extended observation and discussion of the module in question in making these claims.) This prompt gives students an opportunity to present and defend their views on, for example, the relevance of social and political issues to the study of pronouncements on language standards and policies.

Most short-answer prompts involved application of learning to very specific linguistic examples, as in the following instance (the first of four prompts following a short text):

Are the words [5 words listed] used in the text as verb or noun? Explain clearly.

(Analysing English examination)

Confining ourselves to Horowitz's definition, we could make a case for classifying all such prompts under his 'critical thinking' subcategory of argumentation. We do not find that procedure insightful, however. Few of these prompts required learners to question assumptions, a capacity we believe many people normally associate with 'critical thinking'. We accordingly modified the categories in Horowitz (1986a) to accommodate the frequent cases in our data where familiarity with concepts, relations, or processes was ascertained through application tasks. For instance, when prompts required students to apply a concept to new data, as in the *Analysing English* example, we decided to subsume these cases under 'familiarity with a concept'. The point we find most notable, and educationally valuable, is the extent to which the examination prompts we analysed call for applications of learning to instances of previously unseen data.

2. Six out of 81 prompts were not readily amenable to analysis in terms of the chosen framework. These prompts called for writing or rewriting of a text according to certain specifications of variety, genre, or register, rather than for the anticipated forms of academic display. They were found across four modules: two writing-intensive electives, one film criticism elective, and the essential module *Studying English in Context*. One rewriting prompt (extracted and visually compressed here) was as follows:

(b) Now read the autobiographical essay below. Then, rewrite it so that it fulfils: (i) the communicative purpose and audience parameters you specified in part (a) above [not reproduced here]; and (ii) the stipulated length requirement of 300 words or less (the original is 527 words long). In rewriting the text, you may delete information which you feel is irrelevant as long as the end-result is a coherent text with clear discourse patterns and smooth information flow.

(Discourse Analysis examination: despite its title,
this was essentially a professional writing module)

In *Studying English in Context*, rewriting tasks provided data for further discussion in a separate prompt. In one example, a passage was provided in Old English, with explanatory notes. The rewriting prompt was 'Provide a translation of the passage in contemporary English. (Feel free to add in as many details as necessary.)' The prompt that followed this rewriting task invited comparison and discussion of differences between the OE and contemporary versions.

One could propose a separate category for rewriting tasks ('demonstrate familiarity with genres, varieties, and registers') but we did not develop this idea. Although we eliminated six writing and rewriting prompts from further analysis, we draw attention to the inclusion of such tasks alongside other academic writing tasks in our data.

3. Other problems for our analysis arose from the conceptual and rhetorical complexity of certain tasks, for example, where a prompt elicits both description and explanation. Relative weighting of these two requirements

was not always apparent to the authors as outside observers. It might not be apparent to student writers either, but we recognise that familiarity with past questions and lecturers' expectations could assist students. (On the importance of classroom context for interpretation of examination and assignment prompts, see Allison and Gupta, 1997; Reid and Kroll, 1995.)

One brief illustration of a complex prompt comes from *Studying English in Context*. The prompt presented a quote from the writer Kingsley Amis, and then proceeded with a comment and two questions:

> Amis seems to be bemoaning the way the English language has been changing in recent years. What are some of the reasons for change? Do you agree with Amis that linguistic change leads to imprecision?

We took this as a single, complex prompt, since the response sought was a single essay. The first question about reasons for changes could be seen, in Horowitz's terms, to elicit students' familiarity with 'relations between concepts' (cause and result). It can also be interpreted, though, as requiring students to summarise 'general' arguments, presented during the module, about *possible* causes of linguistic change. The subsequent evaluative question explicitly calls for a point of view, and implicitly (within this context of study) for supporting arguments. Although the wording asks whether students agree with a claim, different students might respond differently to the invitation, some confining themselves largely to demonstrating awareness of (and agreement with) stock arguments they have learnt, others developing more of a personal stance and discussion. Overall, we independently classified this prompt as mainly eliciting 'familiarity with argument', but were less sure how far it called for 'critical thinking' and a capacity to develop an academic discussion, as opposed to awareness of other people's arguments.

In sum, our analysis highlighted a high proportion of prompts (many being text-based) that required students to apply known concepts to new data, sometimes with explanation and supporting arguments, and a small but interesting subset of prompts calling for writing or rewriting tasks, either as stand-alone tasks or as a basis for further comparison and discussion. On some modules (including *Studying English in Context* as well as certain electives) we found more complex prompts in which students would need to combine description and evaluative commentary in extended writing. There were striking differences across individual modules (e.g. *Analysing English* called mainly for familiarity with applications of concepts, sometimes with an element of explanation as well, in 14 cases out of 18; the other first-level module, *Studying English in Context*, had only 2 such cases out of 11, but more often assessed familiarity with relations and argumentation). Observed trends across module levels were less clear, but electives at third level tended to include more prompts calling for argumentation than was the case for essential modules at first level.

Besides examinations, the importance of assessment in the modular system is reinforced by written assignments, supplemented in some cases by 'quizzes' or class tests, for continuous assessment (CA) purposes. Short-answer items are again prominent on some elective modules (e.g. in theoretical phonology and syntax) as well as two essential modules. The relationship between CA and formal examinations, noticeable in all modules, is often consolidated by the inclusion of past examination questions as assignment prompts. On several modules, though (including *Studying English in Context*, at first level; *Critical Discourse Analysis*, at third level; *Genre Knowledge and Specialised Communication*, at Honours level), CA includes other tasks, unfortunately too lengthy to cite or describe fully here, in which students select and investigate genres or texts of interest to them, looking into aspects of lexical choice, or generic structure, and present findings to the class. (Allison, 1998, documents learners' engagement with text analysis on another module.) Consequently, CA task specifications range from short answers or general essay prompts to detailed instructions over the development and presentation of a term paper or a research proposal. As with examinations, there is considerable variety across modules at the same level, again including the two first-level modules, but no clear increase in writing task complexity across the different module levels. If anything, it is content demands rather than rhetorical demands that vary across levels until the Honours year, where the 12,000-word thesis constitutes a research investigation and a writing task of unprecedented scale.

REPORTED VIEWS OF TEACHERS AND LEARNERS

We elicited views of students and English Language (EL) teachers through open-ended questionnaires and in follow-up interviews. As we were more concerned to be receptive to our respondents and to generate comments than to impose consistency, procedures were allowed to vary, especially for interviews, which ranged from recorded exchanges to note-making and even to dialogue by e-mail. Our questionnaires were designed to elicit comments reflecting respondents' views, interpretations, and emphases, again without unduly constraining the shape of responses. Our wording was sometimes naïve (e.g. referring to 'good writing'): we wanted to start from commonplace notions and see what respondents said about them. A small piloting phase helped us ascertain whether questions served these purposes without confusing respondents, and led only to very minor changes in layout or wording.

Questionnaire prompts 1 and 2 are reproduced, and other prompts are summarised, when we present results. The prompt wording is shown for student questionnaires; staff versions were adapted to refer to 'your students'. Follow-up interviews (several weeks later) normally began by recalling certain questionnaire responses and encouraging speakers to elaborate on comments, views, and reservations in their responses. This approach was both purposeful and conversational (Kvale, 1996).

Student questionnaires were obtained, in free time following tutorials, from 44 volunteers on the essential first-level module *Studying English in Context*, approximately 17% of 265 students taking the module. Questionnaires were also collected voluntarily from 121 students following the third-level elective *Semantic and Pragmatic Analysis*, about 88% of a cohort of 138: the high return rate reflected provision of class time. Another 26 questionnaires were obtained (avoiding duplication) from students following a third-level elective on professional writing. Students chose whether or not to provide names and contact information for possible interview follow-up. For analysis, 44 third-level questionnaires were extracted to facilitate comparison across student samples: 40 respondents were from the module on semantic and pragmatic analysis, and 4 (also interview volunteers) from the writing module. The staff sample consists of named questionnaires returned, mostly by e-mail, by 18 out of 23 language staff (excluding two EL staff involved in our research project), a return rate of 78%.

Fourteen EL teachers were eventually interviewed (11 recorded, 3 unrecorded at their request), as were 14 students (9 recorded, 5 through e-mail dialogue at their request). Six student interviewees were on the first-level module, and 8 were on third-level modules.

In view of the relative diversity in sampling and elicitation procedures, we maintain caution when comparing discourse data obtained from first-level and third-level student respondents and from staff. We are none the less confident that the main lines of our investigation reflect broadly representative views among the various groups. This confidence is based on the amount of data and the range and richness of views expressed, as well as on a general compatibility of questionnaire and interview responses for individuals. Most interview data provided clarification, fine-tuning, and elaboration, with occasional shifts in emphasis, but hardly any contradiction of comments in the questionnaires.

We now summarise the main lines of responses and follow-up interview comments, in varying degrees of detail, on five questionnaire prompts. Where we provide numbers, the intention is to report discourse trends succinctly and revealingly, not to claim greater objectivity.

Prompt 1: What are some essential elements of good writing? Do students and teachers match in their expectations of what good writing is? If not, what are the main differences in expectations? In student questionnaires, this prompt elicited a wide range of adjectives and other expressions, mainly noun phrases, describing good writing (see first box). Staff questionnaire comments emphasised the following adjectives: *clear* (8 respondents), *appropriate* (4) and *grammatical* (3). Other adjectives included those listed in the second box. Observed differences are of some interest, especially references by staff to writing that was *witty, stylish, elegant, clever, readable,* or *polished,* which sometimes appear to be at variance with other calls for clarity and simplicity. At the same time, we should not read too much into such data. The inclusion by students but omission by staff of *relevant* seems noteworthy, but we found conceptually comparable staff comments such as *a clearly discernible line of argument.* Most elements of good writing suggested by students were also attested in staff data (except for *lingo, main theme,* and *perceptions*).

Adjectives

Common to Levels 1 and 3	*Level 3 only*	*Level 1 only*
Good (applied to 'sentences') *Strong* ('command of language') *Direct* and *simple, precise* and *concise,* *appropriate* (applied to 'genre and vocabulary') *Fluent* and *interesting, relevant, coherent* and *well-developed* ('arguments')	*Succinct, logical* and *unambiguous,* *understandable,* *informative,* and *creative.*	*Convincing*

Noun Phrases

Grammar, vocabulary, and *sentence* *structure;* *Style* and *lingo;* *Genre, organisation,* and *main theme;* *Content* and *knowledge;* *Evidence* and *arguments;* *Perceptions, ideas,* and *stand* (personal views).	*Planning* and *presentation; claims,* *justifications,* and *thesis; humour.*	

Adjectives used by one or two staff respondents, not found in the student data:	*Adjectives used by students but not staff:*
adequate, free (of some stated defect); *witty, stylish, elegant, clever, readable,* *polished; sustained* (argument), *mature* (perspective), *critical* (thinking, stance), *legitimate* (reasoning).	*strong, easy, direct, concise, fluent, relevant,* and *well-developed* (Levels 1 and 3) and *succinct, unambiguous, understandable,* and *informative* (Level 3).

There appears to be some overlap, but also some divergence in staff–student expectations. Respondents' perceptions of agreement or mismatch were somewhat diverse and often uncertain. Many comments were qualified, as in *Most students probably don't give much thought to* . . . (staff questionnaire). Mismatches were sometimes elaborated upon during interviews. The following extract from a student response is of interest to us:

> I think most of the time they do match . . . (but one thing) which I think may not help sometime is that when students write they don't have a preconceived idea of (the) particular topic or the genre of the topic [right] so the writing style may differ from the prototype that is already there [right]. So the lecturer obviously have that kind of knowledge but the students may not have that kind of knowledge [hmm] so it should not be perceived as a short-, shortcoming on the students' part but rather as a progressive kind of thing [right], yeah.

This student appears to be gently resisting 'deficit' messages (see Lea and Street, 1999), and suggesting that academic socialisation is a gradual process.

Prompt 2: Do you think your writing has developed in your time at NUS? If so, identify some aspects of your writing in which you have seen some improvement. If not, why do you think you have not improved in your writing skills? Level 1 student questionnaires: Yes (24), No (12), uncommitted (8). Level 3: Yes (35), No (3), uncommitted/uncertain (6). Staff: Yes (8), No (4), uncommitted/uncertain (6). These summaries conflate various degrees of emphasis or qualification in replies. The higher level of agreement among the student respondents on third-level modules deserves mention. So does the fairly widespread doubt or uncertainty of staff. All 'no' staff respondents taught courses in either syntax or phonology, generally described as less writing-intensive. Staff respondents attributed their own uncertainty to insufficient time in the Department, or to insufficient familiarity with modules and student performance at different levels.

This item gave rise to very interesting qualitative findings in the student data. The areas of improvement listed by student respondents on third-level modules were quite distinct from first-level. We have arranged these comments for easy comparison as follows: (a) general; (b) vocabulary; (c) grammar; (d) aspects of academic writing; (e) planning of academic writing; (f) awareness of reader/communication. In some cases we have grouped comments into subsets (using semicolons), again to assist comparison.

(a) *better assignment, better language usage, feel for language* (level 1); *better understanding of language, more professional* (level 3).

(b) *vocabulary, new words, use of words* (level 1); *choice of words, complicated words* (level 3).

(c) *sentence structure, grammar* (level 1); *tenses, conjunctions* (level 3).

(d) *style, academic style; clarity; objectivity, more factual knowledge; more critical; individual opinions, views; thesis* (level 1); *academic style; clarity, clear expression, simpler in style and presentation; objectivity, extracting main ideas; critical thinking; original ideas; thesis, research, coherent argument; better grounds, supporting claims, substantial backing; citation, transitions* (level 3).

(e) *planning, development of ideas* (level 1); *organisation, presentation, arrangement of ideas, structure, subtitles* (level 3).

(f) *comprehensible writing* (level 1); *target audience, different writing for different needs, suit expectations, specific needs* (level 3).

The third-level data suggest wider awareness of research and argumentation, and of audience expectations. Third-level comments are often more specific (e.g. *tenses* and *conjunctions* rather than just *grammar*). Some of the more 'technical' requirements (such as *citation, supporting claims, transitions, subtitles*) may in some ways approximate more closely to the demands of full academic writing, but also make it more challenging for students to formulate and sustain their own viewpoints as they write.

Students who perceive that their writing has not improved often invoke curricular features: lack of emphasis on writing (as opposed to content); not enough essays or assignments for practice. This is much more marked in first-level responses, where students may have had limited opportunities to write at university (e.g. *I have not seen an improvement in my writing skill since written assignments are quite rare. In addition, I don't get feedback from tutors as I would in Sec. School or JC* (=Junior College). *There is not much emphasis on writing at NUS.*). The very few third-level responses are similar in their concerns. Teacher responses are more evenly divided between (a) acknowledging lack of instruction/guidance/teacher attention and (b) commenting on student values and behaviour (e.g. *There are many reasons for the apparent lack of progress. Our students read very little, and write even less . . .*).

Prompts 3–5 (not reproduced here) concerned sources of information on good writing, usefulness of guidelines and feedback. Although responses on sources were fairly similar, students reported a wider range (including magazines, newspapers, and friends) whereas staff concentrated mainly on guidelines given in classes. Vagueness in expectations was a factor mentioned by both staff and students. Another difficulty is that students may not understand what tutors are asking for (noted by level-3 student); this may arise when staff expectations contrast with past practice in schools (noted by staff member). A (small) majority of students and staff indicated that guidelines were given, and helped to clarify expectations.

Teacher feedback was considered important to very important by large majorities of students and staff. Comments on this topic were often emphatic (e.g. *Extremely!!!* – level-1 student; *I think it's EXTREMELY important . . .* – staff member). Many students mentioned that some kind of consultation session would be desirable (14 level-1 students, 25 level-3 students; also 3 staff). Staff proposed written comments and class discussions; students suggested more feedback in tutorials and less time between assignments and consultation. Another possibility noted by students (both levels) was greater use of e-mail consultation, though one staff interviewee using this mode observed how onerous it could become for the teacher.

A feature of staff questionnaire comments on student ideas about good writing was that students sought unsuitably to impress. Adjectives used in this connection were *fancy, convoluted, archaic-sounding, impressive sounding, elegant and profound sounding* (stuff that doesn't mean anything), *long-winded, pompous, pedantic, complicated, purple* (prose); interview data added *highfalutin*, and a student used *bombastic*. It is interesting to contrast these concerns with occasionally more favourable responses to writing that is *witty* or *polished*.

One linguistic frame proved revealing. The frame 'seem(s) to' plus verb (or *be*), not found in the student questionnaire data, yields eight instances in the staff data for Prompt 1 (seven different respondents). Seven of these staff comments involve students (or some students) as subject and theme. All seven instances attribute to students a belief or attitude of which the writer apparently disapproves, for example: *Students seem to have a mental model of a standard academic essay for all occasions.* Interview follow-up on this particular comment linked it to a staff member's perception of student inhibitions about writing, conveyed through student questions in the form 'are we allowed to . . . ?'.

CLOSING DISCUSSION

Our closing remarks summarise outcomes in four areas that carry implications for further research and for professional deliberation, both locally and more widely. Pedagogic implications of our investigation include fuller sharing and questioning of perceptions, insights, and reasons, which our study has helped to achieve in its setting.

Writing development

There is evidence that students' notions of writing development become more elaborate, in terms of awareness of academic discourse, as they experience the EL curriculum. Most students also believe their writing improves. Some of these outcomes may reflect instruction on EL elective modules directly connected with writing. Staff views were on the whole more cautious, but again tended to relate writing improvement to work on writing electives. Some writing tasks do appear to involve students in research processes, but others place more emphasis on familiarity with known concepts and known arguments, and on concerns for consistency and backing as an essay develops.

The EL curriculum

The curriculum in question exhibits considerable variety but uncertain progression, partly because of the range of elective module choices. Students and teachers are aware of different expectations among EL lecturers and modules, and across academic subjects. They are often avowedly unaware of the overall EL curriculum, students for evident reasons, several teachers because they only teach at one or two levels and remain unfamiliar with other areas of specialisation. Writing tasks vary greatly across modules. Many tasks call for applications of learning to new data. Issues for ongoing discussion in the situation include how far and in what senses students are expected to write 'critically' and to develop arguments, and whether writing development should be a central curricular aim or a possible incidental outcome.

Communication between students and staff

Communication is reported to be generally good, but sometimes appears problematic from the student perspective, especially on level 1 modules. Students' calls for more consultations (notably in comments on ways to improve feedback) appear to reflect at least three things: concerns over vagueness in spoken guidelines given by tutors; greater convenience of e-mail consultation; preferences for less 'stiffly formal' exchanges of views. Timetabled consultation hours are actually under-utilised (staff comment in interview). There is room for more pedagogic experimentation in providing structured consultations (e.g. linking these to self-help checklists, as suggested by a staff member) and in encouraging the use of a wide range of consultation opportunities.

Awareness of academic expectations

Both staff and students comment on the importance of clear writing and note problems in this regard. One issue concerns simplicity as opposed to attempted sophistication in writing styles. A complication is that some academic genres (and some individuals) do not value simplicity as highly as others; another is that people may mean different things by 'simplicity'. Another issue concerns the level of explicitness that is expected when students write for their teachers – and when teachers set out guidelines for their students – such as the need to spell out intermediate steps in reasoning, and not to assume too much reader cooperation. It will sometimes be necessary to set higher expectations, that student writers do not yet meet, as a teacher becomes a critical reviewer, rather than the all-knowing person who can fill in all the gaps in students' arguments. Other questions concern levels of intellectual engagement with material, including the importance some teachers attach to learning to be 'critical' and what this may mean. Finally, our review of students' and teachers' comments underscores the importance, and difficulty, of larger questions about the legitimacy or otherwise of academic expectations over what and how to write, about the constraining power of these expectations, and about their impact on pedagogic and research practices.

ACKNOWLEDGEMENTS

The authors would like to thank all colleagues and students who contributed to this study. We are grateful to Dr Susheela Varghese for her collaboration during preliminary investigations, and to our Research Assistant, Tiew Lee Ching, who assisted with recording and transcription. We thank the editor and series editor for constructive criticisms of an earlier version of this chapter.

NOTE

1. This study forms part of a funded research project (RP970010) at the National University of Singapore.

Chapter 15

The L2 case discussion in business: An ethnographic investigation

Jane Jackson

INTRODUCTION

The number of university students studying business through the medium of English as a second or foreign language continues to grow worldwide. Since one of the most common methodologies used in schools of business is the case method, non-native speakers are apt to find themselves in case-based courses at some point in their education. At the heart of this problem-based methodology is the analysis of a case – a detailed description of an actual dilemma facing a person in a company (Barnes, Christensen, and Hansen, 1994; Maufette-Leenders, Erskine, and Leenders, 1997). In this mode of learning, students are encouraged to slip into the shoes of a manager or other business professional facing a crisis and to collaboratively seek out a solution. By way of a full-class case discussion, the business professor typically acts as a facilitator to guide the students in their analysis. The overall aim is for students to relate their theoretical knowledge to the real world of business. In the process, they can refine the interpersonal, analytical, problem-solving, and decision-making skills they will need for success in the competitive world of business (Barnes et al., 1994; Hammond, 1980; Erskine, Leenders, and Maufette-Leenders, 1998). Not surprisingly, this interactive approach is also now widely used in the preparation of lawyers, health care providers, social workers, teachers, and many other professionals.

Several recent ethnographic studies have centred on the use of lectures in a second- or foreign-language context (Benson, 1994; J. Flowerdew, 1994; Flowerdew and Miller, 1996, 1997); there has, however, been a dearth of research on the challenges involved with using the case method in an EFL setting. While guides for case leaders address diversity issues, they are based on anecdotes not on research. Consequently, there is scant information about the linguistic/discoursal features of case discussions and the impact of the culture and environment on the behaviour of the participants. Thus, this ethnographic study is an attempt to better understand case-based learning and provide information of value to content professors, L2 students, and ESP course developers.

Rationale for study

At a bilingual (Chinese–English) university in Hong Kong, I was asked to design an English for Specific Purposes (ESP) course for first-year business administration/accounting students. To develop a relevant, meaningful course, I needed to have a good understanding of the teaching and learning situation in the content classroom. In preliminary interviews with business professors, many expressed frustration with their attempts to engage their Chinese students in case discussions. While some had opted for lectures because of this, others were persevering with case-based teaching, believing that it can help students to develop the skills they will need in their future careers. It is in this context that I began investigating the communication taking place in English-medium case-based courses in business.

Ethnographic approach

My study followed an ethnographic approach, drawing on a variety of qualitative data to provide a detailed description of the case-based learning situation (Hammersley and Atkinson, 1983; Watson-Gegeo, 1988). This 'thick' description (explanatory, interpretative account; Geertz, 1973) took into consideration the values, roles, assumptions, attitudes, and patterns of behaviour of the participants in case-based business classes in this EFL setting. In the process, I sought to better understand the ways the professors and their students interact with each other and with the case material (video and reading), and how interaction and learning does or does not take place.

In university settings where students and professors share the same language and cultural backgrounds, a common set of assumptions and experiences may guide the behaviour of all participants. In situations where professors from the West are teaching in Asian countries, the possibility of cultural misunderstandings naturally increases. By bringing the cultural assumptions and expectations of professors and students to light, ethnographic research can provide a basis for improving the learning situation (Flowerdew and Miller, 1996, 1997). In the context of this study, it helped to demystify the genre of case discussions in business and provided insights into better ways to help induct non-native speakers into this unfamiliar mode of learning.

The purpose of the present study was to provide an interpretative-explanatory account of the discourse and interaction that took place in English in a business case discussion at a Hong Kong university. By providing an account of the experiences of an expatriate professor in Hong Kong and his Chinese students, I hope that the findings will be of interest for those trying to understand professor–student behaviour in case discussions in other second- or foreign-language settings.

Research goals

During this phase of my study, my research goals were developed and refined as I became more familiar with the teaching situation and the socio-cultural context. A pilot study with another management course in the previous semester also helped me to set the following guiding questions:

1. How and why are cases presented and analysed in this English-medium strategic management course?
2. What are the American professor's and his Chinese students' views about case-based learning?
3. What is the typical linguistic/discoursal structure of the case discussions?
4. What conditions seem to enhance or detract from the students' willingness to actively participate in case discussions in English?
5. What adjustments might be made in similar business courses to better engage non-native speakers in case discussions?
6. What are the implications for the design and delivery of the ESP business communications course for first-year business administration/accounting students?
7. What are the broader implications for professor and NNS student training for case-based learning and teaching?

METHODOLOGY

The study reported here is drawn from a much larger body of data collected over more than three years, and with a greater number of professors and Chinese students at the same university in Hong Kong (Jackson, 1998a, 1999a). This chapter focuses on one of the four case-based management courses that I observed for a full semester. This phase of my study targeted a final-year, undergraduate case-based management course, *Business Policy and Strategies*, that is compulsory for all business administration/accounting students. The section selected for study was taught in English by an American professor, a native speaker of English. I began by investigating the management professor's views about case-based learning as well as the beliefs and attitudes held by his students. I also observed and videotaped eight case discussions and then carried out a detailed analysis of the verbal and nonverbal communication that took place in the Swatch case discussion, near the end of the course.

Research instruments/procedures

Throughout a 14-week semester, data collection about the case-based learning experience in this management course consisted of:

- 'The use of cases in business administration courses at CUHK', a 77-item questionnaire for the business professor adapted from instruments developed by Anderson and Lawton (1993) and Miles, Biggs, and Schubert (1986). It employed a six-point Likert scale for closed questions and included a section focusing on the way he used cases in his course *Business Policy and Strategies*. Questions were designed to identify his perceptions of the benefits and limitations of the case method in business courses in this context as well as the special challenges he was facing in the strategic management course;

- 'Learning through business cases', a 91-item questionnaire for the students to determine their views about this mode of learning. Like the professor's questionnaire, this instrument was adapted from earlier ones by Anderson and Lawton (1993) and Miles et al. (1986);
- semi-structured interviews as well as informal discussions with the American business professor before and after the course to gain a more in-depth understanding of his perceptions about case-based learning in his management course as well as in business administration courses in general;
- semi-structured interviews in Cantonese with five Chinese students in the course (2 males and 3 females, representing a range of behaviour in the case discussions) to gather their views about case-based learning in their management course;
- a semi-structured interview in English with the sole international exchange student in the class, an American male who is a native speaker of English;
- observation of eight hour-long case discussions in the strategic management class;
- field notes describing less formal discussion with and observation of the professor and his students;
- video-recordings and transcriptions of eight case discussions (two cameras were used with one camera focused on the professor and the other one on the students to capture as much of the interaction as possible);
- a lexical analysis of all of the case readings/discussions using *WordSmith Tools*;
- a discourse analysis of one of the case discussions, the 'Swatch' case, focusing on the verbal and nonverbal behavior of the participants including their questions and responses;
- other artefacts of the case-learning situation, such as seating chart, textbook (Wright, Kroll, and Parnell, 1996), handouts, and course syllabus.

Having data from a variety of sources and subjects ensured a strong element of triangulation which is essential in ethnographic research. Through regular contact with the management class I was able to 'build up trust with respondents, learn the culture, and test for misinformation introduced by both the researcher and researched' (Davis, 1992: 606). Hypotheses were mainly generated from the observations of the case discussions and then carefully cross-referenced with data from other sources. Following the recommendations of Atkinson (1994), Flowerdew and Miller (1992), and Van Lier (1988, 1989), I have tried to avoid cultural stereotyping by being as rigorous as possible in making inferences and interpretations based solely upon the data.

RESULTS AND DISCUSSION

Profile of subjects and their learning environment

The *Business Policy and Strategies* course was taught in English by an American professor (NS) who was in his mid-thirties. Before coming to Hong Kong, he had taught business courses in the United States for five years. At the time of this study, he was in his second semester at this Hong Kong university and was teaching the strategic management course for the first time in this context.

Thirty-six of the 37 students enrolled in the strategic management course were Chinese; the remaining student was a male exchange student from the United States who was a native speaker of English. Thirty of the class members (17 female and 13 male students, including the exchange student) completed a comprehensive survey about case-based learning in business. Five (2 males; 3 females) of the Chinese students were also interviewed in Cantonese about the use of cases in their strategic management course. These interviewees were selected to represent a range of behaviours in the case discussions, that is, they included students who never spoke as well as the few that answered the professor's questions more frequently. In addition, the views of the exchange student were gathered in an interview in English.

All of the students in this course were studying full-time and were in their final year of undergraduate studies; they had an average age of 21.4 years. None of the Chinese students had ever lived or studied in an English-speaking setting. All of these students had gone through the Hong Kong secondary school system during the time when instruction was usually conducted in a mixture of English and Cantonese (Johnson, 1998). Since Hong Kong is a primarily Cantonese-speaking society, the students would have had limited opportunity to use the language outside of school (Falvey, 1998).

Only six of the students who completed the survey had had previous practical experience in business and this consisted primarily of entry-level summer jobs. Before taking this case-based course, the students had studied cases in an average of 4.5 business courses.

This management course met for three hours on Monday mornings for fourteen weeks. The setting for the course was a traditional classroom with students seated in rows of movable desks. Throughout all case discussions, the students remained in rows facing the professor, who led the case discussion in front of a large whiteboard. For each case discussion, one video camera was focused on the professor, who wore a lapel microphone, and the other camera was focused on the students. The sessions were videotaped by professional technicians from the university who routinely taped classes on campus. Thus, they were as unobtrusive as possible.

In the first class meeting, the professor introduced the students to his approach to case-based learning. By way of a locally based caselet, a brief case, he made it clear that he would often call on students individually during the case discussions. To facilitate this, he prepared name cards with the students' photos and drew up a seating chart.

In the course under study, eleven Western-based cases were analysed by the students in full-class case discussions with each session lasting approximately an hour. In each, the professor used the whiteboard to highlight key headings/points and frame the discussion.

Before examining the interaction in the Swatch case, the following section provides additional contextual information about the case-based learning situation in the course, focusing on the attitudes of the participants towards this mode of learning, their perceived roles and expectations in case discussions, and the use of English as the medium of instruction.

Perceptions about case-based learning

Positive aspects

The American professor holds very positive views about the value of case-based teaching in business administration programmes. He believes that cases are an important teaching tool and that by analysing them, students can improve both their problem-solving and decision-making skills. By way of the survey, he indicated that cases can be especially useful in helping students to: apply theories to real-life situations in business, appreciate the complexity of business operations, deal with ambiguities and conflicting information, integrate the activities of the various functions of a business organisation, develop their communication and persuasion skills, and solve practical problems systematically.

Using the same six-point scale as in the professor's questionnaire, the Chinese students responded quite positively to similar statements about the use of cases in their business courses. Overall, they believe that analysing business cases is a useful activity that is particularly helpful in 'identifying problems in business' and in 'bringing together learning from different areas of business'.

In response to the following open-ended question, 'What do you like most about studying cases?', the majority of the Chinese respondents commented that it 'allows the application of theories and concepts to solve problems.' A quarter noted that by studying cases 'they learn material beyond the text-book so that it broadens their horizons'. A similar number commented that case analysis 'can help prepare them for the real world of business'. (For a more extensive analysis of their responses see Jackson, 1999b.)

Negative aspects

The professor's only negative comments about cases related to the special difficulties involved with using them in Hong Kong; that is, the lack of high-quality locally based management cases and the reticence of Chinese students in case discussions. While he acknowledged that many do not have confidence in their ability to participate fully in these events, he is convinced that the experience will gradually help them become more self-assured and independent.

In response to an open-ended question about what they disliked most about studying cases, just under a half of the Chinese students volunteered that they do not like analysing cases that are not based in Hong Kong; several commented that 'lack of background information makes the analysis difficult'. Furthermore, only a few of the 29 Chinese students felt confident or very confident in their ability to 'understand the cultural background of Western-based cases'. This is significant since only the introductory caselet was locally based.

Roles of participants in case discussions

The professor

In response to the question, 'What do you think are the roles and responsibilities of your professor in full-class case discussions?', the interviewees primarily viewed the professor as a leader who should guide the discussion. In fact, the Chinese equivalent of this term was used by almost all of the students who were interviewed.

Kwan Yu's response was typical: 'The professor should act as a leader, initiate students to think and give us directions because the case may have many areas which we could discuss. It is not possible for us to discuss all of them in class so the professor should specify which aspects we should focus on.'

The students

Interviewee responses to the question, 'What do you think are the responsibilities of students in full-class case discussions?' were rather perplexing. While all of the Chinese students felt that students should express their views in discussions, they do not follow this in practice. In fact, they rarely speak out in class unless singled out by the professor and, when they do, their responses tend to be as brief as possible, making it very difficult for their professor to engage them in discussion.

One of the male interviewees made the following comment about the role of students: 'Students should actively take part in expressing their ideas; they should speak out whenever they have an answer in mind. They should also be well prepared for the discussions. In this way, they can express their ideas more quickly. I think students should contribute their ideas in case discussions in class because people may have different point of views. It is good for the case discussions if students share ideas with one another.'

The last sentence of the student's comment is intriguing. Student–student exchanges did not occur during the full-class case discussions under study. Also, the professor usually had to single out a student to get a response. If students did not agree with a comment, they rarely indicated this in class. In the survey, 10 of the 28 students admitted that they were reluctant to disagree with classmates during the full-class case discussion. They were even more reluctant to disagree with their professor. In fact, more than half admitted that they would not want to speak up in such a situation. Thus, while the American management professor is hoping to be challenged in class, his Chinese students may be too uncomfortable to openly question him or their classmates.

Table 15.1 The perceptions of the Chinese students in the 'Business Policy and Strategies' management course

Using a scale where 1 = strongly disagree and 6 = strongly agree:

In my business courses, I feel confident in my ability to . . .

	M	SD
1. write up case reports in Chinese	4.04	1.12
2. write up case reports in English	4.54	1.00
3. present cases orally in Cantonese	4.54	1.30
4. present cases orally in English	4.19	0.74
5. understand case material in English	4.57	1.03
6. understand the cultural background of Western-based cases	3.50	1.00
7. discuss cases in Cantonese	4.57	1.26
8. discuss cases in English	3.86	0.80

In my business courses, I am reluctant to . . .

	M	SD
1. express my ideas in Cantonese in small group discussions	2.43	1.20
2. express my ideas in English in small group discussions	3.50	1.32
3. express my ideas in Cantonese in full-class case discussions	2.70	1.20
4. express my ideas in English in full-class case discussions	3.46	1.00

N = 29

Medium of instruction in case-based classes

By way of the survey and interviews, the professor conveyed his belief that Chinese students are reluctant to speak up in the full-class case discussions because they lack confidence and have difficulty expressing their ideas in English. While he feels that their written case reports are generally satisfactory, their oral reports in English are weak perhaps due to insufficient opportunity for the students to practise English outside class.

Students were asked to evaluate their own confidence level with regard to the use of English and their mother tongue in case study analysis. As shown in Table 15.1, students actually feel quite confident in their ability to prepare and present case reports in either English or Chinese. While they feel quite secure in their ability to read case material in English, they admit that they have difficulty comprehending Western-based cases because of the references to companies and situations that are unfamiliar to them. In the open-ended segment of their questionnaire, they also noted that they had difficulties understanding the idioms in the case readings.

In the survey, the Chinese students indicated that they are much more reluctant to express their ideas in English than in their mother tongue in both small group and full-class case discussions. They are more at ease presenting oral case reports, probably because they can make use of a prepared script. Taking part in spontaneous discussions with little time to reflect is certainly more challenging for students, especially when their comments must be made in English, a foreign language.

A MICROANALYSIS OF THE 'SWATCH' CASE

Rationale for the selection

In order to develop a better understanding of the case discussions as experienced by the students and the case leader, I will focus now on a more detailed analysis of a case discussion that took place in the twelfth week, near the end of the semester. My observation of this case discussion is supplemented by my field notes, the case reading, two videotapes of the interaction (one focused on the professor and one on the students), a complete transcript, a lexical analysis of the case reading and discussion, a discourse analysis of the questions and verbal/nonverbal responses, and interviews with the professor and six students about this learning experience. Thus, the data includes both quantitative and qualitative input in a variety of forms.

The Swatch case was selected because the reading, case video, and discussion exhibited aspects found in most of the other sessions and did not display any features that made it stand out as unusual. Also, this case discussion took place near the end of the course, so the students were familiar with their professor and his style of leading case discussions. Moreover, since almost all of the case discussions had been videotaped, by this stage, the participants seemed quite at ease with the video cameras and my presence as an observer.

The lexical density of the case discussion was also similar to the other cases that were discussed in this course. Using *WordSmith Tools*, the average type/token ratio for all of the case discussions (including professor/student discourse) was found to be 39.09%. In all of the cases, the average type/token ration for the professor's discourse only was 38.81%. The type/token ratios for the Swatch case were similar with 39.98% for all of the discourse (professor and students) and 40.05% for the professor's discourse only. As he was trying to establish rapport with his students and bridge the professor–student divide, he frequently used informal discourse in the discussion. He also appeared to make an effort to simplify his language as illustrated in the following excerpt in which he was encouraging students to categorise various firms and products and their target population:[1]

P   I remember how many times I've told you that there are many industries where- there is a cluster of firms in one category. And everybody says, 'This is the only way to do it.' Computer business was very much like that for many, many years where there were- certain type of computers clustered at the high end of the market and nobody dared to enter the low end. Everybody was terrified of PCs twenty years ago. PCs? You're kidding me! How can- how can anyone own a computer at home? That was Xerox's problem, too. Xerox- invented the Macintosh basically but then they said, 'Who can own a computer? My gosh! That's crazy!' 'Coz in the old days- computers were giant- big, huge things. You know they filled half of a room. I mean just- ah the logic there just wasn't there. They couldn't conceive of computers anywhere but here. ((P knocks on board)) Okay. So- my question to you was that- are we doing this again in other industries. Okay. That's what I always want to ask you. Draw an analogy to a new industry.

You know. The one you're in maybe. Some day you know- are the- are the people doing this? Are things clustered here? Or here or here? You know and where- where other segments of the market are just- being ignored because people don't want to admit that- ((softly)) it's possible. Okay. Good.

With more than half of the cases in this course, the professor showed a video just before the full-class case discussion in order to provide additional input about the company under study. Just before the Swatch discussion got under way, the students viewed a short video about global strategy that made reference to the dilemma of the Swiss watch company.

The case reading

At the beginning of the course, the students were given a syllabus which listed the cases that they were required to prepare for. For the twelfth week, the students were assigned the reading: 'The Swatch in 1993' by Arieh Ullmann (Wright, Kroll, and Parnell, 1996: 367–90). It provided a historical overview of the Swiss watch industry, focusing on the success story of the Swatch brand of watches. The case highlighted the fierce competition the company was facing and concluded with executives of the company expressing fears about the future of Swatch. In this open-ended, 'decision' case, the readers were encouraged to slip into the shoes of the Swatch executives to work out ways to ensure the continued success of their brand of watches.

The case reading included thirteen exhibits (illustrations of the components of the watch, a bar chart, and several tables depicting financial data) to provide additional information about the management and marketing of this product. The length of the case and the number and type of graphics were typical of the cases that the students had been assigned in this course. Further, to provide a measure of the lexical density of the case reading, *WordSmith Tools* was used to determine the type/token ratio. The mean was 52.83%, which was similar to the other readings.

As in the other case-based sessions, the students were asked to read the case on their own and then work in small study groups outside of class (maximum of six students) to prepare for the full-class case discussion with the professor. According to the students, Cantonese was primarily used in these out-of-class meetings.

The overall structure of the full-class case discussion

The discussion of the Swatch case lasted 55 minutes and followed a format that was similar to earlier sessions. The professor adopted an informal, friendly style, smiling and gesturing throughout. And, as usual, he began by focusing the students on the facts of the case before moving on to ask them to identify and analyse the problems the company was facing.

P   After having seen the video and read the case, what- in your view, what is the initial situation in the Swiss watch industry - initial- meaning before Swatch came? What was happening in the industry?

MS   Um.. before the production of the Swatch=
P   =Yeah! Yeah. Right. in – in in
      the 19- 1950s, you know around that time
MS   Well, actually Swiss=
P   =Mm=
MS   = was I-I think according to the generic table refer to
      the (inaudible) and actually the Swatch uh before the Swatch, the Swiss
      watches was rather an highly manual watch because the-
P   Okay
MS   there was no od- uh.. They don't use the machine to mass production
      the-
P   Okay
MS   the:: the watch
P   Okay. Right. So the Swiss Swatch industry- you're giving me a generic
      strategy already which is question two but um.. that's all right. Ah that's
      all right.

Throughout the discussion, the professor tried to make the case seem more
relevant to students by making references to the promotion and distribution
of watches in Hong Kong. He also encouraged his students to link the case
with an earlier one they had studied.

P   What case is this close to::: broadly speaking, conceptually? Another com-
      pany went through this type of exercise in a way. Um.. mm.. not exactly
      the same but it- broadly speaking- it was a product that was very expensive
      in general and then .. they identified a new niche. What company was
      that? Do you remember? Which- which case did – did a company go
      through a very similar- What do you guys think?
MS   Um
P   We've done about- seven or eight cases. Right? Which one is – which one
      is closest to this one?
FS   Um
P   Which – which case had was- was companies- where companies focused in
      a very high price and focused end of the market and then realized that
      there were some other niches around?
MS   Um..
P   Which one? How about Carnival? Okay?

In this sequence, the professor did not get the desired response after a series
of questions so he volunteered the answer himself and continued on to
another point.

At the end of the discussion, he asked the students to formulate possible
solutions to the dilemma and then to extend the findings to other industries.

And they [the Swatch executives] never expected to sell as many [Swatch watches]
as they have. I mean they- they for many years, they got very lucky. The watch
became a fashion statement. Okay and- and opened up to a very broad audience.
And again I ask you the same question. Are there other industries that are doing
this that are stuck in one of these boxes? ((referring to grid on the whiteboard)). In
the industry that you're going to be in someday and that have an opportunity ((P
knocks on board)). Okay? ((P laughs)) That's what I'm saying. Okay. Good Good.

There were no comments so he went on to end the session with an assignment.

As in the other case discussions, the professor was in full control of the direction of the case discussion. Since the students did not jump in with their own questions or comments, it was the professor's questions that determined the direction and flow of the discussion. In particular, he made use of repetitions of questions, reformulations (restating a previous question using different words), and extensions (adding a few more details to a previous question) as in the following exchange with Lyndon (a Chinese student) and Michael (the American exchange student):

P	Okay but I mean- do you think it was tough competition? [for the Swatch company?] I mean- were companies getting wiped out? Ah.. ah people getting laid off? O::r- or ah.. what- you know- Ah when-when you- when you look at the factory, um.. ah you know those factories in the- in the video. What type of factories do they look like? Do they look like factories that- that are changing all the time and going out of business, getting knocked down? Who do they look like to you? ((P laughs))
Lyndon	Actually they 'relies' on the labor skill... eh... ((laughter))
P	Yeah! Yeah! I mean- those factories. Right. Yeah. I mean- it's a labor-intensive bus- Those- those factories look like um..look like country homes, don't they? I mean- don't they look like almost like museums. ((laughter)) Almost. Right? Right- does th- does that look like the type of factory that's changing all the time and going out of business and getting bought out? No! The competition was- what's the word I'm looking for? Brendan, what's the- What's the word Porter used?=
Michael	=He said low but I don't think that's the word you're looking-
P	Yeah! Thank you- thank you Michael. But ah remember, it was ah.. genteel.

Because the professor's questions played such a pivotal role, I decided to examine them more closely to see if they could shed further light on the students' behaviour. To categorise the questions, I modified a typology of questions that was developed by Christensen (1991), a renowned specialist in case discussion leadership at the Harvard School of Business. I also added comprehension-type questions that might be asked in a foreign-language context, drawing on the work of Long and Sato (1983). A detailed analysis of the questions and verbal/nonverbal responses in the Swatch case revealed that the professor asked 369 questions, 99% of which focused on the identification of problems the company faced. Eighty-four per cent of the questions were closed and the most frequent type of question was 'information-seeking' such as 'Is Swatch lower cost than these guys?' and 'What are the two, broadly speaking the two technological pats that are mentioned in the case and on the video?' There were few or no questions of the following types: challenge, action, priority/sequence, or prediction. For example, 'Now wait. Why should the company divest? Why would you want to get rid of them?' (challenge), 'What do you recommend this guy to do? What is your solution?' (action), 'What is the first thing that the guy should do? And the next?' (priority/sequence), and 'What is the future for the company?' (prediction). Thus, the professor's questioning techniques may also partially account for the brief responses and the limited expression of students' views (Jackson, 1999c, 1999d, in press).

Interpersonal features

Another interesting feature of the discourse of the case discussion was the professor's persistent attempts to bridge the gap between himself and his students by establishing a relaxed atmosphere intended to foster consensus. As in his other case discussions, he made several references to his life in Hong Kong to personalise the discourse. In fact, as the following example illustrates, he sometimes adopted a self-depreciation stance to further remove himself from the pedestal of exalted professor.

> I've never owned a Swatch before coz I'm too - I'm too cheap to buy one. Let me see. ((laughter)) I'm really- ah a little tight .. but anyway- ((laughter))

His jokes and references to American brands of watches, the K-Mart and Wal-Mart (department stores), and T-birds (a type of car), however, were less successful. On many occasions the only one who shared his laughter was the American exchange student. During these times, the Chinese students either sat quietly with no expression or whispered in Cantonese to their neighbours. Translations of these segments revealed that they were trying to find out what their professor was talking about. For example, in the following excerpt, he switched from a discussion of the uniqueness of Swatch watches to limited edition cars in the States; in the process, he lost much of his audience. In interviews, several of the Chinese students commented that time was wasted when they went 'off topic' in class. While the professor was hoping to clarify concepts and have the students make applications to other industries, they did not see the connection and were frustrated by the reference to objects that are not part of their world.

> P   They're [Swatch watches] so limited. Interesting. Very interesting. Limited-
>   have- have- have the auto-makers ever done that before? Have the auto-
>   makers ever done that? Can you ah- Michael [the American exchange
>   student] is shaking his head yes. Absolutely. I mean the auto-makers
>   have been excellent at doing this- producing what they call limited edition
>   cars. Where can you buy a T-Bird, ah- the Thunderbird? That's my
>   favourite car. I just found out that they're going to stop manufacturing
>   and I was really- You know, I suffered when I heard that. You know. ((P
>   laughs))
> SS   ((Some students talk to each other in Cantonese)) Kou hai dole kong
>   mug? ((What's he talking about?))
> P   And- and ah- they would produce a limited edition. They would only
>   produce ten thousand of them. And if you really like T-Birds, it was a
>   good thing to have a limited edition. It was nice. ((Michael smiles and
>   nods his head while many of his Chinese classmates show no reaction.))
>   You know, I don't know why. I mean I guess you drive around and it says

limited edition on the back ah- Well- marketing is so much about perception and- this case is- is mainly two things. Okay? I mean it's mostly- eh..
the- the interesting marketing approach they use ..

As has been mentioned in previous research on lectures in a foreign-
language context, the use of jokes and analogies can be problematic when
the professor and students do not share the same cultural background
(Flowerdew and Miller, 1995, 1996; Jackson and Bilton, 1994).

Students' participation in the case discussion

Observations of case discussions throughout the semester revealed that students rarely volunteered an answer and if the professor wanted a response,
he usually had to single out a student or the class would remain silent. The
discussion of the Swatch case was no exception. Thus, the professor had to
continually exert a great deal of energy to try to engage his students. His
frustration with this situation was evident in one of his interviews:

> I'm finding there are only two or three students who will speak up in class. You
> know, you want to encourage other people to speak, but you also have an
> obligation to the whole class to keep some discussion going and if some people,
> I mean some people, won't even raise their hand to say 'yes' or 'no' – If you ask
> a yes or no question, they won't raise their hand with either a yes or no!
> Nothing! You know that's half the challenge, I have to figure out how to get to-
> how to encourage people. That's been my biggest problem.

An interview with the American exchange student brought to light his
views about this phenomenon. Like the professor, Michael noted the students' reluctance to speak up and attributed it primarily to difficulties with
the language and a lack of confidence. He also noted that he had had several
informal discussions with his classmates which convinced him that they actually had many valuable ideas about the cases that were simply not expressed
in their full-class case discussions.

> You know, it's hard to say, but I think maybe they [his Chinese classmates]
> don't participate, not because they don't have ideas, but because there is a
> language barrier there. Even though they do know the language, it's still very
> difficult to communicate ideas fluently sometimes, with the vocabulary, and in
> business the language can get very technical. And I can imagine myself in this
> situation in other languages as well, so I mean I'm pretty much putting myself
> in their shoes so I think sometimes it's the language that prevents them from –
> ... Some may not be active orally, but, ah, still participating very actively by
> listening and drinking in a lot. . . . I sense that confidence may be a problem
> for some of them . . . Some of them are very brilliant, and you know it, because
> you talk to them outside of class, and they have these wonderful ideas, and you
> wonder sometimes why they don't bring it up in class. And I, I think it's less a
> lack of confidence than they sense an inability to speak as proficiently in Eng-
> lish as someone else.

Like the American exchange student, applied linguists in Asian settings have
long been intrigued and perplexed by the reluctance of Chinese students to

take an active role in formal classroom settings. Cortazzi and Jin (1996), Littlewood (2000), and Liu and Littlewood (1997), for example, have examined this phenomenon and highlighted the complex nature of factors that contribute to this 'passivity' in English-medium classes. In particular, they cite insufficient opportunities to speak in class during the school years, the impact of Confucian values that discourage students from challenging teachers or other students, and the fear of 'losing face' in front of classmates. In this study, an exploration of the views of the Chinese management students revealed similar concerns. Like the students in Littlewood's survey (2000), most wanted to take a more active role but they, too, felt certain constraints and inhibitions.

In fact, the Chinese student interviewees gave a wide range of explanations for their reticence in case discussions, including several that the American professor and student had not considered. One of the male Chinese students noted the following: 'First of all, maybe students are shy and do not want to be the focus of attention. Secondly, they do not have confidence in their ideas. Therefore, they do not want to volunteer ideas in case discussions.' In both the open-ended question on the survey and in interviews, students frequently expressed concern about the value of their points and some made reference to their poor level of English.

Kwan Yu, a male student who was often called on in class, attributed the reticence to linguistic factors but also went on to add that the traditional school system in Hong Kong does not prepare students for case-based or problem-based learning. He further noted that most Chinese students would be ill-at-ease in challenging the ideas of the professor or other students. This might partially explain why there were very few questions or challenges directed at the professor. There were also no student–student exchanges during the eight case discussions that were observed, including the Swatch case.

Kit, who was reticent during the Swatch case discussion as he was in all of the others, explained his behaviour in this way: 'If my ideas have not been mentioned before, I would speak up. Otherwise, I wouldn't. I cannot say I often volunteer, but I'm not wholly passive.' These comments are very intriguing. Students who were actively listening and following the 'discussion' may not have regarded themselves as passive, even though they may certainly have seemed this way to their American professor who was trying valiantly to keep the 'discussion' moving along. For instance, in one of his interviews, the professor commented that 'you get ten students who really seem to be paying attention and have really read the case and are taking notes and everything. And then you get twenty students that I can't really tell . . .' As Kit has pointed out, though, the Chinese students may not be quite as unresponsive as they appear to their professor.

The only student who initiated a question in the discussion was the American exchange student. As in the other case discussions, the Chinese students preferred to leave the questions to the professor. If they misunderstood a comment their professor or one of their classmates had made, they either remained silent or whispered to their classmates in Cantonese to get an explanation. Also, as in many of the other sessions, the students waited until the professor ended the class before gathering around his desk to freely ask questions about the case.

In the full-class case discussion, not only did the Chinese students rarely volunteer a response, but when they were singled out for a question, they usually replied with as few words as possible, sometimes after consulting their neighbours in Cantonese. This practice, however, made it very difficult for the professor to keep the discussion going smoothly. He often followed up with probes to extract more information from the respondents but the words did not flow easily.

In interviews, the Chinese students were asked about this and their answers were very revealing. Kwan Yu emphasised the value of directness rather than talking at length. 'I would like to be as brief as possible. It is always best to speak out the main points only.' Fiona agreed, referring to anything more than a few words as a 'speech'. None of the students wanted to be seen as 'show-offs' by dominating the discussion. Clearly, the American professor and his Chinese students have very different views about what it means to 'dominate' a case discussion. While the professor is struggling to get the students to express their views, they feel constrained by their perceptions about appropriate discoursal behaviour in this context.

When the professor was asked to compare case teaching in Hong Kong with the United States, another possible source of conflicting expectations was revealed.

> I guess in the strategy classes back in the US, the students will make more assumptions and... ah.. they will .. maybe they will be a little bit more creative; they'll look past the questions and the case a little bit more.. and ah make more comparisons with other companies and things and- and students in Hong Kong are usually hesitant to do that. They think that they're- you know- not answering the question and going too far outside of the case. You know they- they just- they just don't do it as often.. from what I can notice.

CONCLUSION

Maintaining student interest and drawing students into case discussions are challenges that business professors experience no matter where they teach. The problem is much more acute, however, when classes are made up primarily of Asian students, who are apt to be more reticent than their Western counterparts, especially when the discussions take place in English in an EFL setting.

While some business professors have abandoned case-based learning in favour of the less challenging, transmission mode of lectures, this does not have to happen. What is particularly encouraging about this ethnographic study is that the students in this management course were quite positive about case-based learning and expressed a genuine desire to take a more active role in case discussions. They did concede, however, that they would need a great deal of encouragement and prodding for this to happen. Non-native speakers who are more familiar with a 'transmission' mode of learning need help to be successfully initiated into a discussion-based pedagogy. For example, the expectations of the professors must be made more explicit and emphasised throughout the semester. In addition, the professors can become more sensitised to the difficulties of their students and adopt more effective strategies to actively engage their non-native students in these learning sessions. Specifically, they could single out individual students for questions, follow up with probes, and use more open-ended, challenging questions. Professors could also promote student–student exchanges in the case discussions.

This chapter highlights the impact of culture on the learning situation. For communication to be effective and a positive experience, the participants must have a deeper understanding of each others' beliefs and expectations. Ethnographic research such as this can provide a basis for improving the case-based learning experience by bringing these differences to light.

Implications for ESP specialists

This ethnographic study helped inform the design and development of a required English language support course for first-year business administration students. This course follows an integrated-skills format and centres around business cases, descriptions of actual problems faced by real companies in business. Instead of providing the students with a lengthy case followed by a full-class discussion, the students are given three short readings about the company and its dilemma from general interest publications. The students then participate in role plays of various business meetings (e.g. news conferences, staff meetings) which are videotaped for feedback and analysis. These communicative events help ready the students for the challenges of unscripted speaking in case discussions in their content courses. Another important feature of this course is that the practical benefits of case-based learning are emphasised and the expectations of case leaders in the content courses are made explicit (Jackson, 1998b).

Implications for case leaders

In addition to providing information for ESP course developers, ethnographic research can provide useful feedback for content professors. For example, a close examination and analysis of the videotapes and transcripts of the case discussions as well as the interview data helped with the formulation of several suggestions that could lead to more interactive case discussions in this context (Jackson, 1999b).

The American lecturer who welcomed me into his class was enthusiastic about receiving feedback about his case discussions. He is developing a deeper understanding and appreciation of the perspectives and difficulties of his Chinese students and has taken a keen interest in their language development. In fact, he is now acting as a content adviser for the ESP business course.

Limitations of study and future research

My study provides a beginning to understanding why Chinese students will or will not participate in case discussion in English. Still, because this chapter has focused on a single case discussion by an American professor in Hong Kong, a significant limitation is the lack of generalisability of my results across other institutions and settings. At this site I have also observed and video-taped fifteen hour-long case discussions by three other business professors in three courses. Following the same ethnographic approach, I am now examining the questioning techniques and interaction patterns in these case discussions. This should deepen my understanding of the learning situation and provide more useful feedback for the participants. Additional research of this nature is needed in Hong Kong to fully understand how the variable features of a case discussion may be manipulated to ensure optimum participation of Chinese students. More research needs to be carried out in different settings to determine appropriate modes in specific cultural environments.

Ethnographic research can be of value to professors in a variety of disciplines who lead case discussions with non-native speakers. It can also provide useful information for ESP specialists and students and thus has the potential to play a significant role in affecting change in both ESP *and* content courses.

ACKNOWLEDGEMENTS

I am very grateful for the cooperation and interest of the professor and students who took part in this phase of my ethnographic study. It would not have been possible without their help. This research was supported by an Earmarked Grant, an external award from the University Research Grants Council of Hong Kong.

NOTE

The following conventions have been used in transcribing case discussions:

Symbols to identify who is speaking:

P	Professor
Name	Names of students, if given
S	Unidentified student (sex unknown)
MS	Unidentifed male student
FS	Unidentified female student
SS	Unidentifed group of students speaking at the same time

P:	Well Ye[s, two.]	Brackets indicate the point at which simultane-
M:	[Oh goo:]d.	ous speech starts and ends.
P:	[How-]	
F:	[When did it]	
P:	Let's examine this=	When there is no audible gap between one
M:	=What?	utterance and the next, equal signs are used.
P:	We added to-	A hyphen represents a 'cut-off' of an immedi-ately prior word or syllable.

(.8) Yes (.2) yeah	Numbers in parentheses indicate elapsed time in silence in tenths of a second.
(.) to get (.) treatment	A dot in parentheses indicates a slight pause, typically less than one-tenth of a second.
P: *Right.* What's *up?*	Underlining indicates some emphasis in delivery, via pitch and/or amplitude.
P: GREAT ENDing	Capital letters indicate that sounds that are much louder than the surrounding talk.
P: So::: S: O:kay	Colons indicate that the immediately prior sound is prolonged or 'stretched'; the number of colons denotes, approximately, the length of the prolongation.
.h I feel that .hhh	A row of h's prefixed by a dot indicates an inbreath; without a dot, an outbreath. The length of the row of h's indicates the length of the in- or outbreath.
	Punctuation marks are used for intonation rather than grammatical function.
P: Finish it today . or else Sam: Issues, P: When? Sam: Look at that!	. denotes a downward contour. , denotes a slight rise in intonation. ? denotes a strong rising intonation. ! denotes an emphatic and animated tone.
I ( ) that	Empty parentheses indicates the transcriber's inability to hear what was said.
Would (you) like it?	Parenthesised words are possible hearings.
((cough)) ((softly)) ((laughter)) ((loud bang)) ((writing on the board))	Double parentheses contain author's descriptions rather than transcription.

Chapter 16

Framing and Text Interpretation Across Languages and Cultures: A Case Study[1]

Joyce Bell

BACKGROUND

Over the last decades, many universities in Australia, as elsewhere, have seen a significant increase in the number of international and migrant students from a non-English-speaking background (NESB). These students are faced with a double cultural shift as they are required to accommodate to a Western lifestyle and culture, and to the culture of the classroom, that is, the different teaching and learning styles (e.g. patterns of discourse and ways of relating to lecturers) used in an Australian university (Ballard and Clanchy, 1991; Cargill, 1996). For some years now there have been concerns among Australian academics about academic literacy (Bradley, 1984) and the appropriateness of the teaching styles used with international students (Burke, 1996; Zuber-Skerritt, 1994).

The research discussed in this chapter relates to two particular groups from Thailand and India who, in the view of their Australian research supervisors, seem to experience a significant cultural/study shift at university in Australia. Comparing their reading traditions and strategies in the home and the host environment is expected to provide some insight into the nature and magnitude of their cultural/study shift.

RESEARCH PROJECT ON THE READING PRACTICES OF THAI AND INDIAN POSTGRADUATE INTERNATIONAL STUDENTS

A review of the literature indicates that the reading practices of postgraduate international students have not received much attention. In particular, little is known about Thai and Indian postgraduate students' reading experiences in their own countries or how their reading practices change during study at an Australian university. My research is currently exploring the adjustments and self-awareness of adjustment when reading in English by these two groups of students. The methodology has involved an ethnographic approach, grounded in a theory of framing and metacognitive theory, using individual interviews, pair think-alouds in Australia, Thailand and India and observations in Thailand and India. The case study reported in this paper is the first of a series of case studies and, as such, cannot be used to generalise in any way but serves to highlight the adaptations that can be made, and indeed are made, by the resourceful student and why these adaptations are necessary. This case study embodies one Thai postgraduate student's accounts (drawn from two individual interviews) of reading experiences, reading practices, and English language education in his home country and in Australia and the extent to which his reading practices have changed between his first semester and his third semester.

Some consideration needs, at this stage, to be given to attributes generally thought by academic staff to be necessary for the successful postgraduate student: reading critically, being able to understand academic language, being aware of discipline-specific discourse patterns, and utilising effective learning strategies.

READING CRITICALLY

Academics around the world claim that critical thinking is an integral part of scholarship at university. Saljo (1982) challenged this view, as have, more recently, Reid et al. (1998). Using a whole range of methodological approaches (e.g. observations in lectures, interviews with staff and students, analysis of methods of assessment), Reid et al. found that, across the disciplines, 'the assumption that success at an Australian university depends upon the need to think critically appears to be false in many instances' (p. 57). Handbooks and course outlines, which they examined, generally seemed to encourage the demonstration of critical analysis of texts and case studies but the educational practices did not always match the rhetoric. The extent to which undergraduate students are encouraged to engage in critical thinking as part of their coursework, and are therefore prepared for the further challenges when reading complex academic texts at the postgraduate level, is not well known. Ramsden (1994) states that, according to student learning research, assessment gives messages about the kind of learning that is required. Assessment methods in undergraduate courses which place a great emphasis on examination may not encourage the development of critical thinking skills. For example, research with students from Hong Kong (Biggs, 1991; Kember and Gow, 1990) and Singapore (Volet and Kee, 1993; Volet, Renshaw, and Tietzel, 1994), where tests and examinations are the only method of formal assessment, has shown that students tend to use memorisation strategies when reading texts. Yet there is strong empirical evidence that students from these countries read, learn, and memorise with the intention of understanding the material, even more so than students from Western backgrounds (Biggs, 1996; Volet and Renshaw, 1996). The extent to which reading for understanding in these contexts also incorporates the notion of analysing critically the study materials is not fully established.

LINGUISTIC COMPETENCE

Critical analysis of text requires more than just functional competence. Participating in discourse analysis requires the necessary/appropriate vocabulary and appropriate background reading. For example, at the purely linguistic level, students may miss cohesive markers and other signposts in texts and, if reading is slow, may not have the time to relate a text to other related texts to further understanding.

Furthermore, students may, of course, have a high level of English language but of a variety more appropriate for intranational use in their own country than in the host country (Pride, 1982). Moreover, Scollon and Scollon (1995) believe that many aspects of Western culture, especially Western patterns of discourse, which ultimately lead to confusion or to misinterpretation in inter-cultural discourse are carried within English as well as transmitted through the process of the teaching and learning of English (p. 4).

Important as the language difficulties may be, there has been an increasing awareness that language difficulties do not account for all the students' experiences and that apparent difficulties with language are really problems relating to understanding of the knowledge presented (Williams, 1989; Barker, 1990). Other difficulties may relate to discipline-specific discourse, unfamiliar text structures, and reading/learning strategies learned in another cultural context. For example, Hinkel (1994) found that (NESB) students who had cultivated discourse traditions influenced by Confucian or Taoist values interpreted texts differently from students from an English-speaking background.

ACADEMIC SUBCULTURES

The specific cultures of universities are not 'universal' but are strongly influenced by the broader socio-cultural influences of the society in which they are located (Ballard and Clanchy, 1991). Furthermore, each discipline has its own subculture, termed 'tribes and territories' by Becher (1989), different teaching and learning styles (such as patterns of discourse and ways of relating to lectures) used at an Australian university (Ballard and Clanchy, 1991; Cargill, 1996). Even in the humanities areas, students from other cultures can feel excluded, according to Becher (1989), 'since the communication here none the less creates what linguists would call its own register – a particular set of favoured terms, sentence structures and logical syntax – which it is not easy for an outsider to imitate' (p. 24).

The difficulty of reading academic texts in the disciplines is compounded by the fact that the structure of academic texts varies according to the cultural background of the writer (Clyne, 1981, 1987a; Hinkel, 1994; Holm and Dodd, 1996; Swales, 1990; Taylor and Tingguang, 1991). The research has shown that good readers seem to use the text structure to facilitate recall of the main ideas in the text as well as an aid to interpreting the whole piece of text

(Leon and Carretero, 1995). Hence students accustomed to reading, for example, German or Chinese texts, may be confused by the different conventions used in English texts. Moreover, research has shown that training in text structures with adult students in academic ESL programmes can lead to significant advancement in text comprehension (Carrell, Pharis, and Liberto, 1989). It has been shown, too, that the orthographies themselves used by cultures other than those using the Roman script can also produce cognitive consequences for readers. For example, Koda's (1995) study showed that students from four different cultural backgrounds where written texts used different orthographic structures (Arabic, English, Japanese, and Spanish) used different information-processing procedures for reading English text.

LEARNING STRATEGIES

All students need to adopt effective reading strategies in order to be successful in the academic environment. Learning strategy studies within and without the language field have shown that effective learners actively associate new information with existing information in long-term memory; they often use metacognitive strategies such as organising, evaluating, and planning their learning. Research has shown that some of the best learners use affective and social strategies to control their emotional state, to keep themselves motivated and on-task, and to get help when they need it (McCombs, 1982, 1988). Cultural background affects strategy choice, according to Oxford (1996). In the area of reading, for example, it has been found that students from Korea and some Arabic-speaking countries often use rote memorisation strategies when reading to learn; compensation or guessing strategies have been shown to rank high amongst Japanese (Watanabe, 1990), Chinese (S.-J. Chang, 1990), and Thai students (Wen and Johnson, 1991).

These strategies are usually linked with reproductive or surface learning as opposed to deep learning. But are Japanese, Thai, and Chinese students really surface learners, as Western academics may have perceived? Large-scale international comparisons of attainment between students of a Confucian heritage cultural background and Western students have shown that the students from the Confucian heritage cultural background rate higher than Australian students on deep learning (Biggs, 1996; Salili, 1996). Radloff (1997) found, too, that Australian students did not demonstrate particularly high levels of self-regulated learning.

On the one hand, then, those studying in the Confucian tradition seem to use memorisation techniques; on the other hand, Chinese students also have been shown to perform at high cognitive levels in academic tasks. Lee (1996) addresses this issue by arguing that, although memorisation is certainly a significant component of learning in the Confucian tradition, it should not be equated to rote learning. Marton, Dall'Alba, and Lai Kun (1996) discuss this ambiguity. They showed, through interviews with teacher-educators and by making comparisons with an earlier study carried out in 1993, that memorisation has different purposes. Memorisation can be associated with rote learning but can also be used to deepen and further understanding. The different approaches to learning, derived from different educational systems, may lead students from Eastern educational traditions to different results than those from Western educational systems (Cheng, 1995, cited in Volet, 1999). It is thus clear that 'the culturally-shaped mental baggage of guest students and their host educators is not always congruent and can lead to ambivalent or difficult transfer of knowledge' (Volet, 1999). For example, students who are unfamiliar with the English-speaking study environment are presented with linguistic and cultural challenges; they must ascertain, not only to what degree critical analysis is required in a discipline, but also how to interpret possibly unfamiliar texts and express their criticality in the discourse appropriate for that discipline. The extent to which the Australian environment requires, for example, Thai and Indian postgraduate students to evaluate the efficiency of their reading/learning strategies in their second language and make adjustments, is not well known. Furthermore, Ballard (1989) argues that postgraduate students often experience greater difficulties than their undergraduate counterparts due to their previous schooling and undergraduate training, which reinforce habits of studying that are not applicable in the Australian setting.

Reading problems, and the expected outcomes, have been cited as one of the most neglected problems facing international postgraduate students (Smith, 1998 cited in Zuber-Skerritt and Ryan). Little reading research has been carried out with NESB postgraduate students, but a recent study by Burke (1996) with postgraduate Australian students whose first language was not English highlighted some of the problems with reading. The participants in the study indicated that new discipline-specific terminology was a major cause of difficulty, causing them to read considerably more slowly than their Australian counterparts, to rely heavily on dictionaries, and to reread a text several times. Carrell (1988) has shown, too, the importance of a reader's background knowledge of the content area of the text (content schemata) as well as the rhetorical structure of the text (formal schemata).

THE USE OF FRAMING IN THE STUDY OF READING

The term 'frame' can be traced back to the work of the anthropologist Bateson (1972), who introduced the term, and to others who built on his work, for example, the sociologist Goffman (1974), the linguistic anthropologist Gumperz (1982), and the social psychologists Schank and Abelson (1977) and more recently Tannen (1993) and MacLachlan and Reid (1994). Tannen defines 'frames' as 'expectations' and in recent work gave examples in which 'speakers reveal expectations about the context and activity in which they are taking part' (1993: 35). Watanabe (1993: 178) explains further that 'frames guide interactants to appropriate interpretations of what is going on in situations at each moment'. Reid recently applied the concept of framing to reading practices. According to Reid, frame analysis assumes that 'interpretation presupposes an ability to recognise the framing devices (mainly linguistic) which convey metamessages – that is messages about messages' (Reid, 1998: xi). Based on Reid's work it can be assumed that readers have expectations about text structure, length of sentences, content of introductions, pictures/tables with links to text, subheadings. Their reactions to the text are expected to reflect their frames of knowledge of the world and their interest in the text. In some cases, the 'application of certain culturally influenced interpretations of text' may create difficulties when tackling reading at an Australian university (Reid et al. 1998: 64).

A study by Tannen (1993) discussed in a chapter of her book *Framing in Discourse* demonstrated that structures of expectations are often culturally determined. Watanabe (1993) and Reid (1999) have also shown that mismatch can occur in cross-cultural encounters. It is possible that the kind of mismatches identified by Reid in his research on international students' reading practices could be traced to the opportunities afforded for reading in students' home countries. Furthermore, the kind and availability of English texts in their own country and English language instruction may also influence their current reading practices in the host country and their ability to adapt their reading.

Four kinds of interpretative framing, assumed to influence the interpretative process in reading, have been outlined by MacLachlan and Reid (1994) as follows (see also Candlin and Plum (1998)):

> *Extratextual* framing occurs when a reader uses his background knowledge and experience to interpret the text;
> *Intratextual* framing is when a reader uses cues, such as headings and subheadings, cohesive devices etc. within a passage to interpret;
> *Circumtextual* framing occurs when a reader takes into account the cover of a book or journal, and peripheral features such as title and abstract to build a picture of the text;
> *Intertextual* framing is when a reader links other readings with his present reading to help make sense of the present reading.

The data for this study were analysed using these four framing variables in order to find out the strategies which a Thai postgraduate student may use when he first arrives at an Australian university and also to assess the extent of change in strategy use across the three semesters and the reasons for those changes.

A CASE STUDY

Somchai's background

In the first interview, the Thai student, Somchai, was invited to introduce himself and talk about his reading experience and English-language learning in his own country. Before coming to Australia, Somchai was a lecturer in the visual arts area from a university in Thailand. At the time the present study was conducted, he was 30 years of age and was studying for a Masters degree at an Australian university. The main language spoken in his home was Thai. He had never lived overseas before. He came to Australia to further his knowledge in art, particularly in the field of jewellery design. Somchai did not express any concerns about the fact that he would be undertaking higher-degree studies in the English language.

Somchai's family background

Somchai's accounts of his family background indicated that reading and English language experiences were encouraged. They would have provided him with the extratextual framing capabilities which he could draw on when studying in Australia. Somchai described his father as 'unusual', explaining that his father read a lot of newspapers 'to understand world, try to understand and adapt, develop himself to the new, to change of the society'. He mentioned also that his father was unusual in that, at the age of 60 plus, he still used a computer. According to Somchai, only 0.1% or 0.2% of Thai people use a computer. His father, he said, used it mainly for designing although sometimes 'he makes short words'. He added that his brothers also used the computer and read many books.

While Somchai's father encouraged reading, his mother, on the other hand, was perceived as being very conservative and, unlike the father, did not use the home computer. Somchai was asked if his mother ever read to him when he was a child. He answered in the negative, explaining that Thai people don't follow this practice. He added, however, that Thai children were often asked to read to the grandmother if she had bad sight or was old. Somchai stated that he himself used to read books about plants to his grandmother. Somchai felt that this practice, although 'very good' did not seem to aid understanding of the written word. As Somchai explained, 'it is very boring for children and then they cannot understand what they read'.

Reflections on English-language learning in Thailand

In Thailand, Somchai learnt English through both formal and informal means. It was expected that both the formal English language instruction and the informal learning would have influenced the application of his extratextual framing capabilities when reading in Australia. He explained the process of learning English and the teaching styles in Thailand. Somchai estimated that he would be 9 years of age before reading competently in Thai. He had started learning English at the age of 5 rather than the normal age of 10 because his father 'tried to push any son to higher education'. He took English classes in Thailand for more than ten years, 1–3 classes per week. Even with the early start with English, Somchai has found considerable difficulty with English which has carried over to his postgraduate years in Australia.

One of his basic problems, Somchai said, was pronunciation. He explained that children are generally taught English with Thai pronunciation and, by the time they are 15, they know it is wrong and have to change but, according to Somchai, it is too late. Generally, children are taught by a Thai teacher, with perhaps a guest lecturer occasionally from Europe and England.

In addition to the formal English language instruction, Somchai furthered his English language learning by informal means. He reported that he learnt his English listening skills from American movies and now finds Australians hard to listen to as 'all most speak without opening the mouth'.

Even though Somchai started English when he was 5, he stated that he still found many books 'complex'. When asked why this was so, he explained that this was due to the system of teaching by translation:

> we study English by translation in Thai, in Thai sentence; we don't study by understanding so we have the problem like when we, when I was 5 years old I study the ABC and about 7 years old I start to make the sentence, study like this and the teacher give you ten sentence and as the homework tomorrow you translate into Thai, then tomorrow they give you the Thai sentence and you translate to English like that so when we study more advanced we found that the sentence is not the same as the basic study; some sentence is long sentence and have subsentence inside it; is difference from Thai sentence.

Somchai then elaborated on the difference between the Thai sentence and the English sentence. 'Thai sentence is like a series, like step by step but English sometimes you must understand the whole sentence and you know the main idea of this sentence and the example . . . in Thai you could take a small part and understand that totally without reading full sentence . . .'.

Overall it seems likely that Somchai's family background would have instilled an interest in reading from an early age. The teaching practices to which he was exposed may not, however, have equipped him sufficiently for postgraduate reading at a Western university.

Reflections on language learning in Australia

Since his arrival in Australia, Somchai had been trying to further improve his English language knowledge through informal means. He said he watched television and movies while studying in Australia, partly because he found books to be expensive in Australia. He stated that he enjoyed watching television programmes such as 'X Files', 'Dark Skies', and 'Burning Zone'. He reported that 'they [movies] are easy to follow because they are American and the pronunciation is clearer'. (Pronunciation is mentioned later as having a bearing on comprehension.) Comedy, he added, could be difficult to follow because of the cultural connotations. At first, for example, he said he could not understand the American comedy, 'Nanny' (shown in Australia), and found her dress 'strange' (the Thai concern with dress) and now he realises she dresses as she does in order to instil competition between the guys.

Already in his first semester, Somchai was aware that peoples of different background expressed the same concepts differently – 'maybe the people of the world are the same, same ideas, same meaning of beauty, the same meaning of aesthetics but different culture . . .'.

It is likely that the informal learning in Australia would give Somchai a sense of English language usage in Australia and would enable him to communicate better with his peers and supervisors.

Somchai's reading practices in the Australian context were elicited in two interviews conducted in his first and third semester at an Australian university. Table 16.1 summarises the types of framing he reported using in each of the two semesters.

Table 16.1 Framing differences between first and second interviews

	First interview	Second interview
Extratextual framing	1	1
Intertextual framing	1	2
Intratextual framing	13	30
Circumtextual framing	1	2

Somchai's interview in his first semester

For the first interview, Somchai had been invited to bring to the interview an academic text which he had read recently. He was then asked questions about his approaches to reading this text. In the first interview Somchai discussed his reading approach in relation to two chapters which he chose from a book entitled *Visual Aesthetics* by J.J. de Lucio Meyer (1973).

Table 16.1 shows that, in his first semester, Somchai used mainly intratextual framing and did not utilise circumtextual, intertextual, or extratextual framing much at all.

Circumtextual framing

Somchai reported only one feature of circumtextual framing. He reported that he had studied the title of the above text and from the wording had assumed that the text would give him a basic understanding of visual arts. Other circumtextual features, such as the colour and layout of the book or the references at the end, which would have given an indication of the type of reading, were not mentioned.

Intratextual framing

Competence in the use of intratextual features such as headings, transitional markers, italics can assist in interpreting the text as a whole. Somchai focused on key words within the text – 'area' and 'space'. The author, Meyer, according to Somchai, explains composition in simple, easy to understand language:

'*we use six months to understand composition in art in Thailand but now when I read this composition, this area plus space, everything is clear...*'.

Somchai was told in his English lessons in Thailand to look for the main points of a passage in the first sentence or the last sentence in the paragraph. However, he said that now he only uses this strategy for a specific purpose, that is for examination learning. He also said he did not mark words or phrases unless he had to remember the words for an examination.

Somchai reported that he read the whole of books, '*looking for the different vision*' as, at this time in his first semester, he found he had been given plenty of time to read. Rather, then, than reading to remember facts for an examination, he read for understanding and '*for catching ideas*'. Keywords mentioned by the lecturer such as 'music', 'arrangement', 'symmetrical' and 'architectural properties' or 'the interior' he said helped him to understand what he was reading: '*some picture pass through my mind and I can guess all of the paragraphs*'.

Regarding the author's vocabulary, Somchai said, '*the word is very simple*', further explaining why some texts were intimidating: '*some books too look like texts, for me a text book mean use very hard words and the sentence and the sentence is long sentence and hard to understand*'.

Somchai seemed to be very aware that the intratextual features, in particular, pictures of art, were an aid to his understanding. For example, he stated, '*the author use example of famous picture or famous sculpture so I can imagine*'.

Extratextual framing/intertextual framing

Drawing on reading of other texts plus one's background knowledge can also assist in interpretation of text. Somchai reported, for example, that reading done in Thailand concerning composition in art helped him to understand reading about this topic in Australia. He said he was surprised to find that, although he understood the general concepts, he had never had the topic so clearly defined before. In fact, when lecturing in Thailand he had found it difficult to explain the topic to his students because the Thai texts seemed more complex. The English written text, in this case, because of the intratextual features, simple structures, examples, and pictures, was easier to understand than the Thai texts he had read before.

Another aspect of extratextual framing can be following through on references when knowledge of other texts is required to make sense of the present text. Somchai stated that he had not had much experience of using references. In Thailand, he said, he checked references on occasion if he was writing a piece of research where '*one book is not enough*'. He explained that it was difficult to follow through with references in Thailand because of the difficulty in borrowing books. The process, he said, was long and complex. For example, he explained that, even if he visited the prestigious Chulalongkorn university library, he could be barred from borrowing when the university chose to admit only its own students. He said he would not necessarily follow up references in Australia; this practice would depend on whether or not he needed more information.

Somchai's responses show that, in his first semester, the intratextual features were important considerations. His understanding of text was clearly stimulated by visual features, by pictures in a text and images which he built in his mind from keywords, some of which may be mentioned during coursework lectures. He seemed to prefer to gain a 'picture' from one book rather than several 'pictures' from a variety of texts which would require comparison. He explained his preference for visual features: '*normally I like to read magazines, design; the nature of design or art is people to accept the visual picture more than try to understand the text so for the magazine is news and have some, a lot, of picture and a little bit of explaining, so easy.*' There was no hint of analysis or questioning of an author's opinion or comparing of one author's opinion with another.

Revering authorship, Somchai read, not to develop his own viewpoint, but to find out what the author's view is as '*he is a very great writer*'. His motivation to read was increased by the desire to help his students on his return to Thailand, and to this end, when new ideas presented themselves in texts, he took note of them to pass on to his students.

In conclusion, Somchai used little circumtextual, intertextual, or extratextual framing at the time of his first interview, preferring instead to concentrate on intratextual features within the text to assist him in interpreting academic text.

Somchai's interview in his third semester

Somchai's second interview took place in his third semester. He was asked similar questions to the first semester so that the responses could be compared to those of the first semester, thus giving insights into any changes in reading practices which Somchai might have experienced. He was asked, in addition, to discuss any changes in his approach to reading of which he was aware. Table 16.1 shows that his use of circumtextual, intertextual, and extratextual framing had not increased much, if at all, but his intratextual framing had increased significantly.

For his second interview Somchai had read a text entitled 'Spirituality: Let the Stones Sing', which discusses how modern man has no vocabulary to describe a holy site. He was directed to the text by his lecturer, who showed him a collection of articles on his topic. He chose this particular text because it was not too long.

Circumtextual framing

As in his first semester, Somchai used circumtextual framing to help him choose this text, having first been shown the collection of articles by his lecturer. Somchai studied the title and said that when he saw the word 'spiritual' he thought this particular paper would be suitable as his research now focuses on spiritual Buddhism.

Extratextual framing

As with the first article, Somchai used little extratextual framing, although he saw some connections with the present article in his past readings of *National Geographic* or *Reader's Digest*, particularly the write-ups about the 'large bird sculpted in the ground in Mexico'. He reported that he could make connections with the same themes of air, space, and earth which occurred in these texts.

Intertextual framing

Intertextual framing had increased somewhat by the third semester through an increase in reading that had taken place for a variety of reasons. Necessity, Somchai stated, had driven him to the library to find books which might explain terms used in his present reading although this practice still takes a long time. Fortunately, he reported that he now felt more confident using the library resources. He said, too, that he read other texts to help him understand more about the general area of art and spirituality. As he said, '*I need to know everything about spirituality.*' In the collection of articles which he was given he also found others which related directly to the one used for this interview. Indicating his awareness of how seeking other sources can assist in the reading of a particular text, he described how another article mentioned the holy rock, '*the rock which Joshua use to sleep on and he dream about God . . . so I can link the idea of spirituality in earth and rock with the very old . . . and I know how the artist use that spirituality in this material*'.

Even in his third semester Somchai said he never followed up references from reference lists of texts, preferring to find texts specific to his needs through the library or at random. He explained that following up references would take too much time: '*some [references] is very interesting but if I stop my reading to find out I lost my time*'. He added, '*Thai people we don't give importance to reference so much.*' As a result he said he found great difficulty in writing in-text quotes because he did not know which book a phrase or term had come from.

Somchai reported that he now used the Internet for further reading, although only infrequently, explaining, '*it is easy to lose focus*'. As well as using the Internet for general articles, he said he now also connected to the libraries of other universities in Australia as well as public reference libraries, although he really preferred to search for books and articles at his own university in Australia.

Intratextual framing

Intratextual framing increased significantly from the first semester and involved some new strategies. Somchai had become aware of the need to build on his vocabulary knowledge and, in order to do this, he sometimes took note of '*special sentences*' which his lecturer had used or which he had noted had created interest among the other students. He mentioned that he was delighted to find, from extended reading, mention of artists which his lecturer had mentioned, or artists of whom he had never heard before.

Another new strategy that Somchai reported concerned the initial reading of a text. He said that he now uses word-by-word reading in the first two paragraphs of texts in order to understand them very clearly. Thereafter, because of the minute work with the first paragraphs, he said he could guess the content of the rest of the text. He said he had become aware of the fact that an author often uses the same terms over and over and therefore it was useful to find out the meanings in the early paragraphs. He said he accomplished this by using an English–Thai dictionary. However, he was aware that the use of the dictionary did not necessarily help him understand the vocabulary for a given context. He explained, '*I can use dictionary to know that but I don't know the correct meaning or the concept of this word.*'

Somchai said he still had problems with long sentences. In order to overcome the problems he said he tried to '*find the structure of the sentence . . . find subject, verb and object and . . . the phrase or other sentence to explain the word or subject*'. He was aware that this technique, too, may have its limitations. For example, he said the use of 'it' can confuse him as he did not always know what 'it' refers to.

When asked about the line which separated the heading from the author in this article, Somchai stated that it was there to separate the author from the heading. He added, '*I like it; it make shorter; it make article to look short and easy to read.*' As in the first semester, Somchai is attracted to articles which appear short, perhaps indicating that he does not have the confidence or ability to read longer, more complex articles at this stage.

At the bottom of the text was printed the name of the journal, *National Painting*. Somchai missed this cue and stated he did not know where the article came from. Perhaps he does not note cues such as this as he has not been in the habit of referencing.

Unfamiliar vocabulary can hinder intratextual framing. For example, Somchai mentioned his difficulty with names. The author of this article is Charles Pickstone. Somchai explained that 'Charles' is considered a normal name to him but names like 'Pickstone' cause problems because they are not familiar to him. He explained what happens when he comes across a difficult name: '*I don't know how to pronounce and when I don't know how to pronounce I cannot pronounce in my mind so I cannot remember and that give me a lot of problem in lecture . . . because the lecturer talking about somebody, some author; I don't know what he is talking about.*' This observation is in line with Rayner and Polltasek's (1989) views, derived after reviewing a large number of studies, that 'associations between the printed word and the appropriate pronunciation are activated during reading and appear to be important in comprehending text' (p. 211).

Somchai gave another useful insight. He mentioned that he could not feel the emotion in an English text as he could with a Thai text. He said, '*when I speak English it is something like pretending; it is not my word, it is something like unreal but when speaking Thai I can put any emotion . . . when I read about Picasso work, Picasso's work about the Korean massacre, the queuing group of people, something like that I got the feeling of why horrible but when I read in Thai word it mean more strong, the feeling is different.'* The emotional level attached to interpretation of text may be an area which some lecturers are not aware of in their students.

Conclusion

The comparative analysis of Somchai's reflections on his reading between his first and third semester showed that, by his third semester, he had not only become more aware of the difficulties which academic texts can present, but had devised strategies for overcoming some of his reading difficulties. His responses indicated that he was certainly aware of the changes that had taken place over time. To him, there were problems with the teaching practices in Thailand, and these had contributed to his current reading difficulties. His responses showed an increased awareness of his reading processes and he was able to articulate which changes in his reading practices had helped him to read faster and with more understanding. In the third semester, he stated that he could read for three hours a day as opposed to one hour in the first semester and was reading three times the material in that time.

The main change appeared to be a significant increase in the use of intratextual framing. For example, in his third semester he read the first two paragraphs of a text word-by-word to achieve full understanding and then guessed the rest of the text. This change did not come about through explicit teaching, but rather through his own observations. After much reading, he had become aware of the fact that an author often uses subject-specific terminology and concepts in the first paragraphs of a text and then repeats them throughout the text.

Somchai was aware, too, that his greater ease in reading was partly due to the fact that his research was now more focused. Whereas in his first semester he read a range of topics, he was now homing in on his research area, the spirituality of Buddhism. This had enabled him to approach the content of texts with more confidence in his ability to understand them.

Somchai reported that in his first semester all reading was 'scary'. Now, at least, he felt comfortable reading magazines and newspapers because he said he realised they were not 'serious'; in other words they were not necessary for his study and so he could just read what he could understand. Newspapers were still a problem because he did not have the necessary social and cultural background to enable full understanding. For example, he could not understand the longstanding dockside dispute in Australia known as the Patrick dockside dispute, because, as he said, '*I do not understand the layers, last year's news, so I cannot understand this situation.*' Academic reading, however, he said was still '*scary*'.

Somchai's final comment in the second interview also revealed his lingering anxieties. He admitted feeling he was still '*riding on the tiger's back*'. He explained that it was dangerous to try and stay on the tiger's back and it was equally dangerous to fall off!

In conclusion, this case study provided some insight into the reading practices of one postgraduate student in his own country and over some time at university in Australia. The use of frame analysis for examining that student's account and reflections on his reading practices was particularly useful to highlight some of the changes which had taken place over time. It also revealed the strategies developed by that student to cope with the situation and his awareness of these strategies.

Even from this small part of the larger study, it can be seen that there are implications for both supervisors/lecturers and postgraduate students. Greater understanding of international postgraduate student difficulties could be brought about through bilingual professional development for supervisors and lecturers working with international postgraduate students. Plum (1998) noted, after analysing the writing of Psychology students, that these students had significant difficulty meeting the varied literacy demands of all the disciplines they were enrolled in and he cited the most important factor accounting for this situation to be the lack of any model of academic writing being demonstrated to the students. Regarding reading requirements, students could be made aware, even prior to leaving their homeland, of the reading requirements of their courses. Strategies and tools to enhance their understanding of texts could be part of early preparation/awareness programmes in the initial part of students' first semester in the country of study.

NOTE

1. A version of this paper is in the March 2000 issue of the ALA journal.

Bibliography

Adamson, H.D. (1993). *Academic competence: theory and classroom practice – preparing ESL students for content courses.* White Plains, NY: Longman.

Ahmad, U.K. (1995). Academic language and culture: some observations on scientific Malay and scientific English. Paper presented at RELC (SEAMEO Regional Language Centre Seminar), Singapore.

Ahmad, U.K. (1997). Research article introductions in Malay: rhetoric in an emerging research community. In A. Duszak (ed.), *Intellectual styles and cross-cultural communication* (pp. 273–303). Berlin: Mouton de Gruyter.

Aijmer, K. and Altenberg, B. (eds) (1991). *English corpus linguistics.* London: Longman.

Alderson, J.C. and Urquhart, A.H. (1985). The effect of students' academic discipline on their performance on ESP reading texts. *Language Testing,* **2**, 192–204.

Ali, M.Z.B.M. (1987). The translation of English scientific texts into Bahasa Malaysia: A study in contrastive textualization. Unpublished doctoral dissertation, Georgetown University.

Allen, J.P.B. and Widdowson, H.G. (eds) (1974). *English in focus series.* Oxford: Oxford University Press.

Allison, D. (1995). Assertions and alternatives: helping ESL undergraduates extend their choices in academic writing. *Journal of Second Language Writing,* **4** (1), 1–15.

Allison, D. (1996). Pragmatist discourse and English for academic purposes. *English for Academic Purposes,* **15**, 85–104.

Allison, D. (1997). *Characterising an English-language curriculum: a study in English for academic purposes (Topics in Language and Literature, 6).* Singapore: Dept. of English Language and Literature, National University of Singapore.

Allison, D. (1998). Investigating learners' course diaries as explorations of language. *Language Teaching Research,* **2** (1), 24–47.

Allison, D. and Gupta, A.F. (1997). Why some questions don't work: evaluating examination prompts in an educational setting. *Language and Education,* **11** (3), 147–62.

Allison, D., Varghese, S. and Wu, S.M. (1999). Local coherence and its limits: a second study of second sentences. *Journal of Second Language Writing,* **8** (1), 77–97.

Allwright, R.L., Woodley, M.-P. and Allwright, J.M. (1988). Investigating Reformulation as a practical strategy for the teaching of academic writing. *Applied Linguistics,* **9** (3), 237–58.

Anderson, W., Best, C., Black, A., Hurst, J., Miller, B. and Miller, S. (1990). Cross-curricular underlife: a collaborative report on ways with academic words. *College Composition and Communication,* **41**, 11–36.

Anderson, P. and Lawton, L. (1993). Case study versus a business simulation exercise: an international comparison of student perceptions of acquired skills. In H. Klein (ed.), *Innovation through cooperation: with cases, simulations, games, and other interactive methods* (pp. 377–86). Boston: WACRA (World Association for Case Method Research and Application).

Angelil-Carter, S. (1997). Second language acquisition of spoken and written English: acquiring the skeptron. *TESOL Quarterly,* **31** (2), 263–87.

Anthony, L. (1999). Writing research article introductions in software engineering: how accurate is a standard model? *IEEE Transactions on Professional Communication,* **42**, 38–46.

Aston, G. (1995). Corpora in language pedagogy: matching theory and practice. In G. Cook and B. Seidlhofer (eds), *Principle and practice in Applied Linguistics: studies in honour of H.G. Widdowson* (pp. 257–70). Oxford: Oxford University Press.

Aston, G. (1997). Small and large corpora in language learning. In B. Lewandowska-Tomaszczyk and P.J. Melia (eds), *PALC'97: practical applications in language corpora* (pp. 51–62). Lódź: Lódź University Press.

Aston, G. and Burnard, L. (1998). *The BNC handbook.* Edinburgh: Edinburgh University Press.

Atkinson, P. (1990). *The ethnographic imagination: textual constructions of reality.* London: Routledge.

Atkinson, D. (1992). The evolution of medical research writing from 1735–1985. *Applied Linguistics,* **11**, 337–74.

Atkinson, D. (1993). A historical discourse analysis of scientific research writing from 1675 to 1975: the case of the philosophical transactions of the Royal Society of London. Unpublished doctoral dissertation, University of Southern California.

Atkinson, P. (1994). *The ethnographic imagination: textual constructions of reality.* London: Routledge.

Bachman, L. (1986). *Reading English discourse: business, economics, law and political science.* Englewood Cliffs, NJ: Prentice Hall.

Bakhtin, M. (1986). *Speech genres and other late essays* (trans. V.W. McGee). Austin: University of Texas Press.

Ball, S.J. (1988). Participant observation. In J.P. Keeves (ed.), *Educational research methodology and measurement: an international handbook* (pp. 310–14). Oxford: Pergamon.

Ballard, B. (1989). Overseas students and Australian academics: learning and teaching styles. In B. Williams (ed.), *Overseas students in Australia: policy and practice* (pp. 87–98). Canberra: IDP.

Ballard, B. and Clanchy, J. (1991). *Teaching students from overseas: a brief guide for lecturers and supervisors.* Melbourne: Longman Cheshire.

Barber, C.L. (1962). Some measurable characteristics of modern scientific prose. In *Contributions to English syntax and philology.* Reprinted in J.M. Swales (ed.) (1988), *Episodes in ESP* (pp. 1–16). Hemel Hempstead: Prentice Hall International.

Barker, M. (1990) *Oriented for success: A source book on overseas student services.* Australian Government Publishing Services, Canberra.

Barlow, M. (1996). Parallel texts in language teaching. In S. Botley et al. (eds), *UCREL* (vol. 9), (pp. 45–56). UK: University of Lancaster.

Barlow, M. (1998). A review of text and corpus analysis. *International Journal of Corpus Linguistics,* **3** (2), 319–27.

Barnes, L., Christensen, C.R. and Hansen, A. (1994). *Teaching and the case method.* Boston: Harvard Business School Press.

Bartholomae, D. (1985). In M. Rose (ed.), *Inventing the university: when a writer can't write* (pp. 134–65). New York: Guilford.

Bartholomae, D. (1986). Inventing the university. *Journal of Basic Writing*, **5**, 4–23.

Bates, M. and Dudley-Evans, T. (1976). *The Nucleus series: English for science and technology*. London: Longman.

Bartholomew, B. (1993). A descriptive framework for identifying schematic elements and patterns in certain science and engineering reports. Unpublished doctoral dissertation, New York University.

Bateson, G. (1972). *Steps to an ecology of mind*. San Francisco: Chandler Publishing Company.

Bazerman, C. (1988). *Shaping written knowledge: the genre and activity of the experimental article in Science*. Madison, Wisconsin: University of Wisconsin Press.

Bazerman, C. (1994a). *Constructing experience*. Carbondale: Southern Illinois University Press.

Bazerman, C. (1994b). Systems of genres and the enhancement of social intentions. In A. Freedman and P. Medway (eds), *Genre and the new rhetoric* (pp. 79–101). London: Taylor & Francis.

Becher, T. (1981). Towards a definition of disciplinary cultures. *Studies in Higher Education*, **6** (2), 109–22.

Becher, T. (1988). *Academic tribes and disciplines: intellectual enquiry and the cultures of the disciplines*. Milton Keynes: Open University Press.

Becher, T. (1989). *Academic tribes and territories: intellectual inquiry and the cultures of disciplines*. Milton Keynes: Society for Research into Higher Education and Open University Press.

Belcher, D. (1994). The apprenticeship approach to advanced academic literacy: graduate students and their mentors. *English for Specific Purposes*, **13**, 23–34.

Belcher, D. and Braine, G. (eds) (1995). *Academic writing in a second language*. Norwood, NJ: Ablex.

Benson, M. (1988). The academic listening task: a case study. *TESOL Quarterly*, **27** (4), 421–45.

Benson, M. (1994). Lecture listening in an ethnographic perspective. In J. Flowerdew (ed.), *Academic listening: research perspectives* (pp. 181–98). Cambridge: Cambridge University Press.

Berkenkotter, C. and Huckin, T.N. (1995). *Genre knowledge in disciplinary communication: cognition/culture/power*. Hillsdale, NJ: Lawrence Erlbaum Associates.

Berkenkotter, C., Huckin, T. and Acketman, J. (1988). Conventions, conversations and the writer: case study of a student in a Rhetoric Ph.D. program. *Research in the Teaching of English*, **22** (1), 9–44.

Bex, T. (1996). *Variety in written English: texts in society: societies in texts*. London: Routledge.

Bhatia, V.K. (1983). Simplification versus easification: the case of legal texts. *Applied Linguistics*, **4** (1), 42–54.

Bhatia, V.K. (1984). Syntactic discontinuity in legislative writing and its implications for academic legal purposes. In A.K. Pugh and J.M. Ulijn (eds), *Reading for professional purposes* (pp. 90–6). London: Heinemann Educational Books.

Bhatia, V.K. (1991). A genre-based approach to ESP materials. *World Englishes*, **10** (2), 153–66.

Bhatia, V.K. (1993). *Analysing genre: language use in professional settings*. London: Longman.

Bhatia, V.K. (1994). Generic integrity in professional discourse. Text and talk in professional contexts. In B.-L. Gunnarsson, P. Linell, and B. Nordberg (eds), *Skriftsrie 6* (61–76). Uppsala, Sweden: ASLA.

Bhatia, V.K. (1995). Genre-mixing and in professional communication. The case of 'private intentions' v. 'socially recognized purposes'. In P. Bruthiaux, T. Boswood, and B. Du-Babcock (eds), *Explorations in English for professional communication* (pp. 1–18). Hong Kong: City University of Hong Kong.

Bhatia, V.K. (1997). Genre-mixing in academic introductions. *English for Specific Purposes*, **16** (3), 181–95.

Bhatia, V.K. (1998). Generic conflicts in academic discourse. In I. Fortanet, J.C. Plamer, S. Posteguillo and J.F. Coll (eds), *Genre studies in English for Academic Purposes* (pp. 15–28). Bancaixa: Fundacio Caixa Castello.

Bhatia, V.K. (1999a). Disciplinary variation in business English. In M. Hewings and C. Nickerson (eds), *Business English: research into practice* (pp. 129–43). London: Longman and the British Council.

Bhatia, V.K. (1999b). Integrating products, processes, purposes and participants in professional writing. In C.N. Candlin and K. Hyland (eds), *Writing: texts, processes and practices* (pp. 21–39). London: Longman.

Biber, D. (1988). *Variation across speech and writing*. Cambridge: Cambridge University Press.

Biber, D., Conrad, S. and Reppen, R. (1994). Corpus-based approaches to issues in applied linguistics. *Applied Linguistics*, **15** (2), 168–89.

Biber, D., Conrad, S. and Reppen, R. (1998). *Corpus linguistics: investigating language structure and use*. Cambridge: Cambridge University Press.

Biber, D. and Finegan, E. (1989). Drift and the evolution of English style: a history of three genres. *Language*, **65**, 487–517.

Biber, D. and Finegan, E. (1994). Intra-textual variation within medical research articles. In N. Oostdijk and P. de Haan (eds), *Corpus-based research into language* (pp. 201–21). Amsterdam: Rodopi.

Biber, D., Johansson, S., Leech, G., Conrad, S. and Finegan, E. (1999). *Longman grammar of spoken and written English*. Harlow: Longman.

Biggs, J.B. (1996). Western misconceptions of the Confucian-heritage learning culture. In D.A. Watkins and J.B. Biggs (eds), *The Chinese learner: cultural, psychological and contextual influences* (pp. 45–67). Hong Kong: CERC & ACER.

Bizzell, P. (1992). *Academic discourse and critical consciousness*. Pittsburgh: University of Pittsburgh Press.

Bloch, J. and Chi, L. (1995). A comparison of the use of citations in Chinese and English academic discourse. In D. Belcher and G. Braine (eds), *Academic writing in a second language: essays on research and pedagogy* (pp. 231–74). Norwood, NJ: Ablex.

Bloor, M. and Bloor, T. (1993). How economists modify propositions. In W. Henderson, A. Dudley-Evans and R. Backhouse (eds), *Economics and language* (pp. 153–69). London: Routledge.

Blyler, N.R. (1991). Reading theory and persuasive business communications: guidelines for writers. *Technical Writing and Communication*, **21** (4), 383–96.

Botley, S., Glass, J., McEnery, T. and Wilson, A. (eds) (1996). Proceedings of Teaching and Language Corpora Conference 1996. *UCREL* (vol. 9). UK: University of Lancaster.

Bourdieu, P., Passeron, J.-C. and Martin, M. (1994). *Academic discourse: linguistic misunderstanding and professional power* (trans. R. Teese). Cambridge: Polity Press.

Bradley, D. (1984). *Problems of Asian students in Australia: language, culture, education*. Canberra: AGPS.

Braine, G. (1989). Writing in science and technology: an analysis of assignments from ten undergraduate courses. *English for Specific Purposes*, **8**, 3–15.

Brett, P. (1994). A genre analysis of the results sections of sociology articles. *English for Specific Purposes*, **13**, 47–59.

Briggs, C.L. and Bauman, R. (1992). Genre, intertextuality, and social power. *Journal of Linguistic Anthropology,* **2** (2), 131–72.

Briggs, S., Clark, V., Madden, C., Beal, R., Hyon, S., Aldridge, P.M. and Swales, J.M. (1997). *The international teaching assistant: an annotated critical bibliography* (2nd edn). Ann Arbor, MI: English Language Institute Test Publications.

British Council (1980). *Reading and thinking in English* (4 vols.). Oxford: Oxford University Press and the British Council.

Brown, P. and Levinson, S. (1987). Politeness: some universals in language usage. (Reprinted with a new introduction, from E. Goody (ed.). *Questions and politeness.*) Cambridge: Cambridge University Press.

Bruce, N. (1989). The roles of analysis and the conceptual matrix in a process approach to teaching academic study and communication skills. In V. Bickley (ed.), *Language teaching and learning styles within and across cultures* (pp. 236–65). Hong Kong: Institute of Language in Education.

Bruffee, K. (1986). Social construction: language and the authority of knowledge: a bibliographical essay. *College English,* **48,** 773–9.

Bruthiaux, P. (1993). Linguistic simplicity and the language of classified ads. Unpublished doctoral dissertation, University of Southern California.

Bunton, D. (1998). Linguistic and textual problems in Ph.D. and M. Phil theses: an analysis of genre moves and metatext. Unpublished Ph.D. thesis, University of Hong Kong.

Burke, E. (1996, March 1). Academic and non-academic differences: perceptions of graduate non-English speaking background students. *TESL-EJ,* **2.**

Burnard, L. (1995). *The British National Corpus Users Reference Guide (SGML version).* Oxford: Oxford University Computing Services.

Burnard, L. and McEnery, T. (eds) (2000). *Rethinking language pedagogy from a corpus perspective.* Frankfurt am Main: Peter Lang Publishers.

Butler, C. (1990). Qualifications in science: modal meanings in scientific text. In W. Nash (ed.), *The Writing Scholar* (pp. 137–70). London: Sage Publications.

Cai, G. (1993). Beyond bad writing: teaching English composition to Chinese ESL students. Paper presented at the College Composition and Communication Conference. San Diego, CA.

Campbell, C. (1990). Writing with others' words: using background reading text in academic compositions. In B. Kroll (ed.), *Second language writing* (pp. 211–30). Cambridge: Cambridge University Press.

Canagarajah, A.S. (1993). Critical ethnography of a Sri Lankan classroom: ambiguities in student opposition to reproduction through ESOL. *TESOL Quarterly,* **27,** 601–26.

Canagarajah, A.S. (1997). Safe houses in the contact zone: coping strategies of African-American students in the academy. *College Composition and Communication,* **48,** 173–96.

Canavan, P.J. (1974). *Paragraphs and themes.* Lexington, MA: D. C. Heath.

Candlin, C.N. (2000). General Editor's Preface to K. Hyland, *Disciplinary discourses: social interaction in academic writing* (pp. xv–xxi). Harlow: Longman Pearson Education.

Candlin, C.N. and Hyland, K. (eds) (1999). *Writing: texts, processes and practices.* London: Longman.

Candlin, C.N. and Plum, G.A. (eds.) (1998). *Researching academic literacies. Framing student literacy: cross-cultural aspects of communication skills in Australian university settings.* Sydney: NCELTR, Macquarie University.

Candlin, C.N. and Plum, G.A. (1999). Engaging with the challenges of interdiscursivity in academic writing: researchers, students and tutors. In C.N. Candlin and K. Hyland (eds), *Writing: texts, process and practices* (pp. 193–217). London: Longman.

Cargill, M. (1996). An integrated bridging program for international postgraduate students. *Higher Education Research and Development*, **15** (2), 177–88.

Carrell, P. (1984). The effects of rhetorical organization on ESL readers. *TESOL Quarterly*, **18** (4), 441–69.

Carrell, P., Devine, J. and Eskey, D. (1988). *Interactive approaches to second language reading.* Cambridge: Cambridge University Press.

Carrell, P., Pharis, B.G. and Liberto, J.C. (1989). Metacognitive strategy training for ESL reading. *TESOL Quarterly*, **23**, 647–78.

Carter, R. and McCarthy, M. (1997). Grammar, tails, and affect: constructing expressive choices in discourse, *Text*, **17**, 405–29.

Casanave, C. (1995). Local interactions: constructing contexts for composing in a graduate sociology programme. In D. Belcher and G. Braine (eds) *Academic writing in a second language* (pp. 83–110) Norwood, NJ: Ablex.

Casanave, C.P. and Hubbard, P. (1992). The writing assignments and writing problems of doctoral students: faculty perceptions, pedagogical issues and needed research. *English for Specific Purposes*, **11**, 33–9.

Chafe, W., Du Bois, J. and Thompson, S. (1991). Towards a new corpus of spoken American English. In K. Aijmer and B. Altenberg (eds), *English corpus linguistics* (pp. 64–82). London: Longman.

Chang, S.-J. (1990). A study of language learning behaviours of Chinese students at the University of Georgia and the relation of those behaviours to oral proficiency and other factors. Unpublished doctoral dissertation, University of Georgia, Athens, GA.

Chang, Y.-Y. and Swales, J.M. (1999). Informal elements in English academic writing: threats or opportunities for advanced non-native speakers? In C.N. Candlin and K. Hyland (eds), *Writing: texts, processes and practices* (pp. 145–64). London: Longman.

Charteris-Black, J. (2000). Metaphor and vocabulary teaching in ESP economics. *English for Specific Purposes*, **19** (2), 149–65.

Cheng, W. and Warren, M. (2000). The Hong Kong corpus of spoken English: language learning through language description. In L. Burnard and T. McEnery (eds), *Rethinking language pedagogy from a corpus perspective* (pp. 133–44). Frankfurt am Main: Peter Lang Publishers.

Chiseri-Strater, E. (1991): *Academic literacies: the public and private discourse of university students.* Portsmouth, NH: Boynton-Cook.

Cho, J. H. (1998). *A stylistic comparison of newspaper editorials written in Korea and the United States.* American Association of Applied Linguistics, Seattle, Washington, March, 1998.

Cho, J.H. (1999). A study of contrastive rhetoric between East Asian and North American cultures as demonstrated through student expository essays from Korea and the United States. Unpublished doctoral dissertation, Bowling Green State University.

Christensen, C.R. (1991). The discussion teacher in action: questioning, listening, and response. In C.R. Christensen, D. Garvin, and A. Sweet (eds), *Education for judgment: the artistry of discussion leadership* (pp. 153–72). Boston: Harvard Business School Press.

Christensen, F. (1984). A generative rhetoric of the sentence. In R.L. Graves (ed.), *Rhetoric and composition: a sourcebook for teachers and writers*, 2nd edn (pp. 110–18). Upper Montclair, NJ: Boynton-Cook.

Clark, W.F. (1997). Investigating transfer of writing sophistication in expository writings of American and Mexican students in their first and foreign languages. Unpublished doctoral dissertation, Indiana University of Pennsylvania.

Clyne, M. (1981). Culture and discourse structure. *Journal of Pragmatics*, **5**, 61–6.

Clyne, M. (1987a). Cultural differences in the organization of academic texts. *Journal of Pragmatics*, **11**, 211–47.

Clyne, M. (1987b). Discourse structures and discourse expectations: implication for Anglo-German academic communication in English. In L.E. Smith (ed.), *Discourse across cultures: strategies in world Englishes* (pp. 73–83). New York: Prentice Hall.

Clyne, M. (1991). The sociocultural dimension: the dilemma of the German-speaking scholar. In H. Schröder (ed.), *Subject-oriented texts: languages for special purposes and text theory* (pp. 49–67). Berlin: Walter de Gruyter.

Čmejrková, S. (1996). Academic writing in Czech and English. In E. Ventola and A. Mauranen (eds), *Intercultural and textual issues* (pp. 137–53). Amsterdam, Philadelphia: John Benjamins Publications.

Čmejrková, S. and Daneš, F. (1997). Academic writing and cultural identity: the case of Czech academic writing. In A. Diszak (ed.), *Culture and styles of academic discourse. Trends in Linguistics. Studies and Monographs*, **104**, 41–61. Berlin.

Coates, J. (1983). *Semantics of the modal auxiliaries*. London: Croom Helm.

Cobb, T. (1997) Is there any measurable learning from hands-on concordancing? *System* 25, 301–15.

Coe, R.M. (1987). An apology for form: or, who took the form out of process? *College English*, **49**, 13–28.

Coe, R.M. (1994). An arousing and fulfillment of desires: the rhetoric of genre in the process era – and beyond. In A. Freedman and P. Medway (eds), *Genre and the new rhetoric* (pp. 181–90). London: Taylor & Francis.

Colina, S. (1997). Contrastive rhetoric and text-typological conventions in translation teaching. *Target*, **9** (2), 335–53.

Connor, U. (1990). Linguistic/rhetorical measures for international persuasive student writing. *Research in the Teaching of English*, **24** (1), 67–87.

Connor, U. (1996). *Contrastive rhetoric: cross-cultural aspects of second language writing*. Cambridge: Cambridge University Press.

Connor, U. (1999). Learning to write academic prose in a second language: a literary autobiography. In G. Braine (ed.), *Non-native educators in English language teaching* (pp. 29–42). Mahwah, NJ: Erlbaum.

Connor, U. (forthcoming). Variation in rhetorical moves in grant proposals of U.S. humanists and scientists. *Text*.

Connor, U. and Johns, A.M. (eds) (1990). Coherence in writing: research and pedagogical perspectives. Alexandria, Virginia: TESOL.

Connor, U. and Lauer, J. (1985). Understanding persuasive essay writing: linguistic rhetorical approach. *Text*, **5** (4), 309–26.

Connor, U. and Mauranen, A. (1999). Linguistic analysis of grant proposals: European Union research grants. *English for Academic Purposes*, **18** (1), 47–62.

Connor, U. and Upton, T. (2000). Cross-cultural differences in politeness: data from an international learner English corpus. Paper presented in colloquium 'Computer learner corpora: uses for research and teaching' at AAAL Conference, 13 March, Vancouver, BC.

Conrad, S. (1996). Investigating academic texts with corpus-based techniques: an example from Biology. *Linguistics and Education*, **8**, 299–326.

Cooper, C. (1985). Aspects of article introductions in IEEE publications. Unpublished M.Sc. dissertation, University of Aston.

Cope, B. and Kalantzis, M. (1993). *The powers of literacy: a genre approach to teaching writing*. London: The Falmer Press.

Cortazzi, M. and Jin, L. (1996). Cultures of learning: language classrooms in China. In H. Coleman (ed.), *Society and the language classroom* (pp. 169–206). Cambridge: Cambridge University Press.

Coxhead, A. (2000). A new academic word list. *TESOL Quarterly*, **32** (2), 213–38.

Crismore, A., Markannen, R. and Steffensen, M. (1993). Metadiscourse in persuasive writing. *Written Communication* **10**, 39–71.

Crookes, G. (1984). *Towards a validated discourse analysis of scientific texts*. MA thesis, University of Hawaii.

Crookes. G. (1986). Towards a validated analysis of scientific text structure, *Applied Linguistics*, **7** (1), 57–70.

Crystal, D. (1997). *English as a global language*. Cambridge: Cambridge University Press.

Curado, A. and Berzosa, M. (2000). Dealing with small representative corpora in ESP. In B. Lewandowska-Tomaszczyk and P.J. Melia (eds), *PALC'99: practical applications in language corpora* (pp. 475–88). Frankfurt am Main: Peter Lang Publishers.

Dagneaux, E., Denness, S. and Granger, S. (1998). Computer-aided error analysis. *System*, **26**, 163–74.

Davis, K.A. (1992). Validity and reliability in qualitative research on second language acquisition and teaching: another researcher comments. *TESOL Quarterly*, **26**, 605–8.

De Beaugrande, R. (1996). The 'pragmatics' of doing language science: the 'warrant' for large-corpus linguistics. *Journal of Pragmatics*, **25**, 503–35.

Degenhart, E.R. and Takala, S. (1988). Developing a rating method for stylistic preference: a cross-cultural pilot study. In A.C. Purves (ed.), *Writing across languages and cultures: issues in contrastive rhetoric* (pp. 79–106). Written Communication Annual, vol. 2. Newbury Parh, CA: Sage.

Dodd, B. (1997). Exploiting a corpus of written German for advanced language learning. In A. Wichmann et al. (eds), *Teaching and language corpora* (p. 131). London: Longman.

Donahue, R.T. (1994). Advancing international studies through contextualism: images of Japanese discourse and society. Unpublished doctoral dissertation, University of Virginia.

Drury, H. (1991). Literacy at tertiary level: Making explicit the writing requirements of a new culture. In R. Christie (ed.), *Literacy in social processes* (pp. 214–27). Deakin, Australia: Deakin University Press.

Dubois, B. (1988). Citation in biomedical journal articles. *English for Specific Purposes*, **7**, 181–94.

Dudley-Evans, T. (1986). Genre analysis: an investigation of the introduction and discussion sections of M.Sc dissertations. In M. Coulthard (ed.), *Talking about text* (pp. 128–45). Birmingham: English Language Research, University of Birmingham.

Dudley-Evans, T. (1994a). Genre analysis: an approach to text analysis for ESP. In M. Coulthard (ed.), *Advances in written text analysis* (pp. 219–28). London: Routledge.

Dudley-Evans, T. (1994b). Variations in the discourse patterns favoured by different disciplines and their pedagogical applications. In J. Flowerdew (ed.), *Academic listening: research perspectives* (pp. 146–58). Cambridge: Cambridge University Press.

Dudley-Evans, T. and St John, M.G. (1998). *Developments in English for specific purposes*. Cambridge: Cambridge University Press.

Dunkelblau, H.S. (1990). A contrastive study of the organizational structure and stylistic elements of Chinese and English expository writing by Chinese high school students. New York University: Ph.D. diss.

Duszak, A. (1994). Academic discourse and intellectual styles. *Journal of Pragmatics*, **21**, 291–313.

Duszak, A. (1997). Cross-cultural academic communication: a discourse-community view. In A. Duszak (ed.), *Culture and styles of academic discourse. Trends in Linguistics. Studies and Monographs*, **104**, 11–39. Berlin: Mouton de Gruyter.

Eason, C.A. (1995). Argumentative essays written by native speakers of Chinese and English: a study in contrastive rhetoric. Unpublished doctoral dissertation, university of Illinois at Urbana-Champaign.

Eggington, W.G. (1987). Written academic discourse in Korean: implications for effective communication. In U. Connor and R.B. Kaplan (eds), *Writing across languages: analysis of L2 text* (pp. 153–68). Reading, MA: Addison-Wesley.

El-Sayed, A.M.M. (1992). Arabic rhetoric and its influence on the English writings of Arab university students. *Indian Journal of Applied Linguistics*, **18** (2), 43–65.

Emig, J. (1969). Components of the composing process among twelfth-grade writers. Unpublished doctoral dissertation, Harvard University.

Emig, J. (1983). *The web of meaning.* Upper Montclair, NJ: Boynton Cook.

Erskine, J., Leenders, M. and Maufette-Leenders, L. (1998). *Teaching with cases.* London, Ontario, Canada: Richard Ivey School of Business, The University of Western Ontario, London, Canada.

Faigley, L. and Hansen, K. (1985) Learning to write in the Social Sciences. *College Composition and Communication*, **36**, 140–9.

Fairclough, N. (1989). *Language and power.* London: Longman.

Fairclough, N. (1992). *Discourse and social change.* Cambridge: Polity Press.

Falvey, P. (1998). ESL, EFL and language acquisition in the context of Hong Kong. In B. Asker (ed.), *Teaching language and culture: building Hong Kong on education* (pp. 73–85). London: Longman.

Ferris, D.R. (1991). Syntactic and lexical characteristics of ESL students writing: a multidimensional study. Unpublished doctoral dissertation, University of Southern California.

Fish, S. (1989). *Doing what comes naturally.* Oxford: Oxford University Press.

Flowerdew, J. (1993a). An educational, or process, approach to the teaching of professional genres. *ELT Journal*, **47** (4), 305–16.

Flowerdew, J. (1993b). Concordancing as a tool in course design. *System*, **21** (2), 231–44.

Flowerdew, J. (1994a). Specific language for specific purposes: Concordancing for the ESP syllabus. In R. Khoo (ed.), *LSP – problems and prospects.* Anthology Series 13 (pp. 97–113). Singapore: SEAMEO Regional Language Centre.

Flowerdew, J. (1994b). *Academic listening: research perspectives.* Cambridge: Cambridge University Press.

Flowerdew, J. (1996). Concordancing in language learning. In M. Pennington (ed.), *The Power of CALL* (pp. 97–113). Houston, TX: Athelstan.

Flowerdew, J. (1999). Problems in writing for scholarly publication in English: the case of Hong Kong. *Journal of Second Language Writing*, **8**, 243–64.

Flowerdew, J. (2000). Discourse community, legitimate peripheral participation, and the nonnative-English-speaking scholar. *TESOL Quarterly*, **34** (1), 127–50.

Flowerdew, J. (in press). Genre in the classroom: a linguistic approach. In A. Johns (ed.), *Genres in the classroom.* New Jersey: Erlbaum.

Flowerdew, J. (2001). Academic writing at the lower proficiency levels. In I. Leki (ed.), *Case Studies in TESOL Practices: Writing.* (pp. 21–33) TESOL Publications.

Flowerdew, J. and Dudley-Evans, A. (1999). Genre analysis of editorial letters to journal contributors. Paper presented at American Association of Applied Linguistics Annual Conference, Stamford, Connecticut, March 1999.

Flowerdew, J., Li, D. and Miller, L. (1996). Cantonese-speaking lecturers' perceptions, problems and strategies in second language lecturing at City University. Unpublished report submitted to City University of Hong Kong Quality Enhancement Committee.

Flowerdew, J., Li, D. and Miller, L. (1998). Attitudes towards English and Cantonese among Hong Kong Chinese University lecturers. *TESOL Quarterly* **32** (2), 201–31.

Flowerdew, J. and Miller, L. (1992). Student perceptions, problems and strategies in L2 lectures. *RELC Journal,* **23** (2), 60–80.

Flowerdew, J. and Miller, L. (1995). On the notion of culture in second language lectures. *TESOL Quarterly,* **29** (2), 345–74.

Flowerdew, J. and Miller, L. (1996). Lectures in a second language: notes towards a cultural grammar. *English for Specific Purposes,* **15** (2), 121–40.

Flowerdew, J. and Miller, L. (1997). The teaching of academic listening comprehension and the question of authenticity. *English for Specific Purposes,* **16** (1), 27–46.

Flowerdew, J. and Tauroza, S. (1995). The effect of discourse markers on second language lecture comprehension. *Studies in Second Language Acquisition,* **17** (4), 435–58.

Flowerdew, L. (1998a). Integrating expert and interlanguage computer corpora findings on causality: discoveries for teachers and students. *English for Specific Purposes,* **17** (4), 329–45.

Flowerdew, L. (1998b). Concordancing on an expert and learner corpus for ESP. *CAELL Journal,* **8** (3), 3–7.

Flowerdew, L. (1998c). Corpus linguistic techniques applied to textlinguistics. *System,* **26** (4), 541–52.

Flowerdew, L. (2000). Investigating referential and pragmatic errors in a learner corpus. In L. Burnard and T. McEnery (eds), *Rethinking language pedagogy from a corpus perspective* (pp. 117–24). Frankfurt am Main: Peter Lang Publishers.

Flowerdew, L. (in press, 2001). The exploitation of small learner corpora in EAP materials design. In M. Ghadessy, A. Henry, and R. Roseberry (eds), *The use of small corpora in language teaching.* Amsterdam: John Benjamins.

Flowerdew, L. and Tong, K.K. (eds) (1994). *Entering text.* Language Centre, Hong Kong University of Science and Technology and Guangzhou University of Foreign Languages.

Foley, J.A., Kandiah, T., Bao, Z., Gupta, A.F., Alsagoff, L., Ho, C.L., Wee, L., Talib, I.S. and Bokhorst-Heng, W. (1998). *English in new cultural contexts: reflections from Singapore.* Singapore: Oxford University Press/Singapore Institute of Management.

Folman, S. and Sarig, G. (1990). Intercultural rhetorical differences in meaning construction. *Communication and Cognition,* **23** (1), 45–92.

Fortanet, I., Plamer, J.C., Posteguillo, S. and Coll, J.C. (eds) (1998). *Genre studies in English for Academic Purposes.* Bancaixa: Fundacio Caixa Castello.

Foucou, P. and Kübler, N. (2000). A web-based environment for teaching technical English. In L. Burnard and T. McEnery (eds), *Rethinking language pedagogy from a corpus perspective* (pp. 65–73). Frankfurt am Main: Peter Lang Publishers.

Fox, H. (1994). *Listening to the world: cultural issues in academic writing.* Urbana: NCTE.

Fredrickson, K.M. (1996). Contrasting genre systems: Contrasting court documents from the United States and Sweden. *Multilingua,* **15**, 275–304.

Fredrickson, K.M. and Swales, J.M. (1994). Competition and discourse community: introductions from Nysvenska Studier. In B.-L. Gunnarsson, P. Linell, and B. Nordberg (eds), *Text and talk in professional contexts* (pp. 9–22). Sweden: ASLA.

Freed, R.C. and Broadhead, G.J. (1987). Discourse communities, sacred texts, and institutional norms. *College Composition and Communication,* **38** (2), 154–65.

Freedman, A. (1994). Anyone for tennis? In A. Freedman and P. Medway (eds), *Genre and the new rhetoric* (pp. 43–66). London: Taylor & Francis.

Freedman, A. and Medway, P. (eds) (1994a). *Genre and the new rhetoric*. London: Taylor & Francis.

Freedman, A. and Medway, P. (1994b). Locating genre studies: antecedents and prospects. In A. Freedman and P. Medway (eds), *Genre and the new rhetoric* (pp. 1–22). London: Taylor & Francis.

Freedman, A. and Medway, P. (eds) (1994c). *Learning and teaching genre*. Portsmouth, NH: Boynton Cook.

Furneaux, C., Locke, C., Robinson, P. and Tonkyn, A. (1991). Talking heads and shifting bottoms: the ethnography of academic seminars. In P. Adams, B. Heaton, and P. Howarth (eds), *Sociocultural issues in English for academic purposes* (pp. 75–87). London: Modern English Publications in Association with the British Council.

Galtung, J. (1985). Structur, Kultur und Intellektueller Stil. In A. Wierlacher (ed.), *Das Femde und das Eigene* (pp. 151–93). Munich: Judicum Verlag.

Garside, R., Leech, G. and McEnery, A. (1997). *Corpus annotation*. London: Longman.

Garside, R., Leech, G. and Sampson, G. (1987). *The computational analysis of English*. London: Longman.

Gavioli, L. (forthcoming). Concordancing and ESP: scientific English. In A. Baldry (ed.), *Multimodality and multimediality in the distance learning age*. Campobasso: Lampo Edizioni.

Gee, J.P. (1990). *Social linguistics and literacies: ideology in discourses*, 2nd edn. London: Taylor & Francis.

Geertz, C. (1973). *The interpretation of cultures*. New York: Basic Books.

Geertz, C. (1983). *Local knowledge: further essays in interpretive anthropology*. New York: Basic Books.

Giddens, A. (1993a). *Sociology* (2nd edn). Cambridge: Polity Press.

Giddens, A. (1993b). *New rules of sociological method: a positive critique of interpretative sociologies* (2nd edn). Cambridge: Polity Press.

Gilbert, G. (1976). The transformation of research findings into scientific knowledge. *Social Studies of Science*, **6**, 281–306.

Gilbert, G.N. and Mulkay, M. (1984). *Opening Pandora's Box: a sociological analysis of scientists' discourse*. Cambridge: Cambridge University Press.

Glaser, B. and Strauss, A. (1967). *The discovery of grounded theory*. Chicago: Aldine.

Gledhill, C. (1995). Collocation and genre analysis: the discourse function of collocation in cancer research abstracts and articles. *Zeitschrift für Anglistik und Amerikanistik*, **1**, 1–26.

Gledhill, C. (1996). Science as a collocation: phraseology in cancer research articles. In S. Botley et al. (eds), Proceedings of Teaching and Language Corpora Conference 1996 *UCREL* (vol. 9), (pp. 108–26). UK: University of Lancaster.

Gledhill, C. (2000). The discourse function of collocation in research article introductions. *English for Specific Purposes*, **19** (2), 115–35.

Gnutzmann, C. and Oldenburg, H. (1991). *Contrastive text linguistics in LSP-research: theoretical considerations and some preliminary findings*. In H. Schröder (ed.), *Subject-oriented texts: language for special purposes and text theory* (pp. 103–36). Berlin: Mouton de Gruyter.

Goffman, E. (1974). *Frame analysis: an essay on the organization of experience*. Cambridge, MA: Harvard University Press.

Grabe, W. (1984). Towards defining expository prose within a theory of text construction. Unpublished doctoral dissertation, University of Southern California.

Grabe, W. and Kaplan, R.B. (1989). Writing in a second language: contrastive rhetoric. In D.M. Johnson and D.H. Roen (eds), *Richness in writing: empowering ESL students* (pp. 263–83). New York: Longman.

Grabe, W. and Kaplan, R.B. (1996). *Theory and practice of writing.* London and New York: Longman.

Graddol, D. (1997). *The future of English.* London: British Council.

Granger, S. (1993). International corpus of learner English. In J. Aarts, P. de Haan, and N. Oostdijk (eds), *English language corpora: design, analysis and exploitation* (pp. 57–71). Amsterdam: Rodopi.

Granger, S. (1994). The learner corpus: a revolution in applied linguistics, *English Today,* **39** (10), 25–39.

Granger, S. (ed.) (1998a). *Learner English on computer.* London: Longman.

Granger, S. (1998b). The computer learner corpus: a versatile new source of data for SLA research. In S. Granger (ed.), *Learner English on computer* (pp. 3–18). London: Longman.

Granger, S. (1998c). Prefabricated patterns in advanced EFL writing: collocations and formulae. In A. Cowie (ed.), *Phraseology* (pp. 145–60). Oxford: Clarendon Press.

Granger, S. and Rayson, P. (1998). Automatic profiling of learner texts. In S. Granger (ed.), *Learner English on computer* (pp. 119–31). London: Longman.

Granger, S. and Tribble, C. (1998). Learner corpus data in the foreign language classroom: form-focused instruction and data-driven learning. In S. Granger (ed.), *Learner English on computer* (pp. 199–209). London: Longman.

Granger, S. and Tyson, S. (1996). Connector usage in the English essay writing of native and non-native EFL speakers of English. *World Englishes,* **15** (1), 17–27.

Green, C., Christopher, E. and Lam, J. (2000). The incidence and effects on coherence of marked themes in interlanguage texts: a corpus-based enquiry. *English for Specific Purposes,* **19** (2), 99–113.

Greenbaum, S. (1992). A new corpus of English: ICE. In J. Svartvik (ed.), *Directions in corpus linguistics* (pp. 171–9). New York: Mouton de Gruyter.

Gumperz, J.J. (1982a) *Language and Social Identity.* Cambridge University Press, Cambridge.

Gunnarsson, B.L., Linell, P. and Nordberg, B. (eds) (1997). *The construction of professional discourse.* London: Longman.

Gupta, A.F. (1994). *The step-tongue: Children's English in Singapore.* Clevedon, Philadelphia: Multilingual Matters.

Guthrie, J.T. (1988). Locating information in documents: examination of a cognitive model. *Reading Research Quarterly,* **23** (2), 178–99.

Hafernik, J.J. (1990). Relationships among English writing experience, contrastive rhetoric, and English expository prose of L(1) and L(2) college writers. Unpublished doctoral dissertation, University of San Francisco.

Halliday, M.A.K. (1973). *Explorations in the functions of language.* London: Edward Arnold.

Halliday, M.A.K. (1978). *Language as social semiotic.* London: Edward Arnold.

Halliday, M.A.K. (1988). On the language of physical science. In M. Ghadessy (ed.), *Registers of written English* (pp. 162–78). London: Pinter.

Halliday, M.A.K. (1989). *Spoken and written language.* Oxford: Oxford University Press.

Halliday, M.A.K. (1994). *Functional Grammar* (2nd edn). London: Edward Arnold.

Halliday, M.A.K. and Martin, J.R. (1993). *Writing science.* London: Falmer Press.

Halliday, M., Strevens, P. and McIntosh, A. (1964). *The linguistic sciences and language teaching.* Oxford: Oxford University Press.

Hammersley, M. and Atkinson, P. (1983). *Ethnography: principles in practice.* London: Tavistock.

Hammond, J. (1980). *Learning by the case method.* Note distributed by the Harvard School of Business, Boston, MA.

Hamp-Lyons, L. (1988). The product before: task-related influences on the writer. In P.C. Robinson (ed.), *Academic writing: processes and products* (pp. 35–46). Basingstoke: Modern English Publications/British Council.

Hamp-Lyons, L. and Heasley, B. (1987). *Study writing: a course in written English for academic and professional purposes.* Cambridge: Cambridge University Press.

Hargan, N. (1995). Misguided expectations: EFL teachers' attitudes towards Italian university students' written work. *Language and Education,* **9** (4), 223–32.

Harris, S. (1997). Procedural vocabulary in law case report. *English for Specific Purposes,* **16** (4), 289–308.

Hasan, R. (1985). The structure of a text in Halliday. In M.A.K. Halliday and R. Hasan (eds), *Language, context, and text: aspects of language in a social-semiotic perspective* (pp. 52–69). Victoria: Deakin University Press.

Hatzidaki, O. (1996). Corpus linguistics as an academic subject. In S. Botley et al. (eds), Proceedings of Teaching and Language Corpora Conference 1996. *UCREL* (vol. 9), (pp. 254–65). UK: University of Lancaster.

Hayes, J. and Flowerdew, L. (1983). Uncovering cognitive processes in writing: an introduction to protocol analysis. In P. Mosenthal, L. Tamor, and S.A. Walmsley (eds), *Research on writing: principles and methods* (pp. 206–29). London: Longman.

Heath, S.B. (1983). *Ways with words: language, life, and work in communities and classrooms.* Cambridge: Cambridge University Press.

Henderson, W. and Hewings, A. (1990). A language of model building? In T. Dudley-Evans and W. Henderson (eds), *Language of Economics: the analysis of Economics discourse* (pp. 43–54). ELT Documents 134. London: Modern English Publications and the British Council.

Herrington, A. (1985). Writing in academic settings: a study of the contexts for writing in two chemical engineering courses. *Research in the Teaching of English,* **19**, 331–59.

Herrington, A. (1988). Teaching, writing and learning: a naturalistic study of writing in an undergraduate literature course. In D.A. Jolliffe (ed.), *Advances in writing research. Vol. 2: Writing in academic disciplines* (pp. 133–66). Norwood, NJ: Ablex.

Heslot, J. (1982). Tense and other indexical markers in the typology of scientific texts in English. In J. Hoedt, L. Lundquist, H. Picht, and J. Quistgaard (eds), *Pragmatics and LSP* (pp. 83–103). Copenhagen: Copenhagen School of Economics.

Hewings, M. and Nickerson, C. (eds) (1999). *Business English: research into practice.* Longman and the British Council.

Hill, S.S., Soppelsa, B.F. and West, G.K. (1982). Teaching ESL students to read and write experimental research papers. *TESOL Quarterly,* **16** (3), 333–47.

Hinds, J. (1987). Reader versus writer responsibility: a new typology. In U. Connor and R. Kaplan (eds), *Writing across languages: analysis of L2 text* (pp. 141–52). Reading, MA: Addison-Wesley.

Hinkel, E. (1994). Native and nonnative speakers' pragmatic interpretation of English texts. *TESOL Quarterly,* **28** (2), 353–76.

Hirvela, A. (1997). 'Disciplinary portfolios' and EAP writing instruction. *English for Specific Purposes,* **16** (2), 83–100.

Hoey, M. (1983). *On the surface of discourse.* London: George Allen & Unwin.

Hoey, M. (1986). Clause relations and the writer's communicative task. In B. Couture (ed.), *Functional approaches to writing research perspectives* (pp. 120–41). London: Frances Pinter.

Hoey, M. (1997). From concordance to text structure: new uses for computer corpora. In B. Lewandowska-Tomaszczyk and P.J. Melia (eds.), *PALC'97: practical applications in language corpora* (pp. 2–23). Lódź: Lódź University Press.

Holm, A. and Dodd, B. (1996). The effect of first written language on the acquisition of English literacy. *Cognition*, **59**, 119–47.

Holmes, J. (1988). Doubt and certainty in ESL textbooks. *Applied Linguistics*, **9** (1), 21–44.

Holmes, R. (1997). Genre analysis, and the social sciences: an investigation of the structure of research article discussion sections in three disciplines. *English for Specific Purposes*, **16** (4), 321–37.

Holyoak, S. and Piper, A. (1997). Talking to second language writers: using interview data to investigate contrastive rhetoric. *Language Teaching Research*, **1** (2), 122–48.

Hopkins, A. (1985). An investigation into the organising and organisational features of published conference papers. MA dissertation, University of Birmingham.

Hopkins, A. and Dudley-Evans, T. (1988). A genre-based investigation of the discussion sections in articles and dissertations. *English for Specific Purposes*, **7**, 113–21.

Horowitz, D. (1986a). Essay examination prompts and the teaching of academic writing. *English for Specific Purposes*, **5** (2), 107–20.

Horowitz, D. (1986b). What professors actually require: academic tasks for the ESL classroom. *TESOL Quarterly*, **20** (3), 445–62.

Horowitz, D. (1989). Function and form in essay examination prompts. *RELC Journal*, **20** (2), 23–35.

Howarth, P. (1998). The phraseology of learners' academic writing. In A. Cowie (ed.), *Phraseology* (pp. 161–86). Oxford: Clarendon Press.

Hoye, L. (1997). *Adverbs and modality in English*. London: Longman.

Hu, Z., Brown, D. and Brown L. (1982). Some linguistic differences in the written English of Chinese and Australian students. *Language learning and communication*, **1** (1), 39–49.

Hull, G., Rose, M., Fraser, K.L. and Castellano, M. (1991). Remediation as social construct: perspectives from an analysis of classroom discourse. *College Composition and Communication*, **42** (3), 299–329.

Hunston, S. (1993). Evaluation and ideology in scientific writing. In M. Ghadessy (ed.), *Register analysis: theory and practice* (pp. 57–73). London: Pinter.

Hunston, S. (1995). Grammar in teacher education: the role of a corpus. *Language Awareness*, **4** (1), 15–29.

Hyland, K. (1994) Hedging in academic writing and EAP textbooks. *English for Specific Purposes*, **13** (2), 239–56.

Hyland, K. (1996a). Talking to the academy: forms of hedging in science research articles. *Written Communication*, **13**, 251–81.

Hyland, K. (1996b). Writing without conviction? Hedging in science research articles. *Applied Linguistics*, **17** (4), 433–54.

Hyland, K. (1998). *Hedging in scientific research articles*. Amsterdam: Benjamins.

Hyland, K. (1999a). Disciplinary discourses: writer stance in research articles. In C.N. Candlin and K. Hyland (eds), *Writing: texts, processes and practices* (pp. 99–121). London: Longman.

Hyland, K. (1999b). Talking to students: metadiscourse in introductory textbooks. *English for Specific Purposes*, **18** (1), 3–26.

Hyland, K. (2000). *Disciplinary discourses: social interaction in academic writing*. London: Longman Pearson Education.

Hyland, K. (2001). Humble servants of the discipline? Self mention in research articles. *English for Specific Purposes.*

Hyland, K. and Milton, J. (1997a). Hedging in L1 and L2 student writing. *Journal of Second Language Writing*, **4** (3), 253–306.

Hyland, K. and Milton, J. (1997b). Qualifications and certainty in L1 and L2 students' writing. *Journal of Second Language Writing*, **6** (2), 183–205.

Hyon, S. (1996). Genre in three traditions: implications for ESL. *TESOL Quarterly*, **30** (4), 693–722.

Inkster, G. (1997). First catch your corpus: building a French undergraduate corpus from readily available textual resources. In A. Wichmann et al. (eds), *Teaching and language corpora* (pp. 267–76). London: Longman.

Islam, M.N. (1994). Contrastive rhetoric: English and Bengali. Unpublished doctoral dissertation, Oklahoma State University.

Ivanic, R. and Simpson, J. (1992). Who's who in academic writing? In N. Fairclough (ed.), *Critical language awareness* (pp. 96–110). London: Longman.

Jabbour, G. (1997) Where is the writer in a frequency list? Using a corpus of medical research articles in teaching. In B. Lewandowska-Tomaszczyk and P.J. Melia (eds), *PALC'97: practical applications in language corpora* (pp. 178–90). Lódź: Lódź University Press.

Jackson, J. (1998a). Essential knowledge for effective ESP teaching: insights from the content classroom. Paper presented at the Regional English Language Seminar, RELC'98, *Language Teaching: New Insights for the Language Teacher*, Singapore.

Jackson, J. (1998b). Leading case discussions in an Asian context. Paper presented at the Fifth Cross National Teaching Forum at the World Association for Case Method Research and Application (WACRA) conference at Marseille, France.

Jackson, J. (1999a). A question of questions in an L2 speech event: the case discussion. Paper presented at the 12th World Congress of Applied Linguistics (AILA'99), *The Roles of Language in the 21st Century: Unity and Diversity*, Waseda University, Tokyo.

Jackson, J. (1999b). Enhancing ESP programming through ethnographic research. In J. James (ed.), *Quality in teaching and learning in higher education* (pp. 121–7). Hong Kong: The Hong Kong Polytechnic University.

Jackson, J. (1999c). Perceptions of Chinese students in an English-medium case-based management course. In H. Klein (ed.), *Interactive teaching and the multimedia revolution: case method and other techniques*, **XI**, 61–108. Boston: The World Association for Case Method Research and Application (WACRA).

Jackson, J. (1999d). Questions as 'speech acts' in L2 case discussions: an ethnographic case study. Paper presented at the American Association for Applied Linguistics (AAAL'99) at Stamford, CT, USA.

Jackson, J. (in press). The power of questions in second language case discussions. In H. Klein (ed.), *Complex Demands on Teaching and Innovation: Case Method and Other Techniques*, **XIII**.

Jackson, J. and Bilton, L. (1994). Vocabulary in science lectures. *English for Specific Purposes*, **13** (1), 61–80.

Jacobs, S. (1990). Building hierarchy: learning the language of the science domains, ages 10–13. In U. Connor and A. Johns (eds), *Coherence in writing: research and pedagogical perspectives* (pp. 151–68). Alexandria, VA: TESOL.

James, G. and Purchase, J. (1996). *English in Business Studies and Economics: a corpus-based lexical analysis.* Hong Kong: Language Centre, Hong Kong University of Science and Technology.

James, G., Davison, R., Cheung, A.H.Y. and Deerwester, S. (1994). *English in Computer Science: a corpus-based lexical analysis.* Hong Kong: Longman Asia.

James, G., Ho, P.W.L. and Chu, A.C.Y. (1997). *English in Biochemistry, Biology and Chemistry: a corpus-based lexical analysis.* Hong Kong: Language Centre, Hong Kong University of Science and Technology.

Jamieson, K.M. (1973). Generic constraints and the rhetorical situation. *Philosophy and Rhetoric,* **6**, 162–70.

Jamieson, K.M. (1975). Antecedent genre as rhetorical constraint. *Journal of Speech,* **61**, 151–67.

Jenkins, S. and Hinds, J. (1987). Business letter writing: English, French, and Japanese. *TESOL Quarterly,* **21**, 327–54.

John, M.J. (1987). Writing processes of Spanish scientists publishing in English. *English for Specific Purposes,* **6** (2), 113–20.

Johns, A.M. (in press). *Genre in the classroom.* Mahwah, NJ: Erlbaum.

Johns, A.M. (1997). *Text, role, and context: exploring academic literacies.* Cambridge: Cambridge University Press.

Johns, T. (1988). Whence and whither classroom concordancing? In T. Bongaerts, P. de Haan, S. Lobbe, and H. Wekker (eds), *Computer applications in language learning* (pp. 9–33). Dordrecht: Foris.

Johns, T. (1991). Should you be persuaded: two examples of data-driven learning. *ELR Journal* (New Series), **4**, 1–16.

Johns, T. (1994). From printout to handout: grammar and vocabulary teaching in the context of data-driven learning. In T. Odlin (ed.), *Perspectives on Pedagogical Grammar* (pp. 293–313). Cambridge: Cambridge University Press.

Johns, T. (1997). Kibbitzing one-to-ones. In G.V. Langley (ed.), *BALEAP professional interest meetings report 1995–1997* (pp. 76–9). London: British Association of Lecturers in English for Academic Purposes.

Johns, T. and King, P. (eds) (1991). *Classroom concordancing (Special edition: English Language Research Journal 4).* Birmingham: Birmingham University.

Johnson, D.M. (1992). *Approaches to research in second-language research.* New York: Longman.

Johnson, R.K. (1998). Language and education in Hong Kong. In M. Pennington (ed.), *Language in Hong Kong at century's end* (pp. 265–76). Hong Kong: Hong Kong University Press.

Jolliffe, D.A. and Brier, E.M. (1988). Studying writers' knowledge in academic disciplines. In D.A. Jolliffe (ed.), *Advances in writing research. Vol. 2. Writing in academic disciplines* (pp. 35–89). Norwood, NJ: Ablex.

Jones, J. (1991) Grammatical metaphor and technicality in academic writing: an exploration of ESL (English as a Second Language) and NS (Native Speaker) student texts. In R. Christie (ed.), *Literacy in social processes* (pp. 178–98). Deakin, Australia: Deakin University Press.

Jones, J., Gollin, S., Drury, H. and Economou, D. (1989) Systemic-functional linguistics and its application to the TESOL curriculum. In R. Hasan and J.R. Martin (eds), Language development: learning language, learning culture: meaning and choice in language: studies for Michael Halliday (pp. 257–381). Vol. XXVII in the series *Advances in Discourse Processes,* R.O. Freedle (ed.).

Jordan, R.R. (1990). *Academic writing course.* London: Collins.

Kachru, B. (1985). Standards, codification and sociolinguistic realism: the English language in the outer circle. In R. Quirk and H.G. Widdowson (eds), *English in the world: teaching and learning the language and literatures* (pp. 11–30). Cambridge: Cambridge University Press.

Kachru, Y. (1997). Cultural meaning and contrastive rhetoric in English education. *World Englishes,* **16** (3), 337–50.

Kachru, Y. (2000). Culture, context and writing. In E. Hinkel (ed.), *Culture in second language teaching and learning* (pp. 75–89). Cambridge: Cambridge University Press.

Kamel, G.W. (1989). Argumentative writing by Arab learners of English as a foreign and second language: an empirical investigation of contrastive rhetoric. Unpublished doctoral dissertation, Indiana University of Pennsylvania.

Kamimura, T. and Oi, K. (1997). Contrastive rhetoric in letter writing: the interaction of linguistic proficiency and cultural awareness. *JALT Journal,* **19** (1), 58–76.

Kaplan, R.B. (1966). Cultural thought patterns in intercultural education. *Language Learning,* **16** (1), 1–20.

Kaplan, R.B. (1972). *The anatomy of rhetoric: prolegomena to a functional theory of rhetoric.* Philadelphia: Center for Curriculum Development.

Kaplan, R.B. (1987). Cultural thought patterns revisited. In U. Connor and R.B. Kaplan (eds), *Writing across languages: analysis of L2 text* (pp. 9–22). Newbury Park, CA: Sage.

Kaplan, R., Cantor, S., Hagstrom, C., Kamhi-Stein, L., Shiotani, Y. and Zimmermann, C. (1994). On abstract writing. *Text,* **14,** 401–26.

Kavossi, M. and Frank, J. (1990). The language culture interface in Persian Gulf states print advertisements: implications for international marketing. *Journal of International Consumer Marketing,* **3** (1), 5–26.

Kember, D. and Gow, L. (1990). Cultural specificity of approaches to study. *British Journal of Educational Psychology,* **60,** 356–63.

Kenkel, J.M. (1991). Argumentation pragmatics, text analysis, and contrastive rhetoric. Unpublished doctoral dissertation, University of Illinois, Urbana-Champaign.

Kennedy, G. (1991). Between and through: the company they keep and the functions they serve. In K. Aijmer and B. Altenberg (eds), *English corpus linguistic* (pp. 95–110). London: Longman.

Kennedy, G. (1995). English as system and probability in academic and professional communication. In P. Bruthiaux, T. Boswood, and B. DuBabcock (eds), *Explorations in English for professional communication* (pp. 139–54). Hong Kong: English Department, City University of Hong Kong.

Kennedy, G. (1998). *An introduction to corpus linguistics.* London: Longman.

Kettemann, B. (1997). Concordancing as input enhancement in ELT. In B. Lewandowska-Tomaszczyk and P.J. Melia (eds), *PALC'97: practical applications in language corpora* (pp. 63–73). Lódź: Lódź University Press.

King, P. (1989). The uncommon core: some discourse features of student writing. *System,* **17,** 113–20.

King, P. (1997). Parallel corpora for translator training. In B. Lewandowska-Tomaszczyk and P.J. Melia (eds), *PALC'97: practical applications in language corpora* (pp. 393–402). Lódź: Lódź University Press.

Knowles, G., Williams, B. and Taylor, L. (1996). *A corpus of formal British English speech: the Lancaster/IBM spoken English corpus.* London: Longman.

Koch, B.J. (1983). Presentation as proof: the language of Arabic rhetoric. *Anthropological Linguistics,* **25,** 47–60.

Koda, K. (1995). Cognitive consequences of L1 and L2 orthographies. In I. Taylor and D.R. Olson (eds), *Scripts and literacy* (pp. 311–26). Dordrecht: Kluwer Academic Publishers.

Kowal, K.H. (1994). The semantics of multicultural discourse: linguistic relativity, contrastive rhetoric, and intercultural pragmatics. Unpublished doctoral dissertation, University of Illinois at Chicago.

Kress, G. (1989). *Linguistic processes in socio-cultural practice.* London: Oxford University Press.

Kubota, R. (1992). Contrastive rhetoric of Japanese and English: a critical approach. Unpublished doctoral dissertation, University of Toronto.

Kubota, R. (1997). A reevaluation of the uniqueness of Japanese written discourse: implications for contrastive rhetoric. *Written Communication,* **14** (4), 460–80.

Kubota, R. (1998). An investigation of Japanese and English L1 essay organization: differences and similarities. *Canadian Modern Language Review,* **54** (4), 475–507.

Kvale, S. (1996). *InterViews: an introduction to qualitative research interviewing.* Thousand Oaks, CA: Sage.

Latour, B. (1987). *Science in action: how to follow scientists and engineers through society.* Milton Keynes: Open University Press.

Lautamatti, L. (1987). Observations on the development of the topic of simplified discourse. In U. Connor and R.B. Kaplan (eds), *Writing across languages: analysis of L2 text* (pp. 87–114). Reading, MA: Addison-Wesley.

Lave, J. and Wenger, G. (1991). *Situated learning: legitimate peripheral participation.* Cambridge: Cambridge University Press.

Lea, M.R. and Street, B. (1999). Writing as academic literacies: understanding textual practices in higher education. In C.N. Candlin and K. Hyland (eds), *Writing: texts, processes and practices* (pp. 62–81). London: Longman.

Lee, D. (1999). *Modeling variation in spoken and written English: the multi-dimensional approach revisited.* Unpublished Ph.D. thesis. UK, University of Lancaster.

Lee, W.O. (1996). The cultural context for Chinese learners: Conceptions of learning in the Confucian tradition. In D.A. Watkins and J.B. Biggs (eds), The Chinese Learner: Cultural, Psychological and Contextual Influences (pp. 25–41). CERC & ACER, Hong Kong.

Leech, G. (1997). Teaching and language corpora: a convergence. In A. Wichmann et al. (eds), *Teaching and language corpora* (pp. 1–23). London: Longman.

Leech, G. and Coates, J. (1979). Semantic indeterminacy and the modals. In S. Greenbaum, G. Leech, and J. Svartvik (eds), *Studies in English linguistics* (pp. 123–38). London: Longman.

Leech, G. and Short, M. (1981). *Style in fiction.* Harlow: Longman.

Leech, G. and Svartvik, J. (1983). *A communicative grammar of English.* London: Longman.

Leki, I. (1991). Twenty-five years of contrastive rhetoric: text analysis and writing pedagogies. *TESOL Quarterly,* **25** (1), 123–43.

Leki, I. (1992). *Understanding ESL writers: a guide for teachers.* Portsmouth, NH: Boynton-Cook.

Leki, I. and Carson, J.G. (1997). 'Completely different worlds': EAP and the writing experiences of ESL students in university courses. *TESOL Quarterly,* **31** (1), 39–69.

Lemke, J.L. (1998). Resources for attitudinal meaning. *Functions of Language,* **5,** 33–56.

Leon, J.A. and Carretero, M. (1995). Intervention in comprehension and memory strategies: knowledge and use of text structure. *Learning and Instruction,* **5,** 203–20.

Lester, J.D. (1993). *Writing research papers.* (7th edn). New York: HarperCollins.

Lewandowska-Tomaszczyk, B. et al. (2000). Lexical problem areas in the PELCRA learner corpus of English. In B. Lewandowska-Tomaszczyk and P.J. Melia (eds), *PALC'99: practical applications in language corpora* (pp. 303–12). Frankfurt am Main: Peter Lang Publishers.

Lewandowska-Tomaszczyk, B. and Melia, P.J. (eds) (1997). *PALC'97: practical applications in language corpora.* Lódź: Lódź University Press.

Lewandowska-Tomaszczyk, B. and Melia, P.J. (eds) (2000). *PALC'99: practical applications in language corpora.* Frankfurt am Main: Peter Lang Publishers.

Lewis, M. and Starks, D. (1997). Revisiting examination questions in tertiary academic writing. *English for Specific Purposes,* **16** (3), 197–210.

Li, X.M. (1992). *'Good writing' in cross-cultural context.* Albany: State University of New York.

Liebman-Klein, J.D. (1992). Toward a new contrastive rhetoric: differences between Arabic and Japanese instruction. *Journal of Second Language Writing,* **1** (2), 141–66.

Lindemann, S. and Mauranen, A. (1999). *'It's just real messy': the occurrence and function of 'just' in a corpus.* Paper presented at the AILA Congress, Tokyo.

Littlewood, W. (2000). Do Asian students really want to listen and obey? *English Language Teaching Journal,* **54** (10), 31–6.

Liu, N.-F. and Littlewood, W. (1997). Why do many students appear reluctant to participate in classroom learning discourse? *System,* **25** (3), 371–84.

Long, E., Fleming, D., Flower, L. and Wojahn, P. (1995). Negotiating competing voices to construct claims and evidence: urban American Teenagers rivalling anti-drug literature. In P. Costello and S. Mitchell (eds), *Competing consensual voices: the theory and practice of argument* (pp. 172–83). Clevedon: Multilingual Matters.

Long, M. and Sato, C. (1983). Classroom foreigner talk discourse: forms and functions of teachers' questions, In H. Seliger and M. Long (eds), *Classroom oriented research in second language acquisition* (pp. 268–86). Rowley, MA: Newbury House Publishers.

Lorenz, G. (1998). Overstatement in advanced learners' writing: stylistic aspects of adjective intensification. In S. Granger (ed.), *Learner English on computer* (pp. 53–66). London: Longman.

Love, A. (1991). Process and product in geology: an investigation of some discourse features of two introductory textbooks. *English for Specific Purposes,* **10**, 89–109.

Love, A. (1993). Lexico-grammatical features of geology textbooks: process and product revisited. *English for Specific Purposes,* **12**, 197–218.

Love, A. (1999). Coming to terms with diversity. In *Proceedings of the 1st international conference on knowledge and discourse,* Hong Kong, 17–21 June 1996. http://ec.hku.hk/kd96proc/authors/papers/love.htm

Love, A. (forthcoming). Coming to terms with diversity. *Discourse and knowledge.* London: Pearson.

Lu, M.Z. (1987). From silence to words: writing as a struggle. *College English,* **49** (4), 437–48.

Lucy, J.A. (1992). *Language diversity and thought: a reformulation of the linguistic relativity hypothesis.* New York: Cambridge University Press.

Lux, P.A. (1991). Discourse styles of Anglo and Latin American college student writers. Unpublished doctoral dissertation, Arizona State University.

Lyons, J. (1977). *Semantics II.* Cambridge: Cambridge University Press.

MacDonald, S.P. (1993). *Professional academic writing in the humanities and social sciences.* Carbondale: Southern Illinois University Press.

MacLachlan, G. and Reid, I. (1994). *Framing and interpretation.* Melbourne: Melbourne University Press.

Malcolm, L. (1987). What rules govern tense usage in scientific articles? *English for Specific Purposes,* **6** (1), 31–43.

Marco, M.J.L. (2000). Collocational frameworks in medical research papers: a genre-based study. *English for Specific Purposes,* **19** (1), 63–86.

Martin, J.E. (1989). Towards a theory of textuality for contrastive rhetoric research. Unpublished doctoral dissertation, Bowling Green State University.

Martin, J.R. (1985a). *Factual writing.* Geelong, Victoria: Deakin University Press.

Martin, J.R. (1985b). Process and text: two aspects of human semiosis. In J.D. Benson and W.S. Greaves (eds), *Systemic perspectives on discourse, Vol. 1* (pp. 248–74). Norwood, NJ: Ablex.

Martin, J.R. (1989). *Factual writing: exploring and challenging social reality.* Oxford: Oxford University Press.

Martin, J.R. (1992). *English text.* Amsterdam: John Benjamins.

Martin, J.R. (1993), *A contextual theory of language: the powers of literacy – a genre approach to teaching writing* (pp. 116–36). Pittsburgh: University of Pittsburgh Press.

Martin, J.R., Christie, F. and Rothery, J. (1997). Social processes in education: a reply to Sawyer and Watson (and others). In I. Reid (ed.), *The place of genre in learning: current debates* (pp. 46–57). Geelong, Victoria: Centre for Studies in Literary Educatiuon: Typereader Publications.

Marton, F., Dall'Alba, G. and Kun, T.L. (1996). Memorizing and understanding: the keys to the paradox. In D.A. Watkins and J.B. Biggs (eds), *The Chinese learner: cultural, psychological and contextual influences* (pp. 69–83). Hong Kong: CERC & ACER.

Mason, A. (1994). By dint of: student and lecturer perceptions of lecture comprehension strategies in first-term graduate study. In J. Flowerdew (ed.), *Academic listening: research perspectives* (pp. 199–218). Cambridge: Cambridge University Press.

Matalene, C. (1985). Contrastive rhetoric: an American writing teacher in China. *College English,* **47**, 789–808.

Matsuda, P.K. (1999). Composition studies and ESL writing: a disciplinary division of labor. *College Composition and Communication,* **50** (4), 699–721.

Mauch, J.E. and Birch, J.W. (1993). *Guide to the successful thesis and dissertation: a handbook for students and faculty* (3rd edn). New York: Marcel Dekker.

Maufette-Leenders, L., Erskine, J. and Leenders, M. (1997). *Learning with cases.* London, Ontario, Canada: Richard Ivey School of Business, The University of Western Ontario, London, Canada.

Mauranen, A. (1993a). Contrastive ESP rhetoric: metacontext in Finnish–English Economics texts. *English for Specific Purposes,* **12**, 3–22.

Mauranen, A. (1993b). *Cultural differences in academic rhetoric.* Frankfurt am Main: Peter Lang.

Mauranen, A. (1997). Another look at genre: will corpus research be relevant? Paper presented at the Nordtext Symposium.

Mauranen, A. (in press, 2000). Reflexive talk in MICASE. In R. Simpson and J.M. Swales (eds), *Corpus linguistics in North America: selections from the 1999 symposium.* Ann Arbor, MI: University of Michigan Press.

Mayfield, J. (1997). The relationship between reading for inferential comprehension in Spanish and reading for inferential comprehension in English among bilingual sixth grade students. Unpublished doctoral dissertation, State University of New York at Buffalo.

Maynard, S.K. (1996). Contrastive rhetoric: a case of nominalization in Japanese and English discourse. *Language Sciences,* **18** (3–4), 933–46.

McCarthy, L.P. (1987). A stranger in strange lands: a college student writing across the curriculum. *Research in the Teaching of English,* **21**, 233–65.

McCarthy, M. (1998). *Spoken language and applied linguistics.* Cambridge: Cambridge University Press.

McCarthy, M. (2000). Discussant in colloquium 'Computer learner corpora: uses for research and teaching', AAAL Conference, 13 March, Vancouver, BC.

McCombs, B.L. (1982). Enhancing student motivation through positive self-control strategies. Paper presented at the American Psychological Association annual meeting, Washington, DC.

McCombs, B.L. (1988). Motivation skills training: combining metacognitive, cognitive and affective learning strategies. In C. Weinstein, E.T. Goetz, and P.A. Alexander (eds), *Learning and study strategies: issues in assessment, instruction and evaluation* (pp. 141–69). New York: Academic Press.

McEnery, T. and Wilson, A. (1996). *Corpus linguistics.* Edinburgh: Edinburgh University Press.

McKay, S. and Wong, S.-L. (1996). Multiple discourses, multiple identities: investment and agency in second-language learning among Chinese adolescent immigrant students. *Harvard Educational Review,* **77**, 577–608.

Meijs, W. (1988). 'All but' and 'if not' in Brown and LOB. In M. Kytö, O. Ihalainen, and M. Rissanen (eds), *Corpus linguistics, hard and soft* (pp. 181–95). Amsterdam: Rodopi.

Melander, B., Swales, J.M. and Fredrickson, K.M. (1997). Journal abstracts from three academic fields in the United States and Sweden: national or disciplinary proclivities? In A. Duszak (ed.), *Intellectual styles and cross-cultural communication* (pp. 251–72). Berlin: Mouton de Gruyter.

Meunier, F. (1998). Computer tools for the analysis of learner corpora. In S. Granger (ed.), *Learner English on computer* (pp. 19–37). London: Longman.

Miles, M. and Huberman, A.M. (1994). *Qualitative data analysis: an expanded source book* (2nd edn). Thousand Oaks, CA: Sage.

Miles, W., Biggs, W. and Schubert, J. (1986). Student perceptions of skill acquisition through cases and a general management simulation. *Simulation and Games,* **17** (1), 7–24.

Miller, C.R. (1984). Genre as social action. *Quarterly Journal of Speech,* **70** (2), 151–67.

Miller, C.R. (1994). The cultural basis of genre. In A. Freedman and P. Medway (eds), *Genre and the new rhetoric* (pp. 67–78). London: Taylor & Francis.

Milroy, L. (1987). *Language and social networks.* Oxford: Blackwell.

Milton, J. (1998). Exploiting L1 and interlanguage corpora in the design of an electronic language learning and production environment. In S. Granger (ed.), *Learner English on computer* (pp. 186–98). London: Longman.

Milton, J. (1999). Lexical thickets and electronic gateways: making texts accessible by novice writers. In C. Candlin and K. Hyland (eds), *Writing: texts, processes and practices* (pp. 221–43). London: Longman.

Milton, J. and Chowdhury, N. (1994). Tagging the interlanguage of Chinese learners of English. In L. Flowerdew and K.K. Tong (eds), *Entering text* (pp. 127–43). Language Centre, Hong Kong University of Science and Technology and Guangzhou University of Foreign Languages.

Mitchell, S. (1996). *Improving the quality of argument in higher education (interim report).* London: School of Education.

Moely, B.E., Hart, S.S., Santulli, K., Leal, L., Johnson, T., Rao, N. and Burney, L. (1986). How do teachers teach memory skills? *Educational Psychologist,* **21**, 55–72.

Mohan, B.A. and Lo, W.A.-Y. (1985). Academic writing and Chinese students: transfer and development factors. *TESOL Quarterly,* **19**, 515–34.

Montano-Harmon, M. (1988). Discourse features in the compositions of Mexican, English-as-a-second-language, Mexican/American Chicano, and Anglo high school students: considerations for the formulation of educational policies. Unpublished doctoral dissertation, University of Southern California.

Morcos, D.A. (1986). A linguistic study of coordination and subordination in the writing of Arabic speaking ESL students. Master's thesis, University of New Orleans.

Mparutsa, C., Love, A. and Morrison, A. (1991). Bringing concord to the ESP classroom. In T. Johns and P. King (eds), *Classroom concordancing (Special edition: English Language Research Journal 4)* (pp. 115–34). Birmingham: Birmingham University.

Munby, J. (1978). *Communicative syllabus design.* Cambridge: Cambridge University Press.

Myers, G. (1989). The pragmatics of politeness in scientific articles. *Applied Linguistics,* **10** (1), 1–35.

Myers, G. (1990). Writing Biology: texts in the social construction of scientific knowledge. Madison: University of Wisconsin Press.

Myers, G. (1992a). 'In this paper we report . . .': speech acts and scientific facts. *Journal of Pragmatics,* **17**, 295–313.

Myers, G. (1992b). Textbooks and the sociology of scientific knowledge. *English for Specific Purposes,* **11** (1), 3–17.

Myers, G. (1994). Narratives of science and nature. In M. Coulthard (ed.), *Advances in written text analysis* (pp. 179–90). London: Routledge.

Nichols, J. (1988). Nominalization and assertion in scientific Russian prose. In J. Haiman and S. Thompson (eds), *Clause combining in grammar and discourse* (pp. 399–428). Amsterdam: Benjamins.

Noor, N. (1998). Word combinations for business English: a study based on a commerce and finance corpus for ESP/ESL applications. Paper presented at Teaching and Learning Corpora Conference 98. Oxford, UK: Keble College.

Norri, J. and Kytö, M. (1996). A corpus of English for specific purposes: work in progress at the University of Tampere. In C. Percy, C. Meyer, and I. Lancashire (eds), *Synchronic corpus linguistics. Papers from the sixteenth International Conference on English language research on computerized corpora* (ICAME 16), (pp. 159–69). Amsterdam: Rodopi.

Nwogu, K.N. (1990). Discourse variation in medical texts: schema, theme and cohesion in professional and journalistic accounts. *Monographs in Systemic Linguistics,* **II**. Nottingham: University of Nottingham

Nwogu, K.N. (1997). The medical research paper: structure and functions. *English for Specific Purposes,* **16** (2), 119–38.

Olsen, L.A. and Huckin, T.N. (1990). Point-driven understanding in engineering lecture comprehension. *English for Specific Purposes,* **9**, 33–47.

Oster, S. (1981). The use of tenses in reporting past literature in EST. In E.L. Selinker, E. Tarone and V. Hanzeli (eds), *English for academic and technical purposes* (pp. 76–90). Rowley, MA: Newbury House.

Ostler, S.E. (1987a). English in parallels: a comparison of English and Arabic prose. In U. Connor and R.B. Kaplan (eds), *Writing across languages: analysis of L2 text* (pp. 169–85). Reading, MA: Addison-Wesley.

Ostler, S.E. (1987b). Contrastive rhetorics of Arabic, English, Japanese and Spanish. Unpublished doctoral dissertation, university of Southern California.

Ovens, J. (2000). Negative forms and functions in academic spoken English. Paper presented at the Second North American Symposium on Corpus Linguistics, Flagstaff, AZ.

Oxford, R.L. (1996). *Language learning strategies around the world: cross-cultural perspectives.* Manoa, Hawaii: University of Hawaii Press.

Pak, C.S. (1996). Newspaper editorials from 'The New York Times,' 'El pais,' and 'El universal': a comparative applied genre analysis (Spain, Mexico). Unpublished doctoral dissertation, University of Michigan.

Palmer, F.R. (1986). *Mood and modality.* Cambridge: Cambridge University Press.

Paltridge, B. (1997). Thesis and dissertation writing: preparing ESL students for research. *English for Specific Purposes,* **16** (1), 61–70.

Panetta, C.G. (1997). Contrastive rhetoric in technical writing pedagogy at urban institutions. *College ESL,* **7** (2), 70–80.

Partington, A. (1998). *Patterns and meanings: using corpora for English language research and teaching.* Amsterdam: Benjamins.

Patton, M.Q. (1987). *How to use qualitative methods in evaluation.* Beverly Hills: Sage.

Peirce, B.N. (1995). Social identity, investment and language learning. *TESOL Quarterly,* **29**, 9–31.

Pennycook, A. (1994). *The cultural politics of English as an international language.* London: Longman.

Pennycook, A. (1996). Borrowing others' words: text, ownership, memory, and plagiarism. *TESOL Quarterly,* **30** (2), 201–30.

Perl, S. (1979). The composing processes of unskilled college writers. *Research in the Teaching of English,* **13** (4), 317–36.

Phillipson, R. (1992). *Linguistic imperialism.* Oxford: Oxford University Press.

Pianko, S. (1979). A description of the composing processes of college freshman writers. *Research in the Teaching of English,* **13** (1), 5–22.

Pickard, V. (1993a). Citing previous writers: what can we say instead of 'say'. Paper presented at RELC Conference, 1993. Singapore.

Pickard, V. (1993b). Should we be teaching refutation? Concordanced evidence from the field of applied linguistics. In N. Bird, J. Harris, and M. Ingham (eds), *Language and content* (pp. 381–401). Hong Kong: Institute of Language in Education.

Pickard, V. (1994). Producing a concordance-based self-access vocabulary package: some problems and solutions. In L. Flowerdew and K.K. Tong (eds), *Entering text,* pp. 215–24. Language Centre, Hong Kong University of Science and Technology and Guangzhou University of Foreign Languages.

Plum, G.A. (1998). Doing psychology, doing writing: student voices on academic writing in Psychology. In C.N. Candlin and G.A. Plum (eds), *Researching academic literacies. Framing student literacy: cross-cultural aspects of communication skills in Australian university settings* (pp. 211–92). Sydney: NCELTR, Macquarie University.

Poos, D. (1999). A question of gender? Hedging in academic spoken discourse. Paper presented at the Michigan Linguistics Society, East Lansing MI.

Posteguillo, S. (1999). The schematic structure of computer science research articles. *English for Specific Purposes,* **18** (2), 139–60.

Pressley, M., Harris, K.R. and Guthrie, J.T. (eds) (1992). *Promoting academic competence and literacy in school.* San Diego: Academic Press Inc.

Pride, J.B. (ed.) (1982). *New Englishes.* Rowley, MA: Newbury House.

Prior, P. (1998). *Writing disciplinarity: a sociohistoric account of literate activity in the academiy.* Mahwah, NJ: Erlbaum.

Prozorova, L. (1997). If not given, then what? Things that come first in academic discourse. In A. Duszak (ed.), *Culture and styles of academic discourse. Trends in Linguistics. Studies and Monographs,* **104**, 305–22. Berlin: Mouton de Gruyter.

Purves, A. (1986). Rhetorical communities, the international student and basic writing. *Journal of Basic Writing,* **5**, 16–24.

Purves, A.C. (ed.) (1988). Writing across languages and cultures: issues in contrastive rhetoric. Written Communication Annual, vol. 2. Newbury Park, CA: Sage.

Purves, A.C. and Hawisher, G. (1990). Writers, judges, and text models. In R. Beach and S. Hynds (eds), *Developing Discourse Practices in Adolescence and Adulthood* (pp. 183–9). Norwood, NJ: Ablex.

Qualitative Solutions and Research Pty. (1994). QSR NUD*IST (Version 3.0) [Computer software]. London: Sage.

Quaouicha, D. (1986). Contrastive rhetoric and the structure of learner-produced argumentative texts in Arabic and English. Unpublished doctoral dissertation, University of Texas at Austin.

Quirk, R., Greenbaum, S., Leech, G. and Svartvik, J. (1985). *Comprehensive grammar of the English language*. London: Longman.

Radloff, A. (1997). A longitudinal study of self-regulation of learning in adult university students. Unpublished doctoral dissertation, Murdoch University, Western Australia.

Raimes, A. (1985). What unskilled writers do as they write: a classroom study of composing. *TESOL Quarterly*, **19** (2), 229–58.

Ramanathan, D. and Atkinson, D. (1999). Ethnographic approaches and methods in L2 writing research. *Applied Linguistics*, **21**, 44–70.

Ramanathan, V. and Kaplan, R.B. (1996). Some problematic 'channels' in the teaching of critical thinking in current L1 composition textbooks: implications for L2 student-writers. *Issues in Applied Linguistics*, **7** (2), 225–49.

Ramsden, P. (1994). Using research on student learning to enhance educational quality. Occasional paper No. 2. Presented at Griffith Institute for Higher Education.

Rayner, K. and Polltasek, A. (1989). *The psychology of reading*. Englewood Cliffs, NJ: Prentice Hall.

Reid, I., Kirkpatrick, A. and Mulligan, D. (1998). *Framing student literacy: cross-cultural aspects of communication skills in Australian university settings*. Perth: Curtin University Press and Centre for Literacy, Culture and Language Pedagogy.

Reid, J.M. (1988). Quantitative differences in English prose written by Arabic, Chinese, Spanish, and English students. Unpublished doctoral dissertation, Colorado State University.

Read, J. (1990). Providing relevant content in an EAP writing test. *English for Specific Purposes*, **9** (2), 109–22.

Reid, J. and Kroll, B. (1995). Designing and assessing effective classroom writing assignments for NES and ESL students. *Journal of Second Language Writing*, **4** (1), 17–41.

Renouf, A. (1997). Teaching corpus linguistics to teachers of English. In A. Wichmann et al. (eds), *Teaching and language corpora* (pp. 255–66). London: Longman.

Renouf, A. and Sinclair, J. McH. (1991). Collocational frameworks in English. In K. Aijmer and B. Altenberg (eds), *English corpus linguistics* (pp. 128–43). London: Longman.

Reppen, R. and Grabe, W. (1993). Spanish transfer effects in the English writing of elementary school students. *Lenguas Modernas*, **20**, 113–28.

Reynolds, D.W. (1996). Repetition in second language writing (composition). Unpublished doctoral dissertation, Indiana University.

Richardson, P.W. (1994). Language as personal resource and as social construct: competing views of literacy pedagogy in Australia. In A. Freedman and P. Medway (eds), *Learning and teaching genre* (pp. 117–42). Portsmouth, NH: Boynton Cook.

Rijlaarsdam, G., Van Den Burgh, H. and Couzijn, M. (1996). *Theories, models and methodology in writing research* (Editors' introduction, pp. ix–xxii). Amsterdam: Amsterdam University Press.

Robinson, J.H. (n.d.). Contrastive rhetoric and the East Asian student. Unpublished paper, University of St Cloud.

Roseberry, R. et al. (eds) (forthcoming). *The use of small corpora in language teaching.* The Hague: John Benjamin.

Rost, M. (1994). On-line summaries as representations of lecture understanding. In J. Flowerdew (ed.), *Academic listening: research perspectives* (pp. 93–127). Cambridge: Cambridge University Press.

Russel, D.R. (1990). Writing across the curriculum in historical perspective: toward a social interpretation. *College English,* **52** (1), 52–73.

Salager-Meyer, F. (1990a). Discoursal flaws in medical English abstracts: a genre analysis per research- and text-type. *Text,* **10** (4), 365–84.

Salager-Meyer, F. (1990b). Metaphors in medical English prose: a comparative study with French and Spanish. *English for Specific Purposes,* **9**, 145–59.

Salager-Meyer, F. (1992). A text-type and move analysis study of verb tense and modality distribution in medical English abstracts. *English for Specific Purposes,* **11**, 93–113.

Salili, F. (1996). Accepting personal responsibility for learning. In D.A. Watkins and J.B. Biggs (eds), *The Chinese learner: cultural, psychological and contextual influences* (pp. 85–105). Hong Kong: CERC & ACER.

Saljo, R. (1982). *Learning and understanding: a study of differences in constructing meaning from a text.* Goteborg: ACTA Universitatis Gothoburgensis.

Samoeil, J. (1996). A comparative analysis of written narrative strategies in texts written by narrative speakers and non-native speakers of English. Unpublished doctoral dissertation, New York University.

Samraj, B. (forthcoming). Introductions in research articles: variations across disciplines. *English for Specific Purposes.*

Santiago, R.L. (1968) A contrastive analysis of some rhetorical aspects in the writing in Spanish and English of Spanish speaking college students in Puerto Rico. Unpublished doctoral dissertation, New York University.

Santos, M.B.D. (1996). The textual organization of research paper abstracts in applied linguistics. *Text,* **16**, 481–99.

Schank, R.C. and Abelson, R.P. (1977). *Scripts, plans, goals and understanding.* New York: Lawrence Erlbaum Associates.

Schröder, H. (ed.) (1991). *Subject-oriented texts: language for special purposes and text theory.* Berlin: Mouton de Gruyter.

Scollon, R. (1991). Topic confusion in English–Asian discourse. *World Englishes,* **10** (2), 113–25.

Scollon, R. (1993). Maxims of stance: channel, relationship, and main topic in discourse. Research Report No. 26. City Polytechnic of Hong Kong, Department of English.

Scollon, R. (1994a). As a matter of fact: the changing ideology of authorship and responsibility in discourse. *World Englishes,* **13**, 34–46.

Scollon, R. (1994b). Cultural aspects of constructing the author. In D. Keller-Cohen (ed.), *Literacy: interdiscplinary conversations* (pp. 213–27). New Jersey: Hampton.

Scollon, R. (1995). Plagiarism and ideology: identity in intercultural discourse. *Language in society,* **24**, 1–28.

Scollon, R. (1997) Contrastive rhetoric, contrastive poetics, or perhaps something else? *TESOL Quarterly,* **31** (2), 352–7.

Scollon, R. and Scollon, S. (1995). *Intercultural communication.* Cambridge, MA: Blackwell.

Scott, M. (1996). *WordSmith tools.* Oxford: Oxford English Software.

Scott, M. (1997). PC analysis of key words – and key key words. *System,* **25** (2), 233–45.

Scott, M. (2000). Focusing on the text and its keywords. In L. Burnard and T. McEnery (eds), *Rethinking language pedagogy from a corpus perspective* (pp. 103–21). Frankfurt am Main: Peter Lang Publishers.

Scott, M. and Johns, T. (1993). *MicroConcord*. Oxford: Oxford English Software.

Seidlhofer, B. (2000). Operationalising intertextuality: using learner corpora for learning. In L. Burnard and T. McEnery (eds), *Rethinking language pedagogy from a corpus perspective* (pp. 207–23). Frankfurt am Main: Peter Lang Publishers.

Selinker, L. (1972). Interlanguage. *IRAL: International Review of Applied Linguistics.* **10**, 209–31.

Shaw, P. (1991). Science research students' composing processes. *English for Specific Purposes*, **10**, 189–206.

Shaw, P. (1992). Reasons for the correlation of voice, tense and sentence function in reporting verbs. *Applied Linguistics*, **13**, 302–19.

Shaw, P. and Liu, E.T.K. (1998). What develops in the development of second language writing? *Applied Linguistics*, **19** (2), 225–54.

Shen, F. (1989). The classroom and the wider culture: identity as a key to learning English composition. *College Composition and Communication*, **40** (4), 459–66.

da Silva, S.-A. (1991). Um estudo da entrevista baseado na analise de genres. *ESPecialist*, **12** (1–2), 121–43.

Simpson, R., Lucka, B. and Ovens, J. (2000). Methodological challenges of planning a spoken corpus with pedagogical outcomes. In L. Burnard and T. McEnery (eds), *Rethinking language pedagogy from a corpus perspective* (pp. 43–9). Frankfurt am Main: Peter Lang Publishers.

Simpson, R. and Swales, J.M. (eds) (in press, 2000). *Corpus linguistics in North America: selections from the 1999 symposium.* Ann Arbor, MI: University of Michigan Press.

Sinclair, J. McH. (1985). On the integration of linguistic description. In T. van Dijk (ed.), *Handbook of discourse analysis: dimensions of discourse* (vol. 2), (pp. 13–28). Academic Press.

Sinclair, J. (editor-in-chief) (1987). *Collins Cobuild English language dictionary.* London: Collins.

Sinclair, J.McH. (1987). The nature of the evidence. In J. McH. Sinclair (ed.), *Looking UP: an account of the COBUILD Project in lexical computing* (pp. 150–9). London: Collins ELT.

Sinclair, J.McH. (1991). *Corpus, concordance, collocation.* Oxford: Oxford University Press.

Smart, G. (1992). Exploring the social dimension of workplace genre and the implications for teaching. *Carleton Papers in Applied Language Studies*, 933–46.

Soucy, A. (1994). Second language, second self: an exploratory study in contrastive rhetoric. *Carleton Papers in Applied Language Studies*, **11**, 1–21.

Soule, M.E. (1985). What is conservation biology? *BioScience*, **35**, 727–34.

de Souza, S.M. (1991). Data collection: the questionnaire. *ESPecialist*, **12** (1–2), 101–20.

Spack, R. (1997). Initiating students into the academic discourse community: how far should we go? *TESOL Quarterly*, **22**, 29–51.

Sperberg-McQueen, C.M. and Burnard, L. (1994). *Guidelines for electronic text-encoding and interchange.* Chicago: Text Encoding Initiative.

Spilka, R. (1993). *Writing in the workplace: new research perspectives.* Carbondale: Southern Illinois Press.

Stalker, J.C. (1990). Official English and the English profession. In H.A. Daniels (ed.), *Not only English: affirming America's multilingual heritage* (pp. 61–8). Urbana, IL: National Council of Teachers of English.

Stevens, V. (1991a). Classroom concordancing: vocabulary materials derived from relevant, authentic text. *English for Specific Purposes*, **10**, 35–46.

Stevens, V. (1991b). Concordance-based vocabulary exercises: a viable alternative to gap fillers. In T. Johns and P. King (eds), *Classroom concordancing* (Special edition: English Language Research Journal 4), (pp. 47–61). Birmingham: Birmingham University.

St John, M.J. (1987). Writing processes of Spanish scientists publishing in English. *English for Specific Purposes*, **6** (2), 113–20.

Stubbs, M. (1996). *Text and corpus analysis: computer-assisted studies of language and culture.* Oxford: Blackwell.

Stubbs, M. (forthcoming). Computer-assisted text and corpus analysis: lexical cohesion and communicative competence. In D. Tannen et al. (eds), *The handbook of discourse analysis.* Oxford: Blackwell.

Sullivan, D. (1996). Displaying disciplinarily. *Written Communication*, **13** (2), 221–50.

Svartvik, J. (ed.) (1990). The London–Lund corpus of spoken English. *Description and research.* Lund: Lund University Press.

Swales, J.M. (1981a). *Aspects of article introductions.* Birmingham: University of Aston, Language Studies Unit.

Swales, J.M. (1981b). Definitions in science and law: a case for subject-specific ESP matters. *Fachsparche*, **81** (3), 106–12.

Swales, J.M. (1982). The case of cases in academic legal purposes. *IRAL*, **20**, 139–48.

Swales, J.M. (1988). *Episodes in ESP.* Hemel Hempstead: Prentice Hall International.

Swales, J.M. (1990). *Genre analysis: English in academic and research settings.* Cambridge: Cambridge University Press.

Swales, J.M. (1995). The role of the textbook in EAP writing research. *English for Specific Purposes*, **14**, 3–18.

Swales, J.M. (1996a). Occluded genres in the academy: the case of the submission letter. In E. Ventola and A. Mauranen (eds), *Academic writing: intercultural and textual issues* (pp. 45–58). Amsterdam: John Benjamin.

Swales, J.M. (1996b). Teaching the conference abstract. In E. Ventola and A. Mauranen (eds), *Academic writing: today and tomorrow* (pp. 45–59). Helsinki: Helsinki University Press.

Swales, J.M. (1997). English as Tyrannosaurus rex. *World Englishes*, **16**, 373–82.

Swales, J.M. (1998). *Other floors, other voices: a textography of a small_university building.* Mahwah, NJ: Erlbaum.

Swales, J.M. (2001). Metatalk in American academic talk: The cases of 'point' and 'thing'. *Journal of English Linguistics*, **29** (1), 34–54.

Swales, J.M. and Feak, C.B. (1994). *Academic writing for graduate students: a course for nonnative speakers of English.* Ann Arbor: University of Michigan Press.

Swales, J.M. and Feak, C.B. (2000). *English in Today's Research World: A Writing Guide.* Ann Arbor: University of Michigan Press.

Swales, J.M. and Malczewski, B. (in press). Discourse management and new episode flags in MICASE. In R.C. Simpson and J.M. Swales (eds), *Corpus linguistics in North America: states of the art.* Ann Arbor: University of Michigan Press.

Swales, J.M. and Najjar, H. (1987). The writing of research article introductions. *Written Communication*, **4**, 175–91.

Swales, J.M. and Rogers, P. (1995). Discourse and the projection of corporate culture: the Mission Statement. *Discourse and society*, **6** (2), 223–42. London: Sage.

Tadros, A.A. (1989). Predictive categories in university textbooks. *English for Specific Purposes*, **8** (1), 17–31.

Tadros, A.A. (1993). The pragmatics of text averral and attribution in academic texts. In M. Hoey (ed.), *Data, description, discourse* (pp. 98–114). London: HarperCollins.

Tannen, D. (ed.) (1993). *Framing in discourse.* Oxford: Oxford University Press.

Tarone, E., Dwyer, S., Gillette, S. and Icke, V. (1981). On the use of the passive in two astrophysics journal papers. *ESP Journal,* 1 (2), 123–40.

Tarone, E., Dwyer, S., Gillette, S. and Icke, V. (1998). On the use of the passive and active voice in astrophysics journal papers: with extensions to other languages and other fields. *English for Specific Purposes,* 17 (1), 113–32.

Tauroza, S. and Allison, D. (1994). Expectation-driven understanding in information-systems lecture comprehension. In J. Flowerdew (ed.), *Academic listening: research perspectives* (pp. 35–54). Cambridge: Cambridge University Press.

Taylor, G. and Tingguang, C. (1991). Linguistic, cultural and subcultural issues in contrastive discourse analysis: Anglo-American and Chinese scientific texts. *Applied Linguistics.* 12:3 pp. 319–36.

Taylor. G. and Chen, T. (1991) Linguistics, culture, and subcultural issues in contrastive discourse analysis: Anglo-American and Chinese scientific texts. *Applied Linguistics,* 12 (3), 319–36.

Tedick, D.J. (1990). ESL writing assessment: subject-matter knowledge and its impact on performance. *English for Specific Purposes,* 9 (2), 123–43.

Thesen, L. (1997). Voices, discourses, and transition: in search of new categories in EAP. *TESOL Quarterly,* 31 (3), 487–511.

Thomas, S. and Hawes, T. (1994). Reporting verbs in medical journal articles. *English for Specific Purposes,* 13, 129–48.

Thompson, G. (1996). Voices in the text: discourse perspectives on language reports. *Applied Linguistics,* 17, 501–30.

Thompson, I. (1985). The given/new contract and cohesion: some suggestions for classroom practice. *Journal of Technical Writing and Communication,* 15 (3), 205–14.

Thompson, P. (1999). Examining PhD theses in a corpus. *Teaching and language corpora 98* (pp. 177–82). Oxford: Seacourt Press.

Thompson, P. (2000). Citation practices in PhD theses. In L. Burnard and T. McEnery (eds.), *Rethinking language pedagogy from a corpus perspective* (pp. 91–101). Frankfurt am Main: Peter Lang Publishers.

Thompson, S.A. and Mulac, A. (1991). A quantitative perspective on the gram-maticization of epistemic parentheticals in English. In E.C. Traugott and B. Heine (eds), *Approaches to grammaticalization,* Vol. 2 (pp. 313–29). Amsterdam: Benjamins.

Thompson, G. and Ye, Y. (1991). Evaluation of the reporting verbs used in academic papers. *Applied Linguistics,* 12, 365–82.

Thurstun, J. and Candlin, C. (1998). Concordancing and the teaching of the vocabu-lary of academic English. *English for Specific Purposes,* 17 (3), 267–80.

Thurstun, J. and Candlin, C. (1999). *Exploring academic English: a workbook for student essay writing.* Macquarie University: NCELTR Publications.

Tirkkonen-Condit, S. (1996). Explicitness *vs.* implicitness of argumentation: An intercultural comparison. *Multilingua,* 15, 257–73.

Toulmin S., Rieke, R. and Janiket, A. (1979). *An introduction to reasoning.* New York: Macmillan.

Tribble, C. (1990). Concordancing and an EAP writing programme. *CAELL Journal,* 1 (2), 10–15.

Tribble, C. (1991). Some uses of electronic text in English for academic purposes, In J. Milton and K.S.T. Tong (eds), *Text analysis in computer assisted language learning* (pp. 4–14). The Hong Kong University of Science and Technology and the City University of Hong Kong.

Tribble, C. (1997a). Improvising corpora for ELT: quick-and-dirty ways of developing corpora for language teaching. In B. Lewandowska-Tomaszczyk and P.J. Melia (eds), *PALC '97: practical applications in language corpora* (pp. 106–17). Lódź: Lódź University Press.

Tribble, C. (1997b). *Writing.* Oxford: Oxford University Press.

Tribble, C. (1998). *Writing difficult texts.* Unpublished Ph.D. thesis, Lancaster University.

Tribble, C. (1999). Genres, keywords, teaching: towards a pedagogic account of the language of project proposals. *Teaching and language corpora 98* (pp. 188–98). Oxford: Seacourt Press.

Tribble, C. (2000). Genres, keywords, teaching: towards a pedagogic account of the language of project proposals. In L. Burnard and T. McEnery (eds), *Rethinking language pedagogy from a corpus perspective* (pp. 75–90). Frankfurt am Main: Peter Lang Publishers.

Tribble, C. and Jones, G. (1990). *Concordances in the classroom.* London: Longman.

Tribble, C. and Jones, G. (1997). *Concordances in the classroom: a resource book for teachers.* Houston, TX: Athelstan.

Trimble, L. (1985). *English for science and technology: a discourse approach.* Cambridge: Cambridge University Press.

Trzeciak, J. (1996). Cultural factors in English academic writing: the problem of non-Native Speaker students. Unpublished MA dissertation, Centre for Applied Language Studies, University of Reading.

Ullmann, A. (1996). The Swatch in 1993. In P. Wright, M. Kroll, and J. Parnell (eds), *Strategic management: concepts and cases* (pp. 367–90). Englewood Cliffs, NJ: Prentice Hall.

University of Malaya (1980). *Skills for learning* (4 vols). Walton on Thames: Nelson.

Van Dijk, T.A. and Kintsch, W. (1983). *Strategies of discourse comprehension.* New York and London: Academic Press.

Van Lier, L. (1988). *The classroom and the language learner: ethnography and second language classroom research.* London: Longman.

Van Lier, L. (1989). Ethnography: bandaid, bandwagon, or contraband? In C. Brumfit and R. Mitchell (eds), *Research in the language classroom. ELT Documents,* **133**, 33–53. London: Modern English Publications/The British Council.

Vassileva, I. (2000). *Who is the author? A contrastive analysis of authorial presence in English, German, French, Russian and Bulgarian academic discourse.* Sankt Augustin: Asgard.

Ventola, E. (1992). Writing scientific English: overcoming cultural problems. *International Journal of Applied Linguistics,* **2** (2), 191–220.

Ventola, E. and Mauranen, A. (eds) (1996). *Academic writing: intercultural and textual issues.* Amsterdam: John Benjamins.

Vihla, M. (1998). Medicor: a corpus of contemporary American medical texts. *ICAME Journal,* **22**, 73–80.

Volet, S. (1899). Motivation within and across cultural-educational contexts: a multi-dimensional perspective. In T. Urdan (ed.), *Advances in motivation and achievement,* vol. 11 (pp. 185–231). Greenwich, Connecticut: JAI Press.

Volet, S. and Kee, J.P.P. (1993). *Studying in Singapore – studying in Australia: a student perspective.* Occasional Paper no. 1. Murdoch University Teaching Excellence Committee, Murdoch.

Volet, S. and Renshaw, P. (1996). Chinese students at an Australian university: adaptability and continuity. In D.A. Watkins and J.B. Biggs (eds), *The Chinese learner: cultural, psychological and contextual influences* (pp. 205–20). Hong Kong: CERC & ACER.

Volet, S., Renshaw, P. and Tietzel, K. (1994). A short-term longitudinal investigation of cross-cultural differences in study approaches using Biggs' SPQ questionnaire. *British Journal of Educational Psychology*, **64**, 301–18.

Waller, R. (1997). *Three functions of text presentation. Notes on transforming*, 2. Milton Keynes: The Open University.

Walvoord, B. and McCarthy, L. (1990). *Thinking and writing in college: a naturalistic study of students in four disciplines*. Urbana, IL: National Council of Teachers of English.

Ward, J.H. (1988). Editing in a bilingual, bicultural context. *Journal of Technical Writing and Communication*, **18** (3), 221–7.

Watanabe, Y. (1990). External variables affecting language learning strategies of Japanese EFL learners: effects of entrance examination, years spent at college/university, and staying overseas. Unpublished Master's thesis, Lancaster university, UK.

Watanabe, S. (1993). Cultural Differences in Framing: American and Japanese Group Discussions. In D. Tannen (ed.), *Framing in Discourse* (pp. 176–209). Oxford University Press, Oxford.

Watson-Gegeo, K.A. (1988, December). Ethnography in ESL: defining the essentials. *TESOL Quarterly*, **22** (4), 575–92.

Wegerif, R. and Stratfold, M. (1996, 13–14 November). EARLI academic writing online course. EARLI News Letter.

Wen, Q. and Johnson, R.K. (1991). Language learning approaches and outcomes: A study of tertiary English majors in China. Paper presented at the Sixth Annual Conference of the Institute of Language in Education, Hong Kong University.

Weissberg, B. (1993). The graduate seminar: another research-process genre. *English for Specific Purposes*, **12**, 23–36.

Weissberg, R. and Buker, S. (1990). *Writing up research: experimental research report writing for students of English*. Englewood Cliffs, NJ: Prentice Hall Regents.

Wichmann, A., Fligelstone, S., McEnery, T. and Knowles, G. (eds) (1997). *Teaching and language corpora*. London: Longman.

Widdowson, H.G. (1978). *Teaching language as communication*. London: Oxford University Press.

Widdowson, H.G. (1998). Context, community, and authentic language. *TESOL Quarterly*, **32** (4), 705–16.

Widdowson, H.G. (2000a). On the limitations of linguistics applied. *Applied Linguistics*, **21** (1), 3–25.

Widdowson, H.G. (2000b). Panellist on discussion: 'Discours de la méthode': opportunities and limitations of corpus linguistics. TALC'2000 Conference, 22 July, University of Graz, Austria.

Wignell, P. (1998). Technicality and abstraction in social science. In J.R. Martin and R. Veel (eds), *Reading Science* (pp. 297–326). London: Routledge.

Williams, G. (1982). *Learning the law*. London: Stevens and Sons.

Williams, G. (1998). Collocational networks: interlocking patterns of lexis in a corpus of plant biology research articles. *International Journal of Corpus Linguistics*, **3** (1), 151–71.

Williams, R. (1985). Teaching vocabulary recognition strategies in ESP reading. *ESP Journal*, **4** (2), 121–32.

Wing On (1996). The cultural context for Chinese learners: Conception of learning in the Confucian tradition. In D. Watkins and J.B. Biggs (eds), The Chinese Learner: Cultural, psychological and contextual influences. Hong Kong: CERC and ACER.

Winter, E.O. (1977). A clause-relational approach to English texts: a study of some predictive lexical items in written discourse. *Instructional Science*, **6** (1), 1–92.

Wisdom, J. (1964). *Gods, philosophy and psycho-analysis.* Oxford: Basil Blackwell.

Wong, S.D. (1992). Contrastive rhetoric: an exploration of proverbial references in Chinese students L1 and L2 writing. *Journal of Intensive English Studies*, **6**, 71–90.

Wright, P., Kroll, M. and Parnell, J. (1996). *Strategic management: concepts and cases.* Englewood Cliffs, NJ: Prentice Hall.

Wu, M.H. (1992). Towards a contextual lexico-grammar: an application of concordance analysis in ESP teaching. *RELC Journal*, **23** (2), 18–34.

Wykel, S.C. (1996). A contrastive study of the rhetorical structure employed in English texts by native speakers of English and native speakers of Spanish. Unpublished doctoral dissertation, University of Texas a Arlington.

Xu, G.Q. (1990). AN ex post facto study of differences in the structure of standard expository paragraphs between written compositions by native and nonnative speakers of English at the college level. Unpublished doctoral dissertation, Indiana University of Pennsylvania.

Yang, H.Z. (1986). A new technique for identifying scientific/technical terms and describing science texts. *Literary and Linguistic Computing*, **1**, 93–103.

Yli-Jokipii, H. (1996). Requests in professional discourse: a cross-cultural study of British, American, and Finnish business writing. Unpublished doctoral dissertation, University of Turku.

Young, L. (1994). University lectures: macro-structures and micro-features. In J. Flowerdew (ed.), *Academic listening: research perspectives* (pp. 159–76). Cambridge: Cambridge University Press.

Zappen, J.P. (1983). A rhetoric for research in sciences and technologies. In P.V. Anderson, R.J. Brockman and C.R. Miller (eds), *New essays in technical and scientific communication* (pp. 123–38). Farmingdale, NY: Beywood.

Zhang, J.Z. (1990). Ranking of indirectness in professional writing. *Journal of Technical Writing and Communication*, **20** (3), 291–305.

Zhu, H. (1992). Cohesion and coherence in Chinese ESL writing. Unpublished doctoral dissertation, Virginia Polytechnic Institute and State University.

Zhu, Q. (1989). A quantitative look at the Guangzhou Petroleum English Corpus. *ICAME Journal*, **13**, 28–38.

Zhu, W. (1992). Forty years of separation: differences in structural complexity between news reports from Mainland China and Taiwan. Unpublished paper: University of Texas-Pan-American.

Zhu, Y. (1997). AN analysis of structural moves in Chinese sales letters. *Text*, **17** (4), 543–66.

Zuber-Skerritt, O. and Ryan, Y. (eds) (1994). *Quality Postgraduate Education.* London: Kogan Page.

Zuber-Skerritt, O. and Ryan, Y. (1998). 'Enhancing Postgraduate Learning and Teaching of International Students' Paper presented at the HERDSA conference. Adelaide.

Author Index

Subject Index